# DIVORCE AND REMARRIAGE

Here is a comprehensive Christian study of singleness, marriage, divorce and remarriage. What is distinctive about it is Andrew Cornes' balanced combination of biblical scholarship and practical experience, prophetic witness and pastoral wisdom, courage and compassion, truth and love. It will, I predict, stimulate much furious re-thinking, and become indispensable reading for everybody who is anxious to develop a Christian mind on these topics. It is thorough, clear, faithful, realistic and passionate.

*John Stott*

# DIVORCE AND REMARRIAGE

## Biblical Principles and Pastoral Practice

**Andrew Cornes**

WILLIAM B. EERDMANS PUBLISHING COMPANY
GRAND RAPIDS, MICHIGAN

Copyright © 1993 by Andrew Cornes

First published 1993 in Great Britain by
Hodder and Stoughton, a division of Hodder and Stoughton Ltd,
Mill Road, Dunton Green, Sevenoaks, Kent TN13 2YA
Editorial Office: 47 Bedford Square, London WC1B 3DP
and in the United States by
Wm. B. Eerdmans Publishing Co.
255 Jefferson Ave. S.E., Grand Rapids, Michigan 49503

Printed in the United States of America

ISBN 0-8028-0577-9

# Contents

# 1

# Divorce and Remarriage Today

NORA: There's another problem needs solving first. I must take steps to educate myself. You are not the man to help me there. That's something I must do on my own. That's why I'm leaving you.

HELMER (jumps up): What did you say?

NORA: If I'm to reach any understanding of myself and the things around me, I must learn to stand alone. That's why I can't stay here with you any longer.

HELMER: Nora! Nora!

NORA: I'm leaving here at once. I dare say Kristine will put me up for tonight . . .

HELMER: You are out of your mind! I won't let you! I forbid you!

NORA: It's no use forbidding me anything now. I'm taking with me my own personal belongings. I don't want anything of yours, either now or later.

HELMER: This is madness!

NORA: Tomorrow I'm going home – to what used to be my home, I mean. It will be easier for me to find something to do there.

HELMER: Oh, you blind, inexperienced . . .

NORA: I must set about *getting* experience, Torvald.

HELMER: And leave your home, your husband and your children? Don't you care what people will say?

NORA: That's no concern of mine. All I know is that this is necessary for *me*.

HELMER: This is outrageous! You are betraying your most sacred duty.

NORA: And what do you consider to be my most sacred duty?

HELMER: Does it take me to tell you that? Isn't it your duty to your husband and your children?

NORA: I have another duty equally sacred.

HELMER: You have not. What duty might *that* be?

NORA: My duty to myself.

HELMER: First and foremost, you are a wife and mother.

NORA: That I don't believe any more. I believe that first and foremost I am an individual, just as much as you are – or at least I'm going to try to be. I know most people agree with you, Torvald, and that's also what it says in books. But I'm not content any more with what most people say, or what it says in books. I have to think things out for myself, and get things clear.

                    ★   ★   ★

HELMER: You are ill, Nora. You are delirious. I'm half-inclined to think that you are out of your mind.

NORA: Never have I felt so calm and collected as I do tonight.

HELMER: Calm and collected enough to leave your husband and children?

NORA: Yes.

HELMER: Then only one explanation is possible.

NORA: And that is?

HELMER: You don't love me any more.

NORA: Exactly.

HELMER: Nora! Can you say that!

NORA: I'm desperately sorry, Torvald. Because you have always been so kind to me. But I can't help it. I don't love you any more.

                    (Ibsen: *The Doll's House*)

These words which were certainly shocking, and designed to shock, in 1879 – only just over a century ago – will today be recognised by literally millions of people. Many husbands and wives have felt precisely this way themselves, even if they haven't been able to articulate it as clearly as Nora. Many have heard friends or family members express precisely these thoughts. Many pastors and Christian leaders have heard almost exactly these words as they have spoken with those whose marriages are breaking up. Nora speaks for an increasing number of people who have felt trapped in their marriages.

In the period 1901–10, the average number of divorces per year in England and Wales was 593[1]. By the 1930s this had risen almost ninefold to 5,096 per year. By the 1960s that figure in turn had increased almost eight times to 39,654, and the 1970s saw an increase of over threefold on the previous decade to an average of 121,991. By 1980 the figure had reached 148,301 and it has not varied much during the '80s (1989: 150,872); but there are few, if any, grounds to be confident that the rise will not continue.

Of course the population of England has been growing during this period as well. Nevertheless the divorce rate has also accelerated dramatically. The rate of divorce per thousand married couples was 2.0 in 1960; this had risen over sixfold to 13.4 by 1985. 'The speed of change is most clearly seen when one considers the divorce behaviour of people married in the same year. For example, 10% of couples married in 1951 had divorced by their 25th wedding anniversary. However, amongst those marrying in 1961 10% had divorced by their 12th wedding anniversary, whilst among those marrying in 1971 and 1981 the analogous durations of marriage were 6 and 4.5 years' (Kiernan and Wicks p.13[2]). Dates of divorces are for decrees absolute; petitions are normally filed six months to a year beforehand, and at least one partner will have determined that the marriage has irretrievably broken down before filing the petition. It is now officially estimated that at current rates 37% of all marriages will ultimately end in divorce.

England has of course not been alone in seeing this rise

---

[1] All UK figures in this chapter are for England and Wales (referred to as 'England' for convenience; Welsh readers, please forgive!) and are from the official figures of the Office of Population Censuses and Surveys, except where otherwise indicated. US statistics are from the Bureau of the Census. EEC statistics are from the Statistical Office of the European Communities. 'Divorces' includes annulments, but these are statistically insignificant, since there are over 300 divorces for every one annulment.

[2] References to other works are given by author and page number only. For commentaries, author alone is mentioned and the page number can be assumed to be *ad loc.* except where indicated. Further details of books cited can be found in the Bibliography.

in divorce. Within the 12 EEC countries, there were 125,300 divorces in 1960, a figure which had risen over 4 times to 534,200 by 1988. But the figures for the UK have increased much more rapidly than those of its European partners. In 1960, the UK total was 25,900, half that of West Germany (48,878) and less than that of France (30,200). By 1988 the UK figure had risen to 165,700, considerably more than any other EEC country. More importantly the UK divorce rate per thousand of the total population was 0.5 in 1960, only just above the average (0.4) and far surpassed by West Germany (0.9) and Denmark (1.5). By 1988, this figure had risen to 2.9 for the UK, only equalled by Denmark, with other countries far behind and the EEC average at 1.6.

The situation in the United States is more serious still. The analogous figure of divorces per thousand of the total population was 4.9 in 1986 (over 3 times larger than the EEC average) and touched 5.3 in 1981. The absolute numbers have also become enormous. In 1960 there were 393,000 divorces in the USA. This reached a peak of 1,213,000 in 1981 and has remained only just below that figure throughout the '80s (1990 estimate: 1,175,000).

In 1920 there was one divorce for every 7 US marriages; in 1940 it was one for every 6 marriages. The subsequent figures are: 1960: one in 4; 1972: one in 3; 1977: one in 2. Perhaps the most striking statistics of all are the comparisons between the number of first-time marriages (bachelor marries spinster) and of divorces in any given year. They are almost equal. In 1975 there were 1,294,000 first-time marriages and 1,036,000 divorces; by 1985 there were 1,310,000 first-time marriages and 1,190,000 divorces.

Marriages have also been lasting less long. In 1984, English law reduced the legal waiting period between marriage and petitioning for divorce from (normally) 3 years to (always) one. As a result, in 1989 one in 10 divorcees had been married for less than 3 years when they received their decree absolute. In 1983, it was only one in 100. The median duration of marriages ending in divorce was 11.5 years when that statistic began to be recorded in 1963; it had dropped to 9.7 years by 1989. The equivalent US figure for the median duration of a marriage ending in divorce was 6.9 years in 1986.

The large majority of divorcees, especially if they are young and especially if they are male, remarry. In England in the one year 1974, for example, 79% of all divorced men in the 20–24 age band remarried; the equivalent figure for women was 47%. This remarriage rate has dropped very considerably since then; the figures for 1983 in the same age band were Men: 19% and Women: 23%. Similarly the rate for all age bands has fallen. In the one year 1974 22% of all divorced men and 14% of all divorced women remarried. By 1989, these figures had fallen to 8% for men and 6% for women.

These declining figures should not be misinterpreted. The number of people remarrying after divorce continues to climb steadily. In 1974, 64,080 male divorcees remarried and 61,660 female divorcees. By 1989 these figures had reached: 84,035 men and 81,702 women. Also, while the remarriage rate for divorcees had fallen to 8% of all eligible (i.e. divorced) men and 6% of all eligible women by 1989, the marriage rate was far lower: 4.5% of all eligible men (i.e. unmarried and at least 16 years old) and 3.8% of all eligible women. Thus, although more divorcees – particularly if they are over 40 and particularly if they are women – are not remarrying, the major change is that divorcees are taking longer between their divorce and a remarriage. Even this is somewhat misleading because the practice of co-habitation has become not only more marked in the population at large, but particularly so among divorcees, so that a new living-together relationship may still begin very soon after – and often before – the decree absolute. It is still the case that an enormous number of those who divorce remarry. In 1961, only 9% of all marriages involved the remarriage of a divorcee; by 1989 this figure had risen to 35%.

In the United States, the figures are still more startling. By 1985 only 54.3% of all marriages were first marriages for both partners; 45.7% involved remarriage for at least one partner, and in 23.4% of all marriages both partners were remarrying. Obviously some of these marriages involved widows and widowers, but the number of widowed people remarrying is dwarfed by the number of divorcees remarrying.

Less research has been done on the percentage of second

marriages that end in divorce, but all are agreed that 'Remarriages [after divorce] are much more likely to end in divorce than first marriages' (Stone p.411). Phypers, with figures available to him from the '70s and perhaps early '80s, writes: 'Three out of ten first marriages [in England] currently end in divorce. Four to five out of ten second and subsequent marriages end in the same way' (Phypers p.120). These figures are almost certainly now conservative. Anne Kelleher in the BBC1 programme *Byline* (10 July, 1989) said that one in three first marriages end in divorce and two in three second marriages end the same way. In fact the figure for first marriages is, if anything, a little conservative, whereas the second figure may be a little high.

In the USA, Tom Jones states that 60–65% of remarriages after divorce end in a second divorce (*Fresh Start* tape: *Re-entry into the Single Life*). Hosier gives the figure as 57% (p.185), although it is not clear whether this includes remarriages after bereavement.

What is certainly true is that although the total number of divorces has recently levelled off somewhat, the proportion of second divorces continues to increase. In 1960, one or both parties had been previously divorced in 9.2% of all divorces granted in England. By 1979, this figure had become 14.7%, and by 1989 24.7%. According to Burgoyne et al., 'over half of those who divorce and remarry in their early twenties will divorce again' (p.39).

The same authors point to another feature of remarriage after divorce: 'In general second marriages which are dissolved end more quickly than first marriages; the median length of second marriages is seven years, as compared with ten for first marriages [both these figures have now become smaller]. Among this group older partners tend to end a second marriage even more quickly . . . Despite popular beliefs, remarriage does not seem to solve the problems generated by divorce' (p.39).

Stone's conclusion is irrefutable: 'The late twentieth century . . . has seen a revolution in behaviour, values and the law, and the rise of divorce from a statistically insignificant oddity to a commonplace event' (p.7). In fact, the statistics tend considerably to underestimate the problem because they only take account of divorces granted and do not include the separated or what Dominian calls 'those who continue to live under the same roof but have ceased to have a marital relationship' (p.16).

## Causes: Sociological

Inevitably, we ask what the causes are of this phenomenal rise in divorce and remarriage. While different writers, as we shall see, lay greater stress on one factor or another, most are agreed that the following changes in popular attitudes and behaviour have made a major contribution:

### 1.   The stress on rights, not duties

Interviewed in *Time* magazine (24 July, 1989), Alexander Solzhenitsyn wrote:

> In Western civilisations – which used to be called Western-Christian but now might be better called Western-Pagan – along with the development of intellectual life and science, there has been a loss of the serious moral basis of society. During these [past] 300 years of Western civilisation, there has been a sweeping away of duties and an expansion of rights. But we have two lungs. You can't breathe with just one lung and not with the other. We must avail ourselves of rights and duties in equal measure . . . When Western society was established, it was based on the idea that each individual limited his own behaviour. Everyone understood what he could do and what he could not do . . . Since then, the only thing we have been developing is rights, rights, rights at the expense of duty.

This is exactly the attitude of Nora in Ibsen's *The Doll's House*. Admittedly she still uses the language of duty. She is leaving Helmer because of 'my duty to myself'. But in reality, it is her *right* to self-development which she is insisting on: 'I must take steps to educate myself', 'I must set about getting experience', 'This is necessary for *me*.'

Bellah *et al.* in their survey of current attitudes in the USA describe the dominant approach to love and marriage, and indeed to relationships more generally, as 'the therapeutic attitude' which 'emerges most fully in the ideology of many practitioners and clients of psychotherapy but resonates much more broadly in the American middle class' and is contrasted sharply, by Bellah, with authentic Christian attitudes. 'In its pure form, the therapeutic attitude denies all forms of obligation and commitment in relationships. The only requirement for the therapeutically liberated lover is to share his feelings fully with his partner.' The therapeutic approach has two basic tenets: a) I must love and accept myself, and no social or religious conventions must be allowed to stifle this knowledge and acceptance of one's self. b) I must not need another person to be complete; 'needing others in order to feel OK about oneself is a fundamental malady'. These tenets are entirely 'incompatible with self-sacrifice'. One of Bellah's interviewees, herself a trainee counsellor, says: 'Being in love . . . can mean . . . being selfish.' When asked for an example, she replies: 'Just thinking about myself and sitting and telling Thomas [her husband]. Not considering what his day was like when he comes home. Just when he comes in, saying I have to talk to him, and sit him down and talk to him . . . There are times when I don't even think about his day, but I can still love him' (pp.98–101).

Anne Kelleher in the British TV programme *Byline* (BBC1, 10 July, 1989) advocates contractual marriage in which a couple can draw up a mutually agreed, and perhaps legally binding, contract with each other which would almost certainly not include permanence in the relationship and might well opt for sexual freedom. She faces the objection that this may be against the interests of the children: 'The children's interests may have to be set aside for the sake of the parents.'

All this has obviously had the profoundest effect on the stability of marriage. 'Marriage . . . is veering away from the framework of mutual duties and rights [cf I Cor. 7:3f] towards the highest possible satisfaction of personal needs' (Dominian p.11). 'As a result, many marriages which would have been regarded as tolerable in the past are today seen as unendurable' (Stone p.414). It is not surprising that in the USA, which puts such enormous stress on individual rights, the divorce rate is higher than in all other Western countries.

## 2. Unrealistic expectations of easy and sustained happiness

Dominian, in an appendix to the Church of England Report *Marriage, Divorce and the Church*, says that nowadays life is less of a struggle. In the past, most couples were concerned with such basic questions as food, poverty and lack of adequate shelter [cf Matt. 6:25–34], but now that these have receded in significance, people are 'freer to concentrate on the next layer of their beings: the psychological, emotional and sexual, opening new vistas of varied expectations in the personal encounter between spouses while simultaneously making greater demands on them' (p.143). Unfortunately, these expectations – egged on by what children have heard about marriage from the first fairy-stories read to them, and have learned about marriage from films and videos and from the highly unrealistic descriptions of marriage often passed on by their parents – are often quite unrealistically high.

Bellah, writing in the *Fresh Start Newsletter* (Summer 1988, p.4), says that many of our problems in marriage stem from the notion of romantic love in our society, 'the notion that there is one person out there who is the perfect person for you, and if you can just find him, you will live happily ever after . . . Nobody will ever quite measure up, and you will go on looking for Mr or Mrs Right forever, never making a lasting commitment.' In fact, Bellah goes on, this very idea can have precisely the opposite effect from the one intended: 'Because our notion of romantic love is unattainable . . . we as a society have developed a deep cynicism about love relationships' so that 'many people become exploitative in their relationships, seeking only momentary pleasure'.

Disillusionment is in fact a phase which all marriages go through. When I was courting, I repeatedly said to my wife-to-be (and meant it!): 'You're perfect; I can't see anything wrong with you', an idea which quite rightly alarmed her greatly. It is very common – in fact, normal – to have a hopelessly idealised picture of your partner in the early days of your relationship. So disillusionment will almost inevitably occur. 'When this stage commences one, and usually both, parties will feel hurt, angry, bewildered and, frequently, resentful . . . we all sympathise with the young lady who bitterly exclaimed: "I took him for better or worse, but he was worse than I took him for."' (Crispin pp. 107, 109).

Marriages have always gone through stages of disillusionment. What marks out our age is that 'we want more from marriage than most of our grandparents ever dreamed was possible' (Flood p.13) and that we are not prepared to be patient and work hard at relationships to make them better. We want happiness and we want it now. Richmond tells a typical story of a woman leaving her husband, not with any other man immediately in view, saying as her parting words: 'I have another chance to be happy and I'm just not going to miss it' (p.29). The basic attitude is: 'My happiness is more important than your happiness, or the children's happiness or anybody's happiness' (p.117). According to Udry, Americans see marriage as just an arrangement for mutual gratification and so 'the kind of marriage Americans believe in simply has high divorce rates' (quoted in Atkinson p.21).

One might think that this combination of high expectations of marriage and a demand for easy and sustained happiness would at least not be present in those who were remarrying after divorce because their experience of marriage would have taught them otherwise. In fact, the very reverse is the case. 'Those who leave one partnership for another often cherish very high expectations of the new relationship. The rhetoric of their accounts and explanations frequently contains many references to the way their new partner has "changed my whole life", increasing their self-confidence and helping them to discover new aspects of their identity. They may also emphasise how their view of marriage itself has changed, partly from the postmortems carried out on former partnerships which play an important part in the conversation of second courtships. . . The discovery that your second partner is not so very different from your first, that your responses are depressingly familiar or even that, constituted of the daily trivia of domestic life, one marriage is very like another, brings its own bitter disenchantment' (Burgoyne *et al.* p.118).

These two first causes – the emphasis on rights not duties, and the expectation of easily-attained happiness – are closely linked. Our forebears were simply not able to enjoy instant solutions to problems in many areas of life, but 'this new demand of instant gratification of individual desires tends to erode the sense of obligation and responsibility both within the family and in society at large, and in consequence leads to a rise in the divorce rate' (Stone p.414).

## 3.  The emancipation of women

Dominian sees this as 'the most important event' in the changes affecting marriage (pp.10f). In the past, husband and wife were economically and socially interdependent. The wife was chained to the home but also had a great sense of responsibility towards those she cared for. She was – and knew she was – essential to the husband for looking after the home and bringing up their (often many) children.

Advances in contraception, in technology for home use and in services (e.g. child-minding) have reduced the demand for work in the home and increased the opportunities and incentives both for work and for leisure outside it (cf Stone pp.415f).

All this has had at least four major repercussions on a woman's perception of marriage. First, it has opened the work-place to her. In 1931 only 10% of married women in England were employed; by 1987 the figure was 68%. In a study of remarriage in Sheffield, J. Burgoyne and D. Clark discovered that for many women going back to work made them question their marriages.

> A measure of financial independence was marked by a growth in confidence and a broadening of their horizons. Even if they did not consciously admit to looking for a potential new partner, their work often brought them into daily contact with men against whom they now began to judge their husbands in a less than favourable light. Work, itself, offered new challenges and enhanced their self-image. Although it is now common for husbands and others to propose 'a little job' as a potential solution to the problems of depression and

social isolation that so often beset housewives, they are often ill-prepared for the transformation that follows (Burgoyne *et al.* p.95).

Second, women have therefore become economically independent and so are freed 'from the traditional fear of economic destitution arising from divorce' (Stone p.416). Or at least they think they are. In practice, women normally come out of divorce settlements in a much worse position than men, especially because vast numbers of divorced husbands fail to pay alimony.

Third, there has been a change of expectation among women about the respective roles of husband and wife within marriage and about the sharing of chores. This changed expectation may also be reflected in how both partners talk about marriage. But the reality does not live up to the expectation. This fact is frequently pointed out by feminist writers, who themselves have had a profound influence on women's expectations. It is amply corroborated by statisticians: 'Despite the rise of female economic activity, most household tasks – cleaning and washing for example – are still done by women, even where the woman works full-time. Most child-care, and 60% of the care of elderly relatives, is also undertaken by women rather than men' (Kiernan and Wicks p.3).

Fourth, women spend far less time on bearing and raising children. At the turn of the century the average number of children was 5; now it is less than half of that. In addition, all sorts of conveniences are available to help care for children. The result is that a married couple have more time for each other – especially with the reduction of hours in the working week – even before the children leave home. When you add to that the change in life expectancy which 'at the turn of the century . . . for a man was 48 years and for a woman . . . 52 years . . . [but had] extended [by the late 1960s] to 68 for men and 78 for women' it is obvious that this puts 'much greater emphasis on the quality of the relationship between the spouses' (*Marriage, Divorce and the Church* pp.142f). Many marriages have not proved able to withstand these extra demands.

The cumulative effect of all these changes is that 'all studies agree that women are less satisfied with family life than men' (Bellah *et al.* p.111). It is not surprising then that it has increasingly been women who have petitioned for, and been granted, divorces. In England during the period 1951–60 women accounted for 55% of divorce petitions or decrees (the official statistics changed from recording petitions to decrees in 1957). This had risen to 67% for the 1970s and to 72% by 1989. 'Surveys in Britain, the United States and Australia have all found that 3 women leave their husbands for every man who leaves his wife' (Crispin p.88).

## 4. The removal of parental support

In the past, many couples lived near their parents and other relatives. They were readily available to give support and advice when asked, or themselves became aware that the marital relationship was deteriorating and took the initiative in talking about it. Not only were parents near, but their opinions and influence carried real weight. This support and advice 'held together many moderately unsatisfactory marriages' (Stone pp.414f).

Much of this has now changed. 'The massive mobility of modern life has removed family supports . . . Apart from nearby relatives and friends, there was support even from the corner grocer who asked how Johnny's birthday party went, and from the local doctor who had brought "Mom" herself into the world' (Freeman p.193). Now couples often live far away from where they grew up and have their roots. Parents are of course easily reached by telephone and by modern means of transport, but their advice is much less frequently sought or heeded. Even when children do confide in their parents, it is normally when they are away from – often, when they have separated from – their partner, and the parents are almost bound, in the absence of the other partner, to see things entirely from their child's point of view.

## 5. The acceptance of divorce and remarriage

In 1936, Edward VIII ascended the British throne. Almost immediately it became clear to the government (although the British papers hushed it up) that he wanted to marry a divorcee,

Mrs Wallis Simpson. He thought that he could keep his private
and public lives separate but, as A. J. P. Taylor writes, 'divorce
still carried a moral stigma and still drove men from public
office. It was especially damaging for a king' (p.399). Baldwin,
then Prime Minister, made it absolutely clear that Edward must
break off his relationship with Mrs Simpson or abdicate. Edward
suggested a compromise: that Mrs Simpson should become
his wife but not the queen. Baldwin consulted the govern-
ments of the Dominions and reported that all of them were
against the idea. He also threatened that if his advice were not
taken, the entire cabinet would resign. Then, on 2 December,
1936, the news of the king's relationship burst in the British
press. Popular opinion was strongly against the king's marriage
and on 11th December he abdicated.

It is very hard to imagine that situation happening today.
'The ancient moral stigma that for centuries lay upon marital
breakdown, and especially . . . divorce has been removed' (Stone
p.415). Indeed it is not unusual nowadays to find divorce,
and marital unfaithfulness, being actively encouraged. In *Uncle
Vanya*, Elena is married to the very insensitive and self-centred
Serebryakov. Vanya is in love with her and makes no secret about
it. She makes a very modern reference to environmental concerns and also shows what many are doing to marriages today:

> ELENA: Everyone's rude about my husband, everyone looks on
> me with pity: 'The poor thing, she has an elderly husband.'
> Oh how I understand this sympathy for me. It's just as
> Astrov was saying a moment ago: you mindlessly destroy
> forests and soon nothing will be left on earth. In precisely
> the same way you mindlessly destroy humans and soon,
> thanks to you, there will be no faithfulness left on earth,
> no purity, no capacity for self-sacrifice. Why can't you
> look calmly at a woman when she isn't yours? Because
> – that doctor [Astrov] is right – in all of you there is a
> demon of destruction. You have no pity either for forests,
> or birds, or women, or one another.
> VANYA (interrupting): I don't like this philosophising!
>        (A. P. Chekhov: *Uncle Vanya*. Author's translation)

If divorce is often actively encouraged today, remarriage of divorcees – which actually was the fundamental issue in Edward VIII's case – is even more so. Frequently divorcees have told me how family and friends have almost immediately encouraged them to look for a new partner. Research bears this out. 'As the Sheffield remarriage study [carried out by J. Burgoyne and D. Clark] indicated very clearly, there is now strong institutional support for remarriage as a means of re-creating normal family life for divorced parents and their children. Many of the couples in this study described how their attempts to find greater fulfilment in a second partnership were encouraged informally by friends and family and, more formally, by professional advisers. For mothers and the minority of fathers with custody of children, a second partnership was often proposed as a solution to both the emotional and financial problems of single parenthood' (Burgoyne et al. p.38).

This advice is confidently given despite the fact that second marriages, particularly if entered into soon after divorce, are even more likely to end in divorce. Burgoyne et al. suggest that part of the reason may be that it is then easier for all concerned – family and friends as well as the divorcee – to come to terms with the divorce. 'It is as if divorce is more manageable if it is treated as a temporary aberration or momentary failure within a conventional sequence of personal and family changes' (p.12).

It is obvious that if divorce and remarriage are becoming much more acceptable – and even being advocated – within society, they will occur more frequently.

## 6. The decline in religion

In Stott's opinion, 'undoubtedly the greatest single reason [for the growth of divorce] is the decline of Christian faith in the West' (*Issues*, p.259). He cites as one piece of evidence that in 1850 4% of English marriages took place in a registry office as opposed to a church, whereas this figure had risen to 51% in 1979. Interestingly, the number of marriages taking place in church (1989: 52%), especially where it is a first marriage for both parties (1989: 69%), has grown during the 1980s, at a time when the divorce rate has almost ceased growing. It would be interesting to know if the two statistics are linked causally.

Stone asks why the British divorce figures are so much higher than those in almost all other European countries. He answers: 'One of the most likely explanations must surely be the marginal level of current English religious belief and practice, as evidenced by very low church attendance' (p.415). This is borne out by a comparative table in *LandMARC* (New Year, 1991) giving latest figures available for different countries:

| | 1981 Church attendance as % of population | 1987 Divorces per 1,000 existing marriages[1] | 1988 % Births outside marriage | 1982 % women aged 20–24 co-habiting |
|---|---|---|---|---|
| Sweden | 4 (Est.) | 12 (Est.) | 51 | 44 (1981) |
| Denmark | 5 (1985) | 13 | 45 | 45 (1981) |
| France | 12 (1987) | 8 | 28 | 12 |
| UK | 13 | 12 | 26[2] | 18 (1987) |
| W. Germany | 21 | 9 | 10 | 14 |
| The Netherlands | 27 | 8 | 10 | 16 |
| Belgium | 30 | 8 | 11 (Est.) | 7 |
| Italy | 36 | 2 | 6 | 1 (1983) |
| Spain | 41 | 0.0 | 10 (Est.) | n/a |
| Irish Republic | 82 | 0.0 | 12 | 2 |

The correlation between low church attendance and high divorce rate is of course called into question by the facts in the United States. Here church attendance is much higher than in almost all European countries but the divorce rate is also substantially higher. It must be added, however, that purely 'social' or nominal church-going is much more common in the United States than in Europe, especially Protestant Europe, and the gap between convictions about God and acceptance of normative Christian morality seems particularly wide.

But what is the Christian understanding of marriage? The rest of this book will seek to answer that question, but C. S. Lewis

---

[1] Amended slightly by using the official statistics of the EEC.
[2] In the same year, 41% of all recorded *conceptions* in England and Wales were outside marriage.

summed it up very clearly and also showed why it is so hard to follow Christ's teaching: 'The Christian rule is: "Either marriage, with complete faithfulness to your partner, or else total abstinence." Now this is so difficult and so contrary to our instincts that obviously cither Christianity is wrong or our sexual instinct, as it now is, has gone wrong. One or the other . . . I think it is the instinct which has gone wrong' (p.85). Anne Kelleher, from an entirely secular viewpoint, confirms part of Lewis' thesis. She advocates a contractual relationship to replace marriage. This is because she believes there are two great drawbacks to marriage: the first is that in marriage you promise to remain married for the rest of your life; the second is that in marriage you promise to have sex with only this one person for ever, which Kelleher dubs wholly unrealistic (*Byline*, BBC1, 10 July, 1989).

As Lewis and Kelleher both acknowledge, our sexual instinct drives us naturally to promiscuity. Unless it is restrained – most frequently by religious convictions and, in Christian terms, reliance on the power of the Holy Spirit – it will lead us inevitably into sexual liaisons after marriage (adultery; Kelleher states that 6 out of ten wives are unfaithful to their husbands, and 7 out of ten husbands to their wives) and sexual relationships before marriage (in biblical terms, fornication; and also, in modern sociological terms, co-habitation).

It is now a majority practice to co-habit before marrying. At the beginning of the 1970s 7% of never-before-married women co-habited prior to their marriage. This had risen to 19% by the late 1970s and 48% by 1987. I would be very surprised if it is not over 50% today. Certainly in my own experience as a parish clergyman, most of the couples I marry are living together.

Co-habitation is even more widely accepted than practised. A MORI poll of 18–34-year-olds carried out for *Reader's Digest* in May and June 1990 reports that 'Respondents were almost united in their condemnation of hard drugs (90%) and in withholding condemnation from unmarried couples living together (96%) or having children (92%)' (*Church Times*, 28 September, 1990).

It has often been argued that this practice, while contrary to Christian morality, makes divorce less likely, since the couple

have had the opportunity to test every aspect of the relationship before committing themselves to marriage. This is another
myth which research is exploding. 'In America there is a clear
inverse correlation between pre-marital co-habitation or "trial
marriage", and later marital stability: those whose marriages
were preceded by a period of co-habitation are *more* likely to
divorce quickly than those who did not live together before
marriage' (Stone p.413). 'Some say that living together before
getting married makes divorce less likely, since people have
had a "trial period" before committing themselves. However,
Sweden and Denmark, the countries with the highest rates
of co-habitation [45% of *all* Danes and 44% of *all* Swedes
in the 20–24 age group are co-habiting at any one time] are
also those with the highest divorce rates. Nearly half of all
marriages end in divorce, most occurring in the first five years
of marriage' (*LandMARC*, New Year, 1991). Stone offers a
number of possible explanations for these facts of which the
most likely, in my opinion, is: 'Those who co-habit before
marriage take the marriage bond less seriously than others, and
are more inclined to regard it as a conditional contract, easily
entered into and easily broken' (p.413).

Among remarrying divorcees, co-habitation is even more
practised. Kiernan and Wicks, at the same time as reporting
that 48% of women marrying in 1987 had co-habited before
their marriage, stated that 'around 7 out of 10 second marriages
are preceded by a period of co-habitation'. Moreover, the median
duration of this co-habitation had considerably increased from
28 months in 1979 to 34 months in 1987. Yet, as we have seen
already, the divorce rate for second marriages rose significantly
in the 1980s and second marriages ending in divorce lasted
considerably shorter than first marriages.

Dominian has a very telling comment on the relationship
between these phenomena and the Christian faith. The first
paragraph of his book *Marital Breakdown* makes the point that
divorce and remarriage were 'widely recognised' before the ad-
vent of Christian teaching. 'Christianity established a new ideal
of life-long indissoluble marriage in Europe and in those parts
of the world where western civilisation has had an influence. But
in the last 300 years, and particularly during the last century,

there has been a gradual lessening of Christian influence . . . So the earlier solutions have been reintroduced. Divorce [and remarriage] is thus a return to a pre-Christian solution to marital failure' (p.9). The sad fact is that many professing Christians have gone along with the abandonment of the Christian view of marriage.


## 7. Early remarriage

The causes that we have already examined relate equally to the breakdown of first and of subsequent marriages. There are also several factors which relate only to second (and later) marriages and contribute significantly to the large percentage of these that end in divorce.

Early remarriage is one factor. In 1981 the official statistics for England showed that 'about half the people who are divorced in any one year remarry within 5 years' (Social Trends, HMSO, 1981). Hosier reports the equivalent figures for the USA as 62% of divorced men and 54% of divorced women remarrying within 5 years (p.184). Freeman makes a bolder claim: 'It has been estimated that the majority of remarriages take place during the first year after divorce' (p.203). Her source dates, however, from 1979 and in view of the lengthening duration of co-habitation before marriage, it is probably no longer accurate. But what may well be true is that a very large number – probably a majority – begin co-habiting within a year of their divorce and that many of these relationships do ultimately lead to marriage.

The facts are, however, that the shorter the period between the divorce and the start of a new relationship that leads to marriage, the greater the likelihood of this second marriage leading to divorce. Bob Burns states that in America 68% of remarriages within 2 years of divorce end in divorce themselves (Second Wind tape).

Divorce is always an emotional bombshell. However much it has been anticipated and even thought through, it almost invariably turns out to be far harder for both partners than either ever imagined. It crushes self-confidence, it rouses anger and guilt, it promotes insecurity, it complicates all inter-personal relationships, especially romantic and sexual ones. Its effects are frequently compared with those of bereavement and, perhaps even more than in bereavement, it takes several years for the emotional wounds to heal. It is therefore at least 2–3 years before most divorcees are ready for a new male-female exclusive relationship. Most enter such new relationships too early, and this is a major contributory factor to the high incidence of divorce in second marriages.

## 8.  Children

In most divorces children are involved. Because the number of divorces occurring in the first few years of marriage is growing, more couples are divorcing before the arrival of children, but still in 1989 there were children involved in 69% of English divorces and children under 16 involved in 55%. Each year during the 1980s around 150,000 children under the age of 16 experienced their parents' divorce, so that now one in 5 children has this experience before reaching the age of 16 and official estimates are that, if 1988–89 divorce rates continue, this ratio will reach almost one in 4. In the 1980s the most marked increase has been in the number of children aged 0–4 affected by divorce: in 1979 it was 24% of all children under 16 of divorcing parents, by 1989 it was 33%.

In the USA, where the average number of children per divorcing couple is considerably lower than in England, probably because the median duration of marriages ending in divorce is significantly lower (1986: 6.9 years), nevertheless over a million children are involved in divorce every year (1980: 1,174,000; 1986: 1,064,000). A 1980 *Newsweek* article reports that 12 million children under 18 'currently' have divorced parents and that 45% of all children will live with only one parent at some time before age 18.

In these circumstances, remarriage is very often seen as the solution. It is argued that the children need a male and female parent, that mothers, especially of young children, need male support, and therefore the best possible outcome is for the custodial parent – normally the mother – to remarry. On a financial level, this does indeed prove advantageous. Most divorced women who are looking after a family are able to offer their children a substantially better standard of living after their remarriage. But at almost every other level, children make a second marriage more difficult and second marriages make life more difficult for the children.

To take the children first, research shows very clearly that while divorce affects almost all children badly (though divorcing parents frequently try to persuade themselves to the contrary and the effects, especially with girls, sometimes only become apparent years later), these effects are much milder where the children continue to see both parents regularly and much more acute where they lose contact with one parent, normally the father. In practice, 'half the fathers who divorce lose contact with their children within two or three years' (Clulow and Mattinson p.17). This tendency is much more pronounced where there has been a remarriage. On the one hand, the ex-husband is now even more reluctant to have contact with his former wife. On the other hand, 'the custodial parent and new partner may try to discourage children from seeing their other parent now that they are a "proper" family once more' (Burgoyne *et al.* p.135). The 1980 *Newsweek* article already cited reports that 25,000 children per annum are 'snatched or hidden from one parent by the other' in the USA. All this has a disastrous effect on the children. 'Three out of four children [feel] rejected by at least one of their parents after divorce, particularly where parents [have] remarried' (Toynbee: 'Children' p.33).

Remarriage often undermines the children's confidence in the love of the custodial parent. 'Mothers hope that what's good for them will be good for their children. It often isn't. Falling in love and marrying makes their children feel excluded, however hard she might try to prevent it. An intense new relationship disturbs children' (Toynbee p.34). 'The dynamics of a second marriage often involve a rewriting of the history of the earlier marriage (or marriages) so that it is seen as a sort of bad dream . . . All of this leaves little space for the children of the first marriage, who may find it very hard to adjust to a parent's re-interpretation of the past' (Burgoyne *et al.* p.135).

This re-interpretation also undermines confidence in the truthfulness of the parent because the truth – or at least a rival interpretation – often emerges later. Toynbee quotes a

typical case of 2 girls now aged 14 and 15: 'Our Mum ran off
with another man one day, and left us alone with Dad. He said
we'd never see her again, because she'd been so wicked. We never
understood how she could have done that to us.' In fact, five
years after the separation, a family friend arranged for them to
meet with their mother who told them she had repeatedly tried
to visit them but 'Dad had turned her away at the door lots of
times. I'm beginning to think he was more wicked than she was,
to keep us from our mother' (p.34).

Parents who remarry frequently try to convince themselves
that their children get on really well with their new partner.
Of course this is sometimes the case, but far more frequently
the new step-parent is seen as an intrusion into the home;
often children continue dreaming of reconciliation between their
parents long after one or both have remarried. A girl quoted by
Toynbee is much more typical than most would like to think:
'My Mum's married again but I hate my stepfather. He has no
right to boss me about. He only does it to throw his weight
around. He wishes we weren't there, and we wish he wasn't.
My Mum gets really upset when we row all the time. My
sister and me used to try to get him so angry he'd hit us,
then we could call the police and have him taken away. But
he never actually hit us' (p.34).

This last quote shows the other side of the coin: how step-
children make the experience of marriage much more difficult
for the new partner. This is particularly so if he or she has not
been married before or did not have children. Men 'find that
they have suddenly acquired many of the economic and social
responsibilities of fatherhood' and resent having to 'compete
with the children for their mother's attention'. Women find that
their standard of living is significantly reduced by payments
to their new husband's former family 'and their life together
may seem to be dictated by his arrangements over access to
his children' (Burgoyne *et al.* p.119). In England, the *Observer*
reports: 'It is the strains of step-parenthood that contribute
to the even higher divorce rate for second marriages – one
in two second marriages fail' (3 September, 1989). The *New
York Times* reports exactly the same for America: 'In the
USA more than 1,000 new stepfamilies form every day, and

fewer than half of these marriages survive' (2 March, 1987).

Phypers concludes: 'It may seem hard to tell a single parent, struggling to bring up 2 or 3 children on a limited income, to wait until the children have grown up before marrying again, but that is often the best advice' (p.122). Custodial parents are more likely to recognise the truth of this; perhaps that is one reason why divorced women are three times less likely to remarry than divorced men (Stone p.420). But non-custodial parents find their relations with their children are just as much affected by their remarriage; sometimes more, because it means that they lose all, or almost all, contact with their children. And this too puts great strains on the new marriage.

## Causes: Political

In addition to the sociological causes we have noted, Stone points to three highly significant political factors that have contributed to the growing incidence of divorce in England and Wales.

### 1.  Two World Wars

Both World Wars encouraged hasty marriages and also meant that husbands and wives were apart from each other for extended periods. 'Each [war] . . . had the short-term effect of a sudden post-war explosion of divorces, mostly initiated by husbands against adulterous wives'; but they also significantly changed attitudes to marriage and therefore had 'the long-term effect of raising divorce rates permanently by a factor of four or five' (Stone p.412).

Thus, in the period 1910–17 the average number of divorces was 696 per year. This rose to 1,654 in 1919 and jumped to an average of 3,306 in 1920 and 1921. While it then settled down, the average figure was 2,995 for 1922–30, over 4 times the pre-war figure. Again, in the ten years 1933–42, the average was 5,729. This rose to 10,012 in 1943, 29,829 in 1946 and 60,254 in 1947. Again the figures settled back down for a time, but still the average for 1951–60 (26,872) was over four and a half times the figure for the decade to 1942.

In 1948, Kirk wrote:

> Undoubtedly, many hasty and often sordid marriages were contracted under the conditions of war, and much marital infidelity grew out of the long separations from one another that husbands and wives had to endure. In part, the increase of business in the Divorce Court is no more than the result of an instinctive demand for the rectification of this distressing state of things. As married life gradually settles down into more normal channels and the psychological impulse to marry in haste . . . abates . . . we may look for a reduction in the number of applications for decrees (pp.v-vi).

History soon proved him wrong.

## 2.   Divorce laws

Three sets of legislation have profoundly affected the availability of divorce in England and Wales during the twentieth century. In 1938 A. P. Herbert's Divorce Reform Act came into force. The main effect of this Act was to extend the legal grounds for divorce from the sole grounds of adultery to include desertion, cruelty and insanity. The numbers of divorce petitions showed an instant leap: from 4,886 in 1937 to 8,254 in 1939. As with all new legal openings for divorce, the figures then settled back somewhat, after the backlog of those waiting for a divorce had been cleared, but still the figure in 1942 (before another great leap) was 7,618, over half as much again as in 1937. The numbers thereafter continued to rise. 'That the Act was [at least partly] responsible is proved by the fact that of the causes for divorce cited by women petitioners in 1950 (the first year for which data are available) over 50% were the new ones of desertion and cruelty rather than adultery' (Stone p.401). The Divorce Reform Act of 1969 came into force on 1st January, 1971, and was subsequently consolidated in the Matrimonial Causes Act of 1973. It introduced a solitary ground for divorce: irretrievable breakdown of the marriage. For the first time, it became possible for the divorce to be petitioned on the evidence merely of the couple's separation. Since this separation had to be for two years with consent or 5 years without consent, it was perhaps inevitable that there would be a small delay in seeing the effects of the Act, especially as from 1957 onwards the official figures recorded the date on which the divorce decree was awarded rather than when the petition was filed. Nevertheless, the effects of the Act were very marked. In 1970, 58,239 divorces were granted. This rose to 74,437 in 1971 and 119,025 in 1972. 1973 saw a slight dip (106,003) but the average for the period 1974–80 was 131,492. Again, it is clear that the Act was responsible to a considerable extent for this increase. For example, as evidence of marital breakdown, it introduced the concept of 'intolerable behaviour'. Women in particular quickly availed themselves of this new legal concept because by 1982 46% of successful women petitioners cited this cause (1989: 54%).

This flood of new divorce petitions simply overwhelmed the legal system.

> With over 150,000 cases to be processed every year, no judge has the time to investigate 'behaviour', and since most suits are uncontested, he has no evidence . . . except the basic statement of the petitioner. The result therefore is not a careful evaluation of the reasons for the breakdown of the marriage, but merely a swift and cheap administrative procedure to churn out hundreds of thousands of no fault divorces on demand (Stone p.413).

The last significant piece of legislation has been the Matrimonial and Family Proceedings Act 1984 which reduced the minimum interval between marriage and filing a petition for divorce from (normally) three years to (always) one year. This represented a much smaller change in the law, but again there was a clear rise in the number of divorces from 147,000 in 1983 to 160,000 in 1985 before settling back a little to 151,000 in 1989, of which 15,231 were decrees actually granted within the first 36 months of marriage. O'Donovan's conclusion seems inescapable: 'In divorce, as in other things, availability seems to create demand' (p.114).

## 3. Legal Aid

Before 1857, the only way one could divorce was by a private Act of

Parliament. The cost was, understandably, very high. There were only 317 such special Acts between 1670 and 1857. Even after laws were introduced to allow for civil divorce, it was only the rich who felt they could afford the legal costs involved. But in the twentieth century, beginning in 1914, Parliament began giving increasingly generous grants of legal aid to the poor. This, Stone believes, may have been the most important contributory factor, on the political level, to the enormous increase in divorces because 'the working class . . . at last obtained access to the divorce market' (p.413).

> Today the divorce rate of manual workers is four times greater than that of professional couples . . . Much of this . . . may merely indicate a shift into the divorce courts of huge numbers of previously unrecorded breakdowns, desertions and private separations, but some of it must surely reflect a real change in working-class matrimonial behaviour . . . Thus divorce, which for centuries has been a privilege exclusively confined to the rich, has now become a legal device most commonly used by the poor (Stone p.412).

## Christian Attitudes

In the current situation, the clergy have very largely lost their nerve and are often painfully perplexed about what they should do. They know the teaching of Jesus which seems to state that divorce is always to be avoided (except in the case of adultery) and that remarriage is not to be considered during the lifetime of a divorced partner (except – so some would argue – for the 'offended' party in a divorce on the grounds of adultery) (Matt. 5:31f, 19:1–12; Mark 10:1–12; Luke 16:18; 1 Cor. 7:10f). Yet their hearts go out to many of their parishioners and friends who are in such pain and who want to get out of a desperately unhappy marriage or are looking for happiness in a second union. Moreover, they don't want to upset their own congregations who increasingly include divorced and remarried men and women, and parents who would like to see their divorced children married again.

Stone notes that in the House of Lords debate on the 1969 Divorce Reform Act, 'the bishops were notable mostly for their silence'. Amongst several possible explanations for this, the first he suggests is 'that the tide of lay opinion was too strong for them'. He adds: 'What is striking about this debate was the contrast with those in 1857 and 1937: this time, no speaker so much as mentioned the . . . theological arguments about the sanctity of marriage according to the words of Christ' (pp.408f).

At a more grassroots level, Phypers gives this accurate description of many ministers: 'Christian leaders too are bewildered and confused with the problems of divorce, and the remarriage of divorcees, in the life of the church . . . Most stumble from one situation to another, leaving confusion and hurt in their wake through their muddled thinking and inconsistent practice' (p.5). Typical of many was the remark of a man, whose ministry I greatly respect: 'I do remarry divorcees but I am not at all happy about it.'

As for the members of our churches, increasingly they do not even understand the problem. They have not heard Christian preaching about divorce and remarriage because their leaders consider the subject 'too hot to handle'. More and more therefore see it in very straightforward terms: God can forgive any sins; certainly there are faults on both sides in any divorce but God can forgive these, there should therefore be no barrier in the way of remarriage. To say otherwise is to treat divorce as the unforgivable sin.

This is very well expressed in the *Church of England Newspaper*'s Letter of the Week for 17 March, 1989:

> The C of E by its attitude declares divorce an unforgivable sin. Murder, adultery, homosexuality etc. which, once repented of, allow a person to become or remain a priest (in some cases without even repenting) is obviously more acceptable to God than the divorcee. This is untenable and there is no theological basis for this position . . . The attitude in the C of E must be changed . . . Its present position usurps the authority of God who has proclaimed, through Jesus, new life and forgiveness for all who accept him.

In the United States any serious questioning about the legitimate grounds for divorce and about remarriage is even less understood. The Episcopal Church in the USA used to forbid the remarriage of divorcees, but by the time the canon law was changed, Episcopalians had almost completely forgotten why remarriage had ever been forbidden and had begun positively to advocate it. In 1971 a well-known Episcopal church hired a ministerial consulting firm to determine what kind of new rector they should be looking for. As a result of surveying the congregation, the firm reported: 'happily married preferred, but divorce no barrier providing remarriage'.

## Coming to Terms with the Biblical Material

Yet the gospels seem stubbornly to maintain that divorce is only to be considered in exceptional circumstances and that remarriage is not an option for the divorcee. The rest of this book will seek to examine the relevant passages and see whether they really *do* say these things; it will proceed by a detailed examination of the biblical texts. But it does also seem appropriate to think briefly about the ways in which Christians routinely seek to come to terms with, and perhaps to avoid, the impact of these sayings of Christ's. Bromiley helpfully mentions several at the beginning of his book *God and Marriage* and I have added two more which I have most frequently encountered.

*1.   'The Bible teaches the ideal'*

'For some writers and readers the biblical material has the rank of an ideal for which we are all to aim but which we cannot realistically hope to achieve, since the pressures and complexities of life prove too strong not only for non-Christians but for Christians too' (Bromiley pp.ix-x). 'Be perfect, therefore, as your heavenly Father is perfect' (Matt. 5:48) is a wonderful standard to be aiming for, but of course we shall never reach it. When, therefore, Jesus says: 'What God has joined together, let man not separate' (Mark 10:9//Matt. 19:6) and states that remarriage is adultery (Mark 10:11f//Matt. 19:9; 5:32; Luke 16:18, cf 1 Cor. 7:10f), this is to be taken as the ideal. We know, as Christ himself knew, that we will not be able to live it.

What Christ taught, these Christians tend to say, is 'the sanctity of marriage' – a wonderfully vague term which allows us to affirm that Christ strongly emphasised the permanence of the marriage relationship while at the same time we avoid all the awkwardly specific statements Jesus made about divorce and remarriage.

In fact, we cannot so easily water down Christ's teaching. It is true that, specifically in the context of divorce, he recognised human 'hardness of heart' (Mark 10:5//Matt. 19:8) but for that reason alone he did not allow men and women to divorce and remarry. On the contrary, he rescinded the permission to divorce which Moses had given (Mark 10:1–12//Matt. 19:1–9). We will fail, but that does not mean we can approve of, or even acquiesce in, such failure to obey Christ.

## 2.   'Life is not black and white'

A minister in the United States felt compelled to refuse a request for marriage because the fiancee had been previously married. A friend of the bridegroom's, who described himself as a 'life-long member' of his church, on whose staff he had served as youth minister, wrote to the minister:

> Divorce and remarriage are realities of today's world and there is a great need for compassion, understanding and healing on the part of the Church's leaders. Relationships are not black and white. Each person has his/her own story. You had the opportunity to minister to Penny[1] [the divorcee] and her children and to promote stability and healing in their lives. You had the opportunity to provide a good and strong relationship for Chuck and Penny as they plan their life together. It is my prayer that God will open your heart and mind to the realities of today's world so that you might have a better understanding of how to meet people where they are and how to meet their needs and more effectively minister to them.

A letter to a Scottish minister in a similar situation simply said: 'Things in life are often not clear cut.'

It is undoubtedly true that each situation is different. It is imperative for the pastor or Christian friend to find out as much as he can about each individual's story, if possible from both partners' point of view. It is also true that what will be

---

[1] All the stories and quotations of individuals in this book are true; their names, and sometimes other details, have however been changed.

pastorally appropriate will vary from couple to couple and person to person. But Christ's teaching on the subject of divorce and remarriage is not painted in shades of grey. It presents a view of marriage which is true of all married couples, Christian or non-Christian, young or old, sinned against or sinning. The only distinction which he does recognise is that between divorce for adultery and divorce where adultery is not the fundamental cause. We shall later examine what exactly he was teaching about divorce and remarriage, but certainly the impression strongly given is that the moral issues involved are not infinitely variable, depending on different life situations.

## 3.   'Christ's instructions are not laws'

Some insist that Christ was not seeking to lay down laws which should be rigidly obeyed. On the contrary, he taught ethical principles and gave moral guidance which will have to be applied to specific situations and will inevitably admit of exceptions.

One of the great strengths of Eduard Schweizer's commentaries is their brief comments about contemporary application. His final words on Mark 10:1–12 reveal precisely this approach: 'Jesus' statement on the subject [of divorce] is very clear, and in the marriage relationship there are times when his straightforward approach to this subject is most helpful.' The clear implication is that there are also times when we can ignore Christ's 'straightforward approach'.

In fact there are strong grounds for believing that Jesus himself and the evangelists did see his teaching as having the status of law for his disciples. Most commentators, for example, see Jesus in Matthew's gospel as the new lawgiver, surpassing Moses. Gundry puts this very clearly: 'As a teacher of righteousness, Jesus legislates the law that his disciples are to obey (5:21–48; 7:24–28; 28:20).' Jesus is 'a new legislator greater than Moses'. Matthew is at pains 'to accentuate the authority of Christ's law' (Gundry: *Matthew* p.7).

John's gospel has a similar emphasis on Christ's teaching as law, in Christ's reiterated admonition to 'keep my commandments' (John 14:15, 21; 15:10) or to 'keep my word(s)' (John 8:31–55; 14:23f; 15:20).

But whatever our conclusion about how much Jesus saw himself as teaching a new law, it is clear that neither he nor the evangelists are encouraging us to be selective about when we apply his teaching, in the way that Schweizer wants us to be. Helen Oppenheimer says trenchantly: 'It has frequently been insisted [by some] that "Christ did not legislate", but to put the matter so can be misleading if it is then assumed that Christ's commands need not be obeyed' (quoted in Atkinson p.147).

## 4. *'The Bible is culturally conditioned'*

Bromiley quotes some Christians who say: 'As Scripture itself conforms to its own age and place, so it may be permissible for us to conform in some measure to our own age and place' (Bromiley p.x). One of the letters quoted above alludes to this: 'Divorce and remarriage are realities of today's world . . . It is my prayer that God will open your heart and mind to the realities of today's world . . .' Fetterman thinks the point is self-evident when applied to divorce: 'To sacred Scripture should be added the strong supports offered by reason and tradition . . . One example might be appropriate here. Jesus explicitly forbade divorce (Mark 10:1–9), yet our denomination explicitly allows it. The reality seems to point to a need for the Scriptures to be interpreted and an acknowledgment that theological understanding develops from age to age' (p.15).

This approach says that the teaching of Christ applies to somebody else (the people of his time) and not to me. It is interesting to see a variation of this theme in the time of Christ himself. Guelich states that the Jews debated the grounds for divorce but that there is no evidence that they ever questioned the right to divorce as such. To reach this position, they interpreted Malachi 2:16 as applying only to the Gentiles to whom God had not given the Law (Guelich on Matt. 5:31).

There is no question that certain specific instructions in the Bible are expressed in terms of the particular culture of their time and need 'translating' into our different contemporary culture(s). It is also true that specific instructions are occasionally argued for by Scripture on grounds that no longer pertain. But the striking fact about Christ's teaching on divorce and remarriage is that he bases it firmly on God's original intention in creating men and women and in instituting marriage. If he regarded anything in this area as culturally conditioned, it was the Mosaic permission to divorce (Mark 10:1–12; Matt. 19:1–12).

## 5.  'There are so many interpretations'

A divorcee wanting to remarry wrote to her minister: 'We are neither blind nor deaf to your sincerely held views, but other equally sincere Christians believe we do not transgress the law . . . Some good Christians . . . spend years deciding whether a word in Greek or Hebrew means this or that. Others . . . interpret them differently.'

It is absolutely true that there are different interpretations of the biblical material and that there are points on which Christians seeking to take Christ's words with the utmost seriousness disagree, although it should immediately be added that these differences can be greatly exaggerated; on the main points the overwhelming majority are agreed, and the major point of disagreement is the admittedly vital one of whether a person may remarry in the case of divorce for adultery. But the sad fact is that many Christians believe that these disagreements allow them to suspend judgment on the teaching of Christ. The argument runs, whether it is consciously worked out in this way or not: 'There are many different interpretations held by different sincere and scholarly Christians. Therefore I cannot be expected to reach a definite conclusion. Therefore I may choose the interpretation and advice which most appeals to me.'

Whenever I hear this line of argument, I am inevitably reminded of a research visit I made to South Africa in the early 1980s. Many whites who at that time held a central or right-wing position were concerned not so much to convince me of their political persuasion but to lead me to accept that 'the situation is very complex'. It undoubtedly was, and is. Yet the hope was that I would feel: 'The situation is complex. Therefore I cannot come to any conclusion. Therefore I should not be critical of the status quo.' I remember being taught precisely this in the 1960s in a school class on South African politics.

Yet in a context (the observance of special days) about which the New Testament is infinitely more ambivalent than it is on the subject of divorce and remarriage, Paul urges Christians to work their way through to convictions: 'Each one should be fully convinced in his own mind' (Rom. 14:5). And in the same context (broadened to include whether to eat food offered to idols), he states: 'Everything [i.e. every action] that does not come from faith is sin' (Rom. 14:23). We cannot allow different Christian views to keep us from reaching conclusions, however provisional, about the content and contemporary application of Christ's teaching.

## 6. 'We were never married in the first place'

Increasingly, I have heard Christians who want to remarry, or who have remarried, put forward this argument to support their proposed action. They believe: 'We weren't married by God', because they married before they were Christians or because they were not married in church. Or they believe: 'We should never have married in the first place, therefore God can never have considered us as married', because they never consulted God about their marriage partner, or because they married against the advice of many Christians or because they married young and didn't understand what marriage involved.

Others call into question what constitutes a true marriage by a *reductio ad absurdum* argument: 'If the Church says that a person may not remarry during the lifetime of his partner, what does this mean for the person who has lived with his girlfriend? May he never (re)marry? And should he go back to his first or his fifth sexual partner?' By raising the issue of what constitutes a marriage, and particularly of multiple sexual partners, they seek to show that the traditional Christian answers in the field of divorce and remarriage are unworkable and ridiculous (cf Mark 12:18–23).

## What is Marriage?

Many of this final set of questions will have to be examined in greater detail in the body of this book, but it seems appropriate at this point to face the question: what constitutes marriage, according to the Bible? Detailed practices vary, especially as regards the marriage ceremony. This could be fundamentally very simple (e.g. Gen. 24:62–67) or much more elaborate (e.g. Ps. 45:8–17). But in essence, and viewed purely from the less important human point of view (cf Mark 10:9//Matt. 19:6), marriage in the Bible must contain four elements. These are, of course, never spelled out in a systematic discussion of what constitutes marriage; it is assumed that readers will know very well who is married and who is not, just as is the case in most situations today. Nevertheless, the following features emerge:

## 1.  Consent

E. Neufeld in *Ancient Hebrew Marriage Laws* states that in the Old Testament an essential element in marriage is 'an intention of the parties to enter into a binding marital union' (quoted in Heth and Wenham p.103). This consent had to be given by both parties, the bride as well as the groom.

Throughout the biblical period, marriages were of course frequently arranged by the parents and in almost all cases parental permission was essential (e.g. Gen. 34:4–6). Often the parents would take the initiative (e.g. Gen. 24:1–4), but nevertheless the couple's consent was essential (Gen. 24:5–8, 57f).

The consent must of course be *to marry*. A woman who is forced against her will to marry has not really married. In the same way, a woman who has consented to co-habit but is then forced against her will to marry has not married. In both cases the marriage is void, and for the same reason: consent has been withheld. This is why the first question asked in the marriage service is: 'Will you have (or: take) this woman/man to be your wife/husband . . .?' to which the response is: 'I will'. This is called the Declaration of Consent.

## 2.  Permanence

'Marriage [in the Bible] is first and foremost a binding covenant' (Heth and Wenham p.103). The binding nature of this covenant was expressed in a 'solemn oath', most likely spoken at the time of the covenant-making/marriage ceremony (e.g. Ezek. 16:8). This was not an oath which could be rescinded at will nor a covenant that could be terminated when desired (e.g. Ezek. 16:59–63). It was essentially an oath to 'cleave' to one's partner (Gen. 2:24 RSV).

This, however, immediately raises questions. The word we now use for a 'solemn oath' is a vow. But what if one or both of a couple make a vow with mental reservations? What if they vow to 'take you to be my wife/husband . . . till death us do part' but at the same time think 'or until one of us can't stand the other any more and we separate'? Numbers 30 makes it absolutely clear that all vows must be performed and that the Lord will not 'release' a person from a vow even if it is a 'rash promise' (Num. 30:6–8). A vow is only nullified if it is *immediately* repudiated by the relevant head of the household. Ecclesiastes specifically and sternly forbids any escape from vows by the person who protests: 'My vow was a mistake' (5:4–7).

English law takes precisely the same line: 'Vows are still vows (even if inadvisedly made), and if the vow is made, English law rightly holds the contracting parties to their public consent as against any private derogation of it' (Atkinson p.170). Lord Stowell stated as long ago as 1811: 'The parties are concluded to mean seriously and deliberately and intentionally what they have avowed in the presence of God and man.'

Another nineteenth-century English peer and judge, Lord Penzance, made a famous definition of marriage: '[Marriage] is the voluntary union for life of one man and one woman to the exclusion of all others'. This of course is a definition under English law. The Old Testament recognises polygamous marriages, but the exclusive nature of marriage is affirmed in the New Testament, and both consent ('voluntary') and permanence ('for life') are required by the entire Bible.

## 3. Public witness

Old Testament marriage was a family affair, not involving priests or Levites and not taking place in the temple or (later) synagogue, but it was essential that the marriage be 'ratified before the public (witnesses)' who would normally be friends and other family members and who would see that the proper 'social and legal customs of the day' were carried out (e.g. Gen. 34:11f) (Heth and Wenham p.104) and even be involved in checking that the bride was, as she said, a virgin (Deut. 22:13–19). Two people could not simply declare themselves married without any involvement of other people. On the contrary, human witnesses were essential, as well as the ultimate witness of all marriages: Yahweh himself (Mal. 2:14).

Kirk sums up the Christian position: 'The essence of marriage, as regards its form, consists in the exchange of vows before accredited witnesses, not in the presence or words of a priest . . . nor in the blessings of the Church' (p.28). This can take the simplest form: 'In Scotland . . . from before the Reformation until 1940, a couple could be married by simply expressing mutual consent in the presence of two witnesses . . . [without any other] form of ceremony, religious or otherwise, as an accompaniment' (*Marriage and Divorce* p.9).

## 4. *Sexual union*

There is disagreement in scholarly circles about whether marriage takes place at the time of the marriage contract or at the time of sexual 'consummation' after the contract. Kirk, for example, believes that 'the moment at which the marriage "begins" (if we may use this phrase) is the moment at which the contract is made, and not the moment at which the union is consummated between husband and wife' (p.19). Others, of which I am one, believe that sexual union is essential to marriage and that without such consummation there is no valid marriage; this will be discussed later in the book. But in any case, this is, in 999 divorce cases out of 1,000, a purely academic question, especially since all are agreed that 'it must be the *intention* of the couple that [sexual union] should come' (Kirk p.19) and that without such intention there is no valid marriage. I have myself once been involved pastorally in the nullifying of a marriage between a US citizen and an immigrant, which was contracted for money in order to allow the immigrant to enter the country. The contract was perfectly valid from a legal point of view, but there was no sexual intercourse, and no intention of engaging in it, and therefore the 'marriage' was declared void.

But sexual union alone does not make a marriage. This is quite clear in both the Old Testament (e.g. Exod. 22:16f; also the distinction between wives and concubines, though the exact legal status of concubines is not entirely clear) and the New Testament (e.g. John 4:17f). It is not true to say that a couple is married in God's eyes by virtue of the fact that they are co-habiting. They are rather, to use the Bible's terms, committing fornication.

But can there be *de facto* marriages when a couple have lived together for many years? Shouldn't they see themselves as married in the eyes of God? It may in many cases be right for them to marry (cf Exod. 22:16f), though not necessarily in every case (1 Cor. 6:12–18; see the discussion of this passage in chapter 2). But Powers is right to say that they are not married if their reason for living together – rather than getting married – is precisely because they don't *want* to get married; which is nowadays the case with the great majority of co-habiting couples. Powers believes, however, that they are married in God's eyes if their intention is to be permanently committed to each other and there is only some obstacle (for example, financial) preventing immediate marriage. These couples, says Powers, should follow due legal process and be legally married, but they are in fact married already (pp.343–5).

That assessment must in fact be mistaken. While there is indeed the intention of permanence, and perhaps private – and even public – vows of permanence, crucially the consent to marry now is not there. They are like an engaged couple, and indeed may well be engaged. The question: 'Will you have this woman/man to be your wife/husband . . . ?' does not mean: 'Do you want to, at some time in the future?' but: 'Is it your determination to do so now?'

A couple, then, must fulfil four conditions in order to be married: they must give their voluntary consent to marry this man/woman, they must promise that the relationship will be permanent, they must do so in the presence of witnesses, and they must consummate (or intend to consummate) their marriage in sexual union. Such marriages are 'joined together by

God' (Mark 10:9//Matt. 19:6). This teaching of Christ's, which represents by far the most important event that takes place at marriage, has nothing to do with whether the wedding takes place in church or in a registry office, whether a minister of religion is present or not, whether the couple are Christian believers or atheists. God joins together every couple in every valid marriage. He has been doing so, according to Christ, since 'the beginning of creation' (Mark 10:5–9//Matt. 19:4–8).

## Books

We have been looking at the wide discrepancy in this area between the teaching of Christ on the one hand and, on the other, the views about divorce and remarriage of most Christians today and the practice of many Christian leaders. Part of the problem has been the books written on the subject. I have of course read an enormous number of books on the subject in preparation for my own writing and have gained immeasurably from them; my debt is constantly apparent in this book. Yet they divide clearly into two types.

Some address in careful detail the biblical, or later theological, material. They examine and comment on the relevant texts. They come to carefully judged conclusions. Yet hardly any of these more scholarly works make any attempt to flesh out what their conclusions will mean in pastoral practice today. Luck writes: 'We will not attempt to apply our theory to practical situations. That task must be left to another book' (p.219). Nigel Biggar gave a very favourable review to Heth and Wenham's *Jesus and Divorce* but his final remarks are:

> The authors acknowledge that the moral position for which they argue on exegetical grounds . . . entails serious pastoral problems; but they rightly insist that the pastoral perplexity should not be allowed to obscure the high moral calling of married Christians to bear witness to the Gospel . . . through persistent, if unrequited, love. Nevertheless, the persuasiveness of their position would have been much enhanced had its pastoral ramifications been explored and defended as thoroughly as its exegetical foundations . . .

for example in the case of 'children whose well-being requires (?) the replacement of a divorced and absent parent' (*Churchman* 104:2 (1960) pp.181f; the question mark is Biggar's).

The other group of books is clearly written out of intimate encounter with other people's, and often their own, divorce (and remarriage). Many are very sensitive and compassionate; most are full of pastoral wisdom. Almost all seek to come to terms with the biblical material but, for the most part, do so in a woefully inadequate way, with their previously held convictions often clearly manipulating the biblical texts.

It is to try to bring these two traditions together that this book has been written. A few years ago, I asked John Stott: 'Some people are telling me it is time I wrote a book; do you think they're right?' 'Not,' he replied, 'until there's a book burning in your bones.' It was good advice, and so I put the idea out of my mind, not being often given to burning bones. But I have come across so many Christian friends and leaders who are simply bewildered by what to do faced with case after case of divorce and remarriage, and I have yet to find a book which deals thoroughly with both the biblical principles and the pastoral practice. My bones have begun to burn.

I hope it is not impertinent to urge readers to study this book with an open mind. Stott, in his book *Basic Christianity*, writes of how we should approach God's revelation. He is writing particularly for the non-Christian who is looking into the Bible's teaching about Christ, but it has always struck me that his words apply equally to the Christian examining some difficult area of biblical truth:

> Jesus promised: 'Seek and you will find' . . . We must seek *diligently* . . . This matter is so serious that we must . . . give our minds to the quest (Heb. 11:6) . . . We must seek *humbly* . . . We must use our mind; but we must also admit its limitation (Matt. 11:25). It is one of the reasons why Jesus loved children. They are teachable . . . We need the open, humble and receptive mind of a little child. We must seek *honestly* . . . Many . . . come to the Bible with their minds already made up. But God's promise is addressed only to the earnest seeker: Jeremiah 29:13 . . . We must seek *obediently* . . .

In seeking God we have to be prepared not only to revise our ideas but to reform our lives. The Christian message has a moral challenge . . . John 7:17 . . . rests on a moral condition. We have to be ready not just to believe, but to obey. We must be prepared to do God's will once he makes it known. The two hardest hindrances to overcome are intellectual prejudice and moral self-will. Both are expressions of fear, and fear is the greatest enemy of the truth (pp.16–18).

It is of course extraordinarily difficult for all of us to come to the subject of divorce and remarriage with an open mind. For all of us it is a highly-charged, emotive issue. Almost all of us now have close family and friends who are divorced and remarried. Many who read this book will themselves have been through the trauma of divorce at least once, perhaps for a second time. It is most particularly difficult to come with an open mind if we are in the middle of painful, personal decisions: if our own marriage has become unbearably difficult and we are thinking about leaving our partner, or if we have been divorced and have fallen in love with someone else.

That is why it is essential, if at all possible, to study Christ's teaching on this issue and to come to settled convictions *before* agonising personal decisions cloud our judgment. It is so much easier to be genuinely open to the hard things God may have to say when our own personal involvement in the issues is comparatively slight. But for those readers who have come to this book precisely because you have desperately difficult personal decisions to take – and indeed for us all – Heth and Wenham are surely right to say in their Preface: 'We beg you to read what follows not simply as a piece of theology but prayerfully' (pp.11f). Only then will we be able to hear clearly what Christ has taught.

I believe it is also important to come to a book of this kind *with an open Bible*. The first half of this book is entitled 'biblical principles'; its aim is to explore the relevant biblical material and see what it has to say. My principal desire is to encourage Christians to grapple with these biblical passages, to see what they teach and what their implications are for those who seek to follow Christ in today's world. It is for this reason that I have asked the publishers to print out the main texts in full. My hope is that readers will constantly be referring back to the primary source – the biblical text – and frequently looking up biblical references that are cited, in order to discover whether the conclusions drawn in this book really are to be found in the Scriptures.

An American church, which described itself as evangelical, was wrestling with questions about remarriage. They invited me to chair a discussion involving their elders and deacons. I sent them in advance a short document which simply pointed out the most important biblical texts dealing with the subject. I appended no comment but only added a short bibliography of books which studied the biblical material. On the evening itself, the discussion was mainly courteous though highly charged, but the great disappointment to me was that the biblical material was left almost completely to one side and that almost all the arguments were either pragmatic or very generalised (e.g. 'I believe in a God who . . .', 'I don't believe God would . . .').

Lastly, I pray that this book will enable readers to *come to a conclusion*. Having an open mind does not of course mean having no opinion. Christians should be noted for their open minds, always ready to receive, sift and (where appropriate) assimilate new evidence, especially where it can be shown to be rooted in the Scriptures. This will mean that we are constantly open to the possibility of being corrected, but it does not mean that we can reach no conclusions. On the contrary, St Paul urges us to work even controversial issues through, until we are 'fully convinced in our own mind' (Rom. 14:5).

Many readers will come to this book uncertain as to how they should respond in different situations of marital breakdown or desire for remarriage, though most will find that they tend towards one view or another. My great desire is that this book will help them to examine the biblical evidence and pastoral issues and to come to conclusions which will form the basis of their own marital behaviour and their pastoral practice. Shortly after C. E. B. Cranfield produced the second volume of his magisterial commentary on Romans, I wrote to thank him for how helpful it had proved in my sermon preparation. I told him that while I sometimes disagreed with him in detail, he almost invariably presented me with all the relevant evidence and enabled me to reach conclusions. My prayer is that this much lesser book will enable readers to examine the biblical evidence and reach their own carefully considered conclusions.

'The late twentieth century . . . has seen a revolution in behaviour, values and the law, and the rise of divorce [and remarriage] from a statistically insignificant oddity to a commonplace event' (Stone p.7). It is this subject which the rest of this book seeks to examine, first studying carefully the relevant biblical material and then working out some of its practical implications for contemporary pastoral practice.

# BIBLICAL PRINCIPLES

# 2

# Marriage

It is all too easy, in seeking to answer these difficult biblical and pastoral questions, to jump straight to those passages which deal with divorce: what exactly does Jesus mean when he says that divorce may be justifiable in the case of 'marital unfaithfulness' (Matt. 5:32, 19:9)? What does Paul mean when he states that a Christian who is being divorced is 'not bound in such circumstances' (1 Cor. 7:15)? To the busy reader, it may seem like pedantry – an unnecessary slowing down of the pace of this book – to begin with a chapter on marriage; and, moreover, to concentrate (as this chapter does) very largely on a single passage in the Old Testament.

Yet Jesus himself – and the other New Testament writers, notably St Paul – force us to do precisely this. When asked a question about divorce, Jesus refused to answer it until first he had explained God's will for marriage (Mark 10:1–12//Matt. 19:1–12). Indeed, he seems to say, it is quite impossible to understand God's mind on the issues of divorce and remarriage until you have come to terms with his mind on the question of marriage. So, to begin anywhere else than with a discussion of marriage in Scripture would not only be to ignore the method by which Jesus revealed his own thinking, but to risk making exactly the same mistakes about divorce and remarriage that the Jews of Jesus' own day made. They began with the biblical passages about divorce (in their case, especially Deut. 24:1–4); he began with the key passage about marriage. And one of the points he was certainly making was that their mistake stemmed from starting in the wrong place: with divorce rather than with marriage.

We dare not fall into the same error. But even granted that, is it really wise to concentrate (as this chapter will) almost exclusively on a passage in the Old Testament, however significant? If we are seeking to form a *Christian* mind on the difficult questions surrounding divorce and remarriage, surely we must turn to the New Testament for answers? The fact is, however, that this very New Testament sends us immediately back to the Old. And not just in a general sort of way. Jesus' explanation of what marriage is all about is really little more than an exposition of key verses from Genesis chapters 1 and 2, and particularly of 2:24. He makes clear what this Old Testament verse teaches about God's plan in marriage and then draws out the implications for divorce and remarriage (Mark 10:6–12//Matt. 19:4–6, 8b–9).

In his book *According to the Scriptures*, C. H. Dodd has shown how the Old Testament passages which Jesus used to describe his own person and ministry proved decisive for the New Testament writers. Since Jesus had, for example, applied Psalm 110:1 and Psalm 118:22f to himself, other New Testament writers not only re-used these same verses but scoured their Old Testament contexts for further references to Christ. The same process seems to have held true in Christian teaching about marriage. Jesus said the relations between husband and wife should be understood by reference to Genesis 1:27 and 2:24. Other New Testament writers not only went back to these verses but also looked more widely in Genesis 1 and 2 to understand both marital relations and, more generally, relations between men and women.

To say this, incidentally, is not to deny that other Jewish writers of the period certainly recognised the importance of these chapters. But it is to assert that the disciples of Jesus were, in this area, following closely and deliberately the practice of their Master. As we shall see, Paul makes a specific point of saying that he has drawn his teaching on divorce and remarriage directly from that of Christ.

And so, with the urging of Jesus and his apostles, we must turn to this key passage in Genesis chapter 2:

(18) The LORD God said, 'It is not good for the man to be alone. I will make a helper suitable for him.' (19) Now the

LORD God had formed out of the ground all the beasts of the field and all the birds of the air. He brought them to the man to see what he would name them; and whatever the man called each living creature, that was its name. (20) So the man gave names to all the livestock, the birds of the air and all the beasts of the field. But for Adam no suitable helper was found. (21) So the LORD God caused the man to fall into a deep sleep; and while he was sleeping, he took one of the man's ribs and closed up the place with flesh. (22) Then the LORD God made a woman from the rib he had taken out of the man, and he brought her to the man. (23) The man said,

'This is now bone of my bones
and flesh of my flesh;
she shall be called 'woman',
for she was taken out of man.'

(24) For this reason a man will leave his father and mother and be united to his wife, and they will become one flesh.
(25) The man and his wife were both naked, and they felt no shame.

This passage comes as the climax of the second account of Creation (Gen. 2:4ff) and as the pivotal section between Creation (2:4–25) and the Fall (3:1–24). What is its teaching about marriage?

## Not Good

It begins with a most extraordinary, and unexpected, statement. So far in Genesis, we have constantly heard how what God has created is 'good' (1:4, 10, 12, 18, 21, 25), culminating in: 'God saw all that he had made, and it was very good.' (1:31). Now, to our amazement, we hear that something is not good. It is not good that the man should be alone.

It is true, and in our society ought to be underlined, that this need for others can be met by human companionship without marriage. Westermann, in his commentary on Genesis, draws attention to the close connection of thought between 2:18 and Ecclesiastes 4:9–12: 'Two are better than one, because they have a good return for their work: If one falls down, his friend can help him up. But pity the man who falls and has no-one to help him up! Also, if two lie down together, they will keep warm. But how can one keep warm alone? Though one may be overpowered, two can defend themselves. A cord of three strands is not quickly broken.' This passage is indeed frequently used in wedding sermons, but in the first instance it refers widely to any good human friendship.

Nevertheless, in Genesis 2 it is obviously essential to the story that God provides a woman – a wife – to fill the man's needs. Early Jewish commentaries in particular stress this point: 'It has been taught on Tannaite authority: whoever has no wife lives without good, without help, without joy, without blessing, without atonement' (Gen. Rab. 17:2 the proof texts are: 'good' and 'help' (Gen. 2:18), 'joy' (Deut. 14:26), 'blessing' (Ezek. 44:30), 'atonement' (Lev. 16:11)). Gen. Rab. 17:5 has the animals passing by the man in pairs and the man rather pathetically commenting: 'Everything has its partner, but I have no partner.'

## A Helper and a Counterpart

So God resolves to make for man the partner that he needs. The English translations of 2:18 tend to sound rather clumsy, e.g. 'a helper suitable for him' (NIV). In the Hebrew there are two rather short words.

The first is relatively straightforward: *'ēzer* means a helper, and it can be understood in the widest possible terms. Von Rad describes it as 'one who is to be for man the embodiment of inner and outer encouragement'; that is, a being who will both help him physically in the tasks he has to perform and support him emotionally in the ups and downs of his life. The Jewish Apocryphal writing Ecclesiasticus captures this beautifully: 'He who acquires a wife gets his best possession, a helper fit for him and a pillar of support' (36:24).

Of course it is true that both Genesis 2:18 and still more clearly Ecclesiasticus 36:24 see the relationship from the man's point of view. It is his need for help, and the support that he can be given, which is in view. There has been a strong reaction against this viewpoint in the late twentieth century, which is in large measure due to the exploitation of women by men, and wives by husbands – an exploitation which, of course, the Genesis text in no way sanctions. Yet some of the reaction against Genesis 2:18 has a sadder cause: a selfishness that is always wanting to claim rights for ourselves and refuses to see nobility in self-sacrificing service of others. But rightly understood, no one should see the calling to be a helper as demeaning, especially as God himself is frequently said to be the helper of human beings (e.g. Exod. 18:4, Deut. 33:29 and, most famously, Ps. 121:1f).

The second Hebrew word in verse 18 is *keneḡdô*, a composite word which may well have been coined for this passage and is certainly only used here. *Neḡdô* means 'opposite him', 'over against him', and points to the fact that the being whom God creates will need to be different from man, complementary to him. The initial *ke* means 'according to' and adds the thought of correspondence, of meeting the man and his needs precisely. Although in Hebrew this is a prepositional phrase, the best English translation is perhaps the noun 'counterpart': a being who is at once like the man and different from him, who has strengths where he has needs, who is 'the perfect fit' (Wenham translates: 'matching him').

And it might be thought that the animals would fit this need. They too are made from the ground (19) just as the man was (7). They too are described as 'living beings' (19) just as the man was (7 – the Hebrew phrase is identical in both verses). Yet, although the man names them and so incorporates them into his world and proves himself their master, they are not the helper and counterpart he is looking for (20). As Wenham comments: the hold-up in fulfilling man's need 'allows us to feel man's loneliness'.

## 'A Piece of Me'

And so comes God's masterstroke. He sends the man into a deep sleep (21), not as some kind of anaesthetic so that the man will not feel the removal of his rib but because what God is going to do is a very solemn act of creation in which God himself will be the master craftsman and it is not appropriate for the man to be an onlooker (cf Gen. 15:12–17).

God forms woman out of the man's rib and 'brings her to the man' (22). And the man's delight is immediate and obvious. Here is precisely the helper and counterpart that he needed. He breaks out into the poetry of verse 23. 'This' – he points to her and uses the feminine form of 'this' three times in the verse: as the very first and last words, and in the middle – 'at last [the Hebrew is stronger than NIV's 'now'] is bone of my bones and flesh of my flesh.' It is an excited discovery. This one could not be more like me because her origin is my own body. Yet she is different from me: feminine when I am masculine (cf 1:27), and so, appropriately, having a name that is different from, though like, mine (the Hebrew *'îš* and *'iššāh* are as alike and yet different as the English 'man' and 'woman').

Yet there is more still to Adam's exclamation. As the Jewish commentator U. Cassuto states: 'In Hebrew, such expressions [bone and flesh] are commonly used to indicate family propinquity.' Where the English uses the idiom 'my flesh and blood' to mean 'my close relative', Hebrew uses the phrase 'bone(s) and flesh' (see, for example, Gen. 29:14; Judg. 9:2; 2 Sam. 19:12f – in each case the NIV 'flesh and blood' is a translation of Hebrew 'bone(s) and flesh'). The man recognises that he and the woman belong to the same family.

## The Heart of it All

And this leads to the crucial verse 24, towards which the whole story has been leading and which of course is the verse that the New Testament so frequently quotes. It is the narrator's comment; indeed, it is his explanation ('for this reason') of the universal phenomenon of marriage. Why did he include 2:18–23? Not particularly because he wanted to tell us about one particular marriage, that of Adam and Eve; not only because he wanted to prepare for the story of the Fall in chapter 3. But principally because he wanted to explain human marriage – marriage of his own day, since the expulsion from Paradise – to his readers. God created men and women in a certain way, to fulfil certain purposes, and this is why marriage is as it is.

Again, what follows is seen from the man's point of view, but here it is not the man's privileges but his responsibilities that are discussed. Before, it was the privilege of having someone to help him (18); now it is his duty – and joy – to be bound to his wife. In Israelite society, it was in fact the woman who left her parental home, while the husband with his new wife continued to live either in or near his parents' house. Nevertheless, it was incumbent on him to leave his parents in just as significant a way as she left hers. In fact – precisely because this is written from the man's viewpoint – her leaving is not mentioned. It is merely implied. Viewed from her perspective, she will also have to leave and cleave, and she in her turn will find that her husband is a helper and counterpart.

## 1. Leaving

If, then, verse 24 focuses on the man, and if in many cases he did not physically move from the parental home, what does his 'leaving' mean? It must mean that he leaves emotionally, psychologically. Up until now, his first loyalty, the first call on his honouring of other people, has been due to his parents. Now it will be due to his wife.

This is an extraordinary statement. For us in the late twentieth century West who pay scant regard to the opinions of our parents, who (in most cases) would not even think of obeying them if their wishes were contrary to ours, who regard the respect paid to parents in, for example, many Eastern countries as desperately restrictive, and who anyway have often moved away from the parental home long before marriage – for us, this leaving of parents seems rather a minor point to make. But to an Israelite it was a revolutionary thought and shows the profound effect that marriage has on all our relationships.

## 2. Cleaving

But marriage was not simply a coming of age, an independence (real, though not of course complete) from parental influence. It was the taking on of a new and principal dependence, of a new and primary duty to honour. And again this is seen – consistently with the whole passage – from the man's viewpoint. It is not the woman who is told to cling to the man (although this is implied); it is the man who is to cling to the woman and give his loyalty to her.

The Hebrew word *dābaq*, rather tamely translated 'be united to' in the NIV, is in fact more accurately, as well as more vividly, rendered 'cleave' or 'cling'. Wenham points out that the word gives us two aspects of marriage as envisaged by the writer. First, it implies a relationship of *passion*, of strong, deeply felt attraction. 'Shechem's heart was drawn to Dinah daughter of Jacob, and he loved the girl and spoke tenderly to her' says Genesis 34:3, and the word translated 'was drawn to' is exactly the same as 'cleave' in 2:24.

Marriages were indeed normally arranged in Old Testament times but that does not mean that they were passionless, mechanical affairs. How could anyone imagine that from a people who include the Song of Solomon amongst their religious literature? And indeed the Wisdom books abound not only in warnings against illicit passion but in the joys of marital love: 'May you rejoice in the wife of your youth. A loving doe, a graceful deer – may her breasts satisfy you always, may you ever be captivated by her love' (Prov. 5:18–19). This aspect of marriage is included in *dābaq*, to cleave.

But, secondly, so is the idea of *permanence*: Moses commands: 'No inheritance in Israel is to pass from tribe to tribe, for every Israelite shall *cling to* [NIV 'keep'] the tribal land inherited from his forefathers' (Num. 36:7, cf 36:9), and Israel is constantly being urged to cling to (NIV 'hold fast to') the Lord (Deut. 10:20, 11:22, 13:4, etc.).

This is not, then, a relationship to be broken. One relationship has indeed been broken, or at least weakened dramatically: the previously dominant ties to one's parents. But those bonds have been loosened in order to tie a still tighter, more fundamental bond: between man and wife. And the word 'cleave' tells us that this bond should be deep and lasting.

## 3. Becoming one flesh

The most important phrase is also the one where the meaning is least immediately obvious: they become one flesh. As this is at the heart of the Bible's understanding of marriage, it is important that we explore it in some depth.

The first thing to emphasise is that the expression is passive. 'Leaving' and 'cleaving' are both active ideas. The narrator explains why men and women do in fact leave their parents and cleave to their marriage partners, and it is a legitimate implication that if married couples have not already done so, they should. But 'becoming one flesh' is not an active concept. It is not something which a couple can or should do; it is something which happens to them. It is true that the Hebrew expression (*hāyâh lᵉ*) can occasionally be used actively (1 Sam. 4:9 is an example: 'Be men' means 'shew yourselves to be men' and literally: 'become men') but this is rare. Much more frequent is the use of this same phrase in Genesis 2:7, 'Man became a living being', where quite clearly no action is being taken by the man; rather, something is happening to him. And equally clearly Jesus understood 'becoming one flesh' in this passive sense (Mark 10:8//Matt. 19:5f). This, then, is not something which the man and his wife can do for their marriage, or can omit to do; it is something which happens to them as they marry.

This is not to deny that they are involved. As we shall see, the consummation of their marriage is part of what causes this to happen, and obviously they can choose to consummate their marriage or refrain from doing so. Nevertheless it is not they who make themselves one flesh. Rather as they marry, of which consummation is a part, so something happens to them: they become one flesh.

Some writers have laid emphasis on the word 'become'. They say this implies a process. The implication, then, is that all marriage partners are only on the way to becoming one flesh and some couples never remotely achieve this. Again, this is to misunderstand the language of Genesis 2:24. The Hebrew phrase does not describe the process, but the accomplished fact, the changed situation. Once more this is clearly the case with the parallel phrase in 2:7 and with Jesus' understanding of 2:24.

Nor should this idea of a process be read into the NIV's translation of the verbs in the future tense: 'will leave . . . will become'. The Hebrew verbs are imperfect which here, as Wenham rightly states, expresses 'repeated customary action'.

The narrator is here describing what regularly happens when men and women marry. It would probably be better, therefore, to translate with the English present tense: 'Therefore a man leaves . . . cleaves . . . and they become' (so RSV).

If then this is a transformation that happens to the marriage partners, and if it is seen not as a process but as an accomplished fact, what is it? It is natural to think immediately of sexual union. This stems partly from a misunderstanding. We are very familiar with the idea that sexual sin seems to head the list of sins of the flesh (e.g. Gal. 5:19–21) and so we make the equation flesh = sex; but the word 'flesh' here is not at all being used in the negative sense which it frequently carries with St Paul.

Partly too we are aware that in the New Testament 'flesh' and 'body' are often synonyms (so e.g. 1 Cor. 6:16) and of course sexual intercourse is the supreme physical or bodily act of marriage. As we shall see, St Paul does indeed say that sexual intercourse is (at least to some extent) the catalyst which brings about this change into one flesh. But the change itself – the 'being one flesh' – is certainly broader than that. It is not that husband and wife are one flesh when they are sexually united and cease to be one flesh when their bodies are apart. In marriage they become, permanently, one flesh.

The key to understanding this is to realise that the Hebrew word *bāśār* (flesh) can, and does here, mean much more than the mere physical, or more particularly sexual, make-up of men and women. Westermann insists that the word means 'human existence as a whole, under the aspect of corporality'. We can illustrate this very easily in English. We use the word 'someone' and the word 'somebody', but both equally mean 'some person'. In the latter case we are talking, to use Westermann's phrase, about 'human existence under the aspect of corporality'.

So it is with the Hebrew. Vawter has expressed this very clearly; he says 'become one flesh' 'should not be too narrowly interpreted as referring exclusively to the physical side of marriage. The flesh of man is his very being itself, his identity, his heart and soul (Ps. 84:2). The union of man and woman in marriage, therefore, is set on the highest and most integral plane: it is a union of persons who together make up a new person.'

And it is possible that there is a further, more specific, meaning. Brown, Driver and Briggs list *bāśār* in Genesis 2:24 under the meaning 'flesh, describing kindred, blood-relations'. It is this which Wenham also argues for. He states that 'one flesh' means not merely 'the sexual union . . . or even the spiritual and emotional relationship . . . Rather, it affirms that just as blood relations are one's flesh and bone, so marriage creates a similar kinship relation between man and wife. They become related to each other as brother and sister are.' The evidence for this view is not only the language itself ('become one flesh', cf 23) but the forbidden marriages of Leviticus 18 and 20 where a man may not marry his wife's mother or sister (20:14, 18:18), nor may he marry those who are not his own blood relatives but have married his blood relatives (18:8, 14–16). In their book *Jesus and Divorce*, Heth and Wenham comment: 'The moment a man married a woman, she became an integral part of his family in the same way in which children born into that family did. Similarly, he became related to her close female relatives and . . . could not marry them' (p.105).

Whether or not that thought is included in Genesis 2:24 has, to my mind, to remain an open question. But what, I believe, is not open to question is this: the phrase 'they become one flesh' shows that something happens to a man and woman when they are married; a transformation takes place of which they are the passive recipients, even though their choice and action set the transformation in motion; this transformation takes place not merely at the physical level, nor merely at the level of the emotions; it takes place at the deepest and most elemental level: they become a unity. The Samaritan Pentateuch, the Septuagint, the Peshitta, the Targum of Jonathan, the Vulgate and the New Testament at 2:24 all read: 'The two of them become one flesh' and while 'the two of them' may have crept in from 25 (NIV 'both') it exactly expresses the meaning of the phrase: no longer two personal entities but one. This decisive change has taken place as they marry.

## Postscript

As a sort of coda to the story, the narrator adds: 'The man and his wife were both naked, and they felt no shame' (25). One of the principal purposes of this statement is, of course, to prepare for the story of the serpent that follows when 'they realised that they were naked' (3:7) and covered themselves with fig leaves.

It represents a state of both ignorance and innocence about sexuality. Already the man and the woman felt a mutual attraction which caused the man to cry out in delight as he saw the woman (23) and which made him the first man to cleave to his wife and, in the consummated marriage, to become one flesh with her (24; there is no thought that 4:1 is the first time they have intercourse). But they are quite unaware that anyone, including God (cf Exod. 20:26), could be offended by their nakedness or titillated by it (cf Gen. 6:1f). They are somewhat like little children who have no sense that anything special is happening when all their clothes are off and who have no idea of what powerful forces sexuality will unleash in their world.

It is quite clear from the development of the story (3:21) and the entire Old Testament's attitude to nakedness that God's intention now is for people to be clothed – 'There is no road back [to 2:25] as the nudists suppose' comments Kidner – or to be more accurate: God's intention now is for people other than a husband and wife in intimate privacy to be clothed. It is true that in 2:25 the man and his wife were ignorant, unaware that continuing nakedness would cause problems for themselves and others. The sad thing about 3:7 is that they had not only understood rightly that they should normally be clothed; but in addition sin had brought uneasiness into their own relationship. They were no longer fully comfortable even being naked alone together. And from that angle the narrator sees the loss of the open sexual relations of 2:25 as a further pitiful result of human sin.

## New Testament Exposition

It is this passage (Gen. 2:18–25), and more specifically verse 24, which formed the basic text for the New Testament understanding of marriage, and there are 3 chapters in particular where our text is commented on and expounded: Mark 10//Matthew 19; 1 Corinthians 6 and Ephesians 5.

## Mark 10:6–9//Matthew 19:4–6

> (6) ". . . At the beginning of creation God 'made them male and female' [Gen. 1:27]. (7) 'For this reason a man will leave his father and mother and be united to his wife, (8) and the two will become one flesh' [Gen. 2:24]. So they are no longer two, but one. (9) Therefore what God has joined together, let man not separate."

Matthew's account shows, in this section, only minor variations which we will refer to in the exposition that follows.

The context is of course a discussion of divorce. 'Some Pharisees have asked Jesus: 'Is it lawful for a man to divorce his wife [Matthew adds: for any and every reason]?' (Mark 10:2//Matt. 19:3). Jesus takes them back – in Mark's account after they have mentioned the Mosaic permission to divorce – to Genesis 1 and 2. As we have said already, he refuses to discuss divorce before he has made plain how God sees marriage, what marriage is all about. And in his use of the Genesis texts, he makes some very significant points.

## At the Beginning

We note immediately that he takes them right back to the beginning. They want to concentrate on the Mosaic legislation, on the permission to divorce which they believe was granted at Sinai (Mark 10:4//Matt. 19:7). He takes them back beyond that to the original creation of humans, to the first male and female: 'At the beginning of creation God [Matt.: at the beginning the

Creator] "made them male and female"' (Mark 10:6//Matt. 19:4).

The important point here is that in Jesus' mind God's will for marriage was made plain before the choice of Israel to be the people of God, before even the choice of Abraham to be the father of the Israelite nation; it was clearly expressed when the first man and woman were created. It is therefore what is commonly called 'a creation ordinance'.

These early chapters of Genesis before the call of Abraham in 12:1ff, and especially chapters 1–3, are used by the New Testament to explain the truth not merely about those who are chosen to be God's people but about humankind, men and women everywhere, whether they acknowledge God or not, and whether they live up to the standards these chapters sometimes set before them or not.

To give just one example, Genesis 1:26f portrays God as creating 'man in his own image' and 'likeness'. The New Testament, then, states as a fact that all men – pagan just as much as Christian 'have been made in God's likeness' (Jas. 3:9). In the same way, God's will for marriage, to which Jesus takes his hearers back, is not just for the Jews, nor just for the Christian people of God. It is for all humankind.

## God Differentiates the Sexes

Having taken them back 'to the beginning', Jesus does not immediately quote Genesis 2:24 but rather Genesis 1:27, the full text of which is: 'So God created man in his own image, in the image of God he created him; male and female he created them.' Jesus just quotes the end of the verse: 'he made them male and female' (Mark 10:6//Matt. 19:4).

In Genesis 1 this differentiation of the sexes clearly has in mind sexual intercourse and child-bearing since the next verse begins: 'God blessed them and said to them, "Be fruitful and increase in number . . ."' (Gen. 1:28). Marriage is not specifically mentioned but it is implied. In the Gospel story, Jesus makes the connection explicit. He follows the quote of Genesis 1:27 directly with a citation of Genesis 2:24 (Mark 10:7f//Matt. 19:5). It was God, Jesus is saying, who right from the beginning of creation differentiated the sexes, and he did so specifically with a view to marriage.

## No Longer Two

So far Jesus has been quoting Genesis but now he draws two all-important conclusions of his own. The first conclusion is very simple: 'So [Greek: *hōste*, drawing out the implications of the Genesis text] they are no longer two, but one' (Mark 10:8//Matt. 19:6).

Jesus denies something and he affirms something. He denies that they are two any longer. What Genesis 2 is saying is not that *in addition to* being two separate individuals they are now *also* one. It is saying that at the most fundamental level, they are no longer, after they have been married, two. Those who would think of marriage aright, with the mind of God, will no longer think of a man and his wife as two separate entities.

This is not to deny of course that they bring different contributions to the marriage – this is precisely what Genesis 2:18 points out with its phrase 'a helper and counterpart for him' – nor is it to deny that each marriage partner has relationships and responsibilities in which the other partner is only marginally, if at all, involved. The intention is not in the least to water down what each individually brings to the marriage. But it is to deny – Jesus specifically denies – that the most important thing about them any longer is their separateness. At the most important level, he says, they are no longer two.

But he also affirms something. They are now, instead, 'one' or, more literally, one flesh (Mark 10:8//Matt. 19:6). Commenting on this verse, Cranfield allows two possible meanings of 'one flesh'. *Sarx* [flesh] is either 'equivalent to *sōma* [body] (cf 1 Cor. 6:16; Eph. 5:28–31) . . . meaning . . . the two become one *person*' or 'in the light of passages like Gen. 29:14, 37:27; Judg. 9:2; Rom. 11:14, the meaning [is] that a man and a woman cease to be merely members of two different families and become one *kindred*'. It would be more accurate to say that the first meaning is definitely there in Jesus' words and the second may also be.

And Jesus' words make absolutely clear when this happens. We have seen that it is possible to misinterpret the word 'become' in Genesis 2:24 and to think of it as a process which may not be complete until some time after marriage. In the conclusion Jesus draws from Genesis 2:24, there is no word for 'become' and it is quite clear from the context that Jesus sees this change from two to one as taking place at marriage. Origen comments: 'It is God who has joined together the two in one so that they are now no more twain from the time that the woman is married to the man' (*Comm. in Matt.* 14.16). Bonnard agrees: 'The man and the woman are not destined to become, some day, one flesh . . . Attached to each other, the man and the woman are immediately one flesh.'

## God-Joined

And Jesus draws a second conclusion from Genesis 2:24 and indeed from his first conclusion. This time the conclusion is signalled with *oun* ('therefore'): 'Therefore what God has joined together, let man not separate' (Mark 10:9//Matt. 19:6).

We will leave until a later chapter what this remark says about divorce or 'separating' marriage partners. For us at this stage, its important assertion is that it is God who joins men and women together in marriage. This is not simply stated about the original couple, Adam and Eve. Rather, it makes the very striking claim that whenever a man and woman marry, whatever the circumstances that have brought them together, it is God who is joining (literally: yoking) them to one another. Bonnard has some very significant comments to make about this statement of Christ's. He points out that by Jesus' day the idea of a marriage bond was already widespread in antiquity, but in different cultures it was held that different people or things made this bond. Xenophon says it is the law. In other cultures or writers it was the parents' will, or the man's, or a reciprocally given consent. But here, in the teaching of Jesus, it is God. So, the idea of a marriage bond as such is not what makes this Christian teaching unique. Rather it is that the marriage partners in this bond 'must be considered as united by God; this is the originality of the Gospel's thought' (Bonnard).

# 1 Corinthians 6:15–18a

The second New Testament passage where Genesis 2:24 is used and expounded is not in fact about marriage at all. Rather, St Paul is attacking the practice of some Corinthian men who went visiting prostitutes, apparently arguing that there was nothing wrong in this. Paul counters with a number of arguments, including this:

> (15) Do you not know that your bodies are members of Christ himself? Shall I then take the members of Christ and unite them with a prostitute? Never! (16) Do you not know that he who unites himself with a prostitute is one with her in body? For it is said, 'The two will become one flesh' [Gen. 2:24]. (17) But he who unites himself with the Lord is one with him in spirit. (18) Flee from sexual immorality.

## Sex Involves the Whole Person

These Corinthian men justified their own position. St Paul is almost certainly quoting their view when he writes twice in one verse: 'Everything is permissible for me' (12). He also probably quotes them when he writes in the next verse: 'Food for the stomach and the stomach for food' (13). Yet his concern in this passage (12–20) is not with morality in general nor with the question of what foods may or may not be eaten by Christians. His concern in the context is quite clearly with sexual immorality and, in particular, visiting prostitutes.

He has no direct quote from the Corinthians on this issue, but it is not difficult to reconstruct from the passage something very like what their line of argument must have been. This is how Fee expresses it: 'Since everything is permitted [12], and since food is for the stomach and the stomach for food [13] . . . and since all bodily appetites are pretty much alike, that means that the body is for sex and sex for the body.' Since sex with prostitutes is 'the most convenient way available' (Barrett), it is morally quite acceptable.

Paul's argument against this position takes a number of forms. In verse 15 he first describes Christians' bodies as 'members of Christ' and then says that by having sex with prostitutes they are making these members of Christ into 'members of a prostitute' (the literal translation of 15; NIV: 'unite them with a prostitute').

This might seem like a very extreme position. Can a casual visit to a prostitute really make a man 'a member of her'? In verse 16, Paul goes on to justify his position. It seems that initially he is doing little more that restate what he has just said: 'Do you not know that he who unites himself with a prostitute is one with her in body [literally: is one body]?' But he is clearly appealing to something they ought to be fully aware of ('do you not know?'), and one word gives away what will follow: *kollaomai* (NIV: 'unites himself with'). This is the word Matthew 19:5 uses to translate 'cleave' in Genesis 2:24 (the Septuagint uses the compound form *proskollaomai*). St Paul is saying, therefore: surely you should know that a man who cleaves to a prostitute in sexual intercourse is one body with her?

And to drive the point home he quotes immediately from Genesis 2:24, 'For it is said: "The two will become one flesh."' This is certainly saying more than just: two bodies unite. It is saying that sex involves the whole person. Again 'body' and 'flesh' (both used in 16) refer to more than just a person's physical make-up; they embrace the whole person. Bruce quotes D. S. Bailey: the statement that casual intercourse with a prostitute nevertheless involves 'being one body' with her 'displays a psychological insight into human sexuality which is altogether exceptional by first-century standards . . . [Paul] insists that it is an act which, by reason of its very nature, engages and expresses the whole personality in such a way as to constitute a unique mode of self-disclosure and self-commitment.' (D. S. Bailey, *The Man-Woman Relation in Christian Thought*, SCM, London, 1959, p.10, quoted in Bruce's commentary on Ephesians p.393).

## Sex is Only Part of Getting Married

Nevertheless, we must not push Paul's point further than he himself takes it. While it is true that in prostitution the client 'cleaves' to the prostitute and 'becomes one flesh' with her, it does not mean that he has married her. If it did, Paul could not add: 'Flee from sexual immorality' (18) which in context clearly includes: flee from the prostitute(s) you have been consorting with.

Sexual intercourse is clearly included in both phrases of Genesis 2:24: 'cleave to his wife' and 'they become one flesh', but as we have already seen, both expressions speak of much more than sexual intercourse alone. What Paul is saying in 16 is that they are much more deeply involved with the prostitute than they imagine. Certainly they are not married to her, but they have gone a long way towards the full union that marriage is. This misalliance, this extramarital union, would be bad enough for anyone; but it is particularly ugly and morally obnoxious when it involves a Christian's body, since that body is a member of Christ (15).

## Ephesians 5:21–33

The third passage which expounds Genesis 2:24 is also the most famous, and as it has much to say about a Christian view of marriage, it is important to study it in some detail:

(21) Submit to one another out of reverence for Christ.
(22) Wives, submit to your husbands as to the Lord. (23) For the husband is the head of the wife as Christ is the head of the church, his body, of which he is the Saviour. (24) Now as the church submits to Christ, so also wives should submit to their husbands in everything.
(25) Husbands, love your wives, just as Christ loved the church and gave himself up for her (26) to make her holy, cleansing her by the washing with water through the word, (27) and to present her to himself as a radiant church, without stain or wrinkle or any other blemish, but holy and blameless. (28) In this same way, husbands ought to love their wives as their own bodies. He who loves his wife loves himself. (29) After all, no-one ever hated his own body, but he feeds and cares for it, just as Christ does the church (30) for we are members of his body. (31) 'For this reason a man will leave his father and mother and be united to his wife, and the two will become one flesh' [Gen. 2:24]. (32) This is a profound mystery – but I am talking about Christ and the church.

(33) However, each one of you also must love his wife as
he loves himself, and the wife must respect her husband.

This is, of course, part of Paul's instructions to wives and
husbands (5:22–33), children and parents (6:1–4) and slaves
and masters (6:5–9) in which he works out, within the specifics
of those relationships, the moral principles which he has been
expounding in different places throughout the Epistle and particularly in 4:17–5:21. His first instruction is to wives.

## Wives: Reproduce your Submission to Christ

The question of whether wives should submit to their husbands
is so hotly debated and raises so many strong feelings that Christians often fail to hear or understand what those with differing
viewpoints are showing to be present in the New Testament
teaching. Paul's last word to *all* Christians, before he turns to
wives and then to husbands, is: 'Submit to one another' (21).
It is true that grammatically this belongs to verses 18–21, which
is all one sentence. There are in fact two imperatives: 'Do not
get drunk . . . but be filled with the Spirit' and all the verbs in
19–21 are participles describing the results of being filled with
the Spirit: 'speaking . . . singing and making melody . . . giving
thanks . . . submitting to one another'. If, then, it is a mark
of being filled with the Spirit that a Christian submits to his
fellow Christian, there must be occasions when a Christian man
submits to the fellow Christian to whom he is closest: his wife.
     And Scripture makes clear what some of these occasions might
be. Most strikingly it says that authority over the husband's body
lies in the hands of his wife: 'The husband should give to his wife
her conjugal rights, and likewise the wife to her husband. For the
wife does not rule over her own body, but the husband does;
likewise the husband does not rule over his own body, but the
wife does' (1 Cor. 7:3–4 RSV) The translation in NIV 'belongs
to' is much less accurate than RSV 'rule'. The word is *exousiazō*
and means 'have authority over'.
     Similarly, while it is true that the man is seen as the overall
head of the household and a bishop /elder must be someone who
does well at 'being the head of' his household (1 Tim. 3:4–5, a

more accurate translation than 'manage'), the same letter says that wives should 'rule their households' (1 Tim. 5:14. Greek: *oikodespoteō*). The very word used shows that it entailed considerable authority and must have included arranging matters which would have an impact on her husband, as indeed the picture of the good wife in Proverbs 31:10–31 makes abundantly clear.

So there will certainly be occasions and situations when the husband has to submit his wishes to those of his wife. Nevertheless, it must be admitted that it is only the wife – both here and elsewhere in the New Testament – who is instructed to submit to her husband (22, 24, cf Col. 3:18; Titus 2:5; 1 Pet. 3:1, 5); the husband is never specifically told to submit to his wife. The contrast between what is demanded of the wife (submission) and what is demanded of the husband (often, as here, love) is striking and consistent.

Some believe it is significant that while children are told to 'obey' their parents (6:1) and slaves to 'obey' their masters (6:5f), wives are told here to 'submit to' their husbands. Since a different word is used, it is argued, Paul cannot have meant anything as strong as that wives should obey their husbands. But it is hard to believe that this is not included in the strong language of 24: 'wives should submit to their husbands *in everything*'. Masson points out that this is a voluntary submission, a wife's love-response to her husband's love. It has nothing degrading about it. It is to 'accept the position she has been given within the family in [God's] creation order'. But it is to 'subordinate oneself' and includes obedience since it would be impossible to 'subordinate oneself in everything' without obeying.

This certainly is how 1 Peter understands a wife's submission. The same verb as in Ephesians comes in both 1 Peter 3:1 and 3:5, and the later sentence reads: 'The holy women of the past . . . were submissive to their own husbands, like Sarah, who obeyed Abraham and called him her master' (5f).

But what if a husband does not fulfil his part of the bargain? If he does not love his wife, is she absolved from being submissive to him? While this book will want to argue strongly from Scripture that a woman has certain 'rights' (however modern that word may be) which must not be trampled on, nothing encourages her to believe that she is no longer duty-bound to submit to her husband if he does not fulfil his Christian duty to love her.

The strong words of 1 Peter 3 where a wife is told to 'be submissive to' her husband and is given the example of Sarah who 'obeyed' are given in a context where it is assumed that some husbands will not be Christians at all (1) and may not therefore feel in any way bound to adhere to the Christian instruction of 7. Indeed, their wives might be tempted to 'fear' them (6). Furthermore, in 1 Peter's list, the instructions to slaves come first (2:18–25), immediately before the instructions to wives (3:1–6). Here it is explicitly stated that slaves should 'submit themselves' (2:18; same word as in 3:1, 5) to their masters and continue to do so even if the masters, for their part, are harsh (2:18) and unjust (2:19). The implication is surely clear: that in other relationships – and specifically in the relationship between marriage partners that follows in 3:1–7 – each partner is to continue fulfilling his or her responsibility even if the other partner behaves inconsiderately and even cruelly (though this is not to deny, as we shall see, that a wife may under certain circumstances initiate divorce).

And, to return to Ephesians, Paul gives the very highest standard by which a woman may judge her submission. She is to submit to her husband 'as to the Lord' (5:22). This may perhaps mean: 'Submit to your husbands since you submit to the Lord.' Bruce puts this interpretation thus: 'Christian wives' submission is one aspect of their obedience to the Lord.' But it is more natural to take Paul's language as: 'Submit to your husbands in the same way that you submit to Christ'; the submission which they give to Christ is to be mirrored in the submission they give to their husbands. This is to set the standard of a woman's obedience extraordinarily high.

## The Husband is the Head of the Wife

And then Paul gives his reason. 'For the husband is the head of the wife as Christ is the head of the church, his body' (23). There has been considerable debate in scholarly circles about the meaning of the word 'head' when used metaphorically in Paul's writings. Some have argued that it means 'source' or 'origin' rather than the traditional understanding: 'authoritative leader'. This may be true in some other passages, but it is clear from the Septuagint that *kephalē* does often mean 'authoritative leader' (Judg. 10:18; 11:8–11; 2 Sam. 22:44f; Ps. 18:43f; Isa. 7:8f) and Bruce is surely right to insist that in this Ephesian context ' "head" has the idea of authority attached to it after the analogy of Christ's headship over the church'. The entire context has to do with submission (21f, 24), and the reason (v.23 begins 'for') why wives are to submit to their husbands is precisely the same as the reason why all Christians – male and female – are to submit to Christ: God has given them an authoritative leader or head. God has given her husband as leader to the wife, and he has given Christ as leader to the Church. Indeed, as we have seen, 1 Peter does not shrink from saying that Sarah called her husband '*Kurios*' ('Lord').

This, then, is the reason why a wife should submit to her husband: the husband 'is' the head of the wife. That simple word 'is' does not mean 'is in a traditional first-century house', or 'is in the best households'. Paul's clear intention is to say 'is in the purposes of God'. In other words, this is the way God has planned the relationship between husband and wife in marriage. This is God's created order.

And then Paul adds, after writing that Christ is the head of the Church, 'of which he is the Saviour' (23). Of course Paul is continuing to talk about Christ, but the question inevitably arises: is Paul saying that the husband is in any sense the Saviour of his wife? And if not, why does Paul include this thought in a clearly marital context?

There is nothing anywhere in Paul's writings which would suggest that he saw the husband as the wife's Saviour. The New Testament uses the word 'Saviour' solely of God or of Christ. Then why include this thought here? Probably, as Masson suggests, because Paul felt it inadequate to describe Christ solely as 'head of the church'; he was much more than that. Therefore, the Church has an added reason for being submissive to Christ as head – he is her Saviour – which the wife does not have as she submits to her husband.

The beginning of the next verse (NIV: 'Now'; Greek: *alla*. Better translated: nevertheless) shows that, despite not having this added reason, it is the wife's responsibility to submit to her husband. Paul recaps: 'As the church submits to Christ, so also wives should submit to their husbands . . .'. And now Paul adds: '. . . in everything' (24). Masson comments that this is to exclude the possibility of a wife giving her submission 'as a whole' and reneging on this commitment 'in detail'. It is a high calling that insensitive husbands have frequently made much harder to fulfil.

## Husbands: Reproduce the Love of Christ

But husbands shouldn't imagine that the instructions given to them are any less demanding, nor that the standard set is in any way lower. The wife is to give to her husband the submission she owes to Christ; but the husband is to give to his wife the love he receives from Christ.

And when Paul goes on to define that love, he speaks immediately of sacrifice: 'Husbands, love your wives, just as Christ loved the church and gave himself up for her' (25). This is the kind of love that should characterise husbands: a love that is defined (here by St Paul) not by God's generosity in creation, nor by his patience at human sin, nor by his humility in the Incarnation, but by the Cross. It is a love in which the husband will constantly sacrifice himself for the sake of his wife.

For what purpose? Paul, having spoken of Christ's self-giving love for the church goes on: 'to make her holy, cleansing her by the washing with water through the word, and to present her to himself as a radiant church, without stain or wrinkle or any other blemish, but holy and blameless' (26f). Clearly, again, the primary reference is to Christ. But Paul has certainly not lost sight of the marriage relationship. The imagery is very definitely marital: for both Greeks and Jews a pre-nuptial bath was part of the ritual of weddings, and the 'presentation' to the groom was the job of the person we would call the 'best man' (in 27 Christ is both best man and groom, cf 2 Cor. 11:2). And the idea of the Church's being 'radiant' (27; Greek: *endoxon*. Masson: 'in all her glory') obviously fits a marital context. Much of this language is echoed in Ezekiel where God speaks of his betrothal and marriage to Israel:

> I gave you my solemn oath and entered into a covenant with you, declares the Sovereign LORD, and you became mine.

I bathed you with water and washed the blood from you and put ointments on you . . . I dressed you in fine linen and covered you with costly garments. I adorned you with jewellery . . . You became very beautiful and rose to be a queen. And your fame spread among the nations on account of your beauty, because the splendour I had given you made your beauty perfect (Ezek. 16:8–14).

So the language is marital, and the words about Christ are of course preceded by: 'Husbands, love your wives . . .' and followed by: 'In this same way, husbands ought to love their wives as their own bodies' (25, 28). I believe it is right, therefore, to see Paul as implying that this same concern for holiness which Christ has for the Church should be part of the husband's love for his wife: he too should be concerned for his wife's holiness. He should long to see her morally pure and beautiful, just as he likes to see her physically attractive. It is part of his care for her total well-being.

## Husband and Wife Make up One Body

And now Paul comes to his reason. He has said that husbands are to love their wives as Christ loved the Church, and he has shown what kind of love that is: self-sacrificing and with a concern for the partner's holiness. Christ's love for the Church is not introduced as the reason why husbands should love their wives but as the standard of love which they should follow. Then Paul once more draws his conclusion from the love that Christ has shown and at the same time gives the reason why husbands should follow Christ's example: 'In this same way, husbands ought to love their wives as their own bodies' (28).

That last phrase 'as their own bodies' introduces Paul's reason for these instructions. And it does so by bringing out a further parallel between the husband–wife and the Christ–Church relationships: the Church is the body of Christ (23), and in the same way the wife is the body of the husband (28). Masson rightly comments: Paul means that husbands should love their wives 'as being their own bodies', not that they should love their wives 'as they already love their own [physical] bodies'. In other words, husband and wife make up one body.

This is made abundantly clear in what follows: 'He who loves his wife loves himself' (28). What seems – and is – a very simple sentence in fact contains what is at the heart of the Bible's view of marriage. This is not the general command: 'Love your neighbour as yourself' applied to the specific situation of marriage. If so, Paul would have needed to write: 'Husbands [should] love their wives *as* themselves'; and of course it is perfectly proper to write this, as Paul indeed does in 33. But in 28 he in fact wrote: 'He who loves his wife loves *himself*.' Here again is Christ's understanding of what happens at marriage: husband and wife have become inseparable; together they form a single being, a single body.

And if so, then of course the husband will love his wife. 'After all, no-one ever hated his own body' (29). It simply doesn't make sense to hate yourself, and that is precisely what a husband who hates his wife is doing. On the contrary, every sane human 'feeds and cares for' his body (29). The second verb (Greek: *thalpō*) is a warm word. Literally it means 'keep warm', and when, as here, used figuratively, it means 'cherish, comfort'. In Anglican wedding services, both husband and wife vow 'to love and to cherish' each other. St Paul says this only makes sense: they are actually cherishing and comforting themselves.

And Paul cannot help introducing again the example of Christ. He adds: 'Just as Christ [feeds and cherishes] the church – for we are members of his body' (29f).

But where does Paul draw all his teaching from? What makes him convinced that husband and wife together form one body? What assures him that we, the Church, form one body with Christ? Paul's answer is Genesis 2:24 which he quotes now: 'For this reason a man will leave his father and mother and be united to his wife, and the two will become one flesh' (31). The context makes it abundantly clear that Paul quotes this not for what it says about 'leaving' or 'cleaving'; all his attention is focused on the statement that 'the two become one flesh'. Indeed Paul has prepared for this by using the word 'flesh' (Greek: *sarx*; NIV: body) in 29.

Then Paul adds: 'This is a profound mystery – but I am talking about Christ and the church' (32). This verse has created a considerable amount of confusion. Up until now, what Paul has said about the relationship between a husband's love for his wife and Christ's love for the Church has been relatively clear. Christ's love is to be the example and standard followed by the husband. It is true that Paul has said some things of Christ's love for the Church which cannot be applied to the husband: the husband is not the wife's Saviour (cf 23), and while the husband desires and works for his wife's holiness, he cannot 'cleanse her by the washing with water through the word' (26). But these distinctions have been relatively clear. Is Paul now saying that he understands Genesis 2:24 to refer exclusively to Christ and the Church, and not to husband and wife?

This would be an odd view in the light of Christ's own use of Genesis 2:24, but to investigate it more carefully we need to look at Paul's language and especially his use of the word 'mystery'. This is a word which Paul uses several times in this epistle, most notably in 3:1–9. There, a mystery is a truth which humans cannot naturally guess or grasp ('not made known to men in other generations' 3:5; 'for ages past was kept hidden in God' 3:9) but which, at a certain moment in time, God reveals ('made known to me by revelation' 3:3; 'it has now been revealed by the Spirit to God's holy apostles and prophets' 3:5) and is then made publicly known to everyone ('to make plain to everyone the administration of this mystery' 3:9).

This meaning, normal in Paul, clearly fits at 5:32. The understanding that Genesis 2:24 teaches that Christ and his Church form one body could not be grasped without revelation, has now been revealed to Paul (and others) and is to be proclaimed, as Paul does here. Yet there are differences from 3:1–9 and from Paul's normal usage. The truth of which Paul speaks in chapter 3 and which he calls a 'mystery' is clearly stated: 'that through the gospel the Gentiles are heirs together with Israel . . . and sharers together in the promise in Christ Jesus' (3:6). In chapter 5, by contrast, the context has nothing to do with Jew and Gentile. Again, in chapter 5 the 'profound mystery' appears to be the interpretation of a particular Old Testament verse. In 3:1–9 nothing is said about the interpretation of Old Testament scriptures.

Is there then another usage of the word 'mystery' which builds on the basic meaning in Paul and fits this present context more exactly? Bruce draws attention to the Qumran community's understanding of Scripture. The Dead Sea commentators say that the text of Scripture is a *rāz*, a word of Persian origin used in the Aramaic section of Daniel and translated *mystērion* (the word in Eph. 5:32) in the Greek versions. This word expresses Qumran's understanding that all of the Old Testament is prophetic but that God only made plain a certain amount to the original writers and revealed the rest of the mystery later. Clearly, the New Testament has great sympathy with this view (cf 1 Pet. 1:10–12). Equally clearly, this usage of 'mystery' fits very well at Ephesians 5:32.

The important point here is the two-stage revelation. The original understanding of the Old Testament writer and his listeners/readers was not false; it was merely incomplete. So, the understanding of Genesis 2:24 as referring to human marriage was certainly not false; it is merely that God has now revealed a further 'profound' meaning inherent in this verse: it also refers to the unbreakable unity of Christ and his Church. M. Barth says that Paul's approach to the Old Testament is often typological: 'he no more denies the literal meaning of the OT texts quoted than does the author of . . . Hebrews by his "typological" interpretation'.

These two understandings of Genesis 2:24 are of course closely linked. At a human wedding, husband and wife become 'one flesh' and are for the rest of their lives to live out a loving marriage relationship. At conversion/baptism, Christians marry Christ and become 'one flesh/body' with him and 'members of him' (30f, cf the marriage language of 1 Cor. 6:13–17; Rom. 7:2–4). Christ and the Church now live out a continuing marriage relationship of love.

Paul has been rejoicing in the Church's oneness with Christ. But he now returns ('however' 33) to his principal theme of human marriage. Just as the last verse of his instruction to wives recapped what he had been saying (24), so now he recaps not only his instructions to wives but to both partners: 'Each one of you also must love his wife as he loves himself, and the wife must respect her husband' (33).

## Conclusions

Of course this chapter does not contain all that could be said about the biblical teaching on marriage; and indeed more will be said as this book continues. But these passages that we have studied do contain the heart of what is said in the New Testament about marriage, particularly when marriage is being discussed in the context of questions about divorce and remarriage. Before leaving this chapter, it may be helpful to draw out the implications for contemporary marriage of these passages and their teaching.

### 1. The Creation story is determinative for human marriage

If we want to understand human marriage, and particularly God's view of husband and wife, then it is to Genesis chapters 1 and 2 – and especially 2:18–25 – that we must turn. This in fact is made clear within Genesis 2 itself. Verse 24 is not a comment on the original couple's marriage ('the man', as Adam is called almost throughout the story, and his wife) but on every marriage ('a man', 24). It is not about human marriage in an ideal state before the Fall, but marriage in the writer's own (post-Fall) day and in every age. The writer of Genesis states, then, that to understand all human marriage, we must read the story of 2:18–23 and see what God was doing in the original marriage.

This is made still more clear by Christ himself in his controversy with the Pharisees (Mark 10//Matt. 19). They appeal to Moses' permission of divorce (Mark 10:4//Matt. 19:7). He says that Moses' permission does not represent God's abiding intentions. To understand God's current view (in the Christian era), which has in fact always been his true view, it is necessary to go back 'to the beginning' (Mark 10:6//Matt. 19:4, 8). You must read God's thoughts about marriage, says Jesus, from Genesis 2.

It is sometimes said that ideas about the indissolubility of marriage may have once been the nearest approximation we could get to the mind of God, but that now, with greater enlightenment and a more subtle understanding of the pressures on marriage, allowing for divorce and remarriage is often the only proper position for the contemporary Church. Without wishing to pre-empt the detailed discussion which will follow, it must be said that there is far more evidence for precisely the opposite view. Clearly Jesus taught that it was Moses' permission of divorce which was culture-bound and passing, and equally certainly he taught that God's mind on human marriage must be read from the Creation story.

## 2.   *In marriage, a new fundamental family unit is created*

Again, this is very clear from Genesis 2 itself. We have seen that the language of verse 23 'bone of my bones and flesh of my flesh' and of verse 24 'they become one flesh' may well imply the establishment of a new relationship as close as – or even closer than – the closest blood relationship.

The phrase 'a man will leave his father and mother' (24) is just as striking. Adam and Eve of course had no human parents, so that the mention of father and mother might seem out of place. It is included because the writer is determined to point out that one of the implications of marriage is that one's most basic family unit is no longer with one's parents, but with one's wife ('cleave to his wife' 24) or husband and children.

Ephesians 5 only underlines this. The fundamental person to whom a wife must relate is her husband, and vice versa. A woman who before marriage has submitted to her parents is now to submit primarily to her husband; a man who has loved his parents generously and sacrificially is now to give his first love to his wife.

To hate or repudiate one's marriage partner is, therefore, as ugly and as contrary to God's will as a child's rebellion against his parents. Of course it may happen, but it is to tear myself away from my closest family.

## 3.   *In marriage, the two become one flesh*

This phrase is absolutely central to the Bible's teaching on marriage – not only to that of the Genesis writer, but to the teaching of Jesus and of Paul also. We have looked carefully at what it means.

To recap: the phrase itself (*'become* one flesh') shows that it is something which God does to a man and woman when they marry, not something which they do to or for themselves. Certainly it includes the sexual act, as 1 Corinthians 6 makes clear; but to say that this is a reference only to the sexual act would be a travesty of biblical teaching. Rather 'one flesh' means 'one person' and Jesus expressed this in a way which is both extraordinarily simple and extraordinarily profound: 'So they are no longer two but one' (Mark 10:8//Matt. 19:6).

It would be hard to find an expression which more completely showed that husband and wife belong inseparably together. Despite the enormous emphasis in the Bible on the parent-child relationship, this is never said of it. Parent and child always remain two individuals. But the most important fact about husband and wife in Christ's teaching is that 'they are no longer two'.

When a couple separates, then, it is not simply that two individuals who may or may not have drawn close together part and pursue their independent lives. It is that a whole, a unity which was constituted by marriage, is unnaturally torn apart, leaving both parties incomplete. This view – so clearly taught by Christ – is again and again borne out by studies of contemporary divorce. However much a marriage may have been a 'living hell in which we were living two completely separate lives', divorce agonisingly reveals that the couple were much more 'wedded' (I use the word deliberately) than they imagined.

## 4.   *In marriage, God joins the partners together*

God, not man. It is God who, in Genesis 2, says: 'It is not good for the man to be alone' (18). It is God who 'makes the woman' (22). And it is 'God himself who, like a Father of the bride, leads the woman to the man' (von Rad commenting on 'the Lord God . . . brought her to the man' 22).

But can we say this of every marriage, or only of those which, it is sometimes said, are 'made in heaven'? We know from the story that Eve was meant by God for Adam; can we say the same of Fred Smith who marries Jane Baker because his parents push him into it when Jane finds she is pregnant? The answer which the New Testament gives is 'yes'. When Jesus was asked about divorce, he said of marriage in general, of all marriages, that in marriage 'God has joined together' the man and the woman (Mark 10:9//Matt. 19:6).

It is not, then, the clergyman or the judge or the registrar who joins a couple together. It is not even the couple themselves (although of course they must give their free consent to the marriage). In the Anglican wedding service, the clergyman indeed says: 'I proclaim that they are husband and wife.' But he instantly adds: 'That which God has joined together, let not man divide.' God has joined this couple together, whether the wedding takes place in church, in a registry or the open air. The clergyman or secular official merely proclaims publicly what God, not he, has done.

Jesus himself made the implications of this truth clear. It is not for man to undo the work of God. If there is to be any dissolution of the marriage, it is for God to undo his own work, not for either of the marriage partners, nor for an ecclesiastical or secular official.

## 5.   *In marriage, loving my partner is loving myself*

Genesis 2 tells me that I 'became one flesh' (24) with my partner when I married her or him. Together, we form one new person. Therefore, to love my marriage partner is to love myself, as Ephesians 5:28f makes clear.

Again, this is not said of any other relationship. Despite the fact that my parents are my own 'bone and flesh', despite the fact that I may look, speak and behave precisely like them while I may be very different from my wife, Scripture never says that I am one with them. Therefore, to love my partner is more important to me even than self-interest. I can love, or show kindness to, a third party because that person may advance my interests. But St Paul speaks more in terms of self-preservation. A person will naturally 'feed and care for his own body' (Eph. 5:29) because he can have no life apart from his body. Similarly, I can have no life worthy of the name if I do not love, nourish and cherish my marriage partner because she and I are an inseparable unity.

## 6. *In marriage, I am to reproduce my relationship to Christ*

This is the essence of Paul's instructions in Ephesians 5. Perhaps the starkest way to put this is that both partners are to view the husband as Christ. This seems an impossibly arrogant male statement until we see how Paul works it out. It is true that the wife is to submit to her husband in the same way that she, as a member of the Church, submits to Christ. But it is also true that the husband is perpetually to 'give himself up' (25) for his wife, and to do so as sacrificially and unreservedly as Christ has given himself up for the husband and for the whole Church.

Of course this is a standard which both partners will fall short of, and they will do so again and again. But it is not a standard that can ever be lowered or compromised – not until the wife is permitted to give only partial submission to Christ himself, or until Christ's love for the Church begins to run out. It is true that when a marriage is in very serious difficulties, one or both partners may set themselves lower temporary aims – to force themselves to talk to each other just for a few minutes, to hold in their anger and not shout at their partner for the next 24 hours – but the Christian can never see these lower aims as anything more than necessary stepping-stones along a path with a much more glorious end: reproducing in marriage again (or for the first time) our relationship with Christ.

# 3

# Singleness

One of the most conspicuous changes in the modern Western world is that more and more people are living single lives. In 1971, for example, 17% of all households in England consisted of one person living alone; by 1990 this had risen to 26%[1]. In the USA, 6.9 million people in 1960 were living on their own. By 1986 this number had more than tripled to 21.2 million, again nearly a quarter of all households. The number of those living alone in the 25–34 bracket went up 346% between 1970 and 1986. The increase for the 34–44 age bracket was 258%.[2]

There are a range of factors contributing to this change. The first, and most commonly perceived, is that people are marrying later. In 1970, the average age at which a woman got married (for the first time) in the USA was 20.6; by 1985, this had risen to 23.0. The corresponding figures for men were 1970: 22.5; 1985: 24.8.

This change in itself has a number of causes but one of them undoubtedly is that it has become economically more possible – and socially more acceptable – for people to be and remain single, a difference in financial and social climate which has affected both sexes but where the change for women is even more marked. This in turn means not only that men and women can afford to – and may be encouraged to – wait longer before getting married but also that they can more readily think about breaking up their marriage and about the singleness that will follow for one or both partners.

---

[1] Source: 1990 General Household Survey, preliminary results.
[2] Source: *US News and World Report*, 3 August, 1987.

Divorce is of course on the increase. By 1985, for example, the number of first marriages in the USA was 1,196,000; the number of divorces was almost identical: 1,190,000 (this figure, of course, includes the break up of 2nd and 3rd marriages). And while this represents an increase on 1984, it is by no means a freak figure; the tendency has been clear for some time. The figures for ten years earlier, for example, are – first marriages: 1,190,500; divorces: 1,036,000. So, an enormous number of people in the Western world now experience at least two periods of singleness: before marriage and after divorce.

And of course for many there is a third period: widowhood. As life expectancy grows, most clergymen are finding that an increasing amount of their ministry is to the retired and specifically to the widows (and widowers) who may spend decades, not just years, in their widowhood.

Yet with this tremendous growth in the numbers of people living single lives, the Church seems to have almost no Christian insights, no theology of singleness. Books abound on the subject of marriage from a Christian viewpoint, yet Christian books that seriously tackle the single life are extremely rare. While preparing for this book, I went into a Christian bookshop in Somerset. 'I've found your section of books on marriage, but do you have a section on singleness?' The lady looked blank. 'Do you mean single-parenting?' she asked. When I explained further, it turned out that they didn't have even one book on singleness; I wasn't really surprised.

Of course some books have been written and some conferences are held, but they almost all share the same characteristics: they examine singleness exclusively from the pastoral angle, they see it as a 'problem' to be 'coped with' and their theological reflection is minimal. I recently attended a conference entitled: 'Being single in the church community'. It was helpful in many ways but none of the New Testament passages on singleness was quoted or discussed at any stage during the day. This appears to be very typical.

Indeed, the Church has been positively unhelpful in this area. Most churches will hear sermons on marriage from time to time, but when have you heard a sermon devoted to the single life? Most youth groups will have talks on relationships and on the Christian view of marriage, but when were the young people encouraged to think about the calling, and advantages, of singleness? And so, in the close-knit communities that are the core of many churches, the single person, especially as he or she gets older, feels left out or a failure.

John Fischer, in a sermon to Peninsula Bible Church, Palo Alto, says how he has heard people say: 'It's impossible to be a mature Christian without being married.' Perhaps that shocks us: a typically extreme Californian position. Yet an article in the *Church Times* in January 1990 laments how every church seems to ask for a married clergyman, preferably with children, and assumes that a single clergyman's ministry is bound to be defective.

Fischer's sermon (preached in 1973) continues: 'The suggestion creeps in . . . that I am incomplete . . . flying around trying to find the airport, so that I can get my feet on the ground and start living [when I am married].' And on the other side of the Atlantic, Margaret Evening speaks for many when she says that many single people feel 'either that they have failed or life has cheated them' (p.16).

And this from the Christian Church! From the very organisation which, as we shall see, brought about a revolutionary change in attitudes towards singleness. There has down the centuries been a very strong tradition within Christendom that has placed a high value on the single life. While there was some reaction against this in the Reformation churches, singleness was still prized highly even in Protestant circles, as the many American communities which renounced marriage show. Perhaps the single life has sometimes in the past been overemphasised. Yet the almost total lack of any sympathy for, or theology of, singleness in contemporary Western Protestantism is truly astonishing. This chapter will seek, in small compass, to explore what the Scriptures have to say on this subject.

## The Old Testament

The Old Testament is not at all positive about being single. In the famous verse which introduces Genesis 2's teaching about how the woman was created to be the first man's wife, 'The

LORD God said, "It is not good for the man to be alone. I will make a helper suitable for him"' (Gen. 2:18). We have seen (in chapter 2) that this need for companionship can, even in the Old Testament's understanding, be met by friends of the same sex. Nevertheless, the Genesis verse clearly introduces a narrative which explains what happens in marriage (verse 24) and the story clearly envisages solitude as an evil which God designed marriage to remedy.

Jewish interpretation of these verses only reinforces this view. I have already quoted Genesis Rabbah on Genesis 2:18: 'It has been taught on Tannaite authority: whoever has no wife lives without good, without help, without joy, without blessing, without atonement' (17:2). And Ecclesiasticus 36:24–26 also takes its teaching from Genesis 2, on which it provides this commentary: 'He who acquires a wife gets his best possession, a helper fit for him and a pillar of support. Where there is no fence, the property will be plundered; and where there is no wife, a man will wander about and sigh. For who will trust a nimble robber that skips from city to city? So who will trust a man that has no home, and lodges wherever night finds him?'

It is clear, then, not only that marriage is a great blessing from God (which the New Testament of course supports) but that a prolonged single life is a disaster in the eyes of the Old Testament and of early Jewish thinkers. When Jephthah rashly promised to sacrifice the first thing he met on his return home and that proved to be his virgin daughter, she had just one request: ' "Give me two months to roam the hills and weep with my friends, because I will never marry". "You may go," he said. And he let her go for two months. She and the girls went into the hills and wept because she would never marry.' (Judg. 11:37f).

The same is true of singleness after being widowed. Isaiah paints a picture of the 'haughty women of Zion', walking flirtatiously, wearing clothes and jewellery that show off their beauty. All this will be destroyed in the day of God's anger: 'Instead of fine clothing, [there will be] sackcloth; instead of beauty, branding.' And to make the calamity worse, 'your men will fall by the sword, your warriors in battle'. Isaiah knows what the response will inevitably be: 'In that day, seven women will take hold of one man and say: "We will eat our own food and provide our own clothes; only let us be called by your name. Take away our disgrace!"' (Isa. 3:16–4:1).

That really sums it up. Singleness in the Old Testament is a 'disgrace', a 'reproach' (RSV). With this the Talmud is in complete agreement: 'The man who is not married at 20 is living in sin' (quoted in T. Chary: *Aggée, Zacharie, Malachie* p.260), and again: 'Any man who has no wife is no proper man, for it is said: "Male and female created he them and called their name Adam"' (b. *Yeb.* 63a).

It is true that Jeremiah was called by God to singleness; but this was not because the single life was considered inherently good. On the contrary, it was for the appalling reason that there was no future for Israelite families. Wives and children – and fathers too – would die and lie unburied 'like refuse lying on the ground . . . Their dead bodies will become food for the birds of the air and the beasts of the earth' (Jer. 16:1–4). Indeed, one of the clearest signs of God's judgment will be that the happiness of marriage will be no more: 'Before your eyes and in your days I will bring an end to the sounds of joy and gladness and to the voices of bride and bridegroom in this place' (verse 9). So, Jeremiah's call to singleness, far from being a special privilege and blessing, was a sign of the curse that God was going to bring to his people (just as Hosea's call to a marriage that God knew would be unhappy was a sign of the hurt which God felt in his relationship with Israel).

## The New Testament

Into this environment the New Testament's teaching on singleness exploded like a bombshell. It is true that the Dead Sea Scrolls seem to demand that a token few of its male community members 'should live under a vow of celibacy for an indefinite period. It seems that they considered themselves to be warriors of Israel, subject to the vows of abstinence that bound men for the duration of a holy war' (P. Brown: p.38), but this was a group who were marginal to Jewish society, they only envisaged this life for a few and their view of the future new Israel was of a married community with numerous offspring ('fruitful in seed'). The Christian view of the future age was very different (cf Luke 20:34–36).

Pliny the Elder also refers to a group of Essenes who had settled at Engedi and practised celibacy, but his very comment reveals what a surprise it was to him to find anyone who thought, still less behaved, in this way. The group was 'remarkable among all other tribes in the whole world, as it has no woman and has renounced all sexual desire' (Pliny: *Natural History* 5.15.73).

We may say, then, that the teaching of Jesus and his apostles about the single life, while it was not wholly without parallel, ran clean contrary to the teaching of the vast majority of their contemporaries. And it has lost none of its revolutionary impact today.

## The Teaching of Jesus

Jesus' own teaching on the subject can most easily be examined by looking at two passages. First, there is a short but very significant passage where he teaches his disciples directly about the single life. And second, there are various sayings in which Jesus lessens the (hitherto supreme) importance of marriage by relativising it.

The direct teaching on singleness comes in Matthew 19 at the end of a discussion on divorce. The Pharisees open the debate with a question: 'Is it lawful for a man to divorce his wife for any and every reason?'(3). Jesus then leads up to the statement:

(9) "I tell you [the Pharisees; everyone listening] that anyone who divorces his wife, except for marital unfaithfulness, and marries another woman commits adultery."
(10) The disciples said to him: "If this is the situation between a husband and wife, it is better not to marry."
(11) Jesus replied: "Not everyone accepts [a more accurate translation than NIV: 'can accept'] this word, but only those to whom it has been given. (12) For some are eunuchs because they were born that way; others were made that way by men; and others have renounced marriage [literally: have made

themselves eunuchs] because of the kingdom of heaven. The one who can accept this should accept it."

## 'This Teaching'

To what does the phrase 'this word' (11) refer? Much the most likely answer is that it refers to what has just been said: the disciples' view that if remarriage after divorce (at least in many, perhaps in all, circumstances) is out for the follower of Christ (cf 9) then the wise course of action is not to marry (10). Jesus – perhaps to their surprise – does not dismiss this view out of hand. On the contrary, for some people this is precisely what God has 'given' (11). He then goes on to explain the various groups of people to whom singleness has been 'given' (12).

The alternative view – that 'this word' means Christ's prohibition of divorce except for marital unfaithfulness (3–9) or his prohibition of remarriage (9) – is unsustainable. It seems impossible that, having introduced his conclusion with the solemn words: 'I tell you' (9), he would then go on to say that some may legitimately refuse his teaching because it hasn't been given to them (this would have to be the meaning of 11 and the end of 12).

Nor can he be saying in 11: 'Not all [people] accept this teaching, but only those [i.e all Christians] to whom it has been given', stating the rather obvious fact that while Christians will observe his teaching on divorce and remarriage, those who are not Christians will not. This would make a strange, unconnected response to their outcry in 10; it also makes 12 (with its connecting 'for') a strange, unconnected follow-on remark.

The traditional explanation is surely the most natural. Jesus is no longer talking with the Pharisees (3); Matthew makes it clear that this discussion is with the disciples (10). They have expostulated because they are concerned for themselves. What Jesus has just said about the permanence of marriage, and especially about remarriage after divorce being a sin (9), seems to them so tough that it would be better not to marry in the first place (10). Jesus replies that this is indeed God's 'gift' to some but not to all (of his disciples). In this he exactly parallels Paul's point in 1 Corinthians 7:7: 'I wish that all men were as I am [i.e. single]. But each man has his own gift from God; one has this gift [i.e. singleness], another has that [i.e. marriage].'

## Three Types of Eunuch

Jesus goes on to explain his remark. Naturally the question arises: To whom has singleness been 'given'? Jesus explains ('for') by mentioning three groups of people to whom singleness has been 'given' (12).

First, he mentions 'eunuchs who were born thus from their mother's womb' (12a literally). He is thinking primarily of those who, through some congenital defect, are physically incapable of marriage. Here, incidentally, is indirect evidence that sexual consummation is an essential part of marriage. Jesus is surely thinking of some physical defect which makes full sexual intercourse impossible (hence the term 'eunuchs'). And the context (10f) means that he is saying that marriage is not possible for such people.

But I believe it is legitimate to extend this beyond the sphere of physical incapacity for intercourse and marriage. This saying of Christ surely applies also to those whose emotional make-up means that marriage is not possible for them. If – as some maintain – homosexual orientation is inherited with our genes and is not (at least in some/many cases) acquired later in life, then such men and women would also come into the group whom Christ describes as 'eunuchs' (i.e. incapable of heterosexual intercourse – the context of the discussion here) and therefore people to whom marriage has not been 'given'.

Second, Jesus mentions 'eunuchs who have been made eunuchs by men' (12b literally). Again, he must be thinking primarily of those in contemporary royal courts who were set to serve and oversee the women of the court and who were rendered incapable of having intercourse with these women. Perhaps too he was thinking of those who had been castrated, or otherwise mutilated, as a punishment for some crime or in war. Earlier Egyptian wall carvings show piles of penises removed from the slain or from prisoners of war, a sort of primitive head count of the vanquished.

But again it seems to be legitimate to extend the application of Jesus' words. Surely we may include those who by seduction or introduction into gay circles have become homosexual in basic orientation. For some of these, the homosexual element of (in their case) a fundamental bisexuality would have remained largely dormant, but now, through the influence of other people, it has become open and dominant.

Margaret Evening wants to extend this further. A Christian homosexual may, she says, feel that singleness has been thrust upon him, but what about the single woman longing for marriage? In our society where the man is still expected to take the initiative, 'has she really got any choice, short of flinging herself at a man?' (p.60).

And the context demands another application: those who while wanting to remain in the marriage relationship have been divorced by their partner. This is what the whole discussion has been about (3ff). These people have been denied the sexual rights that marriage confers – they 'have been made eunuchs' – by men.

But the first two examples of those who remain single have been leading up to the third: 'eunuchs who have made themselves eunuchs for the sake of the kingdom of heaven' (12c literally). Our natural reaction is to think immediately of those Christians who have taken vows of celibacy (monks, nuns, Roman Catholic clergy and others who have felt a definite call to remain single) and perhaps also those who have so limited their opportunities for courtship with suitable partners that marriage has become impossible (many single missionaries, especially those working in societies where the vast majority are not Christian; those who have spent many years caring for aged and infirm parents).

I believe this wider application is certainly legitimate. The disciples raised the question of whether it might be right never to get married (10) and Jesus continued to open up the issue by talking about singleness quite generally. Nevertheless, Matthew presents 10–12 quite clearly in the context of a discussion about divorce (3ff) and especially remarriage after divorce (9). The obvious explanation is therefore that Jesus had the divorced primarily in mind. These people had either divorced their partners or been divorced. By contemporary law (whether Jewish or Roman – or, indeed, by twentieth-century Western law), they were free to remarry. Yet in response to Christ's expressed will (9), Christians voluntarily forgo their legal right because they know that the morality of 'the kingdom of heaven' conflicts at this point with the possibilities open to the non-Christian.

## Acceptance

To all these three groups, the single life has been 'given' (11), and the context clearly means: given by God (cf also 1 Cor. 7:7). While congenital defects (12a) will be swept away by God in the future age, yet the singleness which results from these defects is something which God has given and – however much of a struggle it is and might continue to be – needs to be accepted. Even the one who has been castrated by an act of violent human evil (12b) needs to recognise, however much he constantly wrestles with resentment, that singleness (the absence, at least, of any full marriage) has become God's will for him, in these evil circumstances. It is what God, in these circumstances, has given.

And exactly the same is true for the Christian divorcee (12c), and also (by extension) for the person whose service for the kingdom of heaven has made marriage impossible. He or she has 'made a eunuch of himself' because he believes this is God's will for him. Even for him it may often be a struggle to recognise that his singleness is 'given' by a good and loving Father. Yet he too must learn to accept it.

And not just accept it with resignation. It is 'given' not imposed. It is a gift. Jesus does not expand, as Paul will, on *how* it is a gift, on what advantages it has. But he does clearly say that it is a gift. Evening insists that singleness 'should not be thought of merely as a giving up, but rather as a taking on, a receiving of a gift' (p.113).

Jesus then closes this discussion with: 'The one who can accept this should accept it' (12d). By this he does not mean: 'If you are able to stay single, that is a definite call to be single.' On the contrary, God gives the gift of singleness to some and the gift of marriage to others (1 Cor. 7:7). The gift of singleness is not given to all who are content to be single, nor the gift of marriage to all who would like to be married. It has in fact frequently been said that one of the best preparations for marriage is to learn contentment in one's singleness and not to be over-eager for marriage.

Nor is Christ saying: 'If you are not able – or willing – to stay single, it is all right to get married.' Verse 9 clearly rules that out. There Jesus is certainly saying that some who want to marry may not do so.

Rather, as commentators almost invariably point out, this is the exact equivalent of Jesus' frequent expression: 'He who has ears (to hear) let him hear' (e.g. Matt. 11:15). Effectively, it is a challenge to obey. The word 'accept' (*chōreō*) means: to understand with a view to a changed life. Lagrange says it means 'to grasp with a view to acting on it'.

Certainly it begins in the mind. Arndt and Gingrich define *chōreō* as, literally, 'have room for, hold, contain' and hence, figuratively, 'grasp (in the mental sense), accept, comprehend, understand'. This in itself is almost as difficult for us in the late twentieth century as it was for Christ's contemporaries. We have to 'make room for' the idea that singleness will be God's gift to many; we have to 'grasp, accept' that remarriage (certainly for many, perhaps for all) will not be God's will after divorce.

But we must go further than that. '*Chōreō* appears to go beyond understanding and points to the capacity to receive and act upon the teaching. Matthew 19:12 . . . exhorts a group of people who have been given an insight or a gift for something to make use of it' (P. Schmidt in NIDNTT 3:742). It is hard enough for us to accept intellectually Christ's teaching on singleness. But many of us will also have to act on this understanding: not simply to refrain from marriage but to live our lives believing that our singleness is God's gift. What is remarkable is that Christ's (and his apostles') teaching on this subject completely revolutionised Christian attitudes to singleness; the early Church in fact went beyond the New Testament in exalting the single state. And what is sad is that this extraordinary new insight which Christ brought has been largely lost in many Christian circles today.

# Jesus on the Relativisation of Marriage

In many ways, Jesus' teaching on marriage (some of which we examined in chapter 2) raises the married state, and especially the marriage bond (which cannot simply be dissolved by a magistrate's decree of divorce), to new heights of significance. Yet by also giving singleness a place of honour, by maintaining that it is a gift given by God to many, Christ provides marriage with a serious rival. As Bromiley puts it, commenting on Matthew 19:11–12, Jesus 'refuses to treat marriage as an overriding absolute in human life' (p.40).

There are also a number of other passages in which Jesus relativises the importance of marriage. It must never come before allegiance to him, and it will not last into the next age.

## Luke 14:25–7 and 18:28–30

> (14:25) Large crowds were travelling with Jesus, and turning to them he said: (26) 'If anyone comes to me and does not hate his father and mother, his wife and children, his brothers and sisters – yes, even his own life – he cannot be my disciple. (27) And anyone who does not carry his cross and follow me cannot be my disciple.'
>
> (18:28) Peter said to Jesus: 'We have left all we had to follow you!' (29) 'I tell you the truth,' Jesus said to them, 'no-one who has left home or wife or brothers or parents or children for the sake of the kingdom of God (30) will fail to receive many times as much in this age and, in the age to come, eternal life.'

Jesus uses very strong language to make a strong point. Clearly he does not literally mean that Christian husbands are to hate their wives (14:26), not when love, even of enemies, is so primary in his thinking and when the rest of the New Testament consistently tells husbands to love their wives (e.g. Eph. 5:25). But it would be a great mistake to assume therefore that Christ means nothing very definite. Rather, as the Matthean parallel makes clear, to 'hate' means 'to love less than' (Matt.

10:37). Jesus demands that his disciples love their wives and children less than they love him.

It is no good our saying: 'We cannot make comparisons when it comes to love. We love Christ and our wife (or husband) in different ways.' Jesus himself makes this comparison and even adds that unless we love him more we are not truly his disciple (14:26).

In Luke 18, he uses similarly strong language. He does not state that all his followers will need to 'leave home or wife . . . for the sake of the kingdom of God' (18:29), but clearly this will be the call of God to some. It seems that it was – at least for a time – for Simon Peter. Peter was certainly a married man (cf Mark 1:30) and, while later his wife did accompany him in his travelling ministry (cf 1 Cor. 9:5), it seems that he initially left her behind when Christ gave the call: 'Follow me' and 'at once they left their nets and followed him', beginning a ministry that took them all over Judea and Galilee (Mark 1:16–18).

Again, we must not mistake Christ's meaning. This is certainly not a call to relinquish marital and family responsibilities on some self-generated notion that God is calling us to evangelism in other parts of the country or the world. Nor is it a demand to leave one's marriage partner if he or she does not share one's Christian faith, a course of action expressly forbidden by St Paul (1 Cor. 7:12–14). Rather, it is a challenge to put the genuine demands of the kingdom of God first, even above our marriages.

Missionary families have found the truth of this promise – because it is a promise that God will more than make up for what we have lost (18:29f) – when husbands and wives have been forced to live apart from each other for an extended period of time. Christian believers have proved the truth of Christ's words when the unbelieving partner has divorced them and given as the reason that their morals and religious beliefs are incompatible.

These two passages in Luke are all about priorities. 'The radical mistake of the human race is that of pushing God into second or third or last place, of putting the will of self in place of the will of God, of giving a higher value to other goals than to the purpose of God' (Bromiley p.37). What Jesus does in the Luke passages is to apply this radical Christian principle to the realm of marriage. It is no longer a case of: 'I must hold on to my marriage at all costs even if it means losing Christ', but rather: 'I must hold on to Christ at all costs even if it means losing my marriage.'

Marriage then, very important as it is in Christ's thought and teaching, slips down the list of priorities.

## Mark 12:18–25//Matthew 22:23–30//Luke 20:27–36

There is another, even more important, way in which Christ relativizes marriage: he says that it belongs to this age only.

Some Sadducees, people who do not believe there will be a resurrection of the dead, came to Jesus with a trick question: a man had six brothers. When he died childless, the second brother followed normal Jewish practice and married his widow. But again there was no child. And so down through all the brothers until they had all married the woman and all died without issue. Now came the question: 'At the resurrection whose wife will she be, since the seven were married to her?' (Mark 12:23).

Jesus will deal with the real issue that they raise – the issue of the resurrection – in a moment; but first he comments on the question of marriage in the post-resurrection age. Matthew and Mark's accounts are very similar; Luke's is a little different and somewhat fuller:

> (Mark 12:24) Jesus replied: 'Are you not in error because you do not know the Scriptures or the power of God?' (25) When the dead rise, they will neither marry nor be given in marriage; they will be like the angels in heaven.'
> (Luke 20:34) Jesus replied: 'The people of this age marry and are given in marriage. (35) But those who are considered worthy of taking part in that age and in the resurrection from the dead will neither marry nor be given in marriage, (36) and they can no longer die; for they are like the angels. They are God's children, since they are children of the resurrection.'

So, marriage belongs to this imperfect age only. Christians who have been widowed are surely right to look forward to a joyful reunion, in the afterlife, with their believing partner. But we are mistaken if we believe that this reunion will mean a re-establishment of our marriage, of our old exclusive relationship.

This does not mean in any way that we shall be the losers. We may presume that an enormous amount that is good about our relationship with those whom we love will not only last but be bettered. And yet marriage itself will not last into the future age. 'Marriage, for all its high significance, has an eschatological limit. Married partners need not be afraid that they will lose the precious thing they already have. They will no longer be married, but in God they will have a more wonderful relationship that transcends the very best that marriage could ever offer, let alone what it can now offer in the sinful situation after the Fall' (Bromiley p.41).

Of course we treasure what we have in marriage now. But if we cannot imagine happiness without marriage we have not yet grasped the supreme happiness of being a 'child of God' (Luke 20:36) in that new age. St John puts this same truth in a different way: we, as part of the Church, will be married to Christ (Rev. 19:9; 21:9ff).

So again, in a very radical way, Jesus relativises marriage. Jewish people found it very hard to imagine any future age except one in which marriage and having children would play a major part. Jesus says that, on the contrary, human marriage will be superseded in the new age and that even in this life many, for a variety of reasons, have been 'given' by God a single life.

## The Teaching of St Paul

J. Héring describes 1 Corinthians 7 as 'the most important chapter in the entire Bible for the question of marriage and related subjects' (quoted in P. Brown p.53). While this may slightly overstate the situation as regards marriage, there is no question that it has the fullest, and most important, teaching on the subject of singleness.

In this chapter, St Paul is clearly responding to questions the Corinthian Christians have put to him and points they have made (7:1). In the latter part of 1 Corinthians, the phrase

'now concerning' (*peri de*) introduces different issues which the Corinthians have raised with him (7:1, 25; 8:1; 12:1) or perhaps which he is raising with them (16:1, 12). In this chapter, therefore, there are two main issues:
1. The issue of sexual intercourse and marital relations (1–16). This is introduced by verse 1: 'Now for the matters you wrote about: It is good for a man not to touch a woman' (literally: NIV's translation 'not to marry' is erroneous and misleading – see below).
2. The issue of 'virgins' (25–38; there is a brief postscript in 39f). This is introduced by verse 25: 'Now about virgins'.

In each case – and in fact each main section contains a number of different situations – Paul's advice is precisely the same: stay as you are. The pivotal paragraph of 17–24, which seems to depart from the subject of marriage and singleness by introducing circumcision (18f) and slavery (21–23), does so only to hammer home Paul's central principle: 'Let everyone lead the life which the Lord has assigned to him and in which God has called him' (17 RSV); 'Each one should remain in the situation which he was in when God called him' (20); 'So brethren, in whatever state each was called, there let him remain with God' (24 RSV).

This is the principle which informs and directs the whole chapter. Its outworkings can be seen again and again (2f, 8, 10f, 12f, 26f, 37, 40). And its implication in the field of marriage and singleness, with which the chapter is primarily concerned, is summed up succinctly in 27: 'Are you married? Do not seek a divorce. Are you unmarried? Do not look for a wife.'

## The Issue of Sexual Intercourse and Marital Relations

(1) Now for the matters you wrote about: It is good for a man not to touch a woman. (2) But since there is so much immorality, each man should have his own wife, and each woman her own husband. (3) The husband should fulfil his marital duty to his wife, and likewise the wife to her husband. (4) The wife's body does not belong to her alone but also to her husband. In the same way, the husband's

body does not belong to him alone but also to his wife. (5) Do not deprive each other except by mutual consent and for a time, so that you may devote yourselves to prayer. Then come together again so that Satan will not tempt you because of your lack of self-control. (6) I say this as a concession, not as a command. (7) I wish that all men were as I am. But each man has his own gift from God; one has this gift, another has that. (8) Now to the unmarried and the widows I say: It is good for them to stay unmarried as I am. (9) But if they cannot control themselves, they should marry, for it is better to marry than to burn with passion.

[The section dealing with this issue of marital relations continues until verse 16, but we will look closely at verses 10–16 in chapter six.]

As we have already noticed, Paul is responding to what the Corinthians have written (1). While he is certainly expounding Christian principles which he sees as universally applicable (see especially 17), yet he is also interacting with their position, and so it is helpful as far as possible to establish what their position was.

The question which immediately confronts us is whether verse 1: 'It is good for a man not to touch a woman' is a direct quotation from their letter. It would seem that Paul does at times quote from their letter: parts of 6:12; 6:13; 8:1 and perhaps 8:4 are most likely direct quotations from what they had written. It is probable that 7:1 is also a quote from the Corinthians. To 'touch a woman' (1) does not mean (despite the NIV translation) 'to marry' but rather: 'to have sexual relations with a woman'. This is how it is used, for example, in Proverbs 6:29. Here then, in verse 1, is a general principle that 'a man' – that is: any man, not just a man before his marriage, but any man married or unmarried – would be better off not having sexual relations with a woman. As St Paul goes on very specifically to say that married men *should* have sexual relations with their wives and vice versa (2ff), it seems impossible that Paul could have made such a general statement. Certainly he speaks very highly of the single state in this chapter, but he could not have said of men in general that it is better for them not to have sexual relations with women.

It is most likely, therefore, that verse 1 represents the position of at least some in the Corinthian Church. Probably because they denigrated the body (cf 6:13, 15:12), some people were teaching that it was unspiritual to have sex with your marriage partner or even to be married at all. It seems that they were saying there should be no sex within marriage (cf 2–6), that marriage partners should divorce each other (cf 10–11) or at least that those married to a non-Christian should divorce their unbelieving spouse (cf 12–16) on the grounds that he or she was unclean (cf 14), and that unmarried people should never marry (cf 8f, 25ff). Fee also suggests that some of the husbands, partly because of sexual frustration because their wives were refusing sex, were frequenting prostitutes, justifying themselves on the grounds that they too thought very little of the body and that, as it was irrelevant to true spiritual life, it didn't matter what you did with it (cf 6:12–20).

Paul has no sympathy with the fundamental idea underlying these positions – if this was indeed that the body is at best irrelevant and at worst evil. Yet he is not completely out of tune with all their conclusions, though he arrives at these from entirely different premises. So his answer is not: 'You are wrong on every count. Marriage is good, and everyone should get married.' Rather, their conclusions are partially wrong: full marital relations are the duty of every husband and wife (2–6). But they are also partially right: singleness is also good and even a better state to be in, for the Christian, than marriage (7–9 and 25ff, especially 38).

## The Married

Paul turns first to those who are married and living together. Immediately he begins to modify, and counter, the Corinthians' position. They have said it is better to abstain from all sexual relations (1). 'But since there is so much immorality, each man should have his own wife, and each woman her own husband' (2). English readers often take the phrase 'have a wife' to mean 'marry' or 'get married to'. Paul would then be saying that everyone should get married.

In view of all he says in the rest of the chapter about the advantages of singleness, it is unlikely that this is Paul's meaning.

But in any case to 'have a wife' (*echein gynaika*) never means to 'marry', 'get married to'. It can mean to '*be* married to' (as it does in 12, 29), but it can also mean to 'have sexually', to 'have intercourse with'. This is its meaning in Isaiah 13:16 (NIV: their wives [will be] ravished: LXX, literally: they [the enemies] will have their [the Israelites'] wives), and is surely (the context dictates this) its meaning here.

Paul emphasises that intercourse is to be with 'his own' wife (*tēn heautou*) or 'her own' husband (*ton idion*). This emphasis may again be because some marital partners were seeking sexual satisfaction elsewhere, as they were being denied sex in their marriages. 'Since there is so much immorality' (2) would tend to support this view. Literally it is: 'because of the immoralities' and the plural rather suggests that immorality was already being practised. Moreover, while the word (*porneias*) may certainly mean immorality in general, it is exactly the same root that Paul has just used for prostitution (6:15, 16 and probably 18 also). Paul is then saying that one reason why husbands and wives should have intercourse with one another is because enforced abstinence has already led to several cases of resorting to prostitutes.

But this of course is not the only reason for marital intercourse. Paul broadens out to say that there is a certain 'debt' (NIV: 'marital duty') which the partners should give each other (3). The context makes clear what this debt is. In marrying, they promised each other their bodies. In fact, they handed over authority over their own bodies to their partner (4). Therefore, they must be prepared to engage in sexual activity with their partner, even sometimes when they themselves are not feeling like it or do not want it.

And here we come across a remarkable aspect of this entire chapter. The Corinthians had seen the issue, in keeping with the vast majority of their contemporaries, entirely from the man's point of view (1). Paul had initially responded from the viewpoint of the man (2a) but had quickly added the same point from the woman's perspective (2b). As he makes his next point, he actually begins with the wife (3a), and on the matter of sex of all subjects! Fee points out that even to this day 'sex is often viewed as the husband's privilege and the wife's obligation'. But not in Paul. Here the obligation is mutual and Paul begins with the husband's obligation to give full sexual dues to his wife. And so throughout the chapter, actually ten times in all, Paul makes it clear that, in marital relations, the obligations, the duties, the responsibilities are (in almost every case) identical for the man and the woman (2, 3, 4, 10f, 12f, 14, 15, 16, 28, 32–34). This is even so in the area of authority, a field which the New Testament might have been thought to reserve exclusively for the husband. 'For the wife does not rule over her own body, but the husband does; likewise the husband does not rule over his own body, but the wife does' (4 RSV). Unfortunately NIV is particularly inaccurate here. Not only does it translate *exousiazō* as 'belong to' instead of 'rule', but it implies, in a way totally unwarranted by the Greek, that husband and wife *share* with their partners authority over their bodies. On the contrary, in the sexual sphere we hand complete authority over our body to our marriage partner, according to Paul.

Paul does allow that there may be occasions when sexual relations are temporarily interrupted in order that the couple may devote themselves more wholeheartedly to prayer. But this should only be by mutual agreement and for a limited period, or else again sexual frustration may break out in sinful ways (5).

And then Paul adds: 'I say this as a concession, not as a command' (6). But what is 'this' which is only a concession? Godet and others refer 'this' back to verse 2. Godet describes verse 2 as 'the general duty of marriage'; he says that verses 3–5 are merely a 'digression' about the practice of marriage, and in verse 7, Paul is saying: 'In speaking as I do [in verse 2] I do not for a moment mean to give you an apostolical command to marry.' But Godet's understanding is not likely. We have seen already that the phrase 'to have a wife' does not mean 'to marry'. And in any case, Paul's precepts in 2 (and in 3 and 5a) are all expressed in imperatives, and 4 is in the form of a very cut-and-dried statement. It is hard to see how these are not 'commands'. The more tentative language comes in the exception because of prayer introduced in 5b. The Corinthians were advocating no sex (1) even within marriage. Paul 'concedes' that temporary abstinence for prayer may be justified, but even this should not be thought of as a command. No married couple who continue uninterruptedly with normal sexual relations should think that they are flouting an apostolic command.

## The Unmarried

Paul only turns formally to address the unmarried in verse 8, but already he has turned to the subject of singleness in verse 7. The Corinthians desired all men to abstain from sex (1). Paul disagrees entirely with them as far as the married are concerned; they are to give each other the 'debt', and privilege, of sex (2–6). However, Paul does have a very high view of the single state, and if it were left to him, he could wish that everyone might be single. 'I wish that all men were as I am' (7) and in the context the natural meaning of this is: single.

There is much speculation about Paul's marital state. Barrett thinks it most probable that he was a widower since unmarried rabbis were very few and Paul was probably a rabbi. Bruce mentions the possibility that his wife may have left him on his conversion to Christianity. Or he may never have married. The question has its own fascination, but does not affect the point that he is making. Insofar as he mentions himself, Paul does not dwell on any past marital state, but on the present: he is single (7, 8).

Yet despite his desire, in view of the advantages of the single life, that everyone should be single, he recognises that this is not God's will for all. God has given different gifts to different people 'one of one kind and one of another' (7 RSV). Commentators have sometimes rather forced their interpretation of this admittedly brief phrase. Conzelmann, for example, thinks that Paul is talking about 'continence' as a gift; but then what is the 'other' gift? He answers this by seeing the gifts as 'freedom from the desire for sexual fulfilment' and 'sexual life in marriage'. But more straightforward and probably more natural is to understand the two gifts as: marriage and singleness (so, for example, Bruce).

Paul, then, recognises singleness as a gift (cf Matt. 19:11) and marriage as a gift. We should not, then, think of the 'normal' state for which no special calling is required, as marriage, and the peculiar state, for which one has to be especially 'gifted' by God, as singleness. While it may be true that God calls more people to marriage than to singleness, we cannot simply assume that one or other must be for us (compare what parents often say to their children: 'when you are married . . .'). Each is a gift, and it is for God to choose which good gift he has given to each one of us – not for St Paul (cf the whole of 7), nor for us.

And then Paul turns to 'the unmarried and the widows' (8). This is a somewhat unusual phrase; since the 'unmarried' clearly includes widows, why mention them specifically? The general word 'unmarried' (*agamos*) can sometimes take on more specific meanings in particular contexts; for example in 11 it means 'unmarried after divorce'. Fee therefore suggests that it means 'widower' here, on the grounds that it makes another pair of men and women ('widower and widow') as so often in the chapter and that then all the cases in 1–16 deal with people who are currently or formerly married and 25–38 take up the issue of those never before married.

Perhaps Fee is being neater than Paul himself. There is no clear indication that *agamos* here means widower. Rather, Paul probably has chiefly in mind those never before married (in contrast to the already married whom he has been discussing in 2–6). He adds the widows because he thinks of those who are again single at the end of their life, and these, even in an age when women quite frequently died in childbirth, were more often women than men. For the self-same reason Paul departs from his usual practice and only mentions women whose partners die in 39f; the issue arose so much less frequently for men (cf also 1 Tim. 5:3–16).

So, to the never before married and the widows, Paul gives his advice. He believes that it is desirable for them to remain single. As yet, he simply states this; he will give his reasons later in the chapter. But he does add his own example. He is not talking from idle theory; he himself is single and is convinced that it is better to stay in this state (8).

There is then a measure of truth in the Corinthians' position, even though their reasons are the wrong ones. But it should not be thought for a moment that Paul is against marriage. On the contrary, many are given the 'gift' of marriage by God (7) and one indication – only one – of this being God's call is if their passions are particularly strong and they are unable to control them (9). It should not be imagined for a moment that Paul thinks this is the only justification for marriage or the only purpose of marriage. In 11:11f he speaks of the mutual dependence of husband and wife, and in 2 Corinthians 11:2f he writes of the 'sincere and pure devotion' that a bride ought to have towards her partner. We have already seen the exalted terms in which Ephesians 5 speaks of married life, and 1 Timothy 4:3 roundly condemns those who forbid marriage.

Nevertheless, this is one important reason why some people should marry. It was clearly a real issue for many Corinthians who were easily led into immorality (2) and whose self-control was often sorely tested (5). It is clearly an issue for many today when our sexual passions are constantly and very deliberately being aroused. For people who find sexual temptation especially strong, marriage is the right place to look for the channelling of their sexual desire. Of a related verse, Conzelmann says: 'This definition of the [I would prefer to say: an] aim of marriage is unfashionable but realistic.'

*The Book of Common Prayer* recognises this. In the marriage service it describes three 'causes for which matrimony was ordained'. Alongside the bearing and nurture of children, and the support the partners can give each other, it gives another cause: 'Matrimony was ordained for a remedy against sin and to avoid fornication; that such persons as have not the gift of continency might marry, and keep themselves undefiled members of Christ's body.' Unhappily, many Christians in the contemporary West postpone marriage until later and later, and meanwhile feel their sexual urges are very strong and look for an outlet in pre-marital sex ('fornication').

## Summary

Paul's teaching so far has been prompted by a question, or some remarks, from the Corinthians about marriage. And therefore verses 1–9 (and the sequel: 10–16) are principally about marriage. Yet in the course of his discussion he has introduced some important statements about singleness.

Certainly Paul recognises that many are 'given' marriage by God; no one should think it inherently less spiritual to get married (7b). Yet it is equally a 'gift' of God to many that they should enjoy the benefits of a single life, and Paul's own preference would be for large numbers to be called to that state (7a). He says 'all' but modifies it with 7b.

Again, marriage is certainly the right way for many (9) but so is singleness; and if you are unmarried at the moment and not under any great inner compulsion to marry, you will do better to remain single (8).

It is not difficult to read Paul's words and seek to explain them. Yet they must have been absolutely revolutionary to most people in his day. They are still revolutionary today, which is why 1 Corinthians 7 is so little discussed or preached about in our churches.

## The Issue of 'Virgins'

Paul goes on in verses 10–16 to speak about divorce (see chapter 6) and then in verses 17–24 discusses the general principle lying behind all his teaching in this chapter (summed up in 20).

With verse 25: 'Now about virgins', he comes on to a new subject, and almost certainly a new issue which the Corinthians had raised with him:

> (25) Now about virgins: I have no command from the Lord, but I give a judgment as one who by the Lord's mercy is trustworthy. (26) Because of the present crisis, I think that it is good for you to remain as you are. (27) Are you married? Do not seek a divorce. Are you unmarried? Do not look for a wife. (28) But if you do marry, you have not sinned; and if a virgin marries, she has not sinned. But those who marry will face many troubles in this life, and I want to spare you this.
>
> (29) What I mean, brothers, is that the time is short. From now on those who have wives should live as if they had none; (30) those who mourn, as if they did not; those who are happy, as if they were not; those who buy something, as if it were not theirs to keep; (31) those who use the things of the world, as if not engrossed in them. For this world in its present form is passing away.
>
> (32) I would like you to be free from concern. An unmarried man is concerned about the Lord's affairs – how he can

please the Lord. But a married man is concerned about the affairs of this world – how he can please his wife – (34) and his interests are divided. An unmarried woman or virgin is concerned about the Lord's affairs: Her aim is to be devoted to the Lord in both body and spirit. But a married woman is concerned about the affairs of this world – how she can please her husband. (35) I am saying this for your own good, not to restrict you, but that you may live in a right way in undivided devotion to the Lord.

(36) If anyone thinks he is acting improperly towards the virgin he is engaged to, and if she is getting on in years and he feels he ought to marry, he should do as he wants. He is not sinning. They should get married. (37) But the man who has settled the matter in his own mind, who is under no compulsion but has control over his own will, and who has made up his mind not to marry the virgin – this man also does the right thing. (38) So then, he who marries the virgin does right, but he who does not marry her does even better.

The question which immediately arises is: who are these 'virgins' about whom the Corinthians have raised a question? The Greek word *parthenos* (25, 28, 34, 36–38) does indeed mean 'virgin', a person who has not engaged in sexual intercourse with another; it is normally used of women but can also be used of men (Rev. 14:4 where NIV translates it 'pure'). There are three main contenders for its meaning in our context:

1. The unmarried. This would not include the divorced or widowed, for whom the term 'virgins' would be wholly inappropriate, but simply the never before married. This is the view of Conzelmann who, however, thinks the word takes on the specialised meaning of 'the betrothed' in the specific case of verses 36–38.

2. The betrothed. Verse 36 speaks of 'his virgin' (NIV: 'the virgin he is engaged to'); verses 37 and 38 both have 'his own virgin' (NIV: 'the virgin' in both cases) and this points to some definite relationship with, and commitment to, the virgin. The most natural explanation is to think of this as an engagement, especially since a distinction is made in verse 34 between 'an unmarried woman' (someone who has never been married) and a 'virgin' (someone, according to this view, who is engaged).

This view has the advantage, over Conzelmann, of keeping the usage of *parthenos* the same throughout the section. Right from verse 25 Paul is answering Corinthian questions about what an engaged couple should do.

3. Unmarried daughters. According to this view, the Corinthians were questioning what Christian fathers should do with their unmarried daughters and whether, in an age of arranged marriages, they should give them away in marriage. It is in this sense that she is 'his (own) virgin' (36–38). Paul, then, refers to the issue in verse 25 but broadens out enormously from it before coming back to the specific question in verses 36–38. This view has given rise to the NIV margin. Detailed refutation of this third view will probably best be deferred until the discussion of 36–38; suffice to say at this stage that there is only one word in 36–38 which really suggests this view and that word is capable of other explanations, that there are several more words and expressions in 36–38 which fit very uneasily with this view, that 'nothing in verses 25–35 even remotely suggests Paul is addressing such an issue' (Fee) and that in the entire section (25–38) no words for 'father', 'guardian' or 'daughter' ever appear.

The choice is, then, between the first two views and the difference between them does not greatly affect our understanding of the passage as a whole. If the meaning is 'the unmarried', then Paul starts by writing about the single in general and narrows it down to the specific situation of the betrothed in 36–38 (this is Conzelmann's position). If, on the contrary, Paul means 'the betrothed' in 25, then he expands to include all single people (certainly in 32–35 and perhaps in 27–35) before coming back to the specific issue of the betrothed in 36–38. On the whole, I believe this second view is more likely, especially in the light of the distinction already referred to between an 'unmarried woman' and a 'virgin' in 34.

## Paul's Judgment

Paul introduces his teaching in this section in an uncharacteristically tentative way: 'I have no command from the Lord, but give a judgment as one who by the Lord's mercy is trustworthy' (25). In part, this is to distinguish what he is about to say from those subjects on which there is a recorded utterance of the Lord (10f). But this is not the way Paul normally writes when he is dealing with an issue on which Christ has not pronounced; and similar phrases are a feature of the chapter (12, 26, 40). Partly, this may be due to his authority, either in general or on this issue, being under attack; verse 40 ('I too') may indicate that some in Corinth were making the claim that they 'had the Spirit of God' and he did not. Nevertheless, this unusual way of speaking needs to be taken seriously. He is giving his apostolic opinion in what follows (this applies to 25–40 and not to the earlier part of the chapter) not passing on a binding command.

Yet the second part of verse 25 also needs to be taken seriously. This is not just anyone's opinion, or even just any Christian's. It is the judgment of one who is conscious that he is 'by the Lord's mercy trustworthy' (25). This theme is also repeated in verse 40, where again he gives his 'judgment' but believes that it is informed by the Spirit of God. We are by no means, then, simply at liberty to dismiss what Paul will say. In addition, those who believe that it was God who oversaw the formation of the New Testament canon may conclude that since this letter, and specifically this chapter, was included, it bears the approval of God that in this matter, as in others, Paul was indeed 'trustworthy' (25) and did indeed 'have the Spirit of God' (40).

So what is Paul's judgment? 'That it is well for a man to remain as he is' (a more literal translation of 26b than NIV which inexplicably introduces 'you'). This principle is in complete conformity with 17–24 and indeed with the theme of the whole chapter: in regard to a person's general affairs, and specifically his marital status, it is best for a person to 'remain in the situation which he was in when God called him' (20).

Paul then works that out in the particular situation which he has in mind: 'Are you bound to a wife? Do not seek release. Are you released from a wife? Do not seek a wife' (27 literally). Probably what Paul is doing here is already opening up the subject more widely and not confining it to the question of the betrothed. Are you already married? – he uses the word 'bound' – deomai – which is his normal term for the lifelong marriage bond: 39, cf Rom. 7:2. Then do not seek a dissolution of your marriage, as some of the Corinthians were probably urging. Are you, on the contrary, unmarried (free from any unalterable commitment to a wife)? Do not seek marriage. As Arndt and Gingrich state, the word for 'released, set free' here (*lelysai* from the common verb *lyō*) does not necessarily imply that the person has been married before, and indeed in the context of the chapter as a whole this is impossible. Clearly Paul is speaking to the same person (as in 27b) when he goes on to say, in 28, that marriage for him is no sin. If 27b were referring to a divorced person, then 27f would be a flat contradiction of 11.

Much more likely is that Paul in 27b is talking to the man who is betrothed but not yet married; hence my paraphrase of his having 'no unalterable commitment to a wife'. Clearly, it is this situation which he has in mind in 28: 'If you do marry, you have not sinned; and if the virgin [Paul uses the definite article, *hē parthenos*: *the* virgin, not, as in NIV *a* virgin] marries, she has not sinned.' 'The virgin' must surely mean the man's betrothed; therefore the man of 28a ('you') who is also described in 27b ('are you released/free from a wife?') must be the man betrothed to her.

An alternative view is that in 27a Paul is still thinking only of the case of the betrothed. Fee translates: 'Are you under obligation to a [future] wife?' and in 27b: 'Are you free from such obligations?' If you are already betrothed, he says, don't break off your engagement (but don't get married either). If you are not yet betrothed, don't seek marriage. What makes this view somewhat less likely is that in 27a Paul says: 'Are you bound to a *wife*?'; if he had betrothal in mind, he would surely have asked: 'Are you bound to a *virgin*?', using the same word as in 25 and 28.

However, there is, in the end, not a great deal of difference between these views, especially since elsewhere in the chapter Paul says both that someone already married should not seek to dissolve the marriage (10ff) and that a betrothed man would do well not to go the whole way into marriage (36–38).

What 27b–28 most certainly are not saying is that while the divorced would be better not marrying (27b), they will not be sinning if they do (28). Luck seeks to get round the obvious contradiction that this would entail with 11 by saying that 11 speaks to the unjustly divorcing whereas 27f speak to the 'innocent party' in a divorce (pp. 184f), but of course there is nothing in either verse, or either immediate context, to make this distinction. As we have seen, both the context of the chapter (verse 11, and indeed the whole principle of: stay as you are) and the immediate context (28) means that 27b must refer to the betrothed.

What Paul adds in 28 is that, contrary to what some Corinthians are probably teaching, it is no sin whatsoever if an engaged couple do decide, contrary to Paul's general guidance (26f), to get married.

Before we leave this paragraph, we should note that Paul gives two reasons for his 'judgment', each of which will be developed in greater detail in succeeding paragraphs. The first is: 'because of the present crisis' (26). The first edition of the RSV translated this as 'impending', which would mean that the crisis was in the future, not the present. We then might be free to say that Paul had got his timescale wrong, the great difficulties of the end times were not suffered by his generation, nor perhaps will they be by ours, and therefore a major element in his reasoning is invalid. It is true that the word for 'distress' (RSV, a somewhat better translation of *ananke* than NIV's 'crisis') is used of the run-up to the final tribulation in Luke 21:23 but that is 'the only known usage of *ananke* in this way in all of Jewish and Christian Literature' (Fee) and it needs the further definition of an adjective in Luke: '*great* distress' (cf Rev. 7:14 'the *great* tribulation', where a different noun is used: *thlipsis*). *Ananke* is of course never used in this way in Paul. This then (in 26) is the ordinary distress that Christians are subject to in the present age (the word is so used on a number of occasions in Paul, e.g. 1 Thess. 3:7).

NIV is right to translate *enestos* as 'present' (26; so also the 2nd edition of RSV). That is how it is consistently used throughout the New Testament, and it is specifically the present in contrast to the future (*mellon*) in 1 Cor. 3:22 and Rom. 8:38.

So Paul views the present time – the Christian age, stretching from Resurrection/Pentecost to the Second Coming – as one of distress, and his point is: 'In the light of the distress we are already experiencing as Christians, you would be wise not to add to the pressures already on you by getting married.' He will expand on this in the paragraphs that follow.

He adds to this a second, very much related, reason: 'Those who marry will face many troubles in this life, and I want to spare you this' (28). He is thinking of ordinary human life ('in this life' is, literally, 'in the flesh'). While Paul would not deny for a moment that marriage brings great consolations (cf Gen. 2:18), he is also very well aware that it brings many heartaches and troubles. Perhaps this is even more the case because they are Christians. All Christians will suffer (cf 2 Tim. 3:12) and it will cause extra pain to the husband when he sees his wife and children suffering. 'I would spare you that' (28), says Paul.

## Reason 1: Marriage Belongs to a Passing Age

And now, after a paragraph in which he has stated his main conclusions (25–28), Paul goes on to treat more fully his reasons for preferring specifically that a betrothed couple should not get married, and more generally that a single person remain single. His first reason is that marriage belongs to a passing age (29–31).

This is stated most succinctly at the end of the paragraph: 'This world in its present form is passing away' (31). The most important final events have already happened: Christ has come, he has died, he has been raised, he has sent his Spirit. Nothing except God's patience now stands in the way of Christ's Second Coming when he will wind up this present world and usher in a new heaven and a new earth (Rev. 21:1). This world, therefore, is on the way out; and marriage, as we have already seen in the teaching of Jesus, belongs to this world.

It is in this sense that Paul can say: 'What I mean, brothers, is that the time is short' (29). This thought is very important to Paul. Most Greeks did not have a concept of a future with a definite end, and while Jews very certainly did have such a concept, for many of them the end was 'off in the vague distance' (Fee). Paul had a well defined conviction. The end of this age had, because of Christ's death, resurrection and sending of the Spirit, been brought near. The time had been shortened (the word for 'short' is in fact a passive participle) and this could not but affect the outlook of those who had recognised it. 'Those who have a definite future and see it with clarity live in the present with radically altered values as to what counts and what does not' (Fee).

So Paul's view is that the time before the end has been shortened (29), this world is passing away (31) and the present is a time of distress for Christians (26). The middle of the paragraph gives the implications of this Christian understanding: 'From now on those who have wives should live as if they had none; those who mourn, as if they did not; those who are happy, as if they were not; those who buy something, as if it were not theirs to keep; those who use the things of the world, as if not engrossed in them' (29b–31a).

What this clearly cannot mean is that the married must live entirely as if they were single people. That would be to say that there should be no sexual relations between marriage partners which, it seems, some Corinthians were maintaining but which Paul was at pains to refute (2–6). Verses 30a and 30b would also contradict Romans 12:15, and the whole section, understood in this way, would suggest withdrawal from the world which is specifically opposed in 5:9f.

Rather, Paul must mean that these things are not to have a dominant grip on Christians' lives, nor to be of absolute importance for them, because Christians recognise that they will not last for ever. By a change of verb in the last two items in the list, Paul spells out more clearly what he means: Christians may still buy but they should not be possessive of what they have bought; indeed it should be as if they have no lasting claim on what they own (30c). They may still make use of purely temporal things, but they should not exploit them to the full (probably the best translation of *katachraomai*. NIV: be engrossed in) as if this world were everything there is to life (31a). From these examples, we see what Paul was saying about marriage in 29 and indeed in the whole paragraph. Certainly Christians can be married but they should not act as if marriage were the be-all and end-all.

Bromiley puts it like this:

The coming of Christ will shortly end the present order, so that even those who have husbands and wives . . . must live out their lives here with the perspective of eternity, when the form of this world will have gone and marriage itself will go with it . . . Important though they may be, these matters [marriage or anything else that belongs to this passing order] are no longer of all-consuming importance, for they are relativised by the new order which Christ's coming will shortly initiate (pp. 58f).

Can we accept this view today? Nearly 2,000 years have gone by since Paul wrote 'the time is short' (29). I think we must acknowledge that this has weakened Paul's argument somewhat. Granted that he made no claim to know when the time of the end would be, yet he does appear to have expected it sooner than it has in fact come.

Yet this weakening of his argument can be overstated. Certainly as his life wore on, if not before, he expected to die before the Second Coming (the clearest reference is 2 Tim. 4:6f which I take to be Pauline), yet the end time continued to be determinative for his life (2 Tim. 4:8). Moreover, the statement in 29 is primarily a theological, not a temporal, one: there is nothing significant due to occur between Christ's death and resurrection and his Second Coming. It is still, therefore, a Christian's conviction that God has shortened the time (29), that this world is on its way out (31) and that the present time is an age of distress (26). And the implication is still that we should not treat marriage as if it were all important.

This has implications for the married (the immediate point in 29): that they should not idolise their marriages or treat them as if they were the most important element in their lives. It also has implications for those who are single, whether currently betrothed or not (the context of the discussion in 25–38): that they should not treat marriage as essential to their happiness or as a relationship without which they will be incomplete.

## Reason 2: Marriage Brings Additional and Conflicting Concerns

Paul now brings forward his second argument for remaining single (32–35). As often in this chapter, he says broadly the same thing to both men and women. First he turns to the man: 'An unmarried man is concerned about the Lord's affairs – how he can please the Lord. But a married man is concerned about the affairs of this world – how he can please his wife – and his interests are divided' (32b–34a). Then Paul turns to the women, using very similar language: 'An unmarried woman or virgin is concerned about the Lord's affairs: her aim is to be devoted to the Lord in both body and spirit. But a married woman is concerned about the affairs of this world – how she can please her husband' (34b). And he concludes with a remark to both sexes: 'I am saying this for your own good, not to restrict you, but that you may live in a right way in undivided devotion to the Lord' (35).

Paul has clearly been broadening out from the single issue of the betrothed. Now he is speaking generally of unmarried men (32), whether or not they are engaged. Turning to the women, Paul begins in the same way: 'an unmarried woman' (34), but he has not forgotten the question the Corinthians set before him and so adds 'or virgin' (34). The issue of the betrothed is still with him.

In this paragraph, Paul reveals two great desires which he has for all Christians and which he is convinced will be best served if Christians are able to remain single. The first desire he expresses right at the beginning of the paragraph: 'I would like you to be free from concern'. 'Concern' is probably the best translation of the word which in various forms (the verb is *merimnaō*) comes five times in 32–34. It is not, here, a uniformly negative idea. On the contrary, it must be a good thing to be 'concerned about the Lord's affairs, how he can please the Lord' (32, cf 34). And similarly, for the husband and wife it is right to be concerned about their marriage partner (33, 34). Yet concern brings worry and tension, and Paul does not want them to pile more and more worries on to themselves (32a). Concern brings troubles (28; a different, more negative, word: *thlipsis*) and 'I want to spare you this' (28).

We must not misunderstand Paul here. He of all people knows not only that suffering cannot be avoided but that it is one of the principal methods which God uses to mould our character (Rom. 5:3–5; 'suffering' is *thlipsis* again). But concern for the Lord's affairs will bring enough maturing troubles of its own (see especially 2 Cor. 11:28). And the Christian is never deliberately to pile troubles on himself out of some misguided Christian zeal. This is especially so when the concerns – and troubles – relate only to things of this world (33, 34). Marriage comes into that category; and this world is passing (31).

Paul has a second great desire: 'that you may live . . . in undivided devotion to the Lord' (35). This is simply not possible for the married man or woman. The married man, in addition to his love for Christ, is rightly concerned about how to bring happiness to his wife (33). This is good and proper, but it does mean that 'his interests are divided' (34), literally: he has become divided. The unmarried man, by contrast, can concentrate all his energies in one direction: how to please the Lord (32). And the unmarried woman can also give all her attention to the Lord's affairs: 'her aim is to be devoted to the Lord [literally: to be holy] in both body and spirit' (34).

Of course the precise situation will vary from case to case. For example, some single people will find the distractions of their unfulfilled sexual impulses so strong that they too, in quite a different way, are concerned with the affairs of this world. For such people, marriage will be the better course (8f, 36). Nevertheless, the single life offers possibilities for undistracted devotion to the Lord which simply cannot be available to the married. Bromiley again sums this up well: 'Marriage . . . is the most intimate and demanding of all human commitments. Hence the possibility of a clash or division of interests is especially high at this point . . . The married who are tempted to put husband or wife or children first find greater difficulty in achieving the primary commitment to Christ which lies at the very heart of faith and discipleship' (p. 59). What married person can deny this?

Nevertheless, Paul is at pains to say that this is by no means a command to stay single. It is not the case that any devoted Christian will be a single Christian. On the contrary, God's gifts are different for each individual (7). And human choice is involved as well. That is why Paul is arguing for the single state here; he is urging those Christians who have the choice – emotionally and because they are not already married – to choose singleness. Yet he writes only 'for your own good', 'not to restrict you' (35). This last phrase is, literally, 'not to throw a noose over you' and is an image taken either from hunting or from war (prisoners were often led with nooses round their necks). Fee comments well on the irony that we have done exactly the opposite of what Paul says; churches have turned his teaching on marriage and singleness into a tight noose: 'Roman Catholicism has insisted on celibacy for its clergy even though not all are gifted to be so; on the other hand, many Protestant groups will not ordain the single because marriage is the norm, and the single are not quite trusted.'

## Application to the Betrothed

Paul has been speaking in general about the single life and comparing it with marriage. He now returns (36–38) to the very specific situation which the Corinthians had raised with him. He is envisaging now a couple who are engaged. In this section, he addresses the man, i.e. the fiancé. Hence the NIV text of 36a: 'If anyone thinks he is acting improperly towards the virgin he is engaged to' (literally: his virgin).

Once more Paul sums up his judgment in a very clear way at the end of the paragraph: 'So then, he who marries the virgin [literally: his own virgin] does right, but he who does not marry her does even better' (38). Both parts of this highly important statement need to be taken seriously. It may seem unnecessary to say that we should take seriously 38a, that it is a good thing to marry. Yet some of the Corinthians seem to have been saying the opposite, and it is easy for us, once we examine what Paul writes in 1 Corinthians 7, to think that he is saying marriage is a weakness, a concession only to the sexually uncontrolled, even half sinful. Not only would that be a travesty of Paul's teaching on marriage in the totality of his writing, but it is equally a quite inaccurate reflection of his teaching in this chapter. Here he has spoken of its disadvantages compared with singleness; in other passages he will speak of its advantages. Yet here too he recognises that marriage is God's gift (7) to many, and that those who marry 'do well' (a literal translation of 38a).

However, if we are to take 38a seriously, we must also take 38b with equal seriousness. Paul is not afraid to weigh up the respective merits of marriage and singleness; he is not shy of answering the question: 'Which is better?' And he comes down unequivocally on the side of singleness: 'He who does not marry does better' (38b literally). As we have said already, this Christian view was revolutionary in its day, being almost unheard of in pagan or Jewish circles. It did, however, take hold of the minds and hearts of Christians who were convinced Paul was right, and the single life was highly honoured and respected in the early Church, sometimes even going beyond the teaching of St Paul. Today this teaching is almost totally unheard, at least in Protestant circles. Who would dare to say that singleness is better than marriage? On the contrary, the unspoken – and often spoken – assumption of almost everyone is that marriage is better than singleness. Yet the apostle Paul says the reverse, and undergirds his statement with arguments which are just as valid today (32–35 certainly; 29–31 arguably) as they were when he first wrote them.

So why marry at all? Paul envisages one situation in which marriage would be the right course of action (36). It is important to stress that it is only one such situation. Other situations might also indicate that marriage is God's gift for that individual. Paul continually harps on the sexual reason in this chapter simply because there was so much immorality already in Corinth (2) and it is quite clear that it had got its grip on members of the church there (6:15ff).

He has just said that he longs for all Christians to live 'properly' (*euschēmon*, 35. NIV: 'in a right way'). Now he contrasts that word with its negative: 'If anyone thinks he is acting improperly' (*aschēmonein*, 36). His passions are getting the better of him, his sexual desires are too much aroused, he is not acting purely with his fiancée.

NIV translates the next phrase: 'and if she is getting on in years' (literally 'if he (or she) is *hyperakmos*'). This word, unknown in Greek literature outside 1 Corinthians 7, is clearly made up of *hyper* and *akmē*. *Akmē* means the highest point or culmination. *Hyper* might, here, be either temporal: 'beyond in time', or intensive: 'fully developed' or 'exceedingly'. If the subject of the verb is the virgin, it would mean she is 'past her prime' (so NIV and Arndt and Gingrich) or 'fully developed sexually' (so Liddell and Scott). If the subject of the verb is the man, it would mean 'with strong passions' (so RSV and Arndt and Gingrich's alternative). The latter seems to be much more likely. The man has been the subject of the previous clause ('If anyone thinks he is acting . . .') and no change of subject is signalled in any way in the text. In the light of Paul's preference for singleness it is also not easy to see why a woman's getting 'past her prime' would be a reason for marriage; by contrast, it is clear that strong passions would be a sufficient reason for marriage in Paul's eyes. Barrett well translates: 'if he is over-sexed'. This is a strong pointer that 'he ought to marry' (36).

There is another factor which should be present. It must be what 'he wants' (36). He – and presumably his fiancée – should want to get married; the section is seen from the viewpoint of the man, but in the light of the constant reciprocity of the chapter as a whole, we may assume that she also expresses the wish to get married (for an example of the woman, even in an arranged marriage, being asked what her wishes are, see Genesis 24:8, 58).

In this situation – as in others which Paul does not discuss – it is not only right (38) but better (9) to get married. This is a counterbalance to 38b. While we must not abandon Paul's conviction that, speaking generally, singleness is better than marriage (38b), yet in many individual instances (and for a variety of reasons) marriage will be better than singleness (9).

However, Paul does not leave it at that. He also envisages the opposite case. Here, instead of wanting to get married (36), the man (and the woman too), informed by the Christian insights of 7f and 25ff, does not want to get married. He 'has settled the matter [literally: taken up a firm stand] in his own mind' (37). He 'has made up his mind not to marry the virgin' (37). And instead of having sexual passions that are getting out of control (36), he is 'under no compulsion', he 'has control over his own will' (37), In this case, the couple will do better not to marry. Paul is far from condemning the couple envisaged in 36. It is no sin for them to marry

(36). But his preference is clearly for the man and woman who are able to stay single (37f).

## An Alternative View

There is an alternative view of the situation envisaged in 36–38, and this finds expression in the NIV margin. Here the man addressed is the father or guardian of the 'virgin', who is his unmarried daughter. The only significant reason for adopting this view is the one word *gamizō* which occurs twice in 38 and is translated on both occasions as 'marry' in the NIV text and 'give in marriage' in the NIV margin. This word does mean 'give in marriage' in its other NT occurrences (Mark 12:25 and parallels; Luke 17:27 and parallel) and in each case is contrasted with *gameō* ('to marry'). Otherwise it does not occur at all outside Christian writings except in a second-century AD grammarian, Apollonius Dyscolus, who also distinguishes between *gameō* = to marry and *gamizō* = to give in marriage.

However, it seems very awkward to imagine that Paul has the father-daughter relationship in mind in 36–38. As we have already noted, the words 'father', 'guardian', 'daughter' are totally absent from the entire chapter. The section is introduced by: 'If anyone [*tis*] . . .'. No reader would think of a father or guardian naturally. The most recent mention of a man (apart from the husband at the end of 34) has been of 'an unmarried man' (32–34).

This reading would necessitate the meaning 'if she is past her prime' or 'if she is fully developed sexually' for *ean ē hyperakmos*, referring to the virgin which, as we have seen, means a change of subject not signalled by the Greek. We have also said that it is hard to see why this would be a reason for saying the marriage 'ought to be' (36 literally), especially since 'fully developed sexually' does not mean 'over-sexed' but merely 'through all the stages of puberty'. Moreover, the fiancé, who according to this theory has not been previously discussed, is abruptly brought into play at the end of 36: 'They should get married.'

But most significantly of all, the language of 36f is somewhat peculiar if used of most fathers. It is just possible that 'if anyone thinks he is acting improperly towards his virgin' (36 literally) could mean that he had promised her to give her in marriage and feels he is not fulfilling his pledge. But the language of 37, especially 'he has control over his own will', is both peculiar and unusually strong (the piling up of descriptions of the man's controlled determination in 37) if it refers to a father contemplating the marriage of his daughter.

If it were not for the one word *gamizō* it is quite clear that the father-daughter understanding of these verses would never have arisen. And there are reasons for believing that Paul may be using the verb in the sense of 'marry' here. 'The strict distinction between verbs in *-eō* and verbs in *-izō* was breaking down in the Hellenistic age' (Barrett) and it may have been precisely because of what he saw as wrong usage of *gamizō* by some writers that Apollonius Dyscolus made his semantic distinction. Paul, then, believing that both words could be used with the same meaning, may simply have introduced *gamizō* for the sake of variety, since he uses *gameō* in 36 and 39. Fee tentatively suggests a further reason: that Paul sees *gamizō* as transitive since it here appears with an object, while *gameō* is without object (intransitive) in the entire chapter.

So the most natural explanation, and the one which fits the language far better, is that Paul is speaking to the fiancé in 36–38 and his advice is that, while the engaged couple of course commit no sin (despite what some Corinthians think) if they do marry, it is preferable ('better') for them to remain unmarried.

Before we leave this section, we should make one further point. Fee rightly stresses that many of the arguments in 25ff – not all, but many – are pastoral: 'those who marry will face many troubles in this life, and I want to spare you this' (28); 'I would like you to be free from concern' (32); 'I am saying this for your own good' (35), etc. In the case of a betrothed couple who are committed to staying single, Paul advises them not to get married (38) but also not to break their engagement: 'to keep her as his betrothed' (37 RSV, more literal than NIV). In our contemporary society, especially where one partner might well not be able to accept singleness so readily and where prolonged engagements are so much less common, pastoral reasons will almost certainly advocate the break-up, rather than the retention, of the engagement.

## Concluding Example: The Widow

Paul refers to one final example before he closes the subject. It is a very specific example (widowhood), yet it allows him to reiterate and sum up many of the themes of the whole chapter:

> (39) A woman is bound to her husband as long as he lives. But if her husband dies, she is free to marry anyone she wishes, but he must belong to the Lord. (40) In my judgment, she is happier if she stays as she is – and I think that I too have the Spirit of God.

Paul addresses the widow. He mentions the woman only (as he does in verse 8 and in 1 Tim. 5) mainly, I suggest, because it is normally the woman who outlives the man, and partly perhaps as a counterbalance to 36–38 where he has been addressing the man.

First, he says that she 'is bound to her husband as long as he lives' (39). The word 'bound' is 'Paul's normal usage for the indissolubility of marriage as long as a mate is living' (Fee). Paul says the same, using the same word, in Romans 7:2. Here, then, is a reminder that, again contrary to what the Corinthians may have been saying, divorce is not to be contemplated by the Christian (a recap of 10–16).

However, if her husband dies, she may marry 'anyone she wishes' (39, an echo of 'he should do as he wants', 36) 'but he must belong to the Lord'. Verses 12–16 spoke of the situation where one partner becomes a Christian and so a Christian finds him- or herself married to a non-Christian. This often produces tremendous tensions and may lead to the unbelieving partner's insisting on divorce (12–16). Partly to avoid any such problems, the Christian widow is only free to marry a fellow Christian.

And she is entirely free to do so. Nevertheless, Paul offers his 'judgment' (40). He uses the same word as in 25, again emphasising that his thoughts on singleness are not a command but advice, yet advice guided, he believes, by 'the Spirit of God' (40). His judgment is that she will be 'happier' or 'more blessed' (*makarios*, the same word that Christ uses in the Beatitudes) if she stays single (40). This of course reiterates for the widow what he has said for the betrothed, and for single people more generally, in 25–38.

## Conclusions

Before we turn to the subject of divorce and remarriage, I want to sum up some of the major emphases of the New Testament teaching we have considered in this chapter, and a few of the implications for contemporary single and married people.

### 1.  Marriage is good

There is nothing in Christ's teaching about the beauty of a single life (Matt. 19:11f) which undermines his teaching about the closeness and splendour of married life (Matt. 19:4–9). There is nothing in Paul's teaching about the very real advantages of singleness (1 Cor. 7) which undermines his teaching about God's gift of marriage (1 Cor. 7:7), the intimacy of marriage (1 Cor. 7:2–6), the sanctifying effect of marriage (1 Cor. 7:14) or the way marriage reproduces the relationship between Christ and his Church (Eph. 5).

It was some Corinthians who thought marriage was too closely connected with evil. It was those who 'followed deceiving spirits' who 'forbade people to marry' (1 Tim. 4:1, 3). This was not Jesus' view, nor Paul's view. On the contrary, Jesus taught that it is God who joins man and wife together (Matt. 19:6); Paul taught that marriage was a gift from God (1 Cor. 7:7). And so the person who marries does a good thing (1 Cor. 7:38a).

Joy at a wedding is a frequent image or symbol in Scripture for the blessedness God brings (e.g. Jer. 16:9). This is not only natural but right. The mistake comes only when we make of marriage more than it was meant to be: when we insist that there can be no happiness without marriage, when we put marriage before our allegiance to Christ (Luke 14:26; 18:28–30), when we cannot imagine eternal joy without being married (Luke 20:34–36 and parallels). This is to promote marriage to a position God never intended and many contemporary marriages are cracking under the strain of the enormous, and often unbiblical, expectations that are being put on them. Our relationship with Christ must be our most important relationship, and it is our marriage to him, as members of the Church, which will last into eternity.

## 2. Singleness is at least as good, indeed better

Jesus' disciples never expected to hear that. When they blurted out: 'If this is the situation between a husband and wife [no divorce and remarriage], it is better not to marry' (Matt. 19:10), they surely expected Christ to say, 'No, no. Of course it is always better to marry.' Instead, he replied that singleness is indeed 'given' to many by God and that it is a most honourable state (Matt. 19:11f). Paul of course said specifically that while a man who marries his intended does well: 'he who does not marry does better' (1 Cor. 7:38), and although this is the clearest place in which he states that the single life is to be preferred to marriage, it is in fact clearly his position throughout the chapter, especially in verses 7, 8, 26f, 32–35, 40.

Every Christian, and particularly every Christian contemplating marriage however far in the future it may be (1 Cor. 7:36–38), should seek to come to terms with this New Testament teaching. It is true that marriage, not singleness, may well be 'better' in our particular case (e.g. 1 Cor. 7:9) but until we have come to see that singleness is at least as much a gift from God as marriage, and that for many people it is the better state, we have not come to see singleness and marriage through New Testament eyes.

## 3. The single life needs to be understood

This calls for understanding. To the contemporary Westerner it is extremely difficult to get our mind – still less our heart – round this idea that singleness is as good as, and even better than, marriage. Our whole upbringing and culture has shouted the contrary. Both Jesus and Paul recognised the problem. It is precisely what Jesus said: 'Not everyone accepts [not 'can accept' as in NIV] this word' and why he exclaims at the end of his teaching on singleness: 'Let him who can accept this accept it' (see Matt. 19:11, 12).

As I have emphasised, the word used here is *chōreō*. It means 'grasp in the mental sense, comprehend, understand'. It was to help his disciples understand why singleness is good that Jesus gave his teaching in Matthew 19:11f; it was to help the Christians at Corinth understand why the single life is preferable that Paul argued it through in 1 Corinthians 7:25ff. And if we in the late twentieth century are to gain a true understanding of singleness in God's purposes we must pore over and seek to understand these crucial passages.

And that comes down to the Church: preaching on these passages, setting them for house group Bible studies, having talks on them in church youth groups and student Christian groups, so that the New Testament's views on singleness become part of the worldview, and the self-understanding, of ordinary Christians.

Responsibility also lies with families: parents, grandparents, uncles and aunts, even older brothers and sisters. If the assumption is always that the unmarried will get married, that marriage is better than singleness, that any older member of the family who is unmarried is only to be pitied, then it is no wonder that we grow up with such difficulties in accepting the Christian view. With our own children, my wife and I try to say: '*If* you get married . . .', to place before them the beauty and advantages of singleness, to help them see that between marriage and singleness there is a real, and not easily decided, choice.

## 4.  The single life needs to be accepted

*Chōreō* is more than just 'grasp mentally'. Its basic meaning is 'make room for' and therefore also 'accept' (Arndt and Gingrich). It is one thing to understand, but Jesus challenges us to go further than that: we are to accept, and therefore be content with, his teaching and its outworking in our lives (Matt. 19:11f). It is the same idea which Paul puts forward when he says that singleness is to be seen positively as a gift from God (1 Cor. 7:7).

But this acceptance is not merely a passive thing. Acceptance can sound much too like 'being resigned to' and that is certainly not the tenor of Christ's or Paul's remarks. Paul commends a person who has weighed up the alternatives, who has considered marriage and singleness, and has chosen singleness having 'settled the matter in his own mind' and who has 'made up his mind not to marry' (1 Cor. 7:37).

Jesus of course recognises that not all can choose marriage or singleness. Some have been rendered incapable of marriage from birth, others because of what men have done to them (Matt. 19:12a,b). Yet these too, hard as it will often be, are to see their singleness as 'given' by God (verse 11). And Jesus also recognises a third category, for whom there is very much a choice: they 'have made themselves eunuchs for the sake of the kingdom of God' (verse 12 RSV).

At a recent conference I attended, a man in his late forties or early fifties spoke about his singleness. He said that he had realised for some years that 'I am very content in my singleness.' He had no expectation of getting married. Yet he also said: 'I cannot say I have been called to be single.' Why? If he was merely saying that he could not be sure he would always be single, that is understandable; but surely a person can say: 'I feel called to be an engineer' who may equally legitimately say five years later: 'I feel called to be ordained.' I believe it is part of the full acceptance of our singleness to see it as a gift – or a call – from God, at least for the time being.

## 5.  The single life needs to be enjoyed and used

It is perfectly clear that Paul, who may well have known what it was to be married (see the earlier discussion of 1 Cor. 7:7f), thoroughly enjoyed his single state. He wished that a great many more Christians would remain single (1 Cor. 7:7); he said that it was good to be single and that he knew this from experience (1 Cor. 7:8). He would surely have laughed off any pity that might have been expressed about his being single.

And then he urges single people to put their singleness – whether it lasts a short time or long – to good use. There are unparalleled opportunities to devote yourself wholly, and without distraction, to the Lord (1 Cor. 7:32–35); there is also the ability to draw away, emotionally rather than physically, from matters connected solely with this world and this age which is passing away (29–31); and there is simply the possibility of being more care-free (28, 32). All these benefits are there for the taking, but they have to be taken and used. They will lie fallow for those who are constantly hankering after marriage (and, to be fair, a very strong hankering after marriage, if it is combined with the opportunity of taking steps towards marriage, may be a sign that marriage is God's gift to that individual: 1 Cor. 7:9, 36).

Paul has spoken of the advantages of singleness for personal holiness (34), detachment from the world and wholehearted attachment to the Lord. Christ himself speaks of another advantage: service in the kingdom of heaven (Matt. 19:12). Again, unparalleled opportunities for Christian service are available to those who have no other calls on their time and no other restrictions on their movements. It was precisely for this same reason – Christian service – that the Church enrolled older women who took a vow not to marry again (1 Tim. 5:3–16).

How very far this is from those who speak of people 'being condemned to singleness'. The single life is a great gift, to be enjoyed and used to the full. Jesus and Paul taught this, the early Church understood and embraced it. It is a jewel – jagged and painful sometimes, but a jewel none the less – needing to be rediscovered by the Church, by individual Christians and by society today.

# 4

# Divorce and Remarriage in the Old Testament

It is often assumed that what the Old Testament has to say about divorce and remarriage is radically different from the teaching of the New Testament. As Jesus quite clearly distanced himself from at least part of the Old Testament divorce material (Mark 10:3–9//Matt. 19:7–9), many writers think it is possible to discuss a Christian view of divorce and remarriage with only the most passing reference to what the Old Testament has to say on the subject. Differences there are. Nevertheless, it is essential to study the Old Testament material, not only because it forms the background to the New Testament discussion and is a uniquely authoritative source for the New Testament writers, but also because it immediately becomes clear that the Old and New Testament positions are much closer than is commonly imagined. This chapter will examine in turn the Law, the Prophets and the Wisdom Literature.

## The Law

Briefly, we must retrace our steps to Genesis chapter 2. No exposition of the Law's teaching on divorce and remarriage would start in the right place – let alone be complete – without a reminder of how marriage is described in the first book of the Law (Gen. 2:18–25 and especially v.24) and what, by implication, it is intended to be. Here I confine myself solely to what this passage has to say about permanence.

In marriage, a man and his wife 'cleave' to each other. It is

not just that their fundamental relationship has ceased to be with
their parents ('leave his father and mother') and is now with each
other. It is that the normal practice of husbands and wives – and,
by implication, their duty – is to cling to one another, to hold
on to one another at all costs. Nothing is to prise them apart.

Moreover, they need to recognise what has happened to them:
they have 'become one flesh'. They have become, at the most
fundamental level of their being, a unity. It is a more important
fact about them that they are now one person than that they
continue to be two individuals.

While divorce is very far from the writer's mind, the implications of his teaching for marriage break-up are obvious. Divorce
can only be what modern psychology confirms: an unnatural
tearing apart of what has been glued together, a very painful
ripping in two of what is now in essence one.

## Restrictions

It is much less surprising, having seen what the Law teaches in
Genesis 2, to discover that nowhere, in all the legal material,
is there any law which directly makes provision for divorce.
Nowhere in the first five books, or indeed the whole Old Testament, do we find anything approaching the formula: 'If a woman
does . . . then a man may send her away.' Divorce law as such
simply does not exist.

This is not to say that no laws deal with divorce. But significantly all the laws which touch on this area (and there are not
very many) are formulated either to restrict divorce or to restrict
remarriage. Driver in his commentary on Deuteronomy, writing
about chapter 24, says: 'The law [Deut. 24:1–4] is thus not,
properly speaking a law of divorce . . . Hebrew law . . . does
not institute divorce [earlier Driver has said it is 'established
by custom'] but tolerates it, in view of the imperfections of
human nature (Matt. 19:8) and lays down regulations tending
to limit it and preclude its abuse.'

# A Law to Restrict Remarriage

It is perhaps inevitable that the first law we turn to is Deuteronomy 24:1–4. In itself it is a rather insignificant law which must have applied directly only to a very tiny minority of people. It is a law which restricts remarriage. But it is important to study it in detail not only because it was the focus of Jewish debate about divorce in Jesus' day, but also because, in passing, it tells us a considerable amount about the Israelite practice of divorce and about what the legislators thought about divorce and remarriage:

> (1) If a man marries a woman who becomes displeasing to him because he finds something indecent about her, and he writes her a certificate of divorce, gives it to her and sends her from his house, (2) and if after she leaves his house she becomes the wife of another man, (3) and her second husband dislikes her and writes her a certificate of divorce, gives it to her and sends her from his house, or if he dies, (4) then her first husband, who divorced her, is not allowed to marry her again after she has been defiled. That would be detestable in the eyes of the LORD. Do not bring sin upon the land the LORD your God is giving you as an inheritance.

It has often been pointed out, and needs to be mentioned briefly again, that the Authorised Version is seriously misleading here. It translates verse 1: 'When a man taketh a wife and marrieth her, then it shall be, if she find no favour in his eyes, because he hath found some unseemly thing in her, that he shall write her a bill of divorcement . . .'. With this translation we seem to have a law of divorce; the law is saying that under certain circumstances (if a husband, because of 'some unseemly thing' in his wife, dislikes her) he must divorce her. But this is not what the Hebrew is saying. The circumstances under which the law applies continue throughout the first three verses; the action to be taken – what the husband must (or must not) do – only comes in verse 4. Stott sums it up well: 'What this law says is that *if* a man divorces his wife, and *if* he gives her a certificate, and *if* she leaves and remarries, and *if* her second husband dislikes and divorces her, or dies, *then* her first husband may not marry

her again' (*Issues Facing Christians Today* pp.262f). Hence the
translation in NIV and all modern versions.

The point of this law, then, is to say that under certain
circumstances – if a man has divorced his wife for 'something indecent', she has remarried and has then been divorced
or widowed – the man may not remarry her. The point of
this law is to restrict remarriage.

## Divorce in Israel

However, it does also tell us – in passing and incidentally –
several things about the practice of divorce in ancient Israel:

### 1.   Divorce was permitted in Israel

Again, we need to stress: it was not directly legislated for, it was
not encouraged; but it was also not prohibited. Otherwise, it
would have been impossible to have a law of this nature.

### 2.   Divorce was permitted in the case of ᶜerwaṯ dāḇār

This is the phrase which NIV translates 'something indecent'
and which literally means 'nakedness of a thing'. Unfortunately,
we cannot be entirely sure what Deuteronomy meant by this
phrase here, and the only other Old Testament occurrence is in
Deuteronomy 23:13–14 (in Hebrew, 23:15) which speaks of the
need to have a place outside the camp for humans to relieve
themselves and cover their excrement so that God may not 'see
among you anything indecent'. Even the Jews of Jesus' own
day do not seem to have been clear what the phrase meant;
there was hot debate about the circumstances envisaged and
allowed in Deuteronomy 24:1.

As it happens, one conclusion that some Jews of Jesus' day
came to must be wrong. The School of Shammai thought
that Deuteronomy 24:1 envisaged divorce for adultery. But the
penalty for adultery in the Mosaic legislation was not divorce
but death (Deut. 22:22; Lev. 20:10; John 8:4f, cf Gen. 38:24)
– or if there was any human doubt in the matter, God's curse
of a terrible, wasting disease (Num. 5:11–31). For precisely the
same reason, 'something indecent' cannot mean pre-marital sex,

either while the woman was engaged (Deut. 22:23f) or at any time before her marriage (Deut. 22:13–21).

A. Isaksson has argued that the phrase means: indecent exposure; the woman has, voluntarily or involuntarily, exposed her private parts (pp.25–7). This would certainly make sense in both Old Testament occurrences (Deut. 23:14; 24:1), would explain the choice of words ('nakedness of a thing') especially in view of the Israelite abhorrence of nakedness (e.g. Exod. 20:26), and in other situations clearly did cause the disgust of the marriage partner (2 Sam. 6:12–20; Ezek. 23:18). However, it seems so very specific and unusual that it makes this whole law – already subject to unusual circumstances – apply to almost nobody. It seems more likely, therefore, that it is of a rather more general, very probably sexual, nature. Driver suggests 'immodest or indecent behaviour'.

### 3.  Divorce involved issuing a certificate of divorce

This certificate is mentioned both in the case of the woman's first divorce (1) and in her second (3). It is also mentioned in Jeremiah (3:8) and Isaiah (50:1) and it seems therefore to have been a requirement for divorce, as it certainly was in later Jewish times.

Murray (p.9) rightly claims that this requirement was to protect the wife, and suggests that it had a variety of purposes:

a) It would 'restrain frivolous, thoughtless and rash dismissal'. Because it was a legal document, it would make the husband think twice before writing it.

b) It gave the woman 'freedom from marital obligations to the husband who sent her away'.

c) It protected her 'reputation and well-being'. Murray does not clearly explain why, but the obvious reason is that if she subsequently remarried, there would be no question of her being accused of bigamy.

Moreover, the certificate of divorce had to be 'given to her' formally (1, 3). The Mishnah even prescribes certain circumstances under which a bill might not be properly delivered to her and then the divorce would be invalid (*m. Git.* 8.1f). So the requiring of a properly validated divorce certificate was to protect the divorced wife against unjust demands (from her first husband) or accusations (from others) and to hinder the husband from flippant divorce.

The Mishnah mentions other factors which would further limit easy divorce and which were probably also requirements in ancient Israel. There were to be at least two witnesses: 'Three kinds of bills of divorce are invalid . . .: one that a man wrote with his own hand but there were no witnesses to it, one to which there were witnesses but which bore no date, and one which bore the date but had one witness only.' (*m. Git.* 9.4). And there was, crucially, a severe financial penalty: each husband pledged an amount of money (*keṯûḇâh*), often very considerable, to be given to his wife if he died or if he divorced her when she was innocent of serious misconduct. Jeremias wryly comments that this must have prevented hasty divorces (p.370).

### 4. Divorce opened the way to remarriage

The woman in Deuteronomy 24 remarries (2) and it does not appear that she has done anything wrong (except perhaps – and it is a big exception – in the eyes of her former husband; see below). The Mishnah, which unlike the Old Testament certainly does legislate directly for divorce, says: 'The essential formula in the bill of divorce is: "Lo, thou art free to marry any man"' (*m. Git.* 9.3).

## Reasons for the Law

In the situation described in Deuteronomy 24:1–4, there is to be no remarriage. Why not? Verse 4 gives three reasons: she has been defiled; it would be detestable in the eyes of the Lord; it would bring sin upon the land. Here the key reason seems to be the first. It is *because* she has been defiled, that this remarriage would be detestable in God's eyes and bring sin upon the land. And yet we are immediately faced with a paradox. Clearly she is not so defiled as to make all remarriage impossible. If it was the circumstances surrounding her first divorce that defiled her, apparently it didn't prohibit her second marriage since this does not seem to be condemned. If it was the second marriage that defiled her, the law seems very specific that it is only her first husband with whom she must not remarry. The implication is that it would be perfectly acceptable to marry a third man. We are forced to the conclusion, therefore, that in saying 'she has been defiled' (4), the law means: defiled, in some way, *in her first husband's eyes*, or defiled *in relation to her first husband*.

It seems to me we are left with two alternatives:

## *1.   Her initial sexual behaviour ('something indecent') is what defiled her*

This possibility is normally overlooked by commentators. It is simply assumed that it is the second marriage which has defiled her. But the strikingly parallel passage of Jeremiah 3:1–13 encourages us to consider a different understanding.

Jeremiah 3 has many points of contact with Deuteronomy 24:1–4. Verse 1 is a clear reference to the Deuteronomic law; verse 8 mentions the certificate of divorce; and the defiling of the land is mentioned in verses 1, 2 and 9 (cf Deut. 24:4). But despite the fact that Israel has remarried (1a), it is not that for which her outraged husband chastises her; it is her sexual promiscuity (1, 6–8) and it is specifically this immorality which, in verses 2 and 9, has 'defiled the land'. Moreover, she is brazen in her sexual sin (3) and, when it suits her, comes rushing back to her first husband (4–5a) but with no intention of changing her ways (5b).

In Jeremiah 3, it would be quite wrong for the offended husband to return to the erring wife (1a). This is precisely what the Deuteronomic law has said (Deut. 24:4). But now a new note is struck, not in Deuteronomy. The wife is told to repent (Jer. 3:12, 14) and if she does so, then the original relationship can be restored (12f) and the first marriage taken up again (14). It is often assumed that this is in contravention of Deuteronomy 24; God is simply breaking his own laws. But an alternative explanation is that Deuteronomy 24:1–4 concerns the situation where the wife is not repentant (as envisaged also in Jer. 3:1a). The wife has sinned against her husband by doing 'something indecent', he has openly declared this by divorcing her. She is defiled in his eyes. Now if he were to take her back without her repenting, he would simply be winking at her sin; this acceptance of her – by him of all people – would be 'detestable in the eyes of the Lord' and would 'bring sin upon the land'.

This explanation is perfectly feasible and has the great merit of tying together Jeremiah 3 and Deuteronomy 24. It may well be correct. Its weakness, however, is that in putting all the emphasis on 'something indecent' (Deut. 24:1) as what defiles her, it makes the second marriage (Deut. 24:2) comparatively unimportant. This leads us to consider a second alternative.

## 2.   Her second marriage is what defiled her

Driver points out that the word for 'defiled' (4, Hebrew root *ṭm'*) is also used in cases of adultery (e.g. Lev. 18:20, Num. 5:13f, 20). Thus while the second marriage cannot be adulterous in the eyes of the law – because, if so, it would surely be more clearly condemned and would be punishable by death – the phrase 'she has been defiled' perhaps tells us that it is adulterous in the eyes of the original husband. 'From the point of view of her first husband, [the second marriage] falls into the same category as adultery' (Driver).

The advantage of this explanation of the important, but some-what elusive, Deuteronomy 24:4 is that it gives full weight to the mention of the second marriage in the law (2f); its disadvantage is, as discussed above, that God then seems to break his own law in Jeremiah 3. A final decision may not be possible, but if the second explanation is correct, as most commentators believe, then it is not just Genesis 2 but Deuteronomy 24 as well which is very close to the New Testament teaching. Driver quotes Keil's commentary: 'The marriage of a divorced woman is thus treated implicitly as tantamount to adultery, and the way is prepared for the teaching of Christ on the subject of marriage.'[1]

---

[1] In a written communication to me, the Rev. Tony Rees asks: 'Why [then] does Deuteronomy forbid the remarried [wife's] returning to the original husband? This ought to be commanded not forbidden.' The answer appears to be that the Mosaic legislation regards adultery as an abominable thing. Ordinarily, adultery is to be punished by death (Deut. 22:22; Lev. 20:10). If remarriage is adultery-in-the-eyes-of-her-husband – then it too is to be treated with the utmost seriousness. The husband may not pretend it never happened and so take her back (Deut. 24:4).

## Laws to Restrict Divorce

The classic passage we have been examining seems to allow the practice of divorce but restricts somewhat the right to remarry. There are also various laws in the book of Deuteronomy which restrict the right to divorce.

*1.   In the case of a captured slave girl*

> (10) When you go to war against your enemies and the LORD your God delivers them into your hands and you take captives, (11) if you notice among the captives a beautiful woman and are attracted to her, you may take her as your wife. (12) Bring her into your home and make her shave her head, trim her nails (13) and put aside the clothes she was wearing when captured. After she has lived in your house and mourned her father and mother for a full month, then you may go to her and be her husband and she shall be your wife. (14) If you are not pleased with her, let her go wherever she wishes. You must not sell her or treat her as a slave, since you have dishonoured her (Deut. 21).

Of course the principal purpose of this law was to protect the captured woman. The marriage is not to take place immediately, perhaps on the sexual whim of an aroused man (cf 11). The woman is to be allowed a decent interval – a whole month – for mourning the loss of her parents (not necessarily by death; she is now entering a family belonging to the enemy nation and cannot expect to see her parents again – indeed, she is 'leaving' them to marry). Above all, if he divorces her ('let her go' is certainly tantamount to divorce and may well bear the express meaning of 'divorce' as the same word does in Deut. 22:19, 29), he must set her free from her slavery and allow her to leave.

While, therefore, divorce is permitted in this case, the effect of the law would certainly be not only to make the Israelite victor slower to marry, but also to make him slower to divorce, since he would thereby lose her entirely, as he would be forced to let her go free.

Again it is important to see the reason why the man must let his wife go free: 'since you have dishonoured her'. The verb is a strong one; RSV translates 'humiliated'. In a sexual context it is used elsewhere of 'violation' (e.g. 22:24, 29) or 'rape' (e.g. Judg. 20:5). It seems then that it is seen as a 'violation' – even of a slave girl – to divorce her for no better reason than that you 'are not pleased with her' (14). Divorce is apparently allowable for sexually indecent behaviour (24:1) but it is despicable (though not legally prohibited) to divorce a captured slave girl simply because you no longer find her attractive. Once more, this is much closer to the teaching of the New Testament than one might at first have expected.

## 2.   In the case of false accusation

(13) If a man takes a wife and, after lying with her, dislikes her (14) and slanders her and gives her a bad name, saying: 'I married this woman, but when I approached her, I did not find proof of her virginity', (15) then the girl's father and mother shall bring proof that she was a virgin to the town elders at the gate . . . (18) and the elders shall take the man and punish him. (19) They shall fine him a hundred shekels of silver and give them to the girl's father, because this man has given an Israelite virgin a bad name. She shall continue to be his wife, he must not divorce her as long as he lives (Deut. 22).

A man wants to get rid of his wife because he no longer likes her; this in turn may be because he does not find her sexually satisfying (13 seems to imply that). And so he hits on a plan: he will claim she was not a virgin when she married him. When this accusation is shown to be slanderous, he forfeits the right to divorce her at any time and presumably for any reason. Marriage must now genuinely be 'till death us do part'.

## 3.   In the case of sexual violation

(28) If a man happens to meet a virgin who is not pledged to be married and rapes her and they are discovered, (29) he shall pay the girl's father fifty shekels of silver. He must marry the girl, for he has violated her. He can never divorce her as long as he lives (Deut. 22).

Again the consequences of the man's initial violation of the girl remain with him for ever. He may never, on any subsequent occasion and presumably for any cause, divorce her.

An interesting example of the flouting of this law is the rape of Tamar by her half-brother Amnon (2 Sam. 13). When he seizes her and urges her to lie with him (11), she begs him instead to ask for her hand in marriage (12f). He nevertheless forces her but then reacts by 'hating her with intense hatred' and telling her to 'get up and get out' (14f). Her reply is: 'Sending me away [*šlḥ*, which is translated 'divorce' in Deut. 22:29] would be a greater wrong than what you have already done to me' (16). Tamar regarded it as clear that Amnon should now marry her, and indeed his refusal to do so constituted a kind of 'divorce' – the very thing which his rape no longer allowed him ever to do.

## Laws to Restrict Remarrying Divorcees

We have seen that the right to remarry after divorce is implied, if not explicitly stated, in Deuteronomy 24. However, certain Israelites were not allowed to marry those who had been divorced.

### 1.   In the case of priests

(5) Priests . . . (6) must be holy to their God and must not profane the name of their God. Because they present the offerings made to the LORD by fire, the food of their God, they are to be holy. (7) They must not marry women defiled by prostitution or divorced from their husbands, because priests are holy to their God. (8) Regard them as holy, because they offer up the food of your God. Consider them holy, because I the LORD am holy – I who make you holy (Lev. 21).

Every Israelite was, of course, to be holy (e.g. 11:44f) but we meet here the higher standard demanded of God's special ministers which we shall find again in the New Testament. Israelite priests had to be still more holy – the word comes seven times in these three verses – than their Israelite brothers, and this meant that they could not marry divorcees.

Our immediate reaction is that it seems harsh to lump prostitutes and divorcees together (7) as if those who have been divorced are necessarily deeply sinful and to be regarded as social outcasts. But this is not at all the view of Leviticus. While a priest's daughter who becomes a prostitute is to be treated with great severity (21:9), a priest's daughter who has been divorced is to be welcomed back as a full member of the priest's family (22:13). It is clear, then, that prostitution and divorce are not seen in the same light at all. Nevertheless, it is a requirement of the profound holiness which priests are to exhibit that they should not marry someone who has had sexual relations with another man: either through sexual immorality or through a previous marriage which has now been broken.

Indeed, Ezekiel says that, in the future which he foresees, the Levitical priests must not even marry non-priestly widows: 'They must not marry widows or divorced women; they may marry only virgins of Israelite descent or widows of priests' (44:22). Only this is compatible with the holiness required of them, and the right to marry divorcees is therefore removed in their case.

## 2.   In the case of the high priest

Leviticus 21 insists that the high priest has been 'dedicated by the anointing oil of his God' (12, cf 10) and then continues:

> (13) The woman he marries must be a virgin. (14) He must not marry a widow, a divorced woman, or a woman defiled by prostitution, but only a virgin from his own people, (15) so that he will not defile his offspring among his people. I am the LORD who makes him holy.

It is not surprising that the standard of holiness for the high priest is even higher than that for the priest: even the widow of a priest is ruled out as his marriage partner. He must only marry someone who has never been married, nor had sexual intercourse of any sort, before. To do so would be to fall short of the holiness required of him and his family and therefore defile the next generation (15) from whom his successor as high priest would come.

## Summary of the Law

To sum up what we have discovered so far about what the first five books of the Old Testament, the Law, have to say about our subject: the Law did clearly envisage that divorce and remarriage would take place. It did not sanction them or legislate specifically for them, but it did not prohibit them either. It assumed they would take place and did not condemn them outright.

Nevertheless it is significant that *all* the individual enactments are not to facilitate, but to restrict, divorce and remarriage. In several circumstances divorce is prohibited entirely, in one circumstance (the only case of remarriage that the Law directly addresses) remarriage is prohibited, in the case of the priests and high priests marriage to a divorcee is prohibited. Yet Old Testament laws are far from all being prohibitive. Many laws are to facilitate an action and lay down the proper procedures.

The Law, then, does implicitly permit divorce and remarriage in some circumstances. Certainly this is true in the case of the 'indecent behaviour' of Deuteronomy 24:1; we have no clear justification, one way or the other, for extending the recognised grounds for divorce or for restricting them. Yet in a legal corpus which has many examples of what today we would call enabling legislation, there is no legislation whatsoever to enable divorce or remarriage, and there are only laws which restrict the ability to divorce and remarry.

## The Prophets: God's Marriage to Israel

It may seem perverse, as we turn to the prophets, to begin with God's 'marriage' to Israel rather than with human marriage, yet it is a very frequent image in the prophetic literature, it occurs much more frequently than any discussion of human marriage and it does indirectly throw much light on God's attitude to human divorce and remarriage, as the prophets understand it. For this reason, it seems best to begin with what is of course a

picture: human marriage and divorce language used to describe
God's relationship with Israel.

It may be helpful to state at the outset how the picture is
very consistently used. Of course different prophets use different
variations on the image with varying emphases; for instance, one
will stress God's outraged anger, while another will depict his
pained love. But overall the message of the picture is this: *God
is a husband who longs for reconciliation with his divorced wife.*

He has divorced her, certainly. Or to be more exact: in some
passages it is unclear whether he has made that definite break or
is simply estranged from her; but in other passages and in some
prophets a legal divorce has clearly taken place. Yet there is no
callousness on God's part, and no anger that has reached the
point where reconciliation is out of the question and not even
desired. On the contrary, God still yearns for Israel and longs
to have her back; he wants the marriage relationship to begin
all over again and he is ready, at the first sign of repentance on
Israel's part and a desire in her for the renewal of the marriage,
to commit himself to her again.

## Hosea

We do not know whether it was Hosea who introduced this
picture of God into prophetic circles, but it dominates his
entire vision and it was certainly he who influenced all the
other prophets who came after him and used this imagery. It is
almost certain, also, that the reason he spoke of God as Israel's
betrayed husband, and felt God's pain so deeply, was that he
himself had married a profoundly unfaithful wife (1:2–3). It is
not absolutely clear whether he divorced her, but certainly he
had lived apart from her (cf 3:1 where God's words begin 'Go
again' – so, rightly, RSV) and he had even to buy her back
(Kidner asks: from debt? or slavery? or a pimp? or the lover of
3:1?) in order that they might be together again (3:2f). It was
this personal experience which lends such fire to the language
of God as betrayed, angry, devastated husband.

But it was not only because Hosea's words were so powerful
that he influenced subsequent prophets. It was that the imagery
was so peculiarly apt, given the nature of Israel's apostasy and the

kind of alternative religion she embraced. McKane comments that Israel's 'involvement in sexual rites associated with the Canaanite cult lends such a peculiar appositeness to the sexual imagery that it is more than a metaphor for idolatry which could be replaced without loss by another metaphor not involving sexual imagery' (*Jeremiah* p.63).

Hosea's use of this image can be summed up as follows:

## *1.   Israel has been unfaithful*

This is expressed in characteristically violent language: God says: 'I will not show my love to her children, because they are the children of adultery. Their mother has been unfaithful and has conceived them in disgrace. She said: "I will go after my lovers, who give me my food and my water, my wool and my linen, my oil and my drink."' (2:4f). 'Let her remove the adulterous look from her face and the unfaithfulness from between her breasts' (2:2).

Again, the anger and the hurt are well understood by Hosea because of his own experience, though the way the book presents the connection between God's feelings and Hosea's is not that Hosea gradually came to see how God must feel because of his own prior marital unhappiness, but rather that God led his servant into such a painful marriage because Israel was so desperately unfaithful and Hosea was to embody the message God was commissioning him to bring: 'When the LORD began to speak through Hosea, the LORD said to him, "Go, take to yourself an adulterous wife and children of unfaithfulness, because the land is guilty of the vilest adultery in departing from the LORD"' (1:2).

So, Israel is God's wife, but instead of remaining faithful to him or even on one rash occasion having a sexual lapse, she has multiplied her lovers (2:5, 7) and given her sexual favours to all and sundry: 'You have been unfaithful to your God; you love the wages of a prostitute at every threshing-floor' (9:1).

## *2.   God has divorced Israel*

Some commentators doubt this. In view of God's obvious love for Israel and his desperate desire for reconciliation, they simply do not believe it would be consistent to depict God as divorcing Israel just as they do not believe that Hosea ever divorced Gomer: 'The punishment [by God of Israel] is not an expression of a broken relationship. On the contrary, it is enforced within the relationship; punishment maintains the covenant. Similarly, Hosea's threats of punishment are proof that his marriage [to Gomer] continues' (Andersen and Freedman).

Yet Hosea's language seems to me to point in the opposite direction. The great diatribe of chapter 2 begins: 'Rebuke your mother, rebuke her, for she is not my wife, and I am not her husband' (2:2). NEB makes this into a question: 'Is she not my wife and I her husband?' but that is not the natural reading of the text. GNB makes it a matter of subjective emotion rather than objective fact: 'She is no longer a wife to me' (Kidner: 'the reality has gone out of the relationship') and this might be possible except that it is not supported by the language that follows.

In particular, Israel describes God as 'my former husband' (2:7; not, as in NIV, 'my husband as at first' – a translation which again seems determined to deny the divorce). This does not necessarily imply that Israel has remarried, this time to the Baals (though RSV's 'my first husband' is certainly a possible translation), but it does seem to state that the first marriage no longer exists.

Just as important, God not only sets out to court Israel again (2:14) but once more to betroth her to himself (three times in 2:19f) which would of course be quite unnecessary if the marriage were still in existence.

Andersen and Freedman maintain that 'the lovers remain "lovers"' (2:5, 7): they are not a new husband. Similarly, Israel is treated as an adulterous wife not as a promiscuous woman who is maritally free but sexually active. Their conclusion is, then, that God and Israel are still legally married even though they are physically and emotionally distanced. My own opinion is that the language of chapter 2 implies almost exactly the opposite: that God and Israel are legally divorced – he is her 'former husband'; he must betroth her to himself again – but that emotionally he has never let her go. That is why he considers that her sexual adventures, despite the divorce, are still adulteries against him. And even she has not severed all the ties with him because when things get difficult she will think she can go back to him (2:7).

### 3.  God wants to be reconciled with Israel

Amazingly, God is prepared to take the initiative. It is he who has been wronged, he who has been betrayed, yet it is also he who starts to 'speak tenderly to her', to bring her back to the 'desert' with its echoes of the honeymoon period after Israel had escaped from Egypt and before she embraced the Canaanite cult in the Promised Land (2:14f). There God will woo her (14), she will begin to respond to him (16f) and he will betroth her to himself all over again (19f).

Yet she must respond. If God is to be reconciled with her, she must 'return' or 'repent': 'Return, O Israel, to the LORD your God. Your sins have been your downfall! Take words with you and return to the LORD. Say to him: "Forgive all our sins and receive us graciously, that we may offer the fruit of our lips"' (14:1f). And the signs are encouraging. Rather like the Prodigal Son, Israel will recognise that life was better with her former husband and will return to him, whether in self-interest (2:7f) or in genuine humility (3:4f; 5:14–6:3).

# Jeremiah

I have often thought of the relationship of the young Jeremiah to Hosea as very similar to the relationship of the young Raphael to Perugino. Early paintings by Raphael are indistinguishable (to all but the expert) from works by Perugino, but later Raphael developed his own, utterly individual style. So the early chapters of Jeremiah are often strikingly similar to Hosea, especially when he uses the husband-wife-adultery image, while later Jeremiah has very clearly developed his own, different style.

In a study of divorce and remarriage in the Old Testament, by far the most important chapter in Jeremiah is part of his earlier prophecies: chapter 3.

> (1) "If a man divorces his wife and she leaves him and marries another man, should he return to her again? Would not the land be completely defiled? But you have lived as a prostitute

with many lovers – would you now return to me?" declares the
LORD. (2) "Look up to the barren heights and see. Is there
any place where you have not been ravished? By the roadside
you sat waiting for lovers, sat like a nomad in the desert. You
have defiled the land with your prostitution and wickedness.
(3) Therefore the showers have been withheld, and no spring
rains have fallen. Yet you have the brazen look of a prostitute;
you refuse to blush with shame. (4) Have you not just called
to me: 'My Father, my friend from my youth, (5) will you
always be angry? Will your wrath continue for ever?' This is
how you talk, but you do all the evil you can." (6) During
the reign of King Josiah, the LORD said to me, "Have you
seen what faithless Israel has done? She has gone up on every
high hill and under every spreading tree and has committed
adultery there. (7) I thought that after she had done all this
she would return to me but she did not, and her unfaithful
sister Judah saw it. (8) I gave faithless Israel her certificate of
divorce and sent her away because of all her adulteries. Yet I
saw that her unfaithful sister Judah had no fear; she also went
out and committed adultery. (9) Because Israel's immorality
mattered so little to her, she defiled the land and committed
adultery with stone and wood. (10) In spite of all this, her unfaithful sister Judah did not return to me with all her heart, but
only in pretence," declares the LORD. (11) The LORD said to
me, "Faithless Israel is more righteous than unfaithful Judah.
(12) Go, proclaim this message towards the north: 'Return
faithless Israel,' declares the LORD, 'I will frown on you no
longer, for I am merciful,' declares the LORD, 'I will not be
angry for ever. (13) Only acknowledge your guilt – you have
rebelled against the LORD your God, you have scattered your
favours to foreign gods under every spreading tree, and have
not obeyed me,'" declares the LORD. (14) "Return, faithless
people," declares the LORD, "for I am your husband . . .".

The literary make-up of this passage is not easy to discern.
There are clearly new beginnings at verse 1 ('declares the LORD'),
verse 6 ('During the reign of King Josiah, the LORD said to
me . . .'), verse 11 ('The LORD said to me . . .') and verse 14
('declares the LORD'). Yet, equally clearly, the same basic
image of husband and adulterous wife/wives pervades the entire

section, in which we must also include 14, because of its continuation of the same imagery (NIV is right to translate *bā'altî*:
'I am your husband' rather than RSV's 'I am your master'
precisely because the marriage imagery is so prevalent in the
passage. Jeremiah uses exactly the same expression in 31:32).
14 is also linked to 12 by its call: 'Return, faithless people'.
Thus while it may have been true, as McKane suggests, that
a redactor (McKane calls him 'the exegete') combined different prophecies, some or all of which originally referred to the
Southern Kingdom of Judah only, what we now have is a series
of oracles, referring principally though not exclusively to the
Northern Kingdom of Israel, in which God is the husband and
Israel and Judah the adulterous wives. It is with the form of the
oracles that we have in the canonical book of Jeremiah that we
must deal, as we seek to discover what light they shed on divorce
and remarriage in the Old Testament.

## 1.   God has divorced Israel

If there was any doubt of this in Hosea, there is none whatsoever in Jeremiah. The human analogy God uses in verse 1
('If a man divorces his wife . . .'), drawing clearly on the law
in Deuteronomy 24:1–4, has no force if God has not divorced
Israel. And as if to dispel any remaining doubt, God states
categorically: 'I gave faithless Israel her certificate of divorce
and sent her away because of all her adulteries' (8).

## 2.   Israel is brazenly unrepentant

Adultery is indeed what Israel has committed – and on a grand
scale. It is bad enough for the former husband when his wife
remarries but worse still when she prostitutes herself among
many men (this *a fortiori* argument is, as Holladay points out,
the force of verse 1). In fact just as the Bedouin sit beside a
desert road trying to sell their legitimate wares, so she sits
touting her sexual favours to anyone who will have her (2).
Every possible Canaanite place of worship – 'every high hill
and every spreading tree' – has seen her adultery (6), and the
Southern Kingdom, far from being appalled, has merely taken its

cue from the North (7f). As we have noted before, this imagery was so peculiarly appropriate not only because Israel and Judah were apostasising, leaving the faithful service of the Lord, but also because their defection to Canaanite practices involved the worshipper in intercourse with cult prostitutes in order to ensure that the land would be fertile.

Yet despite all she has done and all the ways in which God has punished her, she remains totally unrepentant. God has withheld the rain Israel so badly needs, yet she shows no sign of shame or repentance (3). Instead, she pouts and flirts, calling God 'my Father' (perhaps, as McKane suggests, a reference 'to the husband in his capacity as instructor of the young wife' just as the father-son image is used of the teacher-pupil relationship in the Wisdom Literature) and 'my friend from my youth' (a lovely description of the marriage partner also used in Proverbs 2:17). But she only wants God to relent and shower her with his gifts; she has no intention of changing her ways (4f). In fact, she never tires of her adulteries (6f).

## 3.  Israel has remarried – or worse

This section is shot through with references to the law restricting remarriage of Deuteronomy 24:1–4. That law prohibits a first husband remarrying his original wife if she has remarried in the meantime. This is precisely the situation envisaged in Jeremiah 3:1: 'If a man divorces his wife and she leaves him and marries another man, should he return to her again?' Deuteronomy 24 also twice mentions a 'certificate of divorce' (1, 3); compare Jeremiah 3:8. The last words of the Deuteronomic law are: 'Do not bring sin upon the land the LORD your God is giving you as an inheritance', and the defilement of the land is a constant theme in Jeremiah 3 (1, 2, 9).

Can we then conclude that Israel is seen as remarrying? Has she remarried Baal (cf Hos. 2:16f)? For Jeremiah the question is probably academic. He uses the language of the Deuteronomic law which envisages a second marriage (and prohibits a return to the original marriage) without ever saying explicitly that Israel has remarried. But if she has not formally remarried, she has done worse: she has given herself to a large number of lovers, in fact to anyone who will have her (1f). From the point of view of defilement (which is what Jeremiah is interested in, cf Deut. 24:4a), therefore, she is at least as defiled in God's eyes as a wife who remarries after divorce for 'something indecent'; in fact, she is still more defiled.

## 4.  God wants Israel back

Yet God wants her back. Though he has begun by saying that any restoration of the marriage is impossible (1), he now calls her to return and says: 'I will frown on you no longer, for I am merciful' (12). Indeed, while he rejects her hypocritical approaches which seek to profit from their (former) relationship (3–5), he says of himself: 'I am your husband' (14).

Yet he cannot re-establish their marital relationship until she repents, and does so genuinely. There is a marked contrast between the 'return' of the end of verse 1 and the 'return' of verses 12 and 14. In verse 1, it is a purely tactical return because Israel sees it is to her advantage to come back to the Lord; but there is no intention of changing her ways. Holladay calls the end of verse 1 an 'ironic exclamation' and translates: 'And to think you would return to me!' Judah too only feigns repentance; it is 'not with all her heart, but only in pretence' (10). But God calls Israel to a repentance that is sincere: 'Return, faithless Israel . . . only acknowledge your guilt . . .' (12f). Then the marriage can be restored, even though this means taking a divorced wife back.

# Ezekiel

Ezekiel uses the marriage image much less frequently than Hosea or even Jeremiah, but when he does use it, it comes in extended parables – almost allegories – describing God's relationship with Israel. We will concentrate especially on one of the two extended parables: chapter 16.

## 1.  The original marriage

Ezekiel begins the story at Israel's birth: she is an unwanted child whom nobody cared for enough even to cut the umbilical cord or wash off the uterine blood. Indeed, she was abandoned and left to 'kick about in your blood' (4–6). God had compassion on her, saved her life and caused her to grow (6f). She became a young girl, passing through the stage of adolescence with her breasts forming and her pubic hair growing (7).

Then God came to her again: 'I looked at you and saw that you were old enough for love' (8). What follows is tantalisingly brief, but fascinating because it probably sheds light on contemporary Israelite marriage customs. First God 'spread the corner of my garment over you'; the reason immediately given is to 'cover your nakedness' (8), but the fact that Ruth asked Boaz to do the same when she was clearly asking for a commitment to get married (Ruth 3:9) suggests that it may have been a symbolic action effecting betrothal.

Next, 'I gave you my solemn oath' (8), clearly a binding promise of very considerable importance. When God sums up his indictment against his wife, Israel, he says: 'You have despised my oath by breaking the covenant' (59). This oath from the man (no equivalent oath from the woman is mentioned, but the whole chapter is seen from God's perspective) seems very close to the modern idea of a vow: the husband commits himself irrevocably to his wife and takes on binding obligations towards her.

In fact, she clearly takes on obligations towards him too. The oath is very closely connected with the covenant which God as husband enters into (8), and while he may be the initiator of the covenant, she clearly also subscribes to it, or at least receives it, because she can be accused later on of breaking the covenant (59). We will examine later in this chapter the idea of a marriage covenant; suffice to say at this stage that it is also mentioned in Malachi 2:14 and perhaps in Proverbs 2:17.

The next fact that God mentions is: 'I bathed you with water' (9). This might be a reference to preparation for courting and, later, intercourse (cf Ruth 3:3) but it might well be, especially in a book that is as shot through with priestly concerns as Ezekiel, the washing away of blood after initial intercourse (cf Deut. 22:17). He also 'put ointments on you' which was also a preparation for intercourse ('Before a girl's turn came to go in to King Xerxes, she had to complete 12 months of beauty treatments prescribed for the women, six months with oil of myrrh and six with perfumes and cosmetics' – Esther 2:12); the Song of Solomon is also shot through with talk of spices and ointment to prepare for love.

Finally, God mentions all the fine clothing and jewellery he gave to his wife, and how he made her a queen (10–13). This corresponds closely with Psalm 45, the royal wedding song, where the bride is clothed in costly and richly embroidered garments before being led to the king (Ps. 45:13–15).

## 2.   The adultery

So the original marriage was a sumptuous one, in which God did everything for his bride that could possibly be expected of him. Yet that did not stop her becoming a prostitute and betraying him with other men at every possible turn. Indeed, she took his gifts – clothing, jewellery and food – and used them in her adulterous religious practices (15–19).

Indeed, the whole chapter is a fierce diatribe against her adulteries; the most violent language is used: 'At the head of every street you built your lofty shrines and degraded your beauty, offering your body with increasing promiscuity to any-one who passed by' (25). 'You engaged in prostitution with the Assyrians too, because you were insatiable; and even after that, you still were not satisfied' (28).

The truth is that she is worse than a prostitute, for prosti-tutes at least get paid for their services, while his wife is so desperate for sexual gratification that she will pay others to have intercourse with her (31–34).

## 3.   The punishment

This is to fit the crime. In her lust, she has been quick to take off her clothes and display her naked body for the pleasures of sexual gratification (36). But God's punishment of her will be to gather round her all those who have ever used her body, those whom she was genuinely attracted to and those whom she detested. And then God will strip her naked. But her nakedness will not now be attractive; it will be shaming in the presence of such a crowd of men. And they will not be sexually excited by her nakedness; on the contrary, they themselves will rip off her clothes and jewels so that they can plunder and destroy her. She will incite their fury and they will come against her, in her defenceless nakedness, with stones and swords and violence. Adulterous wives deserve this, says Ezekiel, and much more (35–42, especially 38).

## 4. The reconciliation

Yet suddenly, and totally unexpectedly, comes reconciliation: 'My wrath against you will subside and my jealous anger will turn away from you' (42). Just when the wife must least expect it – immediately after hearing the words: 'I will deal with you as you deserve, because you have despised my oath by breaking my covenant' (59) – she hears: 'Yet I will remember the covenant I made with you in the days of your youth, and I will establish an everlasting covenant with you' (60).

This is not a remarriage, because there has been no mention of a divorce, despite Israel's promiscuity. Rather, it is a renewal, and a strengthening, of the original marriage covenant (8) that has never been abrogated. God, having vented his anger and punished Israel, enters into an even stronger and more binding covenant with her, and he doesn't wait for her to repent first. Rather, her shame and repentance will come as a response to his extraordinary love for her (61–63).

There is a very similar, and even more violent, parable in chapter 23 where Ezekiel presents two sisters: Oholah (= Samaria, the capital of the Northern Kingdom) and Oholibah (= Jerusalem, the capital of the Southern Kingdom). Both are again shameless prostitutes and both are very severely punished. They are God's wives (4) but again divorce is never mentioned. Neither, in this very bleak picture, is reconciliation.

## Isaiah

The later chapters of the book of Isaiah take up the imagery of God as husband and Israel as rejected wife but, in keeping with the tenor of the chapters as a whole, go on to speak in glowing terms of the future of the relationship.

## 1.   *The divorce*

At the beginning of chapter 50, the familiar imagery is taken up in just one verse, the opening verse of an oracle:

(1) This is what the LORD says: "Where is your mother's certificate of divorce with which I sent her away? Or to which of my creditors did I sell you? Because of your sins you were sold; because of your transgressions your mother was sent away . . ."

Some commentators try to make out that God is, in this verse, repudiating the very idea that he has divorced Israel. This is her accusation, but it is untrue. North, for example, heads this section: 'Separation, not Divorce' and maintains that the question 'Where is your mother's certificate of divorce with which I sent her away?' expects the answer 'There never was one!' He admits that '*šillaḥ* (send away) is used almost as a technical term for divorce' (e.g. Deut. 24:1–4, Mal. 2:16) but says that it can have 'a wider content of meanings' and here refers to separation.

However, the verse ends: 'Because of your transgressions your mother was sent away'. This 'sending away' at the end of the verse must mean the same as the 'sending away' in the initial question. There is no doubt that in the initial question it refers to divorce because it is occasioned by a 'certificate of divorce'. Thus it must be the case that God is stating: I did indeed divorce your mother.

It may possibly be that the questions represent Israel's petulant accusation of God. But if so, as Westermann points out, God in the rest of verse 1 agrees that he has repudiated Israel and argues that he was justified in so doing. Here, then, is God's divorce of Israel which we have met in other prophets.

## 2.   *The recall*

(1) "Sing, O barren woman, you who never bore a child; burst into song, shout for joy, you who were never in labour; because more are the children of the desolate woman than

of her who has a husband," says the LORD. (2) "Enlarge the place of your tent, stretch your tent curtains wide, do not hold back; lengthen your cords, strengthen your stakes. (3) For you will spread out to the right and to the left; your descendants will dispossess nations and settle in their desolate cities. (4) Do not be afraid; you will not suffer shame. Do not fear disgrace; you will not be humiliated. You will forget the shame of your youth and remember no more the reproach of your widowhood. (5) For your Maker is your husband – the LORD Almighty is his name – the Holy One of Israel is your Redeemer; he is called the God of all the earth. (6) The LORD will call you back as if you were a wife deserted and distressed in spirit – a wife who married young, only to be rejected," says your God. (7) "For a brief moment I abandoned you, but with deep compassion I will bring you back. (8) In a surge of anger I hid my face from you for a moment, but with everlasting kindness I will have compassion on you," says the LORD your Redeemer. (9) "To me this is like the days of Noah, when I swore that the waters of Noah would never again cover the earth. So now I have sworn not to be angry with you, never to rebuke you again. (10) Though the mountains be shaken and the hills be removed, yet my unfailing love for you will not be shaken nor my covenant of peace be removed," says the LORD, who has compassion on you (Isa. 54).

Once again, North tries to maintain there has never been a divorce. He bases his argument entirely round his understanding of verse 6. He claims that the 'call' there is the initial invitation into marriage rather than a 'calling back' after divorce. He also translates the last part of the verse: 'Yet who can disown the bride of his youth?', making it into an 'exclamatory question', rather than a third description of the woman at the time of the Lord's call (as in NIV and most translations).

Yet North himself admits that the Hebrew construction is not what one would expect of an exclamatory question, and the language in the rest of the oracle simply prohibits his assertion that there has been no divorce. Right from verse 1, Zion is described as a 'desolate woman', Brown, Driver and Briggs rightly point out that here the word used (šômēmâh) is placed in opposition to 'her who has a husband' and therefore must refer to someone who is no longer (or never has been) married.

In verse 6 itself, the woman (the Hebrew noun can mean 'woman' or 'wife') is described as 'deserted' or 'forsaken'. This is exactly the word which Genesis 2:24 uses of 'leaving' one's father and mother in order to cleave to one's wife. Genesis clearly intends that a husband should never 'leave' his wife, nor a wife her husband, yet that is exactly what any person does who deserts his/her partner (Prov. 2:17; same word).

In verse 7, God uses precisely the same word when he admits that: 'For a brief moment I abandoned you'. God has clearly forsaken/deserted/abandoned the wife with whom he had a relationship. Indeed, so complete has the rupture been that it can be described as 'widowhood' (4, cf 49:19-21 where Israel is described as both bereaved and rejected). There can be no doubt then that Zion's relationship with God has been brought to an end; she has been divorced.

But now God 'calls' her back (6); he wants to 'bring her back' (7) and he will again be her husband (5). This is not yet explicitly a remarriage; rather, it is a gathering of her again to himself and a renewal of his relationship with her. This is spoken of as a 'covenant' (10) but not a covenant that brings her from divorced singleness or widowhood to marriage; it is, rather, a covenant that brings her from enmity with God (8a) into peace with him. Hence it is called 'my covenant of peace' (10).

And this new covenant will be as strong as the covenant with Noah. Just as God swore never again to cover the earth with flood waters, so he promises never again to repudiate Zion, never to take his steadfast love from her (9f). He will show her 'everlasting kindness' (8).

## 3.  The remarriage

(4) No longer will they call you Deserted, or name your land Desolate. But you will be called Hephzibah ['My delight is in her'] and your land Beulah [Married], for the LORD will take delight in you, and your land will be married. (5) As a young man marries a maiden, so will your sons marry you; as a bridegroom rejoices over his bride, so will your God rejoice over you (Isa. 62).

This image again comes in a longer oracle. Zion is currently 'deserted' (exactly the same word translated 'deserted' in 54:6 and 'abandoned' in 54:7 and used, as we have seen, for 'leave' in Gen. 2:24) and 'desolate' (the same word is used of the land here and of Zion herself in 54:1). This continues the picture of the abandoned, divorced woman.

In chapter 54 God calls her back. It is possible that remarriage is envisaged, but there is no language there which explicitly states that. In chapter 62, however, the language of marriage forms the heart of the prophet's message. The land will henceforth be called 'Married' (4) and just as a bridegroom rejoices over his newly married bride, so God will rejoice over Zion to whom he has been remarried (5). Admittedly there is a difference: the young man envisaged in verse 5 is marrying for the first time. But this is not the case with God. Already there has been a long tradition in prophetic circles that God was married to Israel but had repudiated her. That is precisely why he finds her, before this remarriage, 'deserted'/'forsaken' (4).

There is a strange additional idea: your sons will marry you (5). This of course, on the literal level, would be incestuous and therefore unthinkable. But at many points in these later chapters of Isaiah, especially when the marriage image is being used, the people of Israel or the inhabitants of Zion are called her children. Thus 50:1 begins: 'Where is *your mother's* certificate of divorce . . . ?' 54:1 states: 'More are the children of the desolate woman than of her who has a husband', cf 49:19–21. Here, then, the image is stretched to speak of the joyful unity that Zion's inhabitants will have and their sense that they belong to her. Nevertheless, the basic image remains: God has remarried the woman (Zion/Israel) whom he divorced.

There is an interesting example of a somewhat similar re-marriage to an original partner in the historical books. Saul's daughter Michal fell in love with David and David too wanted to marry her. So 'Saul gave him his daughter Michal in marriage (1 Sam. 18:20–27). However, while David was on the run, Saul dissolved the marriage and gave Michal to another man, Palti, instead (1 Sam. 25:44). David never recognised this second marriage and, as part of his negotiations to become king of the northern tribes, he insisted that Michal be taken away from her new husband (the word is used in 2 Sam. 3:15) and restored to him (2 Sam. 3:12-16).

All this leads to an inevitable question: in a study of human divorce and remarriage, why spend so much time on the marriage of God to Israel? What light does this image throw on the human marriage relationship? Schillebeeckx answers the question well. He states that in the prophetic literature marriage is used as an illustration of God's covenant with Israel. But it could not be so used unless there were similarities to the human marriage covenant which were either obvious anyway or were revealed. Insofar as the illustration revealed new things in marriage which had not previously been perceived, they do shed new light on human marriage which the people of God need to take into account. Indeed, human marriage partners were supposed to learn how to behave by thinking about God's dealings with his marriage partner Israel. So, Ezekiel 23 speaks of the terrible punishment God is going to bring on his two wives, Oholah/Samaria and Oholibah/Jerusalem and almost the last word in the chapter is: 'Thus will I put an end to lewdness in the land, that all women may take warning and not commit lewdness as you have done' (48 RSV) (Schillebeeckx pp. 31-34, 48).

Some have argued that because God's reaction to his wife Israel is wholly unexpected (see, for example, Hos. 2:13f), it cannot be taken as normative for human marriage. God may be prepared to forgive and seek reconciliation, but the prophets do not, it is said, expect humans to do the same. It is absolutely true that God's behaviour towards his marriage partner is supreme evidence of his grace, utterly undeserved on her part. Yet, as we shall see from Malachi, God makes similarly shocking demands of human marriages – so shocking in fact, that later scribes felt compelled to tone them down.

Thus the study of God's marriage to Israel does have significant implications for human marriage in God's purposes. Most of these are probably already obvious. We will, however, delay a summary of them until after we have looked at prophetic material on human marriage.

## The Prophets: Human Marriage

The great passage on this subject is Malachi 2:10–16. Unfortunately it is a notoriously difficult text and it is essential to work slowly through to what the prophet was (probably) saying. Nevertheless, while some details have to remain obscure, much of the thrust of Malachi's message is not seriously in doubt. This is the NIV text:

> (10) Have we not all one Father? Did not one God create us? Why do we profane the covenant of our fathers by breaking faith with one another? (11) Judah has broken faith. A detestable thing has been committed in Israel and in Jerusalem: Judah has desecrated the sanctuary the LORD loves, by marrying the daughter of a foreign god. (12) As for the man who does this, whoever he may be, may the LORD cut him off from the tents of Jacob – even though he brings offerings to the LORD Almighty. (13) Another thing you do: You flood the LORD's altar with tears. You weep and wail because he no longer pays attention to your offerings or accepts them with pleasure from your hands. (14) You ask: "Why?" It is because the LORD is acting as the witness between you and the wife of your youth, because you have broken faith with her, though she is your partner, the wife of your marriage covenant. (15) Has not the LORD made them one? In flesh and spirit they are his. And why one? Because he was seeking godly offspring. So guard yourself in your spirit, and do not break faith with the wife of your youth. (16) "I hate divorce," says the LORD God of Israel, "and I hate a man's covering himself with violence as well as with his garment," says the LORD Almighty. So guard yourself in your spirit and do not break faith.

The word that runs right through this passage is: breaking faith (*bāḡaḏ*); it comes in verses 10, 11, 14, 15, 16. This is the accusation that holds the passage together and provides its theme: 'Judah has broken faith' (11).

## The General Sin (Malachi 2:10)

Malachi begins with the overarching sin: we (he identifies himself with Judah) have broken faith with God and one another (10). His opening questions are there to show that we owe allegiance to God. Some commentators take the 'Father' to be a reference to Abraham, reminding the Jews that they had a common human ancestry, but in view of the parallel phrase in the next line ('Did not one God create us?'), it is much more likely that this is a reference to God as their common Father. He has already been pictured as a Father to Israel in 1:6 and is thought of as Israel's Father in other Old Testament passages (e.g. Exod. 4:22, Hos. 11:1, Isa. 1:2, 30:9).

God is, then, the Father who brought Israel into existence. He is also the one who created Israel (10, cf Isa. 43:1, 15). Clearly they should obey him as obedient children and grateful creatures. But instead they have 'profaned the covenant' and (by implication) broken faith with God.

Yet this is not where the emphasis lies. Malachi's stress is on the fact that we owe allegiance to one another. The reason for stressing that God is one (twice in 10) is precisely to stress our equality together before him (the first phrase is, literally: 'Is there not one Father for us all?'); because we have one Father, we are a community of brothers ('breaking faith with one another' is, literally, 'we break faith each with his brothers'). Hence God's covenant can be called 'the covenant of our fathers' not because they made it but because God made it with them, our common ancestors, and because we are all equally their descendants, we are all equally bound by the covenant.

Yet the basic sin of Judah is that, though bound by covenant to God and one another, though owing allegiance to both, her people have in reality broken faith with both. Indeed they have broken faith with God by breaking faith with their brothers.

## The First Specific Sin: Mixed Marriages (Malachi 2:11–12)

As Malachi begins to move to specifics, he first reiterates the general accusation: Judah has broken faith (11). Then he moves, in his indictment, into the marital realm: 'Judah has . . . married the daughter of a foreign god' (11). By putting it this way, Malachi shows clearly the basic problem with mixed marriages. It is not primarily a racial matter (though that does sometimes enter into the Old Testament assessment of these marriages); principally, it is a religious issue. These women owe their allegiance to 'a foreign god' rather than the God of Israel. And it is the bringing in of this foreign religious element which breaks faith with the community of Israel: 'profaning the covenant of our fathers' and 'breaking faith with one another' (10).

This is also why 'Israel' and 'Jerusalem' are mentioned in verse 11. This 'detestable thing' (a word – tô'ēḇâh – often associated in the Old Testament with idolatrous practices) has been done in the Promised Land and in the Holy City. It is also probably why 'the tents of Jacob' are mentioned in verse 12; this was the place where the holy community lived and from which all evil ought to be eradicated.

Mixed marriages were, of course, a problem faced, probably a little later, by Ezra and Nehemiah and it seems appropriate to treat them at this point. The relevant chapters in the book of Ezra are 9 and 10, and they open with the leaders of the people coming to Ezra and saying: 'The people of Israel, including the priests and the Levites, have not kept themselves separate from the neighbouring peoples with their detestable practices . . . They have taken some of their daughters as wives for themselves and their sons, and have mingled the holy race with the peoples around them. And the leaders and officials have led the way in this unfaithfulness' (9:1f).

This news was taken with the utmost seriousness by Ezra. He tore his tunic and cloak, pulled out his hair and 'sat appalled' for many hours. Then he began a prayer of abject self-abasement, confessing the enormous guilt of Israel's perpetual sinfulness and specifically of this sin (9:3ff; 10:1, 6).

Ezra's reasoning is entirely straightforward: the very life of the community is at stake. As he looks back over recent history, he knows that it was precisely because of Israel's disobedience that the horrors of the Exile took place. Now God has been remarkably generous to them in enabling them to start again in their home country, and they are about to throw it all away again by disobeying the clear commands of God forbidding mixed marriages. This is bound to bring renewed destruction on them (9:6–15).

Drastic situations need drastic remedies. Shecaniah proposed that the only 'hope for Israel' was to divorce the foreign wives, and Ezra and the leadership agreed with this. Arrangements were made and a list was drawn up of the 121 men who had married foreign wives. Each case was carefully examined and the divorces presumably took place (10:2–44). The men were expressly disobeying God in marrying in the first place (10:2, 10); they had, therefore, now to 'send away' (10:3) their wives.

Nehemiah met precisely the same problem (13:23–30) and it should not surprise us – as it seems to surprise some scholars – that the disobedient practice of marrying those of alien race and religion quickly reappeared; Israel frequently turned over new leaves but was not noted for keeping to her good resolutions. Nehemiah was a man of violent emotions and reacted in a characteristically violent way (25) but he also did two other things: he made them take an oath not to make any more mixed marriages (25) and he 'purified the priests and Levites of everything foreign' (30). This last may be a reference to making them divorce their wives, though this is nowhere explicitly stated.

Nehemiah has less to say than Ezra about why mixed marriages were so disastrous. He draws his reasons from the history of Solomon. It seems once more that the problem was not in the marriages themselves; it was that his foreign wives 'led even him into sin' (26); in other words, the reason why mixed marriages were 'unfaithful to God' (27) was because the new wives, with their alien religion, led the Israelites into unfaithfulness to God. This too was why it was dangerous for the children to be growing up 'not knowing how to speak the language of Judah' (24). It wasn't simply hurt national pride; it was that the words in which their religion was expressed were becoming unintelligible to them.

To return to Malachi, he also saw mixed marriages as a great threat to Israel, a 'desecration of the sanctuary the LORD loves' (2:11). He did not, however, advocate divorce, and we do not know what he would have thought of that solution to the grave danger Judah had placed herself in. Instead, he asks for something still more drastic: God's destruction of the Israelite concerned (12). Only this punishment fits the sin; only this will purge the evil of the man's 'breaking faith' both with God and with the endangered community of Israel.

## The Second Specific Sin: Divorce (Malachi 2:13–16)

Malachi now comes on to 'another thing' (13), literally: 'This second thing you do'. This argues against the view, held for example by Luck, that the Israelites divorced their wives (13–16) *in order to* marry foreign wives (11f) and that Malachi is only really attacking this one (combined) practice. On the contrary, Malachi presents to Judah two different examples of their breaking faith: some are contracting mixed marriages, others are divorcing their wives. Both are equally detestable to God, and both are examples of breaking faith with God and with one another (10).

Malachi now explains what this second sin is. He begins with the Israelites' complaint: they are very upset because God is not accepting their offerings (13). Verhoef suggests that they may have drawn this conclusion because of the failure of their crops (cf 3:10–12). In any case, they demand to know why this is happening (14a). And Malachi gives God's reply: it is because they have 'broken faith' (the theme word again) with their wives. And how have they done so? By divorcing their wives (16).

In this context, the wife is described in three ways. First, as 'the wife of your youth' (14, 15). This, or a very similar, phrase is used elsewhere in the Old Testament in the context of a marriage that is at risk or has broken down: 'The adulteress . . . has left the partner of her youth' (Prov. 2:16f, cf Jer. 2:2; Isa. 54:6). It is also used to evoke tenderness towards one's wife through the remembrance of the early days of love: 'May you rejoice in the wife of your youth' (Prov. 5:18, cf Jer. 3:4; Joel 1:8). Perhaps in Malachi it has both nuances: the marriage has broken up, yet the phrase recalls the sweetness of first love and therefore urges reconciliation.

Secondly, the wife is described as 'your partner' (14). The word here (*ḥᵃbertkā*) means 'the one to whom you are united/ with whom you are joined together'. This may very likely be an allusion to Genesis 2:24 where the man 'cleaves' to his wife and together they 'become one flesh', especially as there seem to be echoes of Genesis 1f in the rest of the oracle.

The third description is the one on which discussion has most often concentrated: 'the wife of your marriage covenant' (14) or 'your wife by covenant' (RSV. The word 'marriage' is not in the Hebrew). 'Covenant' is of course a very common concept in the Old Testament; indeed, the word used here is exactly the same as that used for the covenant at Sinai in verse 10. It is used once or twice elsewhere in the Old Testament specifically of a marriage covenant: Ezekiel 16:8, 59–62. Proverbs 2:17 may be another example, though the phrase (literally 'the covenant of her God') could refer to the covenant at Sinai (so, e.g. Kidner) or to the (marriage) covenant made before God (so NIV text). We do not know exactly what constituted an Israelite marriage ceremony, but it seems that – by Malachi's day at least – some form of covenant was involved, though this may have been 'taken as read' rather than always formally entered into (compare, for a later period, Tobit 7:13f).

In the same context, God is described as 'acting as the witness between you and the wife of your youth' (14). This may just mean: witness in the legal case which is being brought against you for 'breaking faith'. Just as likely, however, it means that God was witness to the original marriage covenant (cf Ruth 4:9–13). In fact, it is very probable that it has both meanings here: God is witness *now* in the legal case against these Israelite men precisely because he was *then* a witness of the original marriage covenant.

This, then, is a very important concept. Marriage is a binding agreement between husband and wife whose witness and guarantor is God. Yet it is possible to draw false conclusions from this idea, and in particular to assume, or argue, that if one partner breaks the covenant, so may the other. This is Atkinson's whole thesis in his book *To Have and to Hold* which is significantly subtitled *The Marriage Covenant and the Discipline of Divorce*. He believes:

1. That the concept of covenant is the heart of the biblical understanding of marriage. 'The fundamental biblical description of marriage is that of a covenant' (Atkinson p.134).

2. That either partner can break the covenant and so cause the destruction of the covenant.

3. That therefore a marriage can be 'destroyed'.

Luck is more outspoken in following Atkinson: 'The continued moral obligation to fulfil one's obligations is conditional upon the fulfilment of the spouse's obligations. Marriage is a bilateral, not a unilateral, covenant' (p.46). 'If the marriage vows are broken, the covenant is off and a divorce writ is only a public statement of the facts' (p.29).

This view is, in my opinion, gravely mistaken. It is certainly true that marriage is sometimes spoken of in the Old Testament as a covenant; we have seen the evidence for this. It is equally true that the vows inherent in the covenant can be broken by one partner: see Ezekiel 16:59 and perhaps Proverbs 2:17, if it refers to a marriage covenant. However, this does not mean that the covenant is irrevocably broken and can be regarded as destroyed. On the contrary, the past breaking of the (vows of the) covenant can and should lead to the renewal and further strengthening of the marriage covenant (Ezek. 16:60–62). This may conceivably be implied in the omission of the past tense ('she was'; in fact, no verb is supplied) in Malachi 2:14: 'though she is your partner, the wife of your marriage covenant'; does Malachi still regard her as the man's wife despite the legal divorce? Atkinson admits that marital lapses do not mean that the marriage should immediately and automatically be regarded as destroyed, but he fails to establish from Scripture that a marriage covenant can ever be finally and completely destroyed.

Secondly, Atkinson rightly states that: 'The primary purpose of marriage is . . . that the covenant relationship of man and wife . . . shall be the image of [God's] covenant relationship with his people' (p.75). Yet we have seen how God acts towards his marriage partner. Despite her gross adulteries and even prostitution, he only abandons her 'for a brief moment' (Isa. 54:7) and is then quick to seek reconciliation and restoration of the marriage. He never finally abandons her or treats the marriage relationship as over once and for all. Chary, in his commentary on Malachi, expresses this idea – the very opposite of Atkinson's – brilliantly:

The whole passage [Mal. 2:10–16] pleads for the stability of monogamous marriage: more than a simple bilateral contract, submitted to the risk of a fragile will, it is a *covenant* [Chary's emphasis] which has God for witness. Malachi has doubtless purposefully used this covenant term to remind that marriage must be as stable as the great covenant which binds God and the people. Only this indissoluble unity which God originally wanted (Gen. 1:28; 2:24) . . . makes possible a line of descendants which is 'a seed of God' [15].

Bromiley points out one of the most important ways in which the partners to a human marriage relationship must mirror God's 'husband-love' for Israel: they 'have to consider that, in spite of romantic views of one another, both are sinful and therefore their love will also have to be *grace* on both sides, a love for someone who really does not merit love' (p.34; my emphasis).

As an aside, I also think that Atkinson is wrong in stating that covenant is the basic biblical concept within which all Scriptures understand marriage. This is certainly not the case in the New Testament, and arguably not true of the Old Testament either. The fundamental concept in Genesis 2, in the teaching of Jesus and in much of Paul's writing, is 'one flesh'; even in Malachi, the phrase 'your partner' (14; literally 'the one to whom you are united') may well be a reference to 'becoming one flesh'. A further fundamental concept in St Paul's writing is that of the marriage bond. Certainly in the New Testament, these are infinitely more important than the idea of a marriage covenant.

## Reasons

Malachi has already, implicitly, given reasons why breaking faith with one's wife is sinful: God was the witness and is the guarantor of your promise of permanence; your wife is 'your partner' with whom you have been joined together; she is your wife by covenant (14).

Now he comes on to give further reasons in verse 15. It is a notoriously difficult verse. A literal translation would be: 'And has not he made one? (or: And One did not do [this]). And a remnant of spirit to him. And what is (or was) the One seeking?

Offspring of God. Be on your guard in your spirit, and with the wife of your youth do not break faith.'

The key question for interpretation is this: is the initial 'one' subject or object?

1. If 'one' is subject, it probably refers back to verse 10, where the initial question is: 'Is there not one Father (or: father) for us all?' The most common explanation, for those who espouse this line, is that verse 10a refers to Abraham. Verse 15, then, echoing (with its 'one') verse 10, also refers to Abraham. Hence the NIV margin: 'But the one (who is our father) did not do this'. In other words, Abraham did not divorce the barren Sarah. The main problem with this explanation is that Abraham is such a poor example of what Malachi is trying to say and surely detracts from, rather than enhances, the force of his argument. It is true that Abraham did not divorce Sarah, but he tried other means (having intercourse with Sarah's servant girl, Hagar) to get the 'offspring of God'. This hardly helps Malachi's case.

2. It is more likely that 'one' is object and that the whole verse is a reference to Genesis 1f.

a) 'Has not he [= God] made [them = a man and his wife] one?' This is, then, a reference to Genesis 2:24 ('they become one flesh') and makes precisely the same point that Jesus was making in Mark 10:6–9; Matthew 19:4–6. It is God who 'makes them one' (Malachi), God who 'joins them together' (Jesus). So neither they, nor any other man, is at liberty to sever the unity that God has made.

b) The reference to Genesis 2 helps to explain the next enigmatic part of verse 15: 'And a remnant of spirit to him'. This is probably a reference to God breathing life into mankind (Gen. 2:7) and means: 'though he [= God] had enough spirit for more wives'. God is not short of life-giving spirit and could certainly have given Adam more wives if that had been his intention, but he gave Adam only one because it was his intention that Adam should remain true to her. It is not an obstacle to this understanding that the word used here (rûaḥ) is not the same word used in Gen. 2:7 (nešāmâh) since the two words are used synonymously (e.g. Job 34:14), and Malachi wants to say, at the end of the verse, 'guard yourself in your spirit' (15, cf 16) for which he uses rûaḥ and for which nešāmâh would not do.

Smith quotes T. J. Delaughter (*Malachi, Messenger of Divine Love*, Insight Press, New Orleans, 1976. p.101) and very clearly sums up what this phrase is saying: 'God has the spirit of life and could have given Adam several wives if he had desired to do so. Monogamy was his intent, however, and it was in order to raise up a godly seed for a covenant people.'

c) The next phrase in verse 15 is also a reference to Genesis 1f: 'And what is the one [now with the definite article = this new unit of husband and wife] seeking?' The answer is: 'Offspring from God.' God had indeed 'created them male and female' in order that they should be 'fruitful and increase in number' (Gen. 1:27f). This is the first thing we are told about them after the story of the Garden (Gen. 4:1). But they could only have 'offspring from God' – in keeping with God's will – if they kept within God's norms. Godly offspring would not come from mixed marriages (Mal. 2:11f) nor to those who, contrary to God's will, divorced their wives. The final exhortation follows very naturally: 'Guard yourself in your spirit and do not break faith with the wife of your youth' (15).

## Conclusion (Malachi 2:16)

God sums up in verse 16 his thoughts on the subject of this second sin. Sadly, this verse also is not without its difficulties. 'I hate divorce' is, in the Hebrew text that has come down to us, 'He has hated divorcing.' The obvious person referred to as 'he' is the divorcing husband. This then yields a translation: 'If [the initial *kî* can mean 'for' or 'if'] he hated when divorcing, it would be as bad as covering his garment with violence.' This must be wrong. It would imply that divorce was perfectly acceptable if there were no hate involved and that would undermine all that Malachi is wanting to say about not breaking faith with 'your partner, your wife by covenant'.

The simplest explanation is that espoused by Verhoef and several others, building on Rudolph. The text of the Old Testament which we have consists of consonants with marks and signs to indicate vowels. 'Vocalisation' (the inclusion of vowel signs) occurred in the first millennium AD and was not standardised until late within the millennium. This effectively means that we can be much more sure about the Hebrew consonants than about the vowel signs. By keeping the consonants precisely as they are and changing only the (later) vowel signs, the verb can be read as a participle: 'hating'. The present tense is frequently expressed by the participle and we must supply the personal pronoun 'I'. This is no strange procedure. Where the Hebrew text does not make sense as it stands, the most obvious solution is to revocalise the text while keeping the (more original) consonants. In this case, the text then translates as 'I hate divorce' which is adopted by virtually all translations of the Bible and is entirely in keeping with the context.

This is strong language. It is probably because later scribes were embarrassed by the strength of Malachi's words (God hates divorce) that they slightly altered the text. 'Evidently the text suffered early at the hands of some who wanted to bring Malachi's teaching into line with that of Deuteronomy 24:1 which permitted divorce' (Baldwin). The 'bad state of the text bears its own witness to the probability that it did originally condemn divorce outright. If so, . . . it would be small wonder if it suffered from scribal efforts to soften it' (R. Mason: *The Books of Haggai, Zechariah and Malachi*, CUP, Cambridge, 1977, quoted in Hugenberger p.52).

NIV is less helpful in its translation of the second part of the verse. There is no repeated 'I hate' in the Hebrew, nor is the man involved in a strange double covering of himself, one metaphorical (with violence) and one literal (with his garment). Rather, the phrase literally reads 'and he covers [or, 'and covering', following the proposed reading of *BHS*] over his garment with violence'. The point of mentioning these two sins (divorce and violence) is that God hates one just as much as the other; the meaning is: 'I hate divorce as much as I hate violence,' or perhaps: 'I hate divorce because it is a kind of violence.' Again, it is wholly natural that Malachi should follow this with a repetition of his main exhortation: 'Guard yourself in your spirit and do not break faith' (16).

## Summary of Malachi

It is unfortunate that this tremendously significant passage has some textual and linguistic problems which do not allow us to be 100% confident about some of the details. Nevertheless, the main message is clear. The whole passage is shot through with the command not to break faith; it begins and ends on that note (10, 16) and comes back to it on several occasions (11, 14, 15).

Applying this within the field of marriage and divorce (13–16), Malachi states that husband and wife are partners in a marriage covenant at which God acted as witness and which he is determined to uphold (14). Further, husband and wife are united as one (14: 'your partner'/the one to whom you are joined. Also probably 15: Has God not made them one? . . . And what is this one seeking?). Precisely because this is what marriage is, God hates divorce as much as murder (16) and will punish a society where divorce is rife (13).

In Jesus' day, rabbinic discussion of divorce centred on the meaning of the law in Deuteronomy 24, but Smith is right in saying: 'This passage [Mal. 2] does not seem to be based on Deuteronomy 24 but goes back to Gen. 1f and is the forerunner of Jesus' teaching' on the subject.

## Summary of the Prophets

We can now look back at the earlier prophets' teaching about God's marriage to Israel and see what light it, together with Malachi, has to shed on divorce and remarriage in the human sphere. All the prophets who use this image start from the assumption that God is married to Israel. He has chosen her, made all the necessary preparations and taken her as his bride (e.g. Ezek. 16). For her part, she has been brazenly unfaithful. She has done more than enough to justify not only divorce but judicial death (e.g. Hos. 2, Ezek. 23). And indeed God did divorce her, but only 'for a brief moment' (Isa. 54:7f). It never entered his head, however, to remarry. Indeed, even while divorced, he regarded her sexual escapades as 'adultery' and clearly considered that she was, rightfully, his wife.

Meanwhile, he longs to be reconciled and intends to be.

Sometimes he seems to say that she must repent first; sometimes her repentance seems to be expected only after the marriage has been re-established (Ezek. 16:60–63). But in either case he expects the marriage to begin again (e.g. Hos. 2:16–20). And there is no question of a half-hearted re-entry into married life on God's part, with his commitment weakened because of Israel's unfaithfulness. On the contrary, he is determined that the marriage commitment will be still stronger, the marriage covenant still firmer (Ezek. 16:60–62; Isa. 54:9f).

It is not hard to see how this ties in with Malachi's attitude to human marriage and divorce. God hates divorce; it is as abhorrent to him as murder. He was forced into the evil of divorce because to have allowed Israel to get off scot free with her brazen prostitution would have been worse. But once the point has been forcibly made – and even before Israel fully acknowledges her sin – he is back with her, wooing her, seeking to restore the relationship and make it stronger. Reconciliation and a strengthening of the ties – perhaps after some hard talking and harder action – is God's way of dealing with his own and human marriage difficulties.

## The Wisdom Literature

We turn finally in this chapter to the Wisdom Literature which, as might be imagined, has a fair amount to say about marriage and, while being very positive about its blessings, is also extremely realistic about its difficulties.

## The Blessings

Proverbs 18:22 in many ways sums up the wise men's attitude to the best in marriage: 'He who finds a wife finds what is good and receives favour from the LORD.' This is spelled out more fully in the Jewish Wisdom book of Ecclesiasticus: 'A woman's beauty gladdens the countenance, and surpasses every human desire. If kindness and humility mark her speech, her husband is not like other men. He who acquires a wife gets his best possession, a helper fit for him and a pillar of support' (36:22–24). This short passage is a compendium of all that is good about marriage in the eyes of the Wisdom Literature which, as usual, sees life from the man's point of view.

It mentions, first, physical/sexual pleasure. There is no greater joy for a man than to look on his wife's beauty. The Wisdom Literature is quite unabashed in talking about this: 'May your fountain be blessed, and may you rejoice in the wife of your youth. A loving doe, a graceful deer – may her breasts [RSV, following a poorly attested text: affection. Literally: nipples] satisfy you always, may you ever be captivated by her love' (Prov. 5:18f). Of course the Song of Solomon is the supreme example of this with its detailed descriptions of the bodies both of the woman (4:1–7; 6:4–9; 7:1–9a) and of the man (5:10–16) and its luxuriant use of sexual imagery.

This, in turn, leads to Wisdom's ideal of family life. Children are seen as a great blessing, and to have the family united at home, seeing even the next generation appearing, is much to be desired (cf Psalm 128:3–6).

Then Ecclesiasticus 36 mentions another kind of beauty in the wife: her gentleness of character (verse 23). This is exactly the same picture that 1 Peter sets before us in its picture of womanly virtue: 'Your beauty . . . should be that of your inner self, the unfading beauty of a gentle and quiet spirit, which is of great worth in God's sight' (3:3f). As for the wife's 'kindness', 'she opens her arms to the poor and extends her hands to the needy' (Prov. 31:20). But this is not at all a rather passive, and even weak, gentleness. On the contrary, she is 'prudent' (Prov. 19:14), which is one of the highest accolades the Wisdom Literature can bestow on a human being; it means that she is both full of insight and understanding, and acts upon what she knows to be the wise approach.

Another important word which the Wisdom Literature uses of the wife (ḥayil) is translated by NIV as 'of noble character': 'A wife of noble character is her husband's crown' (Prov. 12:4a); and the great poem in Proverbs 31 begins: 'A wife of noble character who can find?' (10). The basic meaning of the word is 'strong' and it is often used in a moral context. Boaz uses the same word to describe Ruth: 'All my fellow townsmen know that you are a woman of noble character' (Ruth 3:11). The best wives are morally strong.

And lastly Ecclesiasticus 36 says that a good wife is a support. In calling her 'a helper fit for him' (36:24), there is a deliberate echo of Genesis 2:18, 20. Ecclesiasticus and Genesis 2:18 (LXX) use an identical phrase: *boēthon kat' auton*. She is also 'a pillar of support'. This is echoed in the Greek of 40:23: 'A friend or a companion never meets one amiss, but a wife with her husband [the Hebrew is: A prudent wife] is better than both.' Friends and companions certainly lend one a great deal of help in life, but one's marriage partner is one's greatest support.

This is really the main burden of Proverbs 31: the woman with (moral) strength of character is such an outstanding support to her husband and family: she is an extremely able businesswoman who, while she knows all about management, is not above a great deal of hard work herself (31:13–19, 21f, 24, 27); she is not, however, so taken up with her business that her own family (21, 27f) or the poor (20) are neglected; she is well spoken of when people talk in public places (31) and, as a result of her excellence, her husband is not only carefree and confident in her ability (11) but he too is much respected in public (23). She is wise and able to instruct others in wisdom (26), and this is not surprising. because above all she brings into her family her fear of the Lord (30) which is the very foundation principle of all wisdom (1:7; 9:10; 15:33).

These, then, are the blessings of a good marriage. It is not surprising that the Hebrew text of Ecclesiasticus 40:19 pronounces: 'Owning livestock and orchards will make you famous, but it is better to have a wife whom you love' (GNB). And even the jaundiced compiler of Ecclesiastes writes: 'Enjoy life with your wife, whom you love, all the days of this meaningless life that God has given you under the sun' (9:9).

## The Difficulties

But the wise men were far from seeing marriage through rose-coloured spectacles. The splendid poem of Proverbs 31 assumes that such a wife is quite rare (10). And the proverb that begins: 'A wife of noble character is her husband's crown' ends with: 'but a disgraceful wife [literally: a wife who causes shame] is like decay in his bones' (Prov. 12:4).

Instead of giving sexual pleasure (the first gift of a happy marriage in Ecclesiasticus 36:22–24), she is sexually promiscuous. This is a very major theme of the early chapters of Proverbs. Young men are warned away from 'the adulteress, from the wayward wife with her seductive words, who has left the partner of her youth and ignored the covenant she made before God. For her house leads down to death and her paths to the spirits of the dead . . .' (2:16–19).

It is disastrous to sleep with another man's wife: as foolish as scooping fire into your lap and walking barefoot on hot coals. 'No one who touches [another man's wife] will go unpunished.' Behind this punishment certainly stands the God of moral order, but there is a more immediate cause: 'Jealousy arouses a husband's fury and he will show no mercy when he takes revenge. He will not accept any compensation; he will refuse the bribe, however great it is.' Instead, he will rain blows on the man who has slept with his wife, and make sure that his reputation is ruined. But clearly his own happiness has been ruined too (6:23–35).

Because Proverbs was written largely to educate – and in this case, warn – young men, it is not flattering to women in the sexual realm. The women envisaged are not single. On the contrary, they are married and far more sexually experienced than the young men they seduce. Whether they do it for money or for sexual appetite is not made clear, but they not only lead these inexperienced ('simple') men to moral death, they take advantage of their husbands: 'My husband is not at home; he has gone on a long journey . . . and will not be home till full moon' (7:19f). This is how the woman entices the young man into adultery; chapter 7 is a brilliant and vivid description of her guile.

What is more, these women show no shame or remorse, either before their husband or anyone else: 'This is the way of an adulteress: She eats and wipes her mouth and she says: "I've done nothing wrong"' (30:20).

And then instead of being gentle and supportive (the second and third gifts of a happy marriage in Ecclesiasticus 36:22–24), she is quarrelsome (literally: a woman of contentions). This phrase comes again and again in Proverbs, for example: 'A quarrelsome wife is like a constant dripping' (19:13, contrasted with the 'prudent wife' of the next verse). 27:15f says much the same and adds that it is impossible to do anything about her irritating manner: 'Restraining her is like restraining the wind or grasping oil with the hand.' She is not only 'niggling and nagging perpetually' (McKane) but she can be ill-tempered and fly into a rage (21:19). Proverbs' verdict is straightforward: 'Better to live on a corner of the roof [or: a desert (21:19)] than share a house with a quarrelsome wife' (21:9; 25:24).

## The Way Ahead

So what is the way ahead in marriage? It promises and can give so much, yet it can also make you want to get away from all human company, most of all your marriage partner's. How should a husband (or wife) react in these circumstances? The only answer we ever hear from the Wisdom Literature is: with marital faithfulness.

The husband must be faithful to his wife.

(15) Drink water from your own cistern, running water from your own well. (16) Should your springs overflow in the streets, your streams of water in the public squares? (17) Let them be yours alone, never to be shared with strangers. (18) May your fountain be blessed, and may you rejoice in the wife of your youth. (19) A loving doe, a graceful deer – may her breasts satisfy you always, may you ever be captivated by her love. (20) Why be captivated, my son, by an adulteress? Why embrace the bosom of another man's wife? (Prov. 5).

There is general agreement that 'your own cistern', 'your own well' and 'your fountain' (15, 18) are all images for 'your wife' viewed in a sexual context. It is not difficult to see why water easily suggests itself as a sexual image, and verse 15 tells a man to 'keep to his own water supply' (cf 20) while verse 18 implies that (if you stick to the instructions of 15–17) your wife's sexuality will be blessed (in fertility).

There is less agreement on the meaning of verse 16. McKane points out the change from the singular in verse 15 ('cistern', 'well') to the plural in verse 16 ('springs', 'streams of water') and sees this as significant. Since there would be no obvious reason for this change if the woman's sexuality was still in mind, it is likely that this is a reference to male semen, for which the imagery is both obvious and apt. The meaning is, then, that the male sperm should be used at home and not squandered in the highways and byways away from home. Verse 17 leads on from this. Male semen is precious; it is to be preserved for one's wife and not squandered by 'the fathering of children for a strange household and a consequent neglect of the building up of one's own house and posterity' (McKane).

Ecclesiasticus has passages which make very similar points. Negatively, it advises never to get into the beginnings of an adulterous affair: 'Turn away your eyes from a shapely woman, and do not look intently at beauty belonging to another; many have been misled by a woman's beauty, and by it passion is kindled like a fire. Never dine with another man's wife, nor revel with her at wine; lest your heart turn aside to her, and in blood you be plunged into destruction' (9:8f). On the positive side, it gives much the same advice as Proverbs 5:16f: 'My son, keep sound the bloom of your youth, and do not give your strength to strangers. Seek a fertile field within the whole plain, and sow it with your own seed, trusting in your fine stock. So your offspring will survive and, having confidence in their good descent, will grow great' (26:19–21, though the text is not entirely secure).

So the husband is to 'be intoxicated with' (a better translation than NIV's 'be captivated by') his wife's love (19) and is to remain absolutely faithful to her, even when there are superficial attractions in shedding his semen elsewhere (16) or sampling the embrace of another man's wife (20).

Equally, the wife must be faithful to her husband. Women are not normally addressed directly in the Wisdom Literature, but it is not hard to gather what a woman's attitude to marital faithfulness should be according to the wise men. The 'wayward wife' is castigated because she 'has left the partner of her youth and ignored the covenant she made before God' (Prov. 2:16f). Husband and wife are to be 'friends', 'intimates' (a better translation than NIV's 'partner'); God's covenant – whether this is his will expressed at Sinai or the marriage covenant to which God was witness – is to be respected and maintained, however exciting or more satisfying it might seem to be 'wayward'.

The striking fact in all this is that, while the Wisdom Literature is often highly pragmatic about difficult choices in life and while it has no illusions about marriage and knows it can be very tough, divorce is never once mentioned. It does not enter the thinking of those who obey the teachings of Wisdom; it is simply not an option.

## Conclusions

I came originally to the study of the Old Testament material on divorce and remarriage with the assumption that it would be very different from the New Testament material. It is true that Jesus appealed to one part of the Old Testament (Gen. 1:27; 2:24) in preference to another (the Mosaic legislation and particularly Deut. 24:1–4)(Mark 10:3–9//Matt. 19:4–9), but I had assumed that the Mosaic law and its presuppositions would dominate the subsequent discussion of divorce in the Old Testament as it certainly dominated discussion in Jesus' day.

A closer study reveals this assumption to be quite wrong. Crucially, Malachi 2 is based on Genesis 1f and not on Deuteronomy at all. Moreover, while there are echoes of Deuteronomy 24 in other Old Testament passages (most notably Jeremiah 3), the Mosaic law is never used, as it was in rabbinic discussion in Jesus' day, to discuss the grounds on which divorce is permissible.

Further, the Mosaic legislation itself, far from being permissive – in the sense of enabling divorce and remarriage to take place – is in fact restrictive: limiting the freedom with which Israelites might divorce and remarry. The resulting picture may be summarised in this way:

*1. While divorce is allowed, the Old Testament never encourages it*

It is true that the law assumes divorce is taking place and seems to countenance it at least when there has been 'indecent behaviour' (Deut. 24:1). Nevertheless any individual law which specifically legislates about divorce only limits its availability.

The law must therefore be seen as restraining divorce rather than enabling it.

As for the prophets, they say that God hates divorce. This is not only so in the famous saying of Malachi 2:16. It is also the clear message that emerges from the prophetic picture of God's marriage to Israel. It is true that God is sometimes represented as having divorced Israel because the radical evil and the sheer brazenness of her adulteries forced him to it, but he seems appalled by what he has done, does not want it to continue for more than the briefest of moments (Isa. 54:7f) and is prepared to restore the marriage relationship even before Israel has repented (Ezek. 16:59–63).

The Old Testament Wisdom Literature, for its part, does not even countenance divorce, despite its very down-to-earth realism about the difficulties of marriage. This is all the more striking in that the later, post-canonical Wisdom Literature does discuss, and even advise, divorce in certain circumstances. This was never, by contrast, part of the teaching of Old Testament Wisdom.

Some contemporary advocates of a more lenient attitude towards divorce in Christian circles seek to maintain that Christ and his apostles never sought to abrogate the Old Testament 'permissions'. I do not believe that the basic assertion is correct; on the contrary, we have to acknowledge that Christ did state that the Mosaic acceptance of divorce had been invalidated for Christians. But in any case these 'permissions', if one views the Old Testament as a whole, are very slight. All the relevant material – including Deuteronomy 24 – must have had the intention, and had the effect, of discouraging divorce. And some parts of the Old Testament go further: divorce is not only discouraged; it is disallowed (Deut. 22:13–19, 28f; Mal. 2:10–16).

## 2.  *Where divorce has taken place, remarriage is allowed but not encouraged*

The law does imply that remarriages are taking place and, by not censuring the practice, seems to allow it (Deut. 24:1–4). However, remarriage is only mentioned in passing and only ever in a context which restricts its availability. We should never forget, in all the discussion of Deuteronomy 24, that the whole purpose of the law was to *disallow* remarriage in certain circumstances. What is more, this is because the woman had been 'defiled' in the eyes of her original husband and we saw that a very likely explanation of this is that it was her second marriage that had defiled her. In addition, the law states that those of whom a higher degree of holiness is required should not marry those who have been previously divorced (Lev. 21:5–8, 10–15, cf Ezek. 44:21f).

In the prophetic literature, remarriage is spoken of only in horror. Israel, who should have been true to the Lord her God, has married a different husband (so perhaps Hos. 2:7, 16f; Jer. 3:1)! This is seen as utterly appalling and, even though divorced, she clearly has no moral freedom to contract a new marital alliance. The only right course of action for her is to repent and return to the Lord.

This is the picture given of the divine marriage to Israel. The prophets do not seem even to countenance remarriage for humans, and again it is simply not discussed in the Wisdom Literature, despite its wide range of human interests. This stands to reason: if divorce is not an option, still less is remarriage.

One frequently hears it said that 'divorce and remarriage were common in Old Testament times'. There is really no evidence for this assertion at all. The nearest we can come to it is that in some rabbinic circles – not all, but some – in Jesus' day, very lax grounds were allowed for divorce, and that divorce was generally considered to open the way to remarriage (*m. Git.* 9.10; 9.3). It is a matter of dispute how much advantage was taken of this ease of divorce. But in any case this evidence relates to Jesus' day and rabbinic teaching, not to the Old Testament. Divorce and remarriage were certainly practised in the Ancient Near East, but in the Old Testament prescriptive material we find divorce restricted or disallowed altogether, and remarriage hardly mentioned. In the historical material we find very little reference to divorce and almost none to remarriage. And in the Wisdom Literature, which recorded and guided everyday life, we find total silence on both divorce and remarriage. This does not give much encouragement to the view that in Israel divorce was easy and remarriage wholly acceptable.

## 3.  Where divorce has taken place, reconciliation is to be sought at all costs

This is the particular contribution of the prophets, since the Wisdom Literature (naturally, since it does not countenance divorce) is wholly silent on the issue and the Law says very little about divorce and in effect nothing about what should happen after it. But that reconciliation is to be sought at all costs is the supreme lesson that humans can, and should, learn from the prophets' picture of God as husband of Israel: he longs for the re-establishment of the marital relationship, he woos her again, he betroths her to himself (Hos. 2:14–23), he calls her back (Isa. 54:6) and he marries her once more (Isa. 62:4f).

God had every reason to wash his hands of his wife, to abandon her for ever; and indeed he did leave her for a time. But very swiftly he began to seek a mending of the relationship, a re-establishment of marital union, even a remarriage. If we are to take him as our guide in human relations, we will never be able wholly to accept a divorce or to resign ourselves entirely to the idea that a divorce is the end of the story. It is true that we may have to wait for some sign of repentance and 'return' on our partner's side, and the wait may continue to the end of our days, but we shall nevertheless do all in our power – sometimes not waiting for full repentance – to bring about reconciliation and a renewal of the marriage.

# 5

# Divorce and Remarriage in the Teaching of Jesus

As in all societies, Israelite practice did not always match up to Old Testament teaching. We know from Malachi, for example, that divorce had in his day become fairly common – common enough for him to point to divorce as one of the key signs of the nation's falling away from God. But in the centuries between the Old and New Testaments, Jewish teaching changed: explicitly sanctioning and in some instances encouraging, or even mandating, divorce. It is essential to understand this Jewish background if we are to grasp the revolutionary nature of Christ's own teaching on divorce and remarriage.

## Divorce and Remarriage in Contemporary Judaism

### *1. The right to divorce*

The right of the husband to divorce his wife – given adequate, and in many cases not very stringent, grounds – was not in question. Davies and Allison summarise the situation in this way: 'Despite the few rabbinic texts which mourn divorce (cf. *b. Git.* 90b), the impression one gains from ancient Jewish sources is that divorce was relatively easy and was not considered a grave misdeed' (*The Gospel according to St Matthew* pp.527f). This may oversimplify a more complex, and hotly debated, state of affairs, but it certainly seems that many Jews felt this way and were taught this.

No judge or court was involved. A man simply had to write out a bill of divorce in his own hand and in the presence of at least two witnesses, he had to date it, and it had to be delivered to his wife – though in certain circumstances throwing it at her in a fit of anger constituted a valid delivery! (*m. Git.* 9.4; 8.1).

In some instances divorce was positively encouraged. The second-century BC book Ecclesiasticus, which we quoted several times in the last chapter, partly confirms the teaching of Old Testament Wisdom in exalting faithfulness in marriage, but it introduces a wholly alien note when it (on occasion) advocates divorce. There is a hint of this already in Ecclesiasticus 7:19 'Do not deprive yourself of a wise and good wife, for her charm is worth more than gold.' The implication that it might be wise to get rid of a wife who is not 'wise or good' is made explicit only a few verses later: 'If you have a wife who pleases you, do not cast her out; but do not trust yourself to one whom you detest' (7:26). This must be the right text. The Hebrew version omits 'who pleases you' but it is almost required by the parallel phrase: 'one whom you detest'. Divorce is surely in mind here ('cast her out' in 26a is clearly a phrase for divorce, and 'do not trust yourself to [her]' is most naturally taken as a parallel phrase with identical meaning). The writer is encouraging divorce on the simple grounds that the husband no longer likes his wife.

This is also advised when the wife is not sufficiently subordinate: 'Allow no outlet to water, and no boldness of speech in an evil wife. If she does not go as you direct, separate her from yourself' (25:25f). This is a distinct development from the Old Testament where, despite the very realistic acknowledgment of unhappy and difficult marriages, divorce is never even hinted at, let alone openly suggested.

In the whole area of divorce there was gross inequality between the sexes. The husband had the right to divorce his wife, but the wife was not able to divorce her husband. She was able, in certain circumstances, to engineer a divorce, 'but even in such instances the divorce remained the husband's act' in the eyes of the law (Lane: *The Gospel of Mark* p.358).

What the wife was able to do was to get the courts to insist on a divorce. If major 'defects' appeared in the husband, he could be 'compelled' (by the court which was petitioned by

the wife) to put away his wife. 'And these are they that are
compelled to put away their wives: he that is afflicted with
boils, or that has a polypus, or that collects [dog's excrements],
or that is a coppersmith or a tanner, whether these defects
were in them before they married or whether they arose after
they married. And of all these Rabbi Meir said: Although the
husband made it a condition with her [to marry him despite
his defects] she may say: I thought that I could endure it, but
now I cannot endure it' (*m. Ketub.* 7.9f).

Another way in which a wife could have herself divorced was
by writing her own bill of divorce – in this case it was apparently
not necessary for her husband to write the whole bill – and
getting her husband to sign it (*m. Git.* 2.5) or 'compelling him
until he says: It is my will' (*m. Arak.* 5.6).

And as so often in history, women of royal blood or connections got their own way, whether by legitimate means or
illegitimate. Herodias deserted her husband Philip in order to
marry Herod Antipas: she simply sent Philip a letter of separation. And Josephus tells us that Herod the Great's sister Salome
sent her husband Costobar a bill of divorce, though Josephus
points out that this contravened Jewish law under which only a
husband could send a bill of divorce (*Ant.* 15.259f).

In the case of adultery, the husband was *obliged* to divorce the
wife. Death by stoning was no longer normally practised (despite
John 8:2–11) but divorce in this situation was mandatory. This
was also true under Roman law. In 18 BC Augustus passed the
Lex Iulia de Adulteriis which made adultery a crime punishable
by banishment; the husband was forbidden to forgive her or
quash the matter, and if he continued with the marriage, he
himself could face prosecution for condoning the adultery.

Nevertheless, there were factors, particularly financial, which
must have restrained over hasty divorce. When a man was betrothed to his wife, he pledged a sum of money to be given
to his wife (or her family) if he divorced her (*m. Ketub.* 4.2).
Jeremias tells what may have been a typical story: 'Rabbi Jose
the Galilean (before AD 135) had a bad wife but he could not
divorce her because the sum of money fixed by the marriage
contract was too high. So his pupils brought him the necessary
money.' (p.371).

What we find, then, is a marked declension from the teaching at least, and probably from the practice, of Old Testament times. Certainly there were various opinions within the Jewish world; as we shall see, not everyone encouraged divorce at the drop of a hat. Nevertheless, the *mechanics* of divorce were not at all complex and a woman could find herself divorced in an instant just because of a fit of temper. For her it was much more difficult. However, if she could show that her husband had one of the prescribed 'defects', she could compel him to divorce her. And the *right* to divorce (at least by the husband), given adequate grounds, was not in question.

## 2.  The grounds for divorce

So what were these grounds? We have already seen that the grounds on which a husband could be compelled to divorce his wife were laid down in detail (*m. Ketub.* 7, 9f). We have also seen that in the second century BC Ecclesiasticus was telling a husband to divorce his wife if he 'detested' her (7:26) or found her speaking out too much or insubordinate (25:25f).

But in Jesus' own day, this was a matter of hot dispute. The key biblical text was Deuteronomy 24:1–4, and particularly the different phrases in verse 1. This is how the Mishnah reports the debate: 'The school of Shammai say: A man may not divorce his wife unless he has found unchastity in her, for it is written: "Because he has found in her *indecency* in anything". And the school of Hillel say: [He may divorce her] even if she spoiled a dish for him, for it is written: "Because he has found in her indecency *in anything*". Rabbi Akiba says: Even if he found another fairer than she, for it is written: "And it shall be if she find no favour in his eyes"' (*m. Git.* 9.10).

Shammai, then, held the strictest view amongst the influential rabbis of Jesus' time. Stott interprets him as allowing divorce for 'a sexual offence of some kind which, though left undefined, fell short of adultery or promiscuity'. This interpretation stems from a belief that Shammai would still be advocating the death penalty in cases of adultery. But, as Stott himself says, 'the death sentence for adultery had fallen into desuetude' by the time of Jesus (cf Matt. 1:18f) (*Issues Facing Christians Today* pp.263, 268). In fact, it is quite probable that Shammai was teaching precisely that specific sexual unfaithfulness is the sole legitimate grounds for divorce. It seems that his later followers broadened out his position to include less serious sexual offences: 'going outside with hair unfastened, spinning cloth in the streets with armpits uncovered and bathing with the men' (*b. Git.* 90 a-b). Nevertheless the grounds were clearly confined even by Shammai's later followers to sexual immorality, and the Mishnah probably points to the fact that the earlier Shammaite view was more restricted: divorce was only permitted where there was sexual infidelity (the *porneia* of the Gospels).

The view is often stated that Hillel's view was dominant in Jesus' day. Jeremias points out that Philo (*De Spec. Leg.* 3.30) and Josephus (*Ant.* 4.253) only mention the Hillelite position on divorce, and he concludes: 'It appears that this must have been the prevailing view in the first half of the first century AD' (p. 370). But this is a precarious conclusion to draw from these two writers. This is especially so in the case of Josephus because he himself tells us that he divorced his own wife because he was 'not content with her nature' (*Vita* 426). So it is very understandable that he should want to champion the Hillelite position.

The 'test' question which the Pharisees put to Jesus ('Is it lawful to divorce one's wife for any and every reason?' – Matt. 19:3) strongly implies that the issue of legitimate grounds for divorce was a matter of debate in Jesus' day. This is precisely what we should expect when Rabbis Hillel and Shammai were giving such different teaching on a very important human subject.

## 3.   The right to remarry

Jewish teaching was both clear and succinct on the right to remarry: 'The essential formula in the bill of divorce is: Lo, thou art free to marry any man' (*m. Git.* 9.3). This, then, is what a bill of divorce achieved. Certainly it dissolved the marriage; but just as importantly, it set the woman free to remarry. Women had never been allowed, in the Israelite world, to take more than one husband. If, then, she did not have written proof that her first marriage had been dissolved, she might be under suspicion of bigamy if she married again. Her bill of divorce was irrefutable evidence that her husband had divorced her; she was not only free to remarry, it was expected that she would. By extension, the man, in an age when polygamy was (except in very rare circumstances) no longer practised, was also free to remarry.

While this right to remarry after divorce was clearly normal in first-century Judaism, it may not have been held by all. In particular, the Qumran community may have forbidden remarriage during the lifetime of a divorced partner. The crucial text is CD 4.21ff: 'The "builders of the wall" (Ezek. 13:10) who have followed after "Precept" . . . shall be caught in fornication twice by taking a second wife while the first is alive, whereas the principle of creation is: "Male and female he created them" (Gen. 1:27). Also, those who entered the ark went in two by two. And concerning the prince it is written: "He shall not multiply wives to himself" (Deut. 17:17).'

Scholarly opinion is divided on the meaning of this passage. M. R. Lehmann maintains that 'bigamy is referred to only'. P. Brown (p.40) more hesitantly suggests the same. But this would have been a highly theoretical prohibition in a world from which polygamy had effectively died out. More likely, then, is Carson's view: 'Among the Qumran covenanters, remarriage [he writes "divorce" but must mean "remarriage" as this is the point at issue in CD 4.21] was judged illicit under all circumstances' (*Matthew*, p.411).

Of considerable interest, also, is the quotation of Genesis 1:27 to back up the prohibition of remarriage (or bigamy), since of course Jesus uses precisely the same passage in his teaching on divorce and remarriage (Mark 10:6//Matt. 19:4).

## 4.   Summary

This is the Jewish background against which Jesus taught and against which his teaching must be seen. There is no evidence that the Jews of Jesus' day questioned the right to divorce. They interpreted Malachi 2:16 as only applicable to the Gentiles to whom God had not given the Law (Guelich: *The Sermon on the Mount* p.203).

They did, however, hotly debate the legitimate grounds for divorce. Shammai and his followers taught that only sexual immorality justified divorce while Hillel and his school were prepared to allow divorce on almost any ground – for example, that the wife had an unsightly mole (*b. Ketub.* 75a).

Almost all Jewish teachers accepted that divorce conferred on both parties the right to remarry, and indeed that the legal document was specifically designed to set the wife free to remarry. It may be, however, that the Qumran community differed from other Jews in this and taught that only death, not divorce, gave the right to remarriage.

## Divorce and Remarriage in Mark

Most scholars still hold that Mark is the earliest gospel, and it is therefore to Mark that we turn first as we begin to examine Jesus' recorded teaching. There is just one passage in Mark's gospel where Jesus refers to divorce and remarriage, but it is a passage where Jesus discusses the issues in some detail:

(1) Jesus then left that place and went into the region of Judea and across the Jordan. Again crowds of people came to him, and as was his custom, he taught them. (2) Some Pharisees came and tested him by asking: "Is it lawful for a man to divorce his wife?" (3) "What did Moses command you?" he replied. (4) They said: "Moses permitted a man to write a certificate of divorce and send her away." (5) "It was because your hearts were hard that Moses wrote you this law," Jesus replied. (6) "But at the beginning of creation God 'made them male and female'. (7) 'For this reason a man will leave his father and mother and be united to his wife, (8) and the two will become one flesh'. So they are no longer two, but one. (9) Therefore what God has joined together, let man not separate." (10) When they were in the house again, the disciples asked Jesus about this. (11) He answered: "Anyone who divorces his wife and marries another woman commits adultery against her. (12) And if she divorces her husband and marries another man, she commits adultery." (Mark 10).

## 1.  The place (verse 1)

Lane describes the journey Jesus took in this way: 'From Capernaum (9:33) Jesus came into Southern Palestine. The order in which the territories are listed (Judea and Perea [NIV: 'across the Jordan']) suggests that he went across the mountains of Samaria into Judea, following the ordinary route for pilgrims on their way to the Holy City (cf Luke 9:51–53). At some point, he crossed over the Jordan into Perea which was part of the territory of Herod Antipas.'

He was therefore on very dangerous territory to have questions put to him about divorce. Antipas had divorced his wife who was a daughter of the King of Petra. He had remarried Herodias who, as we have already noted, had divorced her first husband Philip. Or rather, because divorce by a woman was, strictly, not possible, it would perhaps be more accurate to say that she had deserted him. The Western text of verse 12 reads: 'And if she *leaves* her husband and marries another'. Some scholars believe this is the original text ('divorce' being later substituted for 'leaves' to make verse 12 more parallel with verse 11 and/or to bring it into line with what Roman law, by which women could divorce their husbands, allowed); if so, it may have been a deliberate reference to what Herodias had done.

## 2.  The question (verse 2)

Mark explicitly tells us that in asking: 'Is it lawful for a man to divorce his wife?' the Pharisees were 'testing' him (2). They were not interested in what he thought, they were only out to trap him.

What were they hoping for? One obvious explanation is that Jesus would say something that opposed divorce or remarriage and so would fall foul of Herod. It was precisely over the question of Herod's marriage to Herodias that John the Baptist had got into trouble, been arrested and finally been decapitated. Mark tells us that the Pharisees were in league with the Herodians against Jesus (3:6; 12:13), so it may well be that they were setting a deliberate trap, that they would ensure that his answer was quickly reported to Herod and that they were hoping it would lead to his death.

An alternative explanation is that they hoped Jesus would lose his popular following. 'Crowds of people' (1) had gathered round him; doubtless many of them held the Hillelite position and were committed – some in their own personal lives – to the idea of relatively easy divorce, and they would turn against a teacher who had strict views on the subject of divorce or remarriage.

A third possible explanation, suggested by Cranfield, is simply that they hoped Jesus would contradict the Mosaic Law. Moses allowed divorce (4, cf Deut. 24:1–4) and if Jesus said that divorce was not permissible they could pounce on this as teaching contrary to the Law (cf Acts 21:28).

Any of these three explanations – or any combination of them – is possible. What all have in common is this: it must have been known (or at least strongly suspected) that Jesus had strict views on the subject of divorce. That is why the Pharisees picked on this subject to 'test' Jesus. Apparently his rigorist teaching was known not only among his immediate, intimate circle, but among the wider public as well – or, at least, among his enemies who had taken pains to discover what his vulnerable points were.

## 3.   The counterquestion (verses 3f)

In a way that is typical of his teaching style, Jesus replies not with his answer but with a question: 'What did Moses command you?' (3). It would be interesting to know what answer Jesus was expecting. Perhaps he was hoping that they would quote to him Genesis 1f since this, rather than Deuteronomy 24, was clearly what was in his own mind (6–9).

It is, however, possible that he was expecting them to respond with Deuteronomy 24. If so, he is simply asking: 'What was the Mosaic legislation on this question?' (Murray p.44). As Gundry points out, Jesus would then be acknowledging that Moses gave a law *about* divorce, not that he *commanded* divorce or mandated divorce in certain circumstances (*Matthew* p.380).

In any case, the Pharisees respond in terms of Deuteronomy 24 – the passage which Hillel and Shammai used in the debate

– and rightly say that Moses 'permitted' divorce (4). This is really the most you can say from Deuteronomy. Moses does not approve of the practice of divorce, nor does he condemn it. He merely mentions it in passing, and from the fact that he does not condemn it, it can be assumed that he 'permits' it.

Schweizer thinks Mark sees more significance in the change of word. Jesus is concerned with God's will and therefore uses both the verb and the noun for 'command' (3, 5. NIV in 5: 'law'). The Pharisees sought 'the greatest possible advantage for [themselves] within the limits of what is permissible' and hence used the word 'permitted' (4). This is perhaps correct, but it seems to me that it is Matthew, rather than Mark, for whom the change of verbs is significant (Matt. 19:7f; see the discussion on this below).

### 4. The moral obligation not to divorce (verses 5–9)

Jesus replies by explaining why the Mosaic legislation of Deuteronomy 24 was given. It was 'because your hearts were hard' (5), literally 'for your hardness of heart'. 'Hardness of heart', a single word in Greek (*sklērokardia*), is used in the Old Testament of Israel's sinful stubbornness (e.g. LXX of Deut. 10:16; Jer. 4:4) and means 'wilful obstinacy against the will of God' (Atkinson p.111). This in turn implies that they knew the will of God, that there is 'some law or obligation that is [being] violated' which must be a reference to Genesis 1f. 'The very judgment respecting hard-heartedness . . . [shows that] the original institution and its binding authority had not been abrogated' (Murray p.31).

So, in his comment on the Mosaic law, Jesus is already drawing a distinction between the 'absolute will of God and those provisions which take account of men's actual sinfulness and are designed to limit and control its consequences' (Cranfield). God's absolute will is expressed in Genesis 1f which Jesus will go on to quote (6–8) and which lead to the conclusion that it is wrong to divorce (9). This will of God for marriage has never been modified or abrogated. However, since men do not live up to the will of God, a law is introduced which does not commend divorce or say that it has now become the will of God under some circumstances, but which regulates it. The law of Deuteronomy 24 deals with 'situations brought about by man's *sklērokardia* and protect[s] from its worst effects those who would suffer as a result of it' (Cranfield). 'Since they persist in falling short . . . Let it at least be within limits' (McNeile: *The Gospel according to St Matthew* p.273).

Is it possible to take this approach today, and to say that, while divorce may never be the absolute will of God, yet it may be the lesser of two evils? That, therefore, divorce could be permitted not only in the case of adultery (cf Matt. 5:32, 19:9) and perhaps some other gross sins such as physical brutality (see the discussion below), but also in any case where it would seem on the surface to be the lesser of two evils: for example, if one or both partners were desperately unhappy in the marriage, or simply bored with each other?

This seems to have been the line taken by some in the early third century in relation to remarriage, and Origen, commenting on the practice, only partially condemns it: 'Already, *contrary to Scripture,* certain church leaders have permitted remarriage of a woman while her husband was alive. They did it *despite what is written*: "A wife is bound to her husband as long as he lives" [1 Cor. 7:39] and: "She will be called an adulteress if she lives with another man while her husband is alive" [Rom. 7:3]. However, they have not acted entirely without reason. Probably this condescension has been permitted out of comparison with greater ills, *contrary to the primitive law reported in the Scriptures' (Comm. in Matt.* 14.23).

This is a very understandable pastoral approach and often stems from the highest motives, as Origen recognised. However, he also pointed out no less than three times that this approach contravened the teaching of the New Testament (see the three phrases that I have underlined). He cannot therefore ultimately approve the practice. And this is not only the case with remarriage (the point at issue for Origen) but also with divorce. Jesus explains the Mosaic 'permission' as a legal enactment to contain the worst effects of Israel's 'hardness of heart' but he then goes on to abrogate the permission.

Murray, in his discussion of the Matthean sentence ('Moses permitted you . . . But it was not this way from the beginning'

Matt. 19:8) says: 'From the beginning there was no such *permission*. It is not simply that the practice was not commanded, not simply that it was not authorised, not simply that it was not approved, but rather that it was not even *permitted*' (p.32, Murray's emphases). And Lane, commenting on Mark 10:5, says: 'The force of [Jesus'] pronouncement here and in the following verses is to obliterate the Mosaic tolerance.'

Jesus' followers, then, may no longer rely on the Mosaic permission and so divorce their wives at will or even in line with the Mosaic conditions; Jesus now says that God's will, as expressed at creation, must prevail – not only as an ideal but in the practicalities of life.

To make this point, Jesus first appeals to Genesis 1:27 (verse 6). He appeals over the head of Moses to the creation pattern ('at [literally: from] the beginning of creation') when God 'made them male and female'. The context of Genesis 1:27 already makes it clear that this was with a view to marriage and we have already seen that the Qumran community drew the conclusion from this text that God forbade remarriage during the lifetime of a partner (or bigamy, CD 4:21ff).

Jesus also makes it clear that the differentiation of the sexes was with a permanent marriage relationship in mind, by instantly going on to quote Genesis 2:24 (verses 7–8a). Because God created the human race male and female ('for this reason', the reason being identical whether it refers back to the quotation in verse 6 of Genesis 1:27 or to Genesis 2:23), a man leaves his parents and his old family, cleaves to his wife and becomes one flesh with her.

Jesus now adds his own conclusion: 'So they are no longer two, but one' (8), literally: one flesh. As we have seen in a previous chapter, the fundamental reality about them is no longer their separate identity – indeed their separateness at the most basic level is denied ('no longer two') – but their unity. Moreover, it is God who has made this unity: 'God has joined [literally: yoked] them together' (9). We have already quoted Bonnard as saying that the idea of a marriage bond is not what makes Christ's teaching unique; on the contrary, it was a widespread concept already in antiquity. What is new is the assertion that the partners within this marriage bond 'must be considered as

united by God; this is the originality of the Gospels' thought'
(*L'Évangile selon S. Matthieu*, p.282).

And then at last Christ answers the Pharisees' original question about divorce. He has refused to do so until they have
understood God's will for marriage; this must come first, and
without it Christian teaching about divorce is incomprehensible.
But having explained the creation ordinance of marriage and
the bond which God himself makes between marriage partners,
Jesus can now give his verdict about divorce: 'Therefore [in the
light of Genesis 1:27 and 2:24 and the fact that the partners
are now one flesh] what God has joined together, let man not
separate' (9). No person – whether either marriage partner or
a third party – is to break apart what God has himself united.

It is important to see what Jesus is saying here. He is not merely
saying that when two people have been bonded together, it will
be difficult, and cause psychological damage, to pull them apart.
He is saying that God himself got involved: God has joined them
together, and therefore to pull them apart is to go against the
express purposes of God. Carson explains this well: 'If God has
joined them together . . . divorce is not only "unnatural' but
rebellion against God' (*Matthew* p.412).

Yet Jesus has not (yet) said that husband and wife *cannot* be
separated, that this is an impossibility. He has only said that they
*must not* be separated. He has spoken only of the moral obligation
not to divorce and stated that it would be a sin against God to
divorce one's partner or to cause the break-up of a marriage. In
the next verses, however, he goes considerably further.

## 5.  The impossibility of any true divorce or remarriage (verses 10–12)

The narrative of Mark now brings them 'into the house again'
where the disciples 'ask Jesus' about what he has just said
(10). This sequence appears on other occasions in Mark and
often leads on to deeper teaching from Jesus or indeed the
punchline which drives home all he has been trying to say
(cf 7:17–23; 9:28f, cp 9:33–37).

In this private teaching, in answer to their questions (10), the
focus now moves from divorce (2–9) to remarriage (11f). He has

said that divorce is wrong because it is separating what God has made one flesh (6–9). He now says that remarriage is wrong because it is adulterous: a man who remarries after divorce commits adultery (11) and in the same way a woman who remarries after divorcing her husband commits adultery (12).

To commit adultery (*moichaomai*) is to have sexual relations when you (or your sexual partner) are married. Where neither partner is married, it is not adultery but fornication which takes place (*porneia*, a general word for sexual sin, but used specifically for fornication when contrasted with adultery). Since Jesus specifically calls remarriage after legal divorce 'adultery', he is saying that whatever has taken place legally in divorce, the partners are still married. This means that remarriage is not only wrong, it is impossible at the deepest level. Jesus makes the astonishing statement – astonishing in his own day and just as amazing in our own – that it is not actually possible to marry again during the lifetime of a divorced partner; it is only possible to commit adultery with a third party, even though from a legal point of view this new 'marriage' has been properly entered into.

Jesus' teaching also means that divorce – at least in the sense in which the Pharisees thought of it – is not only wrong (9) but is impossible. Again, it is of course perfectly possible to secure a divorce that is valid from the legal point of view. But it is not possible to undo what God has done. God has joined a man and his wife together (9). He has created a marriage 'yoke' (9) or unity (8) or bond (1 Cor. 7:39). Since, even after divorce, to marry someone else is to commit adultery (11, 12), clearly this marriage bond still remains, even after legal divorce. Therefore full divorce – in the sense of the 'dissolution' or elimination of the marriage bond – is not something which any legal process is capable of achieving. Only death dissolves the bond (Rom. 7:3; 1 Cor. 7:39).

It is sometimes said that because most Jews of Jesus' day clearly believed that legal divorce conferred the right to remarry, Jesus would have had to make it very clear if he meant to say that legal divorce was permissible under certain circumstances (Matt. 5:32; 19:9) but that it did not destroy the marriage bond and that therefore remarriage was out of the question. This is a valid point, but it is precisely what Jesus did do in calling remarriage 'adultery'. This was the consistent way in which Jesus spoke about remarriage after divorce (cf Luke 16:18; Matt. 5:27–32; 19:9) and shows clearly that he taught that contemporary Jewish thinking was wrong: 'full' divorce – in the sense of destroying the marriage bond and opening the way for remarriage – is impossible. God has joined man and wife together, and this joining not only must not be undone (9); it cannot be undone (11f).

## 6.  The wife (verses 11f)

This was of course utterly revolutionary teaching. But there was further revolutionary teaching on the position of the wife.

Jesus taught that a man who divorced his wife and remarried committed adultery 'against her' i.e. his first wife (11). Jewish law did not recognise any such possibility. A woman could commit adultery against her husband by having an extra-marital affair. A man could commit adultery against another man by having an affair with that other man's wife. But if the woman was unmarried, then the sin of the man was merely fornication (since intercourse is only permitted within marriage) and not adultery (since the woman was not married). It was not possible, under Jewish law, for a man to commit adultery against his own wife.

Yet this is precisely what Jesus affirms. A wife, according to Jesus, has just as great a right to fidelity as a husband. It is just as much adultery against her if he has an affair as it is adultery against him if she has an affair. Or to state more accurately what Jesus says: If the man remarries having divorced his wife, this is an offence against her and specifically the sin of adultery (11). She is just as much sinned against in this case as he would be if she remarried after divorcing him (12).

And here is the second extraordinary feature. Mark, uniquely among the Gospels, records Jesus not only forbidding the man to divorce and remarry (11) but forbidding the wife the same thing (12). St Paul also states that Jesus told wives not to divorce their husbands (1 Cor. 7:10). This was impossible under Jewish law, according to which – as we have seen – a wife could sue the courts for divorce but could not directly divorce her husband.

Some scholars think, therefore, that this is an anachronistic adaptation of Jesus' teaching by the early Church: he, speaking within a Jewish culture, spoke only against divorce and remarriage by the man (11); they added a parallel saying about the woman (12) when Christianity had spread into the Gentile world.

This conclusion is, however, not necessary. It is perfectly possible that this is a dig at Herodias who, as we have seen, abandoned her husband and married Antipas. This would be even more likely if the Western text of verse 12 is the correct one: 'And if she *leaves* her husband and marries another, she commits adultery' (see the discussion above).

Equally possible is that Jesus was deliberately making reference to a custom in the Roman world. He is speaking of a creation ordinance (6–9) which applies equally to all mankind. The disciples would have been clearly aware of what went on in the outside world and Jesus might well have been alluding to that world. Moreover, it would not be long before he was sending them into that world. 'In his private instruction to the Apostles [10–12] . . . the Lord completed his teaching by a reference to the practice of the pagan and Hellenized circles which must have been already familiar to the twelve and with which they would shortly be called to deal' (Swete).

## 7.  Summary

We have seen that it was apparently well known that Jesus had strict views on divorce. This is why the Pharisees picked this issue with which to 'test' Jesus (2). He, for his part, refused to discuss the issue of divorce without first explaining the Scriptural teaching about marriage. This he took from God's creation ordinance (6a) explained in Genesis 1f. He quoted Genesis 1:27 and 2:24 and then summed up this teaching in two statements of his own: man and wife are essentially a unity after being married (8) and God joins them inextricably together (9). It is not merely wrong, therefore, to prise them apart (9); it is impossible. Divorce cannot break the unity or dissolve the bond, and the proof of this is that any legal remarriage is in fact adultery (11f). The man has no more freedom in this than the woman: he too commits adultery against his divorced wife if he marries another woman (11). And even though Roman law allows a woman to divorce, it too cannot break her oneness with her husband, so that in her case also remarriage would be adultery (12).

## Divorce and Remarriage in Luke

Luke does not record the discussion with the Pharisees in Perea; instead, he gives us an isolated saying which is not given its context in Christ's ministry nor found within a dialogue.

> Anyone who divorces his wife and marries another woman commits adultery, and the man who marries a divorced woman commits adultery (Luke 16:18).

With a number of slight changes in vocabulary and syntax, 18a is identical in content to Mark 10:11. It may be that this is Luke's account of the saying that was the climax of the discussion initiated by the Pharisees (Mark 10:2–12) and an echo of that may be that the last interlocutors whom Luke has mentioned are precisely the Pharisees (14). But we have shown that Jesus' strict views on divorce must have been already known to his opponents, and it may be that Luke records an earlier saying on the subject.

In any case, both parts of the saying are principally concerned with remarriage. They do of course incidentally speak about divorce but the focus is on remarriage which is again twice described as adultery. The first part of the saying says what we have already seen in Mark: legal divorce cannot break the marriage bond because (and this is Christ's point) remarriage after divorce is in fact adultery.

The second part of the saying adds a complementary, but quite new, point: it is also adultery for a single man to marry a divorced woman (18b). The whole saying is addressed to the man. Jesus says: it is wrong to marry another woman after divorcing your wife (18a); it is just as wrong to marry (for the first time) a woman who has been divorced (18b).

Why? Exactly the same Greek word (*moicheuei*) and exactly the same reason is given in both cases: it is adultery. In other words, the divorced woman's first marriage still exists despite the legal divorce and therefore true remarriage is actually impossible in reality, and in God's eyes (as opposed to those of the law of the land), it can only be adultery.

## Divorce and Remarriage in Matthew

Matthew records two passages in which Jesus gives teaching about divorce. One is his equivalent of Mark 10:1–12; there are some significant differences from Mark, and the Matthean parallel therefore needs to be studied in detail. The other passage is unique to Matthew and comes within the Sermon on the Mount:

> (27) You have heard that it was said: "Do not commit adultery". (28) But I tell you that anyone who looks at a woman lustfully has already committed adultery with her in his heart. (29) If your right eye causes you to sin, gouge it out and throw it away. It is better for you to lose one part of your body than for your whole body to be thrown into hell. (30) And if your right hand causes you to sin, cut it off and throw it away. It is better for you to lose one part of your body than for your whole body to go into hell.
>
> (31) It has been said, "Anyone who divorces his wife must give her a certificate of divorce." (32) But I tell you that anyone who divorces his wife, except for marital unfaithfulness, causes her to commit adultery, and anyone who marries a divorced woman commits adultery (Matt. 5).

### 1.   The context

After the Beatitudes (1–12) and the sayings about salt and light (13–16), a new section begins at 17. Jesus rebuts an accusation that he has come to abolish the Law (17a); on the contrary, he upholds and fulfils the Law (17a–17b). He insists not only that his followers must practise and teach the Law (19) but that they must go further in their practice than the scribes and the Pharisees (20).

In the rest of the chapter, he works out in detail some specific examples of this general teaching. In a number of similar sections he either quotes the Law and goes on to bring out the range and depth of its implications or he quotes a Pharisaic distortion of the Law and goes on to correct it. It is a characteristic of these sections that the quotation from the Law or from the Pharisees is introduced by: 'You have heard that it was said' (*Ēkousate hoti errethē*: 21, 27, 33, 38, 43). The first two words are omitted in 31: *Errethē de*, and Jesus' authoritative teaching is introduced by: 'But I tell you' (*Egō de legō hymin*: 22, 28, 32, 34, 39, 44).

Jesus begins his specific examples with the sixth commandment (21) and corrects the misunderstanding that this law only has in mind the act of murder. On the contrary, anger and insulting words fall just as much under God's judgment (22). Jesus not only draws out this more far-reaching implication of the sixth commandment, but also goes on to say what to do if you have already broken God's law in this area (23–26).

Now in the second section of specific examples, Jesus turns to the seventh commandment (27). This time he corrects two misunderstandings. The first misunderstanding is very like that dealt with in 21–26. It is not just the sexual act which the law has in mind. On the contrary, it is just as concerned to prohibit the deliberately lustful look at a woman. This may not be the outward act of adultery; but inwardly, in a man's thoughts and his fantasy ('in his heart'), he has already approached her sexually and committed adultery (28). Again, Jesus goes on to say what to do if you have already broken God's law in this area and know the ways in which you habitually are 'caused to sin' (29f).

Then Jesus corrects a second misunderstanding in the same area of sexual morality. He introduces this by the shortened phrase: *Errethē de* (31); this is a sub-section of the discussion of the seventh commandment (27–32). This time he quotes not Scripture itself, but what the Pharisees were teaching, what they thought the Scripture taught: 'Anyone who divorces his wife must give her a certificate of divorce.' This is, of course, a reference to Deuteronomy 24, but it is neither a direct quote from Deuteronomy 24 (compare 27 which directly quotes Exod. 20:14), nor is it the teaching of Deuteronomy 24 at all. This would be legislation *enabling* divorce, stipulating how divorce should take place, which is precisely what the Deuteronomic law was not. As we have seen, there is no law that enacts for divorce in the entire Pentateuch and Deuteronomy 24 is actually a law restricting the right to remarry.

However, Jewish rabbinical discussion saw Deuteronomy 24 as legislating for divorce and merely debated the grounds that 24:1-4 allowed. Jesus corrects this misunderstanding. By bringing his teaching on divorce and remarriage into relation with the command against adultery (27), he reveals that God's law is both much more profound than the Pharisees thought, and much more morally demanding.

## 2.   The first statement (verse 32a)

His own teaching is introduced, as normal, by the phrase: 'But I tell you' (32). As in all the occurrences of this phrase in chapter 5, the 'I' is emphatic (*Egō de*). This is the authoritative teaching which Jesus gave and which set him apart from the Jewish teachers (7:28f).

Jesus' saying in 32 essentially falls into two statements. The first is: 'Anyone who divorces his wife . . . causes her to become an adulteress.' At this stage, we will defer discussion of the exception clause ('except for marital unfaithfulness') mainly because it is clearly an aside, not the main point of Jesus' saying, and it is very easy to miss the main point because so much attention is focused on the exception; but also because the exception *is* very important – particularly in the context of late twentieth-century debate – and merits careful consideration on its own.

The first words of this first statement of Christ's are identical to Luke 16:18a (*Pas ho apolyōn tēn gynaika autou*: everyone who divorces his wife). The end of the statement, however, is quite different. Luke has: 'and marries another woman commits adultery'. Jesus, in Matthew 5, does not mention any remarriage on the part of the man; he mentions instead the divorced woman's remarriage, but he does not use marriage terminology. Instead he describes it as what it is, according to Jesus, in God's eyes: adultery. The divorcing husband 'causes [his wife] to commit adultery' (32).

The verb for 'commit adultery' (*moicheuthēnai*) is in the passive. Lenski has tried to maintain that this means: 'makes her be stigmatised as an adulteress' (when she is really not one), but this suggestion has received almost no support because passive verbs are simply not used in this way: 'The idea of merely subjective judgment on the part of others is not inherent in the passive' (Murray p.24). Rather, as Arndt and Gingrich point out, the active (*moicheuō*) is used with a direct object to mean 'commit adultery with' (e.g. in 28). This explains the passive in 32: 'makes her to have adultery committed with her'. It is her new husband who is primarily thought of as the one committing adultery: 'it may be that in the act of adultery, the woman is considered as more passive than the man' (Murray p.22).

The assumption is that, after being divorced, she will remarry. It is untrue to say that it was impossible for an adult woman to return to a single life (cf Luke 2:36f), but it was certainly difficult. Indeed, as we saw in chapter 3, singleness was generally frowned upon within Judaism. So it was a safe assumption that, unless convinced that she was doing the wrong thing, a divorced woman would remarry.

Some have argued from this that Jesus believed it was all right for her to remarry; since he assumes it, he must approve it or at least be indifferent to it. But on the contrary, he calls it adultery, and adultery against the very man who divorced her. It might be assumed that she could not sin against him since he had done her the wrong of divorcing her in the first place (as we shall see, Jesus puts the blame squarely on the shoulders of the divorcing husband). But this assumption proves quite false. It is indeed true that he wronged her by divorcing her. But now she and her new husband wrong him by remarrying. It is again the understanding of marriage, divorce and remarriage that we have found consistently in Jesus' teaching: 'If her remarriage is considered to be adultery, the implications are clear. The bill of divorce does not dissolve the first marriage . . . The original couple are still married in spite of a "legal" bill of divorce' (Guelich). 'If the woman commits adultery by remarriage, this is so because she is still in reality the wife of the divorcing husband' (Murray p.25).

But the guilt for the sin is her (first) husband's. He 'causes her' to commit adultery; he drives her to it. Admittedly, she should not get remarried, but the greater sin – though it does not excuse her action or make the remarriage all right – is her husband's for divorcing her in the first place. 'This view stands without parallel in Judaism' (Guelich).

The teaching of this first statement (without the exception) is well summed up by two commentators: 'The sin of remarriage on the part of the divorced woman is not by any means minimised . . . It is the sin of adultery that Jesus is condemning in the whole of this sub-section [27–32] of his discourse . . . What he says of the husband who divorced the woman is that he is sinfully involved in [or rather: primarily responsible for] this moral tragedy' (Murray pp.24f). 'The divorced woman . . . commits adultery by remarrying, and her first husband ought to prevent it by not freeing her and giving her economic reason to marry another man . . . Throughout, it is assumed that a second marriage is adulterous' (Gundry).

## 3.  The exception (verse 32a)

There is no question that the main thrust of Jesus' point lies in his statement without the exception, and not in the exception clause; he is talking about situations where there *is* adultery (27, 28, 32a, 32b) and his emphasis in 32a is on remarriage after (wrongful) divorce. The exception is an aside. Nevertheless, it is there, and we must of course explore what it contributes to Jesus' teaching.

The phrase 'except for marital unfaithfulness' (*parektos logou porneias*; literally: apart from the thing (or: matter) of immorality) is a quotation from Deuteronomy 24:1. There are two differences, however. Deuteronomy speaks of 'nakedness of a thing' as the grounds on which a man had divorced his wife; Matthew transposes the word order to: 'the thing of immorality'. This transposition of the word order was also followed by the school of Shammai. The Mishnah quotes them as speaking of *d<sup>e</sup>bar 'erwâh* ('a thing of nakedness') rather than *'erwat dābār* ('nakedness of a thing') (*m. Git.* 9.10). Almost certainly, then, Jesus is represented as quoting Deuteronomy 24:1, using the word order that Shammai's followers were using in the contemporary debate.

And instead of the word for 'nakedness', Jesus uses the word *porneia* (LXX here has *aschēmon pragma*). What does it mean?

It is a broad and general word used for sexual immorality. Arndt and Gingrich define it as: 'prostitution, unchastity, fornication, of every kind of unlawful sexual intercourse'. Some scholars have tried to make out that it refers, here, to incest and therefore that Jesus did not allow divorce on any grounds where there had been a valid marriage; he was merely saying that where a marriage had been legally contracted with a near relative (Romans had less strict 'tables of affinity' than Jews) it was incestuous, and therefore null in God's eyes, and therefore should be legally dissolved. This would not be a divorce in God's eyes since the marriage, being with a relative within the forbidden degrees, was invalid in the first place.

We have said already that *porneia* is a broad word and can take on more specific meanings (such as 'prostitution' and 'fornication') where the context demands it. In this way, it can indeed take on the meaning of an incestuous relationship or unlawful marriage. It has that meaning in 1 Corinthians 5:1; it may have that meaning in Acts 15:20, 29; 21:25, where the four things which Gentile converts were to abstain from, in order not to offend their Jewish fellow-Christians, are (it is argued) all to do with ceremonial purity and all come from Leviticus 17 and 18. If this is correct, *porneia* in the Jerusalem decree in Acts 15 and 21 means intercourse or marriage with close relatives (cf Lev. 18:6–18).

However, this is by no means the normal meaning of *porneia* and it should only be translated in that way where the context demands it. There is no such demand, or even suggestion, in the context of Matthew 5 or 19, and therefore we must give it its normal meaning of illicit sexual intercourse. Obviously adultery is principally in mind but Heth and Wenham are right to say that here it probably also includes incest, homosexuality and bestiality – those sexual sins punishable by death in Leviticus 18 and 20 (p.137). It is probably for this reason that the more general word *porneia* is used in preference to the more specific *moicheia* (adultery). Gundry also suggests that the general word is used 'because a general expression ['nakedness of a thing'] occurs in Deuteronomy'.

The question obviously arises: why is this exception clause here (and in a slightly different form in Matthew 19:9) and not in Mark or Luke? It has often been suggested that Matthew thought Jesus' teaching (which, according to this hypothesis, was: no divorce under any circumstances) was too hard and so softened it, allowing divorce in the case of marital infidelity. This solution to the problem is in fact unlikely in the extreme, given the uncompromising nature of Jesus' moral teaching throughout the gospel of Matthew, not least in the Sermon on the Mount. 'There is no tendency in Matthew . . . to relax requirements of the law . . . The argument that the Matthean church, faced with hard cases, here resorted to a casuistry is without parallel elsewhere in the Gospel' (Atkinson p.130).

A more likely explanation is that, as we have seen, both Jewish and Roman law *demanded* divorce in the case of adultery; a Christian would therefore be breaking the law if he did not divorce an adulterous wife. Divorce in these circumstances was also mandatory in at least some circles within the early church. Hermas (writing some time between AD 90 and 150; the date is disputed) wrote:

'If the husband knows of [an adulterous wife's] sin and and his wife does not repent but persists in her immorality (*porneia*) and the husband continues to live with her, then he becomes guilty of her sin and a partner in her adultery.' 'What then,' I said, 'sir, shall the husband do if his wife persists in this passion?' 'Let him divorce her,' he said, 'and let the husband remain single' (*Mandate*, 4.1.5f).

It is argued then that, given the current legal situation, it was simply assumed by Jesus (in his teaching recorded in Mark and Luke) that divorce would take place – or at least was permissible – in the case of adultery (cf also Jer. 3:8); and either Jesus himself or Matthew brought out what everybody knew already.

Of particular interest here is the exception clause in Matthew 19. The passage in the Sermon on the Mount (Matt. 5:27–32) is not exactly paralleled in the other Gospels and therefore it is quite possible that Jesus brought out the exception (based on well-known Jewish and Roman law) on this occasion while not having mentioned it at other times. But Matthew 19 records the same incident as Mark 10; Matthew has Jesus mention the exception (19:9); Mark does not (10:11).

Did Jesus himself say it or not? The interesting fact is that if Jesus did mention it, then Mark's sources remember the saying without the exception clause, thus showing yet again that the main thrust of Jesus' teaching, and what stuck in his disciples' minds, was not the exception but the forbidding of divorce and of remarriage.

And yet Jesus was certainly not one simply to toe the line of current rabbinic or Roman law, and his approach was different from that of society around him. Jewish and Roman law said that a husband *must* divorce his wife for adultery (cf Matt. 1:18f). We should not assume that Jesus taught the same. In Matthew 19, the Pharisees ask: 'Why then did Moses *command* that a man give his wife a certificate of divorce and send her away?' (7). Jesus, it seems, deliberately changes the verb: 'Moses *permitted* you to divorce your wives . . .' (8). Again, in the story of the woman taken in adultery, Jesus' verdict is reported as simply being: 'Neither do I condemn you. Go now and leave your life of sin' (John 8:11). So it seems that Jesus differed from the Jewish legal authorities in that while they said that husbands *must* divorce adulterous wives; he merely said that they *may* do so. The reason for Matthew's exception is to exculpate the husband – given the current legal situation – from sin when he divorces his wife for adultery. But this is not Jesus' ideal, which is: it is better still not to divorce even when there is adultery (so Mark and Luke) (cf Heth and Wenham pp.123–6).

What this means in practice is that adultery should not be jumped on too quickly by the offended partner as the foolproof and complete justification for initiating divorce proceedings today. Schweizer adds a pastoral note: 'The very infidelity of one of the parties can, for example, bring about a crisis in which both may communicate with one another and thus find the way back together.' If the offended partner reaches too quickly for a divorce, he 'would then be missing the chance, given him by God, of recognising the failure on his part that has driven his partner to infidelity and miss the chance of doing something about it'.

So, for Jesus, divorce in the case of adultery is not mandatory, but it is – according to Matthew 5 and 19 – allowed.

Is Jesus then reinstating the Mosaic permission to divorce which Jesus himself abrogated (Mark 10:4–9)? This cannot be the case because Matthew 19, which includes the exception clause (9), also shows Jesus clearly abrogating the Mosaic permission (7–9). Jesus' teaching is in fact very different from that of Deuteronomy. On the one hand he relaxes the penalty for adultery (already Jewish law had made divorce the penalty rather than death (cf Deut. 22:22); Jesus further relaxes the penalty in saying that even divorce is not mandatory); on the other hand he stiffens the grounds for divorce. He allows it only for *porneia*, i.e. illicit sexual intercourse. The Pentateuch makes this punishable by death (Deut. 22:22; Lev. 20:13, 15f) and therefore Deuteronomy's 'nakedness of a thing' (24:1) must have been some lesser sexual indecency. This lesser sin is no longer sufficient grounds, in Jesus' eyes, for divorce.

However, we must come back to the point that the exception clause is very much an aside in 32a: an important exception to the rule of no divorce under any circumstances, but no more than that. 'What is of paramount importance is that . . . it is not the exception clause that bears the weight of the emphasis in the text. It is rather that the husband may not put away *for any other cause* . . . Preoccupation with the one exception should never be permitted to obscure the force of the negation of all others' (Murray p.21. Murray's emphasis).

For this reason it is impossible to draw any conclusions about remarriage after divorce for *porneia*. This question was simply not in Jesus' mind when he made this statement (32a). He was concerned to show that remarriage after wrongful divorce would be the cause of adultery (32a) and would therefore come under the prohibition of the seventh commandment (27). He was also concerned to show that the guilt lay principally, though not exclusively, with the husband who should not have divorced his wife in the first place. He was not in any sense answering the question: may the woman (or the man) remarry without committing adultery if the wife was legitimately divorced (because she had committed adultery)? 'Matthew writes nothing about the question of remarriage by the husband who has divorced his wife for unchastity . . . To be sure, the Jews took the right of remarriage after divorce as a matter of course. But it is not for nothing that Matthew's Jesus demands a surpassing sort of righteousness (19f, cf 1 Cor. 7:10f)' (Gundry).

### 4. The second statement (verse 32b)

Jesus goes on to speak of one more form of adultery: 'Anyone who marries a divorced woman commits adultery' (32b). He is making an absolutely general statement. NIV and NEB quite gratuitously tie this statement to the last by assuming that the woman of 32b is the same as the woman of 32a, i.e. a woman wrongfully divorced ('anyone who marries a woman *so* divorced (2nd edition: *the* divorced woman) commits adultery' NIV). There is nothing whatsoever in the Greek to make this connection. The Greek simply says: 'And whoever marries a divorced woman commits adultery'.

Apart from minor differences of vocabulary and syntax, this is saying precisely the same as Luke 16:18b, and the teaching about what legal divorce achieves is therefore the same. 'Apparently the divorce bill (Deut. 24:1; Matt. 5:31) which according to *m. Gittin* had as its essential formula: "Lo, thou art free to marry any man" has not in reality cancelled anything' (Davies and Allison).

> The only reason for which this remarriage [in 32b] can be regarded as adulterous is that the first marriage is still in God's sight regarded as inviolate. The divorce has not dissolved it . . . [Husband and wife] are still in reality bound to one another in the bonds of matrimony and a marital relation or any exercise of the privileges and rights of the marital relation with any other is adultery. Whatever the law of man may enact, this is the law of Christ's kingdom . . . If the woman commits adultery by remarriage [in 32a], this is because she is in reality the wife of the divorcing husband (Murray p.25).

Because this seems to many people a hard saying (the woman concerned not being able in New Testament times effectively to contest the divorce and therefore being divorced, very likely, against her will) and because Jesus does give an exception to his rule of no divorce in 32a, it is worth asking whether Jesus might have had any unspoken exception in mind. In particular, could a woman ever marry again during the lifetime of her divorcing partner?

Could an exception be made if her husband divorced her for any reason other than adultery on her part? She might well be a thoroughly innocent person with whom her husband was simply bored. But quite clearly Jesus does not allow an exception in this instance. Certainly he lays all the blame for the gross injustice at the husband's door, but he clearly states that for her to remarry would be adultery (32a). This is of course because her original marriage bond still exists.

Could an exception be made if her husband divorced her *because* she had committed adultery? In *his* case we have already seen that 32a does not address this question directly and no answer can be found in 27–32. In *her* case, however, the answer is surely: no. The Old Testament picture of adulterous Israel shows clearly that if she is guilty, she should repent and seek reconciliation (e.g. Jer. 3:12–14). This is precisely what Hermas also demanded of the adulterous and divorced wife:

> 'If then,' I said, 'sir, after the wife is sent away, the woman repents, and she wishes to return to her own husband, she will be taken back, won't she?' 'Indeed,' he said, 'if her husband will not take her back, he sins and brings upon himself a great sin . . . This is the reason why you were commanded to remain single, whether husband or wife, because in such cases repentance [by the adulterous and divorced partner] is possible' (*Mandate*, 4.1.7–10).

Could an exception be made if her husband divorced her for adultery when she had not in fact committed it? Again, no. He should not have divorced her in the first place (32a) and he must now restore the marriage relationship.

Could an exception be made if her husband had divorced her for any reason other than adultery on her part and then himself remarried? It is hard to see how. If his remarriage in this situation is adultery, that is because the original marriage still exists. If then the woman is still, in God's eyes, married to her (original) husband, her remarriage would also be adultery. It would simply, in God's eyes, be one adultery on top of another.

Finally, could an exception be made if her husband divorced her for adultery and then himself remarried? Here, as yet, we have to answer: we don't know. We have already said that we cannot be sure whether 32a permits remarriage by the man in the case of divorce after the wife's adultery. This, therefore, must for the time being remain an open question. We should stress, however, that understandable as these questions are in the light of very painful pastoral problems, Jesus' second statement (32b) not only does not answer this last question; he does not even raise it. The statement itself makes no exceptions and does not even hint at any exceptions. This is very understandable given Christ's basic premise: legal divorce does not dissolve a marriage.

## 5. *Summary*

Jesus is bringing out the implications of the seventh commandment (27). It is all too easy to see this simply as a prohibition of the sexual act when you yourself are married or when your sexual partner is a married woman. However, in God's eyes the deliberately lustful look is also adultery 'in your heart' (28) and remarriage is also adultery. This is so when you yourself are marrying after divorcing your partner or (to follow more exactly what Jesus says) after being divorced by your partner (32a), even though the fault lies principally with the divorcer (32a); it is also adultery in God's eyes when you, having not been married previously, marry a divorcee (32b).

While the stress in 32b is on remarriage, the main emphasis in 32a is on divorce. Divorce is wrong and leads others into sin, but – as an aside – divorce is permitted in the case of *porneia* (32a). This may be mentioned because contemporary law compelled a husband to divorce his adulterous wife, and Jesus' followers would not be condemned for obeying this law. However, Jesus does not insist on divorce in this instance; his teaching elsewhere (Matt. 19:7f; John 8:11) suggests that he was only permitting it.

In this single case of permitted divorce, would remarriage be allowed to the non-adulterous partner and perhaps – after his remarriage, when marital reconciliation was no longer possible – to the adulterous partner? To this vital question, which we long to have answered, the text unfortunately gives no reply. 'The question of freedom after a lawful divorce is just not addressed, and we cannot wring from the text what it will not give' (Davies and Allison).

## Matthew 19:1–12

The other passage in Matthew on divorce and remarriage is, if anything, even more significant. It is Matthew's account of the incident recorded in Mark 10:1–12. If any passage in the Gospels will answer the question with which we left Matthew 5, it will be this one.

> (1) When Jesus had finished saying these things, he left Galilee and went into the region of Judea to the other side of the Jordan. (2) Large crowds followed him, and he healed them there. (3) Some Pharisees came to him to test him. They asked, "Is it lawful for a man to divorce his wife for any and every reason?" (4) "Haven't you read," he replied, "that at the beginning the Creator 'made them male and female', (5) and said, 'For this reason a man will leave his father and mother and be united to his wife, and the two will become one flesh'? (6) So they are no longer two, but one. Therefore what God has joined together, let man not separate." (7) "Why then," they asked, "did Moses command that a man give his wife a certificate of divorce and send her away?" (8) Jesus replied, "Moses permitted you to divorce your wives because your hearts were hard. But it was not this way from the beginning. (9) I tell you that anyone who divorces his wife, except for marital unfaithfulness, and marries another commits adultery."
>
> (10) The disciples said to him, "If this is the situation between a husband and wife, it is better not to marry." (11) Jesus replied, "Not everyone can accept this teaching, but only those to whom it has been given. (12) For some are eunuchs because they were born that way; others were made that way by men; and others have renounced marriage because of the kingdom of heaven. The one who can accept this should accept it."

### 1.   The place (verses 1f)

This is exactly as in Mark. Jesus arrives in Perea (NIV: 'the other side of the Jordan') and therefore in dangerous territory as far as his teaching on divorce and remarriage is concerned. He is

in an area ruled by Herod Antipas and his wife Herodias, both
of whom have divorced former partners in order to marry each
other.

## 2.    The question (verse 3)

This is slightly different from Mark. Mark has: 'Is it lawful for
a man to divorce his wife?' (10:2). The question in Matthew
is: 'Is it lawful for a man to divorce his wife for any and every
reason [*kata pasan aitian*]?' This puts the question firmly within
the contemporary debate about the grounds for divorce. Is Jesus
going to repudiate the lax Hillelite position? Is he going to side
with the Shammaites, or perhaps be even more strict, and
so make himself unpopular with Antipas and probably also
among the 'large crowds' (2)?

But once more the Pharisees are not really interested in
Christ's answer. Just as in Mark, Matthew tells us that the
question was put to 'test' or tempt him (3). Origen, writing
in the early third century, comments: 'I think that the Pharisees
put forward this word for this reason that they might attack him
whatever he might say; as for example, if he had said, "It is
lawful", they would have accused him of dissolving marriages
for trifles; but if he had said, "It is not lawful", they would have
accused him of permitting a man to dwell with a woman, even
with sins' (*Comm. in Matt.* 14.16). The latter is much more likely
because, as we have seen, it is almost certain that the Pharisees
already knew Jesus had strict views on the subject.

## 3.    The moral obligation not to divorce (verses 4–6)

In Mark, Jesus counters with a question (10:3) and only after
they have replied with a paraphrase of parts of Deuteronomy 24
(thus giving an inaccurate impression of what the Deuteronomic
law was all about) (4) does Jesus give his real answer (5–9). In
Matthew, he comes in with his answer straight away (4–6).

He says almost exactly the same as in Mark. There are a few
changes. He calls God 'the Creator' (4. Mark: 'at the beginning
of creation') and thus underlines that what he is about to say

about marriage and divorce is God's creation ordinance which therefore applies to all humankind; this expresses his original intention and his unchanging and universal will. In Matthew Jesus also adds 'and said' at the beginning of 5 (absent in Mark) and thus clearly attributes the words of Genesis 2:24 to God himself whereas in Genesis they only appear as the words of the human author. In both these cases Matthew is not saying anything which Mark would have disputed – Mark too represents Jesus as appealing to God's creation ordinance and he certainly believed that Genesis 2:24 was the word of God – but Matthew's account simply brings out these issues more clearly. Further, the phrase 'and be united to his wife' is certainly there in Matthew (5) while the textual evidence for its presence in Mark (10:7) is rather more shaky.

Otherwise the two accounts are almost identical. In Matthew, as in Mark, Jesus quotes Genesis 1:27 (4) and then Genesis 2:24 (5) and he draws his own conclusion about the nature of marriage: husband and wife, in marriage, have become something different from what they were before; they are no longer, at the most important level, two independent human beings; they have become, essentially, a unity (6).

On this conclusion about the purpose for which God created men and women (Gen. 1:27) and his will for marriage (Gen. 2:24) and about the change in a couple's position that marriage effects (Gen. 2:24; Matt. 19:5b-6a), Jesus builds another conclusion. This time it is not about marriage but about divorce (6b). Since ('Therefore') in marriage husband and wife have become a unity – they are 'one flesh' (6a), they are 'joined together' (6b) – and since it is God who has affected this change in them – this is why 'the Creator made them male and female' (4), it was he who said in Genesis 2:24 that a man would 'be united to his wife and the two will become one flesh' (5), it is he who has 'joined [each couple] together' (6) – therefore no one – neither the couple themselves nor a third party – is to separate them (6).

Once more we have here the moral obligation not to divorce. So far in the passage Jesus has not said that true divorce – with the right to remarry – is impossible (we have met this elsewhere in Jesus' teaching) but he has said that it is morally wrong to divorce. Commenting on all of verses 3–9, Bonnard writes:

Our conclusion is the following: the fundamental affirmation of the pericope is found incontestably in 6b, which excludes every sort of repudiation, separation or divorce; . . . divorce, even without remarriage, because it legalises a notorious infidelity; separation of body because it artificially maintains at the legal level a marriage bond deprived of its indispensable expression: physical communion. There really is only one thing to say which corresponds to all the biblical teaching: man must not separate what God has united! (6b).

## 4.   The counterquestion (verse 7)

In Mark, Jesus brings up the question of the Mosaic legislation by asking: 'What did Moses command you?' (10:3) – though he was certainly thinking of Genesis 1f and it is quite possible that he hoped their minds would turn to this material. In Matthew, by contrast, it is the Pharisees who now take the initiative and come up with Deuteronomy 24: 'Why then,' they ask, 'did Moses command that a man give his wife a certificate of divorce and send her away?' (7).

They think they've got him! He has taken up a position which can be shown, they believe, to be in direct contradiction to Scripture. The whole situation is very similar to Matthew 22:41–46, only there it is Jesus who is seeking to show up the Pharisees and show how mistaken is their understanding of the Messiah. There he puts the initial question (22:42); here they do (19:3). There they give what they believe to be the Scriptural answer (22:42); here he does (19:4–6). There he counters with another Scripture to disprove their understanding (22:43–45); here they do, to discredit his teaching (19:7).

## 5.   The reply (verse 8)

Jesus replies: 'Moses permitted you to divorce your wives because your hearts were hard. But it was not this way from the beginning' (8). Basically this is the same point as Jesus makes in Mark (10:5) but there is one significant difference. In Mark, Jesus asks: 'What did Moses *command* you?' (10:3) and, after they have replied with a version of Deuteronomy

24, he calls the Deuteronomic passage 'this *command*' (*entolē*; NIV: law)(10:5). They reply to Jesus' question by saying: 'Moses *permitted*' (10:4). In Matthew, the language is reversed. The Pharisees ask: 'Why did Moses *command* . . .?' (7) and Jesus replies: 'Moses *permitted* . . .' (8).

The change of verb in Mark may perhaps be significant. Jesus may be asking: 'What are the Mosaic provisions?' or 'What is the Mosaic legislation on this question?' and he was perhaps expecting a reply from Genesis 1f. They reply with Deuteronomy 24 and correctly acknowledge that this cannot be said to be a command to divorce or legislation for divorce; it is at best indirect permission to divorce.

I am not certain whether Mark saw the change of words in this way; it may just have been a change of vocabulary for variety's sake. It seems to me much more likely, however, that Matthew invests significance in his change of verbs. In Mark 10:4 the Pharisees are not correcting Jesus' understanding; they are merely answering his question. In Matthew 19:8, however, Jesus is clearly correcting the Pharisees, and therefore his use of a different verb may well be deliberate; he wants to make the point that Moses certainly never commanded divorce. On the contrary, he only permitted it. Deuteronomy 24:1-4, or rather the implicit permission to divorce in some circumstances contained in that law, was given by way of concession, not command (cf 1 Cor. 7:6).

In Matthew, Jesus then goes on to reiterate 'But it was not this way from the beginning' (8, cf 4f). He underlines once more that God's creation ordinance was quite different and in this whole section (4–8) abrogates the Mosaic permission.

Murray makes the point that all the Gospels (Matthew, Mark and Luke; John does not discuss the question) abrogate all Mosaic grounds for divorce. *Porneia* was not a Mosaic ground for divorce since, as we have seen, adultery and other acts of extramarital sexual intercourse were punishable by death. 'The burden of the emphasis . . . both in Matthew 19:3–9 and in Mark 10:2–12 is upon the abrogation of the Mosaic permission in Deuteronomy 24' (Murray pp.51f).

## 6.   The further point (verse 9)

Jesus is not content to answer their objection; he wants to drive
his point home. To do so, he turns the focus from divorce (6–8)
to remarriage after divorce (9). He introduces his words by 'I
tell you' (*legō de hymin* 9, cf 5:32); this will be an authoritative,
and important, pronouncement from Jesus.

As in 5:32a, he introduces an exception as an aside (to which
we must return), but as in 5:32a it is absolutely clear that his
main emphasis is not on the aside/exception but on the rest of
the sentence: 'I tell you that anyone who divorces his wife . . .
and marries another woman commits adultery.' Clearly he is
reinforcing his main teaching: that husband and wife must stay
together. Since God himself makes them a unity (4–6), not only
must they not divorce (6) but they must not remarry (9). To do
so would be adultery because the original unity which God made
has not been, and cannot be, broken, whatever legal formalities
of divorce have been gone through.

In Matthew, this statement is made publicly as part of the
discussion with the Pharisees; in Mark, it is made privately,
'in the house' with the disciples (10:10f). But otherwise the
saying (after the initial 'I tell you') is word for word identical
except that Matthew adds the exception clause and omits Mark's
'against her' (10:11). In practice, however, 'against her' must
be understood, as it can only be against his wife that he is
committing adultery.

So again Jesus says that remarriage is not only wrong, it is
impossible. It is not possible to contract a true marriage – a marriage in God's eyes – while your divorced partner is still living. It
is only possible to commit adultery. This is because the first marriage still exists. It may be for this reason that Matthew continues
to call Herodias 'Philip's wife' after she has divorced Philip and
been remarried to Herod Antipas (Matt. 14:3f//Mark 6:17f, cf
Luke 3:19). And it is not only wrong to divorce one's partner;
it is actually impossible in any full sense. You may be able to
break the legal ties, you may be able to live apart, but you cannot
destroy the marriage; your unity with your partner still exists in
God's eyes; the marriage bond can only be broken by death.

## 7.  The exception (verse 9)

As in 5:32, but unlike Mark, Matthew's account introduces an exception. The phrase 'except for marital unfaithfulness' actually uses different wording from 5:32 (here: *mē epi porneia*, there: *parektos logou porneias*: some texts in 19:9 use the same words as in 5:32 but it is likely that these are imported from chapter 5 and that *mē epi porneia* is the original text). The wording of the exception in 19:9 is not a quotation from Deuteronomy 24 but the meaning is otherwise identical to that of the exception in 5:32, and both phrases share the vital word *porneia*.

Clearly, then, Jesus allows – he does not command – divorce where there has been illicit sexual intercourse. But is he also allowing remarriage for the partner who has not committed adultery where there has been divorce for adultery? Essentially, two positions are possible. Either Jesus allows separation, including legal divorce, in the case of adultery (this has traditionally been known as: separation from bed and board, *'a thoro et mensa'*) but maintains that the marriage bond is still in existence and therefore even in this instance remarriage would be adultery: or he allows full divorce in the case of adultery, a divorce which dissolves the marriage bond and therefore opens the way for remarriage. The former position has always been that of the Roman Catholic Church and is also found in the Church of England's canon law which forbids remarriage; the latter position is espoused by many in the Free Church tradition. The issue cannot, however, be decided along denominational lines, but only on the basis of a careful study of the biblical text.

One of the principal arguments used for the latter position is the use of the word *apolyō* ('divorce'). It clearly means 'full divorce' (a convenient shorthand for: divorce which breaks the marriage bond and therefore confers the right to remarry) in 3, 7 (NIV: 'send away'), 8. 'It is unwarranted to understand the same verb a few verses later in some other way, unless there is some compelling contextual reason for the change' (Carson). But this is the whole point: there *is* a compelling contextual reason for the change. Jesus' principal concern in 9 is not with the exception but with the man who divorces for a

reason other than adultery and remarries. There is no disputing
the fact that Jesus calls this remarriage adultery. That means
that his divorcing (*apolyō*, 9) does not effect 'full divorce' but
only 'separation divorce' (a shorthand for: legal divorce which
does not break the marriage bond and therefore does not confer
the right to remarry). Those who want to argue for full divorce
in the case of a divorce that is justified (i.e. for adultery) point out
(rightly) that *apolyō* means full divorce in 3, 7 and 8 and, in their
opponents' view, means separation divorce in 9; they maintain
that there is no justification for this change of meaning.

But Heth and Wenham rightly point out that these same
people actually require Jesus to use *apolyō* with two different
meanings in the same verse! They must maintain that *apolyō* in
9 means full divorce where *porneia* is involved, and separation
divorce where *porneia* is not involved (p.134).

The fact is that the Jews who were speaking to Jesus only conceived of full divorce. Jesus, however, had a different idea. Legal
divorce could take place but not break the marriage bond. It
could only achieve separation divorce. And he makes his position
abundantly clear by calling remarriage after divorce adultery.

If then, the argument from the changed use of the word *apolyō*
will not stand, what other argument is put forward by those
wishing to maintain that Jesus taught full divorce in the case of
adultery? The other main, and more important, argument stems
from the syntax of the sentence. Murray puts the argument like
this: The governing thought of Jesus' statement, expressed by
the principal verb, is 'commits adultery'. For this to make any
sense, remarriage is essential because, if we omit the idea of
remarriage, claiming it is an aside, and read: 'Anyone who
divorces his wife, except for marital unfaithfulness, commits
adultery', we end up with a nonsense; there can be no adultery
without a remarriage. It is this thought of committing adultery by
remarriage that is the ruling thought in this passage and the
exception must therefore be an exception to the ruling thought
and to the principal verb. In other words Jesus is saying: A
person commits adultery by remarrying after divorce, except
that a person does not commit adultery by remarrying after
divorce for adultery (Murray pp.39–41).

This is a strong argument and is a perfectly natural way to

understand the verse seen in isolation. The only major weakness in the argument as it stands is to say that the exception *must* be an exception to the ruling thought. This is not the case. It may well be, but it does not have to be. The exception could simply be to the phrase that immediately precedes it: 'anyone who divorces his wife'. If this second understanding is correct, it would certainly have clarified the matter if Jesus had been reported as saying: 'Anyone who divorces his wife and marries another woman commits adultery except that a man may divorce his wife for marital unfaithfulness but remarriage will still be adultery.' This, however, would have given a great deal more weight to the exception and Jesus' interest is clearly not in the exception but in the situation where a man divorces his wife without proper justification.

So, both interpretations of Matthew 19:9 are possible and the syntax of the sentence, taken by itself, might lead us to believe that Jesus allows remarriage (and is saying that the marriage bond has been destroyed) in the case of divorce for adultery. How are we to decide between these rival interpretations?

We must begin by looking more carefully at the sentence itself and at the sentence within its preceding context. What is the point of the sentence itself? It is to say that remarriage after divorce (at least in certain circumstances) is forbidden because it is adulterous. This is indeed the governing though. The ruling idea is *not* that remarriage after divorce is sometimes permitted nor even that divorce is sometimes permitted; once again we must stress that the exception, though highly significant, is an aside.

And what is the point of the sentence in its context? It is to add weight to Jesus' reply to the question put to him by the Pharisees (3). It is *not* right to divorce for any and every reason (cf 3) because God the Creator, right from the beginning of creation, made the marriage union (4–6a) which not only should not be broken (6b–8) but cannot be broken, because to remarry after divorce is adultery (9). The whole point of verse 9 in its context is to reinforce the command *not* to divorce.

Now without taking away from the whole thrust of his argument, Jesus wants to slip in permission to divorce in the case of adultery perhaps because it created a real crisis of conscience for those who knew that Jewish (and Roman) law demanded divorce in the case of adultery. So, as an aside, he adds the words: *mē epi porneia* (except for marital unfaithfulness).

Where are these words to be put? Murray claims that their present position (after 'anyone who divorces his wife') is the 'natural position' if Jesus was wanting to make an exception to the whole sentence (i.e. if Jesus wanted to say: it is *not* committing adultery to remarry after divorcing your wife in the case of adultery). Murray even asks: 'Where else could the exceptive clause be put?' if it is to apply to the entire sentence (p.41). The simple answer to this question is that placing the exception almost anywhere else would have made Murray's position much stronger, even unassailable.

Because this is such an important point, it is worth working carefully through the other options. If Matthew had written: 'Anyone who divorces his wife and marries another, except in the case of marital unfaithfulness, commits adultery', Murray's case would be all but proven. In this case the divorce and remarriage would be tied very closely together and the strong implication would be that to divorce-and-remarry is not adultery in the case of marital unfaithfulness.

If Matthew had written: 'Anyone who divorces his wife and marries another commits adultery, except in the case of marital unfaithfulness', Murray's case would be unanswerable. The exception clause would then clearly modify the verb 'commit adultery' and the sentence would clearly be saying that divorce-and-remarriage do not constitute adultery in the case of marital unfaithfulness.

But as it is, the exception phrase comes after the verb 'divorce' and modifies the clause 'anyone who divorces his wife'. This is the obvious – indeed the only – position in the sentence that Matthew could put the phrase if he wanted to say that divorce is permissible in the case of adultery but remarriage is not. This is Gundry's conclusion: 'It would be a mistake to think that Matthew allows the husband [in the case of his wife's adultery] to remarry . . . In the word order of 19:9 the exceptive phrase immediately follows the mention of divorce but precedes the mention of remarriage by the husband. Had Matthew been concerned to establish the right of the husband to remarry under the exception, he would hardly have . . . put the exception only after the matter of divorce in 19:9' (pp.90f). Murray himself admits that: 'Such a rendering does in itself make good sense and would solve a great many difficulties in . . . the accounts given in the three Synoptic Gospels' (p.39).

It also makes more sense of the specifically Matthean material. Bromiley makes the point that in Matthew 5:31f 'the Mosaic law is obviously transcended' and in 19:8 'the Mosaic concession is no less obviously withdrawn', so how can Jesus be reinstating the Mosaic concession of full divorce even in a 'narrower' form (narrower because full divorce is now being granted only on the grounds of *porneia*)? 'The story [in Matthew 19] seems to make no final sense if Jesus finishes up by endorsing the Mosaic law which at first he so bravely describes as a concession and replaces with the original creation principle' (pp.44f). Bromiley's point is not proven – Jesus *could* be rescinding the Mosaic ground for full divorce and replacing it with what Bromiley calls 'narrower' grounds – but Bromiley is right in saying that the passage as a whole makes much more sense if Jesus is rescinding the whole concept of full divorce which the Mosaic legislation permitted.

## 8.   Summary so far

Jesus was asked a question about divorce (3). The way the question is phrased ('Is it lawful for a man to divorce his wife *for any and every reason?*') shows that Jesus is being asked to comment on the contemporary debate: will he side with the Hillelites or the Shammaites, or have some novel approach of his own?

In reply, Jesus appeals straight to the early chapters of Genesis. Like the Qumran community, he appeals to Genesis 1:27, but he draws his major teaching from Genesis 2:24: when a couple get married, they become a unity and it is God who 'yokes them together' in this way (4–6). The conclusion is inevitable: if God himself makes the bride and groom one then no one is to prise them apart, not even the couple themselves (6).

In answer to the objection that Moses 'commanded' divorce (7), Jesus admits that he 'permitted' it but abrogates this permission by referring again to God's creation ordinance (8). To reinforce his prohibition of divorce, he brings in the question of remarriage (9). We should never forget that this sentence (9) is not about when it is *permissible* to remarry. It is precisely the opposite. It is about the *wrong* of remarriage. Jesus is saying that it is wrong to divorce and remarry because that is adultery. We are asking a question (is it permissible for the partner who has not committed adultery to remarry after divorce for adultery?) which the text did not set out to answer. Nevertheless, it is a burning pastoral issue today, and we must therefore not duck it.

So far we have studied Jesus' statement itself (9) and its place in its preceding context. We have looked at arguments in favour of the view that Jesus here allows remarriage after divorce for (the other partner's) adultery and arguments against. The arguments against may be marginally stronger, but most fair-minded critics would have to say they were fairly evenly balanced.

But the preceding context is not the only context of a statement. There is also what immediately follows, and there is the tradition of interpretation principally as it occurs in the Bible itself and then as it occurs in the earliest interpreters. Four factors convince me that Jesus was teaching: it is always wrong to remarry in the lifetime of your divorced partner. These are: From the immediately following context:

1. The surprise of the disciples (10).
2. The reply to their surprise from Jesus (11f).

From the interpretation within Scripture:
3. The interpretation of Christ's teaching by St Paul (1 Cor. 7:10f).

From the earliest non-Scriptural interpretation:
4. The interpretation of Christ's teaching by the early Church.

We will look at the first two and the last factor in the rest of this chapter, and at the third factor in chapter 6 (on this paragraph, cf Schillebeeckx pp.153–5).

## 9. *The surprise (verse 10)*

The disciples immediately respond to what they have just heard Jesus say. 'The disciples said to him, "If this is the situation between a husband and wife, it is better not to marry"' (10). They are flabbergasted; they clearly never expected this, and they protest with an idea (then it is better not to marry) which they hope Jesus will instantly repudiate.

This surprise is quite incomprehensible if Jesus was allowing remarriage after divorce for adultery. He would then be saying nothing revolutionary but merely expressing views that were entirely in line with the well-known school of Shammai; he would simply be siding, in the contemporary debate (cf 3), with one of the influential schools[1]. 'The remark of the disciples (10) confirms the view that Christ forbade divorce even in the case of the woman's unchastity . . . After being Christ's disciples so long, they would not hold that what even Jews of the stricter school of Shammai maintained respecting the marriage tie was an intolerable obligation' (Plummer).

We have seen already that it was probably widely known that Jesus held strict views on divorce; that is why the Pharisees chose this subject to 'test' him (3//Mark 10:2). His disciples therefore expected him to side with Shammai on divorce. And indeed on divorce itself he did: he permitted divorce in the case of infidelity (9). But then he went on to say that there should be no remarriage, even in the case of adultery! This is what they (and Matthew) understood; it is what bowled them over.

Lagrange makes the same point and (writing in 1923) adds a contemporary note. He says the disciples would not have kicked up a fuss if Jesus had been merely confirming Shammai's interpretation. 'It must be then that they were aware that Christ had just laid down a much stricter law: that marriage is indissoluble, and while the husband has the right to repudiate his wife by reason of her adultery, he can no longer take another one. One cannot be surprised that the Apostles found this law hard since still today it raises protests which

---

[1] Stott, following Hurley, says that the disciples were surprised because Jesus 'abrogated the [Mosaic] death penalty for sexual infidelity and made this the only legitimate grounds for dissolving the marriage bond' (*Issues Facing Christians Today* p.268). If this were all that Jesus was saying, it would cause no surprise. As far as we know, no influential Jewish school was advocating the death penalty for adultery by Jesus' day, and the dissolution of the marriage bond in cases of infidelity was precisely Shammai's widely known position.

have resulted in so many modern legal enactments that have tragically abandoned the Christian law.'

## 10.  The reply (verses 11f)

Jesus then replies to the disciples' surprised reaction. Almost certainly they expected him to refute their idea or 'word' (11, literally, NIV: teaching). But on the contrary, he goes on to teach the positive value of singleness (11f).

We have already examined this saying of Christ's in detail (chapter 3). We need only repeat at this point that while it certainly does speak of singleness (under the image of being a eunuch) in general, it must be seen in the context of the discussion of divorce and particularly remarriage. Clement of Alexandria (c. AD 150–215) made precisely this point. He was combatting Gnostics who used Matthew 19:12 to prove that marriage itself was sinful (cf 1 Tim. 4:1–3). Clement countered by saying that the Gnostics, in explaining Matthew 19:11f 'do not realise the context. After his word about divorce some asked him whether, if that is the position in relation to woman, it is better not to marry; and it was *then* that the Lord said: "Not all can receive this saying, but those to whom it is granted." What the questioners wanted to know was whether, when a man's wife has been condemned for fornication [*porneia*], it is allowable for him to marry another' (*Stromata* 3.6.50).

This, then, is the context in which Jesus speaks about a singleness that, viewed from the human point of view, has been thrust upon one ('made that way by men', perhaps including the woman (or man) who has been divorced against her will) or voluntarily shouldered ('for the sake of the kingdom of heaven', referring especially to those who, in obedience to Christ's teaching, refrain from remarriage after divorce)(12); this same singleness, viewed from God's point of view, has been 'given' (11) to divorcees. This certainly is teaching that many will find hard (cf 10), and the challenge is to 'accept' it (12, cf 11) in the power of God.

In one sense, Christ does correct the disciples. Their statement is a completely blanket one: if there is no divorce except for adultery, and more particularly if there is no remarriage even after adultery, it is better not to marry in the first place (10)! No, says Jesus, because not all are called to a life of nothing-but-singleness. But this *is* the calling of those 'to whom it has been given' (11). These are not – in the context – those temperamentally able to sustain a life of singleness; they are those in particular – the context demands this – who have been divorced. These are the ones who 'accept' singleness for the sake of the kingdom of heaven.

To sum up: The disciples are amazed at Jesus' reply. They expected him to take a strict line and to side with the school of Shammai. But they have understood him to say something much more strict. Shammai allows divorce for adultery and remarriage in that case. Jesus is not allowing remarriage even in the case of adultery; he is saying that even in the case of adultery the marriage bond still exists. Jesus does not in any way contradict their understanding of his remark. On the contrary, they are correct to say he is mandating singleness for those who have been divorced even in the case of adultery. He goes on to say that this has been 'given' to divorced people by God (both to the divorcers and to the divorcees) and must – however tough this may seem – be 'accepted' fully by them.

## Divorce and Remarriage in the Early Church Fathers

From earliest post-New Testament days, Christian writers wrote about divorce and remarriage. Almost always their teaching is about remarriage – rather than merely about divorce – thus reflecting the Gospel material. In almost every case they write *against* remarriage (contrast our modern preoccupation with when remarriage might be permissible) and mention no exception. When writing about divorce they do quite frequently mention the permission – which they quite often make into a command – to divorce where there has been adultery. The overwhelming majority of them do not allow remarriage in these circumstances. Some specifically prohibit it; others simply say: there should be no remarriage after divorce. They mention no exceptions.

Some might say that this is an argument from silence. If

these early writers were confronted by Matthew 5 or Matthew 19 would they not have made an exception? Perhaps they were speaking in general terms as Jesus does in Mark and Luke, and they wanted to establish the general principle without dwelling on the single exception? But the significant fact is that they clearly did know Matthew 5 and Matthew 19. They frequently quote them; some of the Fathers make their remarks on divorce and remarriage in their commentaries on Matthew; they not infrequently mention the exception as it relates to divorce; but only one or two (and those are later writers) mention any exception to Christ's ruling of: no remarriage. As we have already said, the vast majority – even in a context of quoting Matthew – either say that all remarriage is wrong (without mentioning any possible exceptions) or raise the issue of remarriage after divorce for adultery and specifically prohibit it.

It would make this chapter overlong to attempt any detailed discussion of all the relevant passages in the early Fathers. For this, reference must be made to Heth and Wenham: *Jesus and Divorce* (chapter one), Crouzel: *L'église primitive*, or Collingwood: *'Divorce and Remarriage'*. Clearly, however, it is incumbent on me to produce some evidence to substantiate the last two paragraphs, and I have chosen to limit myself to the second century AD (that is: the first hundred years of post-New Testament writing) and to the six Christian authors who wrote on the subject during that period.

## 1.  Hermas (dates uncertain but writing some time between the end of the first century and AD 150)

Hermas asks his heavenly guardian:

(4) . . . 'If a man is married to a woman faithful in the Lord and he finds her involved in some adultery, does he sin if he continues to live with her?' (5) 'As long as he knows nothing of it,' he said, 'he does not sin. But if the husband knows of her sin and his wife does not repent but persists in her immorality and the husband continues to live with her, then he becomes guilty of her sin and a partner in her adultery.' (6) 'What then,' I said, 'sir, shall the husband do if his wife persists in this passion?' 'Let him send her away [*apolyō*],' he

said, 'and let the husband remain single. But if after sending away his wife, he marries another, he also commits adultery himself.' (7) 'If then,' I said, 'sir, after the wife is sent away the woman repents, and she wishes to return to her own husband, she will be taken back, won't she?' (8) 'Indeed,' he said, 'if her husband will not take her back he sins and brings upon himself a great sin. Rather one must take back the one who has sinned and the one who repents, but not often, because there is only one repentance for the servants of God. Therefore, for the sake of repentance the husband must not marry. This is the proper course of action for wife and husband. (9) Not only,' said he, 'is it adultery if anyone defiles his flesh, but also whoever acts as the heathen do commits adultery. So if anyone persists in such actions and does not repent, then depart from him and do not live with him, otherwise you also are sharing in his sin. (10) This is the reason why you were commanded to remain single, whether husband or wife, because in such cases repentance is possible.' (*Mandate*, 4.1.4–10).

Here, Hermas (in common with many of the early Fathers) agrees with the Roman law in mandating divorce in the case of (persistent) adultery and his reason for this command also agrees with the Roman law: he will become 'a partner in her adultery'(5). However, Heth and Wenham point out that he is 'in direct opposition to the civil law of Rome' by forbidding remarriage after divorce for adultery (6, 8–10) and by making it a Christian duty to receive back a repentant wife (7f). Another difference from contemporary society is that he applies all this not only to a husband with an adulterous wife but also to a wife with an adulterous husband (10). In all these matters where he differs from Roman law and practice, he shows how profoundly he has been influenced by New Testament teaching on divorce and remarriage (Heth and Wenham p.24).

Hermas is one of the early writers who specifically addresses the question of whether it is permissible to remarry after divorce for adultery. His answer is a clear: no (6, 8–10). It is true that his main reason for this is to allow the adulterous partner to repent (8, 10) and the question inevitably presents itself: what if the opportunity for repentance is past, i.e. if the adulterous partner has remarried?

The significant fact, often overlooked, is that repentance is not the only reason Hermas puts forward for remaining single. He also says that for the partner who has not been unfaithful to marry again would be adultery (6, 9). He thus clearly shows that, in his understanding, neither a partner's unfaithfulness nor divorce-for-unfaithfulness breaks the marriage bond. This remains, and it is still adultery to remarry even when your partner has been unfaithful.

## 2.   Justin Martyr (converted c.130; died c.165)

In his *First Apology* (c.150), Justin quotes – one after the other – Matthew 5:28f, Matthew 5:32b (or Luke 16:18b) and Matthew 19:11f and then immediately adds: 'And so those who make second marriages according to human law are sinners in the sight of our Teacher' (*1 Apol.* 15). There is an outside possibility that this could refer to remarriage of any kind, even after the death of a partner, but most scholars agree with E. R. Hardy that 'the reference is . . . to remarriage after divorce' since the context of the Matthean quotations demands this (Hardy in Richardson: *Early Christian Fathers* p.250).

Two points are worthy of note here. One is that Justin makes a distinction between what is possible 'according to human law' and (by implication) what is possible according to 'our Teacher's' law. Human law recognises a valid second marriage; 'our Teacher' calls this 'sin'. Secondly, Justin quotes from Matthew 5 (certainly verses 28f and probably verse 32) and Matthew 19 (verses 11f) and yet makes no exception to his statement that 'our Teacher' regards remarriage as 'sin'.

In his *Second Apology* (2.1–7) Justin says that Christians must separate from adulterous partners. He describes a case where both partners were sexually unfaithful. The wife became a Christian and gave up her infidelity; the husband persisted in his adultery. She wanted to divorce him but was persuaded by friends to wait in the hope that he might change. When he went from bad to worse, she divorced him. Justin clearly approves of what she did. There is, however, no mention of remarriage. In the light of the material in the *First Apology*, the assumption must be that she would not be free to remarry.

## 3.   Athenagoras (writing c.177)

Athenagoras the Apologist addressed his *Legatio Pro Christianis* to the Emperors Marcus Aurelius Antoninus and Lucius Aurelius Commodus. He says that a Christian man must either

> remain as he was brought into the world, or else . . . abide in one marriage and no more, for a second marriage is a fair-seeming adultery. 'Whoever shall put away his wife,' Scripture says, 'and shall marry another, commits adultery.' It does not allow him to divorce the one whose maidenhead he had [ended], nor to bring in another wife beside her. One that robs himself of his first wife, even if she be dead, is a covert adulterer, thwarting the hand of God – for in the beginning God made one man and one woman – and destroying the unity of flesh that was meant for the propagation of the race (*Leg. pro Chr.* 33).

The New Testament clearly teaches that it is preferable to remain single after the death of one's partner (I Cor. 7:8f, 39f; I Tim. 5:9–15) but nevertheless clearly allows remarriage in this situation (Rom. 7:1–3). Athenagoras goes beyond the New Testament in saying that someone remarrying after the death of his wife is 'a covert adulterer'. Nevertheless, he is deeply influenced by the New Testament teaching. He quotes directly one of Christ's sayings on divorce and remarriage (either Mark 10:11 without the final words 'against her' or Matthew 19:9 without the exception clause) and he backs up his argument against remarriage by saying what God did 'in the beginning' and by indirectly quoting Genesis 1:27 and 2:24 (cf Mark 10:6–8//Matthew 19:4–6).

He clearly says that remarriage is wrong and allows no exceptions. If his direct quotation is from Matthew 19:9 he may well have left out the exception clause because he was convinced that the exception applied only to the question of divorce and not to the question of remarriage (which is the subject Athenagoras is discussing). To him remarriage is 'fair-seeming adultery' – 'fair-seeming' because it was allowed by Roman law, but adultery because the marriage bond still exists, unobliterated by divorce.

## 4.   Theophilus of Antioch (writing c.180)

Theophilus wrote:

> The gospel voice provides a stricter teaching about purity
> when it says, 'Everyone who looks upon another person's
> wife to desire her has already committed adultery with her
> in his heart' [Matt. 5:28]. 'And he who marries,' it says,
> 'a woman divorced by her husband commits adultery, and
> whoever divorces his wife except for fornication makes her a
> partner in adultery' [Matt. 5:32] (*Ad Autolycum*, 3.13).

The interesting point here is that Theophilus quotes Matthew
5:32b (in a form closer to Luke 16:18b) and then quotes 5:32a after
that. Some scholars have suggested that this inversion is deliberate
to make the point that while remarriage to a divorcee is adulterous
in all circumstances, divorce is permissible where there has been
*porneia*; we cannot be sure whether this deduction is correct.

## 5.   Irenaeus (writing c.185)

In *Adversus Haereses* 4.15.2, Irenaeus briefly alludes to Christ's
remarks that the Mosaic permission was given because of men's
hardness of heart and that it cannot be made compatible with
God's original law. He also refers to Genesis 1:27. He does not,
however, mention remarriage.

## 6.   Clement of Alexandria (c.150–215)

In *Stromata* 2.23.145, Clement deals with divorce and remarriage at some length. The key passage is: '[The fact] that Scripture counsels marriage, and allows no release from the union,
is expressly contained in the law: "You shall not put away your
wife, except for the cause of fornication"; and it regards as fornication, the marriage of those separated while the other is alive.'
Clement is clearly forbidding remarriage. He says so at the
beginning of this passage ('Scripture . . . allows no release from
the union') and he says so at the end ('[Scripture] regards as
fornication the marriage of those separated while the other is
alive'). Since he is keen to show that 'Scripture' says this, he

sandwiches a quotation from the Gospels between the two prohibitions of remarriage. It might be thought, since he wants to say that all remarriage is prohibited, that he would quote Mark or Luke. Instead he quotes Matthew, with the exception clause ('except for the cause of fornication' is *plēn ei mē epi logō porneias* and looks like a conflation, from memory, of Matthew 5:32 and 19:9). It is clear then that he regards Jesus' words as allowing divorce in the case of adultery but not allowing remarriage under any circumstances.

We have already quoted a second passage in Clement where he relates Matthew 19:11f to its context and specifically to 19:9. He says that the Gnostics, who were calling marriage a sin, misinterpret Matthew 19:11f because they 'do not realize the context . . . What the questioners [in 19:10] wanted to know was whether, when a man's wife has been condemned for fornication [*porneia*], it is allowable for him to marry another' (*Stromata* 3.6.50). Clement is insistent that Matthew 19:11f must be understood in close connection with 19:9 but leaves a little vague what that connection is. The most natural explanation, as we have seen, is that the people who 'have renounced remarriage [literally: made themselves eunuchs] for the sake of the kingdom of heaven' (19:12) are divorcees who, in obedience to Christ, have refrained from remarriage. If this is, as seems likely, Clement's understanding, then he is teaching that Jesus specifically prohibits remarriage – even for the non-adulterer – after divorce for adultery, since Clement states that Jesus is answering the question: 'Whether, when a man's wife has been condemned for fornication, it is allowable for him to marry another?'

## 7. Beyond the second century

All Christian writers up to the end of the fifth century speak in exactly the same way, some of them dealing with the subject very extensively, some of them dealing with it in commentaries on the text of Matthew. The only clear exception is Ambrosiaster (second half of the fourth century) who does allow remarriage to the husband whose wife has been divorced for her adultery (but not to the wife if the situation is reversed!) and to either husband or wife if they are Christians and deserted by a pagan partner. One or two other writers (e.g. Basil of Caesarea, also later fourth century) are not entirely clear; their writings are too succinct or too obscure to form a definite judgment. But the overwhelming majority – including most of the great names in early theology (a few do not discuss the issue) – clearly state that remarriage after divorce is prohibited.

## 8.   Summary

It is true that the early Fathers are not part of the canon of Scripture and do not have the authority of the biblical writings. What they say is not binding on the Christian and we have discussed them here not so much because of the value of their own teaching (real though this is), but because they are the earliest interpreters of the words of Jesus – hence their inclusion in a chapter on 'Divorce and Remarriage in the Teaching of Jesus'.

It is also true that the Fathers were more ascetic than the New Testament. We have seen that Athenagoras goes further than the New Testament in condemning remarriage even after the death of a partner and that Hermas, while saying – contrary to the culture of his day – that a husband should take back an adulterous wife who has repented, adds 'but not often, because there is only one repentance for the servants of God' (*Mandate*, 4.1.8). This only underlines that they are not authoritative for us and that we must treat some of their conclusions with caution. It certainly does not mean that we can sweep aside wholesale their understanding of the New Testament texts, the earliest interpretation in Christian history.

The fact is that they both knew and frequently quoted Matthew 5 and 19. They clearly see these exception clauses as permitting (several see them as mandating) divorce in the case of adultery but none of them (except the lone Ambrosiaster) make even the slightest mention, when discussing Matthew 5 or 19, of an exception to the prohibition of remarriage. 'Not even the text which offers most grounds for this suggestion (Matt. 19:9) is quoted by any writer prior to the sixth century – even among those commentators who explicitly discuss it – as vindicating the practice [of remarriage after divorce for adultery]' (Kirk p.44).

Their normal practice, when speaking of remarriage (which is normally their focus, rather than divorce by itself), is to prohibit it entirely. No exception is mentioned. This is so despite the fact that the exception of divorce for adultery is mentioned quite frequently. As we have seen (e.g. Clement), it is not uncommon to mention the absolute prohibition of remarriage in the same context as the exception that allows divorce for adultery is mentioned or quoted.

There are of course several Fathers who specifically raise the question of remarriage after divorce for adultery, and all (the only clear exception again being Ambrosiaster) prohibit it. In our period we have seen this in Hermas (*Mandate*, 4.1.6, 8–10) and Clement (*Stromata*, 3.6.50). Chrysostom, Augustine and other later writers are absolutely clear on the matter. Plummer in his commentary on Matthew quotes Augustine's succinct comment: 'Only for fornication may a man divorce an adulterous wife, but while she is alive he may not marry another' (p.82).

This, then, is how the Fathers interpreted the words of Jesus. They are not infallible, yet, as Heth and Wenham point out, they 'had a built-in cultural, social and linguistic grid in their thinking which the twentieth-century reader must labour to reconstruct if he wants to interpret the Greek New Testament accurately. Being closest in time to the composition of the Gospels, the Fathers are most likely to have understood the original intentions of the writers in matters of Greek grammar and syntax' especially if Greek was their mother tongue (p.20). And their virtually unanimous testimony, stated or implied, is that Christ in the Gospels – and specifically in Matthew – forbade remarriage after divorce in all circumstances, including when divorce was for adultery.

## Conclusions

### 1.   *Christ's teaching is binding on his followers*

He introduces his teaching on the subject with the solemn: 'But I tell you' (Matt. 5:32; 19:9), a mark of his conscious authority (cf 7:29). He even has the boldness to abrogate the permission to divorce and remarry – indeed a piece of legislation (Mark 10:5) – which Moses wrote in the Old Testament (Mark 10:3–9//Matt. 19:4-8). Even the phrase 'The one who can accept this should accept it' (Matt. 19:12, cf 11) is by no means, as we have seen, a statement that 'you can take this or leave it' but rather a phrase parallel to: 'He who has ears, let him hear' (e.g. Matt. 11:15). It is a challenge to be taught by Jesus and to accept his (admittedly tough) teaching.

This point – that Christ's teaching is binding on us his followers – should not even have to be made. But it is remarkable how many people try to evade Christ's teaching on this very issue of divorce and remarriage. The most common argument is that Christ abolished the old law (Mark 10:3–9//Matt. 19:4–8) and was not intending to bring in a new law. There are senses in which this is true: it is arguable as to whether Christ would want the civil law in a secular state to prohibit all remarriage after divorce; it is also certainly true that Christ's new life is not a crushing burden of dos and don'ts that are even more overwhelming than those of the Pharisees. But it is a totally false deduction to go on and say that Jesus' teaching was merely advice, the explanation of an ideal which we need not live up to if our circumstances or our temperament do not permit. Atkinson quotes Helen Oppenheimer: 'It has frequently been insisted that "Christ did not legislate" but to put the matter so can be misleading, if it is assumed that Christ's commands need not be obeyed' (in Atkinson p.147). Rather, Christ spoke with authority and expected his followers to obey his words (Matt. 7:24–27).

As to the 'crushing burden' of these commands of Christ's, there is not the slightest hint in the Gospels that he allows his followers to be obedient only up to a point. Bromiley again and again stresses that the difference between Christ and the Pharisees (or life without Christ) is that Christ not only makes demands but enables his followers to keep his commands. Jesus 'does not . . . lay on [his disciples] a burden that they cannot carry. Instead he opens up for them the possibility of doing willingly and effectively that which previously, even out of the strictest sense of duty, they could not do' (pp.45f).

We must therefore adapt our pastoral practice to the teaching of Jesus, and not let very real pastoral concerns warp our reading of the Gospels or even allow us to dismiss Christ's words altogether. Too often a Christian group will struggle with Christ's teaching on remarriage and conclude: 'But it doesn't work like that.' Helen Oppenheimer, in a more so-phisticated way, says the same thing: 'Indissolubility of some sort is the most obvious interpretation of Christ's teaching on marriage . . . Dissolubility of some sort is the most obvious interpretation of some of the facts of human life' (p.239). She states specifically that she is trying to base her answers to the questions about divorce and remarriage on *both* Scripture *and* experience. Yet, as she sees it, these two are in opposition to one another. By contrast, Christ certainly wants us to work out his teaching in our experience, but he does not expect his followers to modify his teaching in the light of what they believe contradictory experience is saying.

## 2.    Christ's teaching is stricter than that of his contemporaries

This is true not only in Mark and Luke, but also – and spe-cifically – in Matthew (even with the exception clause). It is in Matthew that Jesus directly speaks of the contemporary teaching about divorce (5:31) and pits his own, much stricter, teaching against it (5:32). It is in Matthew that the Pharisees put their question in such a way as to engage Jesus in the contempo-rary rabbinical debate (19:3). We have seen that the rabbinical schools contained not only the laxer ideas of Hillel but the stricter view of Shammai who allowed divorce only for sexual infidelity. Yet it is in Matthew that Jesus' words – again with the exception clause – are so strong and demanding that they shock not only the crowds but his own disciples (19:9f). And it is once more in Matthew that Jesus says, in the most solemn terms, that his disciples' righteousness [must] surpass that of the Pharisees and the teachers of the law (5:20).

It should not surprise us, then, that his teaching is so shocking to our contemporaries. Admittedly few of us would want to go as far as Hillel and allow divorce even for a trifle: we have been too much influenced by Christ and his apostles for that. But most people in the West today would feel that even Shammai's teaching was too extreme because they would want to broaden the grounds for legitimate divorce to include e.g. 'marital break-down'. Yet on this issue – as on many others – Christ is much more demanding, and has much higher standards, not only than those of contemporary society but also than those of the popular, rather innocuous, image of him.

## 3. Divorce is never God's will

It is necessary to insist on this. So much debate today – and this book reflects the trend – focuses on the exception that Jesus made. Yet that was most definitely not where his emphasis lay. He was asked whether it is lawful for a man to divorce his wife (Mark 10:2//Matt. 19:3) and the whole emphasis of his answer – just as much in Matthew as in Mark – is that divorce is *not* lawful.

God originally made humans male and female with a view to marriage; at the beginning of creation he instituted marriage: an event (it *is* also a process but Christ is speaking here about what happens at the moment a man marries a woman) when each partner leaves his/her original family, forms a new family with the partner to whom he/she cleaves, and – most importantly – is made 'one' with his/her partner. It is God who joins the couple together as one. The implication is obvious: no one is to sunder this God-given oneness (Mark 10:6–9//Matt. 19:4–6).

It is true that if one partner commits adultery, the other may separate himself/herself in legal divorce (Matt. 19:9; 5:32), but even this is only permitted; it need not happen if the offended partner decides to maintain the marriage.

It is, then, never God's will that there should be a divorce, because it is God's will that the oneness should not only exist (it will do, despite legal divorce) but be lived out (in marital fidelity). Jesus does, however, sanction – not command – divorce in the case of adultery, and in that case only.

## 4. Legal divorce does not destroy the oneness of marriage

Couples can – though they should not, except in the case of adultery – live apart. They can – though again they should not, except where there has been adultery – become legally divorced: separating out their finances and making custody arrangements for the children. But what they cannot do is destroy the oneness God gave them when they married. They can undo their own work (of getting legally married); they cannot undo the work of God.

It is the issue of remarriage which shows this most clearly and it is for this reason that, in the context of discussing divorce, Jesus talks about remarriage (Mark 10:11f; Matt. 5:31f; 19:10–12). Remarriage, Jesus teaches, is adultery. This can only be because the original marriage – the oneness, the joining together – still exists.

This is why a divorced Christian, even when reconciliation is no longer possible, must continue to think: 'I am married and therefore not free to contemplate marriage to anyone else.' While married, he could never think of marrying a second partner. His legal divorce changes nothing in God's eyes and therefore should change nothing in his: he is still married, he is not free to contract a second marriage.

Exactly the same applies to a single person who is attracted to a divorcee (Luke 16:18; Matt. 5:32). If he met a woman who was legally married, he could never think of marrying her; he would need to ask God's help to overcome his attraction or, if this proved impossible, he would need to break off the friendship. Exactly the same applies when he meets a divorcee. She is still married in God's eyes; she should consider herself so, and he should consider her so. Any steps leading to marriage are therefore not to be contemplated. This of course seems extraordinarily hard to many today, but it is the indisputable teaching of our Lord.

## 5.   Does divorce for adultery destroy the oneness of marriage?

One question is, however, in dispute: did Christ teach that divorce for adultery (not adultery itself) destroys the oneness of marriage, and that the offended partner (not the adulterous partner whose duty is to seek reconciliation) may therefore remarry? Mark and Luke of course give no hint that there are any exceptions to Christ's teaching about no remarriage. Matthew, however, gives an exception to Christ's teaching about no divorce (which Mark and Luke do not mention); could it be that in Matthew Christ also allows for remarriage after divorce for adultery; and therefore teaches that divorce for adultery irrevocably breaks the marriage bond?

We have seen that Matthew 5:32 does not allow us to answer that question. The exception clause there is so completely an aside. Matthew 19:9 is, by almost unanimous consent, the only saying on which such an idea could be built. So far we have looked at the sentence itself and concluded that while it *may* teach that the man who divorces his wife for marital unfaithfulness and marries another does not commit adultery, the exception clause is an aside (not where Christ's main emphasis lies) and is in the natural (and only possible) place to teach: a man may divorce his wife for marital unfaithfulness, but anyone who divorces his wife and marries another woman – for whatever reason – commits adultery.

We have looked at the preceding context and seen that the whole emphasis is on the fact that it is not lawful to divorce. Christ speaks of the oneness that God gives in marriage and wants to make the point that a mere legal divorce cannot destroy this oneness. He therefore adds that remarriage is adultery (19:9). The exception about the right to divorce is very much an aside, added so as to give the full picture. It is, in itself, possible that Christ believed this also conferred the right to remarry in these circumstances, but it would be dangerous to draw that conclusion from an exception which is very much not the main thrust of his argument.

The succeeding context in any case makes such an interpretation very unlikely. The disciples are thunderstruck by what they have heard (19:10). This is incomprehensible if Jesus had merely reiterated the well-known position of Shammai which was part of the contemporary debate (cf 19:3). Moreover, far from roundly correcting them, Jesus goes on to speak of the value of a singleness which God has 'given' and in context this must mean a singleness after divorce, even the kind of divorce that Jesus (and Shammai) allowed. Christ's uniqueness as compared with Shammai was not in a stricter ruling over divorce, but in prohibiting remarriage – and saying that the God-given oneness remains – even where legal divorce is justified.

# 6

# Divorce and Remarriage in the Teaching of Jesus and of St Paul

In chapter 3 we looked at the very significant passage on marriage and singleness: 1 Corinthians 7. We examined it in detail but deliberately reserved verses 10–16, the section on divorce and remarriage, for this chapter.

Before looking at these verses in detail, we should briefly recap what verses 1–9 tell us about both the Corinthians' and Paul's own position. 'It is good for a man not to touch [meaning 'to have intercourse with', not as in NIV 'to marry'] a woman' (1) is almost certainly a quotation from the Corinthians' letter ('the matters you wrote about' – verse 1). It is the position of at least some of the Corinthians that it is best if every Christian refrains from any kind of sex.

Paul in part agrees with them. If he were to have his choice (7a), Christians would remain single (7f); it is 'better' that way (25ff, especially 38). But in part Paul strongly disagrees with them. He agrees with their teaching as it relates to those who are currently single (8f, 25–40; or rather: he comes to similar conclusions for different reasons). He disagrees with their teaching as it relates to those who are married (2–7, 10–16). They seem to have been suggesting that husband and wife should refrain from intercourse, that abstinence was more spiritual. Paul disagrees (2–6). Some of them also seem to have been suggesting that husbands and wives should divorce (cf 10f) or at least that a Christian married to a non-Christian partner should divorce the non-Christian (cf 12–16). Paul strongly repudiates both positions and comes to his refutation of them in verses 10–16.

# The Question of Divorce

(10) To the married I give this command (not I, but the Lord): A wife must not separate from her husband. (11) But if she does, she must remain unmarried or else be reconciled to her husband. And a husband must not divorce his wife.

## 1.   The Speaker

Before Paul gives his readers Christian teaching on the subject of divorce and remarriage, he tells them who is speaking to them: 'Not I, but the Lord' (10). Paul is, here, not merely speaking on his own apostolic authority, he is quoting from the teaching of the Lord Jesus Christ.

This is very rare in Paul's writings. He quotes from Christ's words much less often than we might expect. Nevertheless there are other examples. Within this letter examples are: 9:14 and 11:23-25, cf 1 Thess. 4:15, 1 Tim. 5:18. And of course there are many more instances where his teaching shows evidence of having been moulded by sayings of Christ without his directly acknowledging dependence. The fact remains, however, that direct quotation – or, as here, a paraphrase – of what is acknowledged to be a saying of Christ's is very uncommon in the New Testament letters. Barrett speculates as to why Paul may have appealed here to Christ's words. It may have been because 'the teaching of Jesus differed sharply from that prevailing in Judaism', in this case from the teaching both of Hillel and of Shammai. Or it may have been because in this instance Christian teaching even differed from the Old Testament (Deut. 24).

In any case, it is clear what Paul hoped to achieve by quoting Jesus directly: his aim was to give added weight and authority to the teaching that follows. Here they will be listening to something more than apostolic authority (1:1, 2:13, etc.); they will be listening to Christ himself. It is because of this direct appeal to the words of Christ that I have entitled this chapter: Divorce and 'Remarriage in the Teaching of Jesus and of St Paul'.

## 2. The addressees

Paul has been addressing 'the unmarried and the widows' (8f).
Now he – or rather Christ himself – addresses 'the married'
(10). As usual in this chapter – and in at least some of the
teaching of Jesus (Mark 10:11f) – he speaks to both the woman
and the man (cf 2, 3, 4, 12f, 14, 15, 16, etc.). What is striking
here is that he addresses the woman first, telling her not to
divorce her husband (10). This is all the more noteworthy
because, as we have seen, women in Jewish society could not
directly divorce their husbands (they could only get the courts
to arrange their divorce, and then only in a few circumstances
– m. Ketub. 7.9f). In Graeco-Roman society, it was possible for
a woman to divorce her husband. Seneca has a splendid passage
on this: 'Is there any woman that blushes at divorce now that
certain illustrious and noble ladies reckon their years not by the
number of consuls but the number of their husbands. and leave
home in order to marry, and marry in order to be divorced?' (De
Beneficiis, 3.16.2). However, even in Roman society, there were
social and especially economic reasons which made it harder
for the woman to divorce, and divorce by the wife was much
less common than divorce by the husband.

This leaves us wondering why Paul majors so heavily on the
wife (10–11a) and adds the husband almost as an afterthought
(11b). The reason may well be that it was the women especially
who were saying that sexual intercourse was to be avoided (1).
We have already seen, in chapter 3, that it was very likely the
women who were denying sexual intimacy to their husbands
(2–6; 'have' in verse 2 means 'have intercourse with' and not
'get married to'). It may well have been this which drove some
of the men to seek sexual satisfaction with prostitutes (6:15–20);
the word for 'immorality' in 7:2, since it both has the same root
as the word for prostitution (porn-) and is in the plural (literally:
because of the immoralities), may also refer to the men's having
sex with prostitutes. Thus 7:2 would then be saying: Since the
men are resorting to prostitutes, each man should be allowed
to have intercourse with his own wife (contrary to the teaching
(verse 1) and practice of you Corinthian women). Needless to

say, this (7:2) is not Paul's only reason for husbands and wives having sex (see, e.g., 3f) but it is one which, he believed, might carry weight with the Corinthian wives.

If we are correct in thinking that it was principally Corinthian women who held the view that 'it is good for a man not to touch a woman' (1), it was probably they too who were suggesting that Christian husbands and wives should divorce (cf 10f) and specifically that Christians should, within mixed marriages, divorce their pagan partners (cf 12–16). It is also very likely the case that, in Corinth then as almost everywhere in the world today, there were more converted women married to unconverted men than vice versa. This may be the reason why, in verses 12–16, although he starts with the man (12) before immediately adding the woman (13), he reverses the order – thinking first of the Christian woman married to the pagan man – in 14 and 16 (but cf 15). It may also be the reason why he begins with, and dwells much longer on, Christ's teaching that the woman should not divorce her husband (10–11a) and only briefly adds the corollary: that the man should not divorce his wife (11b).

## 3. The command

What Paul lays before these women and men is a 'command' (10, contrast 6). It is a command which comes with all the authority of Jesus. The command is that there is to be no divorce: 'A wife must not separate from her husband', 'And a husband must not divorce his wife' (10, 11).

As mirrored in the NIV's English, Paul uses two different words here: to separate oneself (chōrizomai) in 10 and to send away (aphiēmi) in 11. It might be thought that the second word, especially since it is used by Paul of the man, means '(legally) divorce' whereas the first word means only 'withdraw from living with' – in other words that they correspond exactly to our modern distinction between 'divorce' and 'separate'. However, there is strong evidence that Paul is using both words interchangeably. In 13 he uses aphiēmi of the woman divorcing the man, and in 15 he uses chōrizomai of both sexes. Fee comments: 'Divorce in Greco-Roman culture could be "legalised" by means of documents; but more often it simply happened [by one partner getting rid of, or simply leaving, the other]. In this culture, divorce was divorce, whether established by a document or not.' It is possible that *aphiēmi* was used more for divorce formally established by legal document and *chōrizomai* more for a divorce that 'just happened'. It would be unwise however to press this point. Heth and Wenham comment that both *chōrizō* and *aphiēmi* 'are found in legal papyri with the meaning of . . . divorce and would have been understood that way by Paul's readers' (p.138). Our modern distinction between separation and divorce would, in any case, probably not have been clearly perceived by Paul and his contemporaries.

It is, however, noteworthy that *chōrizomai* is the passive of the word Jesus uses in Mark 10:9//Matthew 19:6 (the passive, here, has a middle meaning: 'separate oneself from'). This is further evidence – especially as it is not the most common word for divorce – that Paul knew the teaching of Jesus on divorce and remarriage, and is quoting it here.

## 4. *The exception*

Christ himself, says St Paul, commands both wives and husbands not to divorce their partners. But within this command – between the command to the wife (10) and the command to the husband (11b) – comes an exception: 'But if she does divorce' (11a).

The teaching that follows is addressed specifically to the woman but it clearly is meant to apply to the man too, especially in this chapter where Paul is constantly pointing out that almost everything he says applies to both sexes. The teaching is, then, that if a Christian does divorce, he/she must 'remain unmarried or else be reconciled to' his/her partner (11a). After divorce only two options are open to the Christian: remaining single or resuming your marriage with your partner.

But what *is* this exception? What situation does Paul have in mind? Barrett says that it shows Paul does not want to apply Christ's teaching too rigidly: 'This (cf 7:6) shows that even where Christian legislation exists, it is not to be interpreted, and was not interpreted by Paul, in a legalistic manner.' In other words: 'I know Christ said this, but of course there will be exceptions . . .'. Fee is a little more subtle. He describes it as 'a concession to reality' and quotes M. E. Thrall (*Greek Particles in the New Testament*, p.81) describing this as 'the alternative [to no divorce] possibility which is permissible but not ideal'. In other words: 'I know Christ said this, but I realise you will not all live up to it; that is all right even if it is not quite the best.' Murray is perhaps the most sober in writing that 'Paul recognizes that human nature is perverse, that even Christians act perversely' and therefore he must provide for 'that evil contingency' (pp.61f), but even that means: 'I know Christ said this, but I know some of you will not obey him, so I'm telling you what to do when you disobey.'

All these suggestions seem to me quite impossible. Paul is not a compromiser. It is very hard to see him under any circumstances introducing teaching in a solemn way ('I give this command') and then immediately saying: 'But if you disregard all this, then . . .', especially before he has even finished giving his command (11b). This is even less likely when the Corinthians are advocating divorce and he is wanting to prohibit it; by allowing the exception he weakly concedes the reality to the Corinthians, again even before he has finished making his point. But if it is very hard to imagine him doing this under normal circumstances, it is absolutely impossible when he is quoting 'the Lord'. Paul simply would not quote half of Christ's teaching – quoting Christ in order to make the point with added solemnity – and then break off in the middle to say: 'But if you disobey Christ's teaching, then this is what you must do'.

But still we need to ask the question: what is this exception? The reality is that Paul is still quoting Jesus. He introduces the quote by the phrase: 'I give this command (not I, but the Lord)' in 10. He closes the quote by the phrase: 'To the rest I say this I, (not the Lord)' in 12. Everything between those two phrases is a quotation (or paraphrase) of Christ's teaching. This means that the exception comes just as much directly from Christ's teaching as the command not to divorce. The RSV has no justification for printing 11a in brackets, not at least if the intention is to imply that this is Paul's teaching, not Christ's. It is not until 12 that we revert to teaching from Paul and leave his quotation of Christ.

So if Paul is still quoting Christ when he speaks of an exception to the rule of 'no divorce', where does he get this exception from? The answer is that he must know one or both of the sayings of Christ that were recorded by Matthew (5:32 or 19:9). Jesus, in Matthew, says clearly that there is to be no divorce (19:6) and then allows one exception: there may be divorce in a case of marital infidelity (19:9, cf 5:32). Paul knows this and includes it in his quotation of Christ's teaching. Christ taught not only that a woman should not divorce her husband and a man should not divorce his wife (1 Cor. 7:10, 11b). He also taught that you may divorce for adultery. Moreover, that exception of Christ's came in a setting where remarriage was being discussed. So Christ also taught (according to Paul here) that if (following Christ's permission) you divorce for adultery, then you must remain single or be reconciled to your partner.

This is what Paul is doing: relaying Christ's teaching about the right marital state after the one exception Christ allowed: divorce for adultery. The only difference is that Christ put it negatively (to remarry is to commit adultery) whereas Paul puts Christ's teaching positively (after divorce, you must remain single or be reconciled). As we have seen, the alternative view – that Paul was saying: 'If (disobeying Christ's teaching) you divorce your partner for a reason Christ prohibits, then . . .' – is impossible.

This also destroys the hypothesis that Paul only knew Christ's sayings on divorce as recorded in Mark (and possibly Luke). This is Barrett's position. But it can only be maintained if 11a is Paul's comment, not Christ's. Since it is very unlikely that Paul would interrupt the quotation from Christ with his own comment, and impossible to believe this when (on this hypothesis) his comment runs in the opposite direction to Christ's teaching, we must maintain that 11a is also part of the quotation of Christ's teaching. Paul may indeed have known the saying of Christ that came to be recorded in Mark (Mark 10:12 is the only one of Christ's sayings on divorce that mentions the wife's divorcing the husband, cf 1 Cor. 7:10) but he also knew the 'exception clause' that was recorded in Matthew, and included it in his quotation of Christ.

Before we leave this exception, we should note one more fact: Christ, as reported by Paul, does not say: 'If she divorces, she must remain unmarried *in order to be* reconciled' with the implication, perhaps, that if she cannot be reconciled (because her partner remarries) then she need no longer remain unmarried herself. On the contrary, only two alternatives are placed before the divorced person: to be reconciled – that is, to resume the marriage – or, if that proves impossible, to remain single. This is the 'command' that Paul brings to us, except that it is not Paul, but Christ himself who is speaking.

## The Question of Mixed Marriages

(12) To the rest I say this (I, not the Lord): If any brother has a wife who is not a believer and she is willing to live with him, he must not divorce her. (13) And if a woman has a husband who is not a believer and he is willing to live with her, she must not divorce him. (14) For the unbelieving husband has been sanctified through his wife, and the unbelieving wife has been sanctified through her believing husband. Otherwise your children would be unclean, but as it is, they are holy.

(15) But if the unbeliever leaves, let him do so. A believing man or woman is not enslaved[1] in such circumstances; God has called us to live in peace. (16) How do you know, wife, whether you will save your husband? Or, how do you know, husband, whether you will save your wife?

Paul now turns from divorce in general to a specific instance: a 'mixed marriage' in which a Christian is married to an unbeliever. If, in the light of their view of sexual relations in general (1), some Corinthians were advocating that all married Christians should divorce (cf 10f), the case would seem stronger still where the partners were not spiritually matched and where the non-Christian might be thought of as defiling the Christian partner (cf 14). Paul now turns to this issue which was almost certainly been raised by the Corinthians in their letter.

---

[1]A better translation than 'bound' (NIV). See pp.251f.

## 1.   The speaker

Paul begins: 'To the rest I say this (I, not the Lord)' (12). This is in deliberate contrast to verses 10f. On this issue of mixed marriages, Paul has no specific quotation from the Lord Jesus Christ on which to draw because Christ in his earthly ministry did not deal with this question, whereas he did deal with the question of divorce in general and with the single allowable exception (10f).

Nevertheless, we should not imagine that this is said tentatively. Paul is not saying that this is merely his own hesitant thoughts, which the Corinthians can take or leave. On the contrary, Paul is, in this part of 1 Corinthians 7, very aware of his own authority (cf 17: 'This is the rule I lay down in all the churches'). He is simply distinguishing between what is 'written in the exercise of apostolic authority and inspiration' and what had been 'written not only in the exercise of apostolic authority' but also with 'the authority of the Lord's own teaching' (Murray p.62).

## 2.   The addressees

Paul says he is speaking 'to the rest' (12). He has already spoken to the married about sexual intercourse (2–6), to the unmarried and widows (8f) and to the married again about divorce (10f). 'The rest' is another group, contrasted with these others. And the context makes it clear that he has in mind those Christians who are married to non-Christians (cf 12,13).

Christian teaching was that a Christian should only marry another Christian (39, cf 2 Cor. 6:14–7:1). So almost certainly the cases envisaged here are of those who married as non-Christians and then one partner was converted after their marriage.

## 3.   The command

Paul's command is very clearly stated: do not divorce (12, 13). This may well have startled the Corinthians. Not only did they

– or at least some of them – believe that all sexual relations were suspect (1); they also believed that the Christian should have no dealings whatsoever with pagans (cf 5:9–13). Since they thought this about general social relationships, and since they (presumably) knew the Christian teaching that Christians should only marry other Christians, it must have seemed very natural to expect that Christians should avail themselves of the legal opportunity and divorce their non-Christian partners.

But Paul teaches precisely the reverse. On the contrary, there is to be no divorce even in the case of mixed marriages. The marriage commitment has been made, the marriage bond has been formed, and the Christian is to continue within the marriage, even though he now, since his conversion, finds himself mismatched spiritually with his partner.

There is here a principle of enormous importance for our contemporary debate: it shows conclusively that conversion does not affect the marriage bond. It is frequently stated in Christian circles today that the teaching of the New Testament on the subject of divorce and remarriage only applies to those who became Christians before or during their first marriage. Thus, following the teaching of Christ, a Christian may not divorce (except in the case of adultery), and if he does divorce he may not remarry (some would only be prepared to say: he may not remarry if his divorce were for reasons other than adultery). If, however (so the argument goes), he was not a Christian at the time of his divorce, then at his conversion the slate is wiped clean, it is as if he had never divorced and he is free to remarry. One passage is frequently quoted to 'prove' the point: 'Where a divorce occurred prior to conversion, remarriage may be permitted' (2 Cor. 5:17). 'When one becomes a Christian, all sin is forgiven, and all condemnation removed (Rom. 8:1)' (*Fresh Start* p.41).

This argument, which one meets very frequently among contemporary Christians, makes a number of very serious mistakes. Most important of all, it assumes that it is the sin (of divorce) which prevents remarriage. If this sin can be removed, by forgiveness, then no barrier to remarriage remains. This view is so obviously flawed that it is amazing how tenacious it is. If sin is really the barrier, what does the time of conversion to Christ have to do with it? Surely sin committed after conversion can also be fully forgiven and removed? In that case – according to the theory – remarriage should be open to all those who divorce, whenever they divorce their partners (before or after conversion) and for whatever reason. Yet very few Christians are prepared to take their view to its obvious conclusion because it runs clean counter to the teaching of Jesus.

It is to that teaching that we need to return. Jesus does not base his prohibition of remarriage on the sin of divorce. He bases it on the fact that remarriage would be legalised adultery. In other words, he bases it on the fact that the marriage bond continues to exist despite the divorce. It is not the (sin of) divorce which makes remarriage impossible for the Christian; it is the (original) marriage (see all the material in chapter 5). Only death dissolves the marriage bond, and therefore only death sets a person free to remarry (1 Cor. 7:39, cf Rom. 7:2f).

Moreover, Jesus explicitly bases his arguments on God's original creation (Mark 10:6–9//Matt. 19:4–8). This is God's will for all humankind: not only for those who knew the Jewish law, nor only for those who had been converted to Christ. If, according to Christ, remarriage after divorce is adultery before conversion (because God 'joins together' all married couples, Christian or non-Christian, and commands all couples not to divorce (except for adultery), and not to remarry because for all couples remarriage would be adultery), then after Christian conversion remarriage after divorce is just as much adultery. And the reason is precisely the same in both instances: the marriage bond still exists. 'In the teaching of Scripture nothing is clearer than the deep-seated cleavage between the children of light and the children of darkness.' Yet Paul does not say that mixed marriages are to be broken up. 'It is precisely here that the sacredness of the marriage bond is attested; the very cleavage between faith and unbelief constitutes no ground for separation or dissolution' (Murray pp.66f).

Conversion does not annul obligations or relationships, and of course 2 Corinthians 5:17 teaches no such thing. Conversion does of course bring us forgiveness of sin, but this only strengthens obligations which we have contracted in our pre-conversion days. Zacchaeus could not repudiate his obligations on the grounds that he had now become a follower of Christ's and his slate was wiped clean (cf Luke 19:8); no more can the Christian repudiate his marriage because he has become a Christian and his divorce took place before his conversion. On the contrary, he now learns from Christ that his original marriage bond still exists, that any remarriage would be adultery and that he should, if possible, seek reconciliation with his wife. If this is not possible, he must remain single (1 Cor. 7:11). The significant change is that he now has God's Holy Spirit to enable him to live up to Christ's teaching (Rom. 8:9–17).

So, conversion does not destroy the marriage bond. This is precisely what some Corinthians were claiming (hence their advocacy of divorce where, after conversion, one found oneself in a mixed marriage) and precisely what Paul was denying. Only death (39), not conversion, breaks the marriage bond. And this teaching of Paul's ties in with the teaching of the whole chapter. We have seen that the central paragraph is verses 17–24 in which the principle is clearly enunciated: remain in the state you were in when you were called (i.e. at conversion). The Christian is to remain married to his or her pagan partner. Indeed, being reconciled (11), if at conversion you were already divorced, would not constitute an exception to the principle of 17–24. It would merely be normalising a situation which had become abnormal: restoring the marital rights and obligations which had been wrongly withdrawn.

## 4.  An objection answered

Paul clearly anticipates an objection and seeks to answer it. As so often in our interpretation of the New Testament, we have to work back from his answer to discover what their anticipated objection must have been.

Paul says: 'For the unbelieving husband has been sanctified through his wife, and the unbelieving wife has been sanctified through her believing husband' (14). Arndt and Gingrich define hagiazō ('sanctify') as: 'include in the inner circle of what is holy, in both religious and moral uses of the word.' So, 'in Paul's usage to be holy (hagios) or sanctified (hēgiasmenos) is normally the distinguishing mark of the Christian' (Barrett), as it is in 6:11, cf 1:30. As Barrett acknowledges, this cannot however be the case here as the husband/wife is described as an unbeliever (12, 13, 15). He or she is clearly not yet 'saved' (16).

The basic problem seems to be that the Corinthian Christians felt they would be *defiled* in God's eyes by their contact with an unbeliever (cf 'unclean' in 14c which is contrasted with 'holy' (*hagios*)). St Peter of course had had to overcome precisely the same scruples about any association with pagans (Acts 10:9-29, especially 14f, 28). Paul now reassures the Corinthians. Far from their being contaminated by contact with their pagan marriage partners, these partners are made clean by their contact with them. It is in somewhat the same way that Paul can describe his contemporary Jews as not yet saved (Rom. 11:14) but holy (Rom. 11:16). They are set apart for God even though they are not yet grafted back on to God's tree (Rom. 11:13-24) or family.

Calvin well sums up Paul's argument in 1 Corinthians 7:14: 'It might seem (judging from appearance) as if a believing wife contracted infection from an unbelieving husband, so as to make the connection unlawful; but it is otherwise, for the piety of the one has more effect in sanctifying the marriage than the impiety of the other in polluting it.'

But how is the unbeliever sanctified? Paul answers: 'in' (*en* twice in 14) the wife/believing husband. 'In' is the correct translation, rather than 'through' (NIV, RSV, NEB) or 'by'. It is possible that there is a reference here to the idea of 'one flesh'. The husband and wife are no longer two but one flesh (Mark 10:8//Matt. 19:6); perhaps Paul alludes to this in saying that the husband is in his wife and the wife is in her husband.

Paul then goes on to give proof of his assertion that the unbeliever is sanctified by contact with the believing partner: 'Otherwise your children would be unclean, but as it is, they are holy' (14). He clearly regards this as beyond dispute. He says in effect: 'You know perfectly well how, within the family, your children are "clean" through their contact with you. It would not even cross your mind that you are defiled by contact with them. Well, it is the same with your husband/wife. The whole family stands or falls together: either your children as well as your partner are unclean, or both your children and your partner are "sanctified". As you know your children are "holy",[1] you can be quite sure that your marriage partner is too.'

## 5.   *The alternative situation*

All this has assumed that the pagan partner wants to continue with the marriage ('is willing to live with' the Christian: 12, 13). But suppose he/she does not? What should the Christian partner do then?

Paul answers: 'But if the unbeliever leaves, let him do so' (15). This is the correct translation; RSV has: 'If the unbelieving partner *desires to* separate'. But the desire is not what is mentioned, it is the action. Literally: 'If the unbeliever leaves, let him leave.' At first sight this might seem rather gratuitous advice. If the unbeliever has already left, or is in the process of leaving, there is not very much the Christian can do about it. The point, however, is that the Christian may well be – and in pastoral experience frequently is – tormented in his conscience. He knows the teaching of Christ: that there is to be no divorce (10f). He knows the teaching of St Paul: that there is to be no divorce even when one's partner is an unbeliever (12–14). Should the Christian, then, put up every possible legal, emotional and financial roadblock to prevent the unbeliever from making the separation permanent?

Paul's answer is: no. 'If the unbeliever wilfully departs, let separation take its course; . . . the believer is not under any

---

[1] It may be, as Godet maintains, that Paul's word for the children (*hagia*: holy) is 'stronger than' his word for the unbelieving partner (*hēgiastai*: sanctified). 'The verb, in the perfect passive [*hēgiastai*] indicated a position in which the subject is placed in the person of [*en*] another, whereas the adjective *hagia*, "holy", expresses a real quality inherent in the subject . . . Until Christian children decide freely for or against the salvation which is offered to them, they enjoy the benefit of . . . provisional salvation . . . And this is a state superior, though analogous, to that of the non-Christian spouse who, in virtue of keeping up his union with his Christian wife, is not himself received into the covenant (*hagios*: holy) but yet regarded as . . . consecrated in the person of his wife' (Godet). The argument would then be from the greater to the lesser: 'You know that your children are actually included (provisionally, until they decide for themselves) in the covenant because of their belonging to your family. Can you not see that you also have a sanctifying effect on your husband with whom you are one flesh?'

obligation to pursue the deserting spouse' (Murray p.68).

And then he goes on to explain: 'A believing man or woman is not enslaved in such circumstances' (15). This is a statement which has caused a great deal of debate and of misunderstanding. Much of the misunderstanding is caused by the mistranslation of *dedoulōtai* (literally: enslaved) as 'bound' (so NIV, RSV). When the English reader sees later: 'A woman is bound to her husband as long as he lives. But if her husband dies, she is free to marry . . .' (39, cf Rom. 7:2), he naturally concludes that Paul is saying: 'If the unbelieving partner leaves, the marriage bond is broken and the Christian is free to remarry.'

But in fact the words used by Paul are quite different. When Paul wants to speak of the marriage bond, he uses *deō* which is the normal verb for 'to bind' (27 where NIV's 'Are you married?' is literally: 'Are you bound to a wife?' (so RSV); 39; Rom. 7:2). Here he uses a totally different word: *douloō* (to enslave). It is misleading to translate this as 'bound'.

If the meaning 'no longer bound by the marriage bond' should be ruled out on linguistic grounds, it should also be a non-starter for contextual reasons. Verse 11 states clearly that an exception is possible to the absolute rule of no divorce but explicitly prohibits remarriage in these circumstances. We have already seen that Paul must have in mind legitimate divorce; it is inconceivable that he would interrupt his quotation of Christ's teaching by saying: 'But if, in disobedience to Christ, you do go ahead and divorce anyway . . .'. This exception should then encompass all legitimate cases; he is explaining in 11f the general principle, of which 12–16 is only a specific example. If it is argued that 11a only envisages divorce for adultery (since this formed part of Christ's teaching during his earthly ministry) and 12–16 is an entirely separate case not covered by 10f, it is hard to imagine that Paul, knowing that Jesus allowed divorce for adultery but prohibited remarriage in that circumstance, would prohibit divorce in the case of a mixed marriage (12f) but allow remarriage if a divorce took place on the unbeliever's insistence. This would mean Paul allowed in the case of mixed marriages what he has just quoted Jesus as forbidding in the case of adultery.

Such an interpretation also fits very ill with the context of the passage as a whole. 'The theme of the chapter . . . has to do with *not* seeking a change in status' (Fee; his emphasis). This is the recurrent idea in section after section of 1 Corinthians 7.

So if *ou dedoulōtai* does not mean: 'not bound by the marriage bond', what does it mean? Fee explains it as: 'not under bondage to maintain the marriage'. Barrett comments: 'not enslaved: that is, to a mechanical retention of a relationship the other partner wishes to abandon'. Robertson and Plummer say: 'All that *ou dedoulōtai* clearly means is that he or she need not feel so bound by Christ's prohibition of divorce as to be afraid to depart when the heathen partner insists on separation' (*A Critical and Exegetical Commentary on the 1st Epistle of St Paul to the Corinthians*, p.143). St Paul is saying, then: 'You do not need slavishly to pursue your partner when he leaves you, and do everything you can to pursue your marital obligations. You may accept the divorce.' This is a far cry, however, from saying: 'You may accept that you are no longer married and are therefore free to remarry.' This meaning cannot be squeezed out of *douloō* and is contradicted by the context (especially 11).

Paul then adds: 'God has called us to live in peace' (15). Some commentators believe that this refers back to verses 12–14. Barrett, for example, thinks that 15a,b is merely an aside. In verses 12–14, then, Paul tells the Christian not to leave his pagan partner. Verse 15a,b speaks of the situation where the pagan insists on leaving. This probably did not form part of the question in the Corinthians' letter. Paul merely adds it for completeness' sake and states: 'In that case you need not slavishly pursue your marriage partner.' Then, after this aside, Paul returns in 15c–16 to their original question: 'You should not divorce your unbelieving partner. God has called us to live in peace.'

Barrett and Fee, arguing for this interpretation, put great emphasis on the particle *de* which links 15c to the sentence before. Greek sentences are normally linked to each other by particles, and Fee gives 'due force' to *de* here by translating it as 'However'. In other words, 15a,b are an aside, speaking of the situation in which the unbeliever insists on separation: 'However – to get back to the issue I am discussing and you asked about – God has called us to live in peace (and therefore we should not divorce our pagan partners).'

But this makes *de* strongly adversative, when actually it is a rather weak particle. It can be translated 'but'; it is equally often translated 'and'; it is frequently not translated at all (so Arndt and Gingrich). It is more likely that it should be translated 'and' here. Paul gives his judgment in 15a: 'If the unbeliever leaves, let him do so.' He then expands on this, giving a reason for his judgment: 'A believing man or woman is not enslaved in such circumstances' (15b). Then he gives a further reason for the same judgment: 'God has called us to live in peace' (15c).

Barrett and Fee both say that this would require the particle *gar* ('for') to introduce 15c (RSV, without justification, inserts 'for'). But this is not in fact necessary, as 15b constitutes a reason for letting an unbeliever go if he insists on it, and 15b is not introduced by *gar*. Also 15c constitutes a further reason for letting go, and it is not introduced by *gar* either. The NIV therefore translates it well. It does not translate the weak *de* and merely has: 'God has called us to live in peace.'

The desire to live at peace with others was close to Paul's heart: 'If it is possible, as far as it depends on you, live at peace with everyone' (Rom. 12:18). It was also a typically Jewish concern. *m. Git.* 5.8 has a whole catalogue of things that are 'enjoined in the interests of peace' and finishes with the need for Jews to maintain peace with pagans: 'They do not try to prevent the poor among the Gentiles from gathering Gleanings, the Forgotten Sheaf and the Corner [of the field] – in the interests of peace.'

This principle cannot of course override weightier moral considerations. It would, for example, run clean counter to both Jesus' and Paul's teaching to claim, on the basis of this principle, that divorce is permissible 'in the interests of peace' where there is unbearable friction in a marriage. On the contrary, initiating divorce is never allowed by the New Testament except on the grounds of adultery. But a divorce thrust upon one by a pagan partner may be accepted, need not be struggled against. And one of the reasons is that a struggle would merely engender more antagonism whereas God wants – wherever it is possible within his moral parameters – to promote peace.

So Paul has said that if an unbelieving partner wants to get out of the marriage, the Christian partner should let him go rather than 'stay and fight the matter out' (Barrett's phrase).

## 6. *The final question*

Paul finishes this section with a question: 'How do you know, wife, whether you will save your husband? Or, how do you know, husband, whether you will save your wife?' (16). But what Paul has in mind here is not entirely clear. Grammatically, the questions could be optimistic (so NEB, in its rather loose translation: 'Think of it: as a wife you may be your husband's salvation; as a husband you may be your wife's salvation') or pessimistic ('How can you be certain that you (as you think) will save your partner?').

Luck is one writer who argues for the pessimistic interpretation. The verse can literally be translated: 'For what do you know, wife, if (or: whether) . . .'. The initial 'for' links 16 back to what has been said previously, and it is most natural to think it links back to the immediately preceding verse (15). It may be, then, that Paul was anticipating an objection to his teaching in 15: 'You are saying that if my unbelieving partner desires to separate, I am to let him go. But I am seeking to lead him to faith in Christ. Will I not be failing in my calling to bring him salvation?' Paul, on this hypothesis, replies: 'What makes you think you will bring him to salvation? You may well not' (see Luck p.172).

A further argument for this understanding of 16 is the strong adversative ('Nevertheless' – *ei mē*) which follows in 17. This makes 17 contrast with 16. So 17 is a strong call to remain in the state you are in, and the 'nevertheless' would be entirely understandable if 16 had been a further reason for allowing a marriage partner to leave if he wants to. The force of the section as a whole would then be: Don't divorce your pagan partner if he will stay (12–14), but allow your partner to leave if he insists (15f); nevertheless it is better to remain as you are (17ff), i.e. married.

Most commentators, however, accept the optimistic interpretation: Paul is saying there is a good likelihood that the Christian partner, wife or husband, will help the unbelieving partner to faith. 'The Greek Fathers all interpret the passage in this sense'

(Barrett). There is also a very similar optimistic question in 2 Samuel 12:22.

The most convincing reason for accepting this interpretation is that it seems much more in keeping with Paul's outlook. In this same letter, he tells us that he uses every means available to 'win' or 'save' as many as he can (9:19–23). It is far more likely, then, that he would use the argument: 'If you follow my instructions, you may "save" your partner', than that he would say: 'Follow my instructions because you are rather unlikely to "save" your partner, so it is not worth, for that reason, clinging on to your marriage.' There is a similarly optimistic expectation of the Christian wife's influence on the pagan partner in 1 Peter 3:1f.

Most commentators then tie verse 16 back to 12–14 (and perhaps to 15c if this is interpreted as a reason for staying together). The force of the section as a whole is then: Don't divorce your pagan partner if he will stay (12–14) – but allow your partner to leave if he insists (15, or just 15a,b) – because by staying you may save your partner (16, or 15c–16).

This may be correct, but it certainly has difficulties. On the one hand: if we are correct that 15c is a further reason for letting go a pagan partner who insists on leaving, then the initial 'for' of 16 (which is in Paul's Greek, though not in NIV, RSV, NEB) leaps over 15 and refers back to 12–14; this is possible but not natural. On the other hand, 17 begins with the strong adversative 'nevertheless'; this is almost inexplicable if 16 is a reason for staying together in the married state, since 17 is saying precisely the same.

Perhaps it is more likely, therefore, that 16 is a further reason – but an optimistic reason – for accepting a separation (even a legal divorce) when the unbelieving partner wants it. Paul will then be saying: 'By not wrangling, by accepting the divorce peacefully (15c), you may impress your partner (because your attitude is so very different from what he might have expected, had you not been a Christian) and so lead to his conversion.' This close connection between 15c (living peaceably with one's spouse) and 16 (the hope of winning them over to Christ) is echoed in 1 Peter 3:1f: 'Wives, in the same way be submissive to your husbands so that, if any of them do not believe the word, they may be won over without words by the behaviour of their wives, when they see the purity and reverence of your lives.'

Heth and Wenham in fact believe that 16 links back to both situations envisaged in 12–15. 'Why should believers live harmoniously with their unbelieving mates either in marriage [12–14] or separation [15]? Because they may very well be the channel through whom God brings their unbelieving partner to faith' (p.141).

## Conclusions

### 1.  Paul is the earliest interpreter of the teachings of Jesus

We are very fortunate. It is extremely rare for Paul to quote Jesus, but he does on this subject of divorce and remarriage (10f). It is also helpful to us in that, while he acknowledges that he is merely passing on the teaching of Jesus (10), he paraphrases it, and thus makes clear his own understanding of Jesus' words.

We have already seen (in chapter 5) the value of early Church interpreters of Christ's sayings because they were very close to the language and culture of the New Testament. St Paul was closer still: closer in time (because 1 Corinthians was written less than 25 years after Jesus' statements about divorce and remarriage), closer in language (because Paul spoke Aramaic (Acts 21:40; 22:2) and, if Christ's sayings had come to him in Greek, also spoke contemporary Greek) and closer in culture (because Paul had been brought up within Palestinian Judaism: Acts 22:3).

He has one further advantage over the early Church writers: he is also authoritative as an interpreter. He frequently claimed to write with the authority of an apostle of God, and the Christian Church has recognised the validity of that claim by including his writings in the New Testament. He does in fact agree with the way in which the early Church writers understood the teaching of Jesus about divorce and remarriage, but he has unique authority as an inspired interpreter of Jesus' teaching.

*2.   Paul interprets Jesus as saying that remarriage is never legitimate in the lifetime of a divorced partner*

In his quotation of the teaching of Jesus, he highlights the two areas about which Jesus spoke: divorce and remarriage. Jesus made clear that there was to be no divorce, and he applied this both to men and women (10, 11b, cf especially Mark 10:11f). He also, however, allowed an exception. The exception that Paul mentions ('but if she does separate': 11) must be the same as the exception which Matthew records Jesus as giving ('except for marital unfaithfulness': Matt. 5:32; 19:9). Any other interpretation of 11a makes Paul interrupt Jesus' teaching (when in fact he makes it clear that he does not return to his own teaching until 12) and means that he is saying: 'But if she disobeys the teaching of Jesus . . .'.

In 11a Paul quotes – or paraphrases – Jesus' teaching on remarriage. It is particularly helpful that he does so in the context of Jesus' exception: he is telling us what Jesus taught should happen when there has been divorce for adultery. Jesus taught that only two options were open to the Christian in this case: either to remain single or to be reconciled to his original partner. Separation may be *de facto* permanent, but the couple 'may never take the position that *finis* is written across their marital relations' (Murray p.78).

*3.   Paul does not add another ground for legitimate divorce*

It is often claimed that the New Testament allows divorce on two grounds: in the case of adultery (so Jesus in Matthew and 1 Corinthians 7:11) and in the case of desertion by an unbelieving partner (so Paul in 1 Corinthians 7:15f). But this is not the case. Paul's whole emphasis in 7:12ff is that there should be no divorce. It was the Corinthians who were almost certainly suggesting divorce in the case of a mixed marriage. Paul for his part prohibits Christians from seeking it. Even if the partner is not 'willing to live with' the Christian, the Christian partner is not to initiate divorce. Paul only says that he need not feel obligated to fight tooth and nail against the divorce (15).

Thus, verses 12–16 are not (as is frequently claimed) an exception to the principle in verses 11f, an exception in addition to the one Christ himself gave which is quoted in 11a. On the contrary, it is a further example of the principle in 11f, namely: no divorce. Even verses 15f are not another exception because they merely advocate acceptance of legal divorce, not the initiation of divorce.

### 4.   Christians may accept a divorce thrust upon them

Paul cites a specific instance, an instance which was doubtless raised by the Corinthians: the case of marriages between a Christian and an unbeliever. He says they are not to divorce (12f). However, he goes on to mention a situation which the Corinthians had probably not raised: what happens if the unbeliever insists on leaving? Then the Christian may not initiate, but may acquiesce in, divorce: 'let him separate' (so 15, literally).

Paul goes on: 'A believing man or woman is not enslaved in such circumstances' (15). But what are 'such circumstances'? Does Paul consider this acceptance of divorce as appropriate only when it is an unbeliever who leaves? Or is acceptance appropriate when any husband (or wife) insists on leaving? I would tentatively suggest the latter because of 15c. It is because of the general principle that 'God has called us to peace' that it is right to accept the unbelieving husband's insistence on leaving. Such reasoning would also encourage acceptance of (at least most) divorces where one partner is absolutely intent on leaving and has indeed left (15: 'If the unbeliever leaves, let him leave').

The Westminster Confession accepts this wider application. It first, rightly, warns that 'the corruption of man' very easily comes up with arguments to support illegitimate divorce and then adds: 'yet nothing but adultery, or such wilful desertion as can no way be remedied by the Church or civil magistrate, is cause sufficient' for divorce (chapter 24, section 6). Where there has been desertion, the Church – and indeed the civil authorities – must seek to bring reconciliation, but where this has proved impossible, divorce may be accepted; the deserted partner need not fight against it.

Once again we need to stress that this is in no way a mandate for divorce, nor is it an encouragement, for a person who wants to get out of his marriage, to push his partner into taking the initiative so that he can then quickly acquiesce in the separation. But it is the New Testament's permission not to contest every inch of the way, not to fight tooth and nail against a divorce on which your partner is insisting, despite your efforts at reconciliation.

## 5. Accepting a divorce does not mean that the marriage bond is broken

Paul says that where the unbeliever insists on divorce, 'the believing man or woman is not enslaved' (15). What does that mean? It is true that the opposite of 'enslaved' is 'free'. If, then, Paul declares the Christian 'not enslaved in such circumstances', it means that he or she is free. But free to do what?

Some people leap to the unwarranted assumption that Paul means: free to remarry. We have seen that much of this misunderstanding stems from a false translation of *dedoulōtai* as 'bound', which is especially misleading in the light of 39 (where the different word *dedetai* is correctly translated 'bound'). But not only does *dedoulōtai* in fact mean 'enslaved'; the context also forbids an interpretation which makes 'not enslaved' mean 'free to remarry'. Bengel comments on 15: 'Let him be divorced. A brother or a sister should be patient and not think that that ought to be changed which he or she cannot change . . . but with that exception: "let her remain unmarried": verse 11' (*Gnomon of the New Testament*).

*Ou dedoulōtai* does indeed mean that the Christian is free; he is free to accept the divorce. He does not have to feel obligated – the 'slave' of self-imposed duties – to fight against it. But this does not mean that he is free to remarry. On the contrary, only two options are open to him: to be reconciled with his partner or to remain single (11). And the reason for this is precisely the same reason that Jesus gave in the Gospels: despite the divorce, despite the acceptance of the divorce by the believing partner, the marriage bond still exists. It can only be broken by death (39).

# 7

# Singleness After Marriage

Increasing numbers of people are experiencing a second – and even third, or fourth – period of singleness. Of course it has always been the case that men and women have known single-ness again after bereavement; the difference in our contemporary society is that people are living longer and, while that means that the death of a partner is tending to come later, it also means that women and men are experiencing longer periods of widow-hood. When one adds to these people the millions who are now getting divorced each year, it is easy to see that vast numbers – especially in the Western countries where divorce rates are so high – are experiencing singleness after having been married.

Yet there is also in our contemporary society an abhorrence of singleness. If you are single, over a certain age and have never been married, you are thought probably to be homosexual. As a matter of fact, this is true for many, especially in a culture where only life as a couple is really acceptable and therefore there have to be strong internal motives for not seeking marriage (or heterosexual cohabitation); indeed many homosexuals, for a whole variety of reasons, feel compelled to enter (heterosexual) marriage. But even if it is the case that many never-married people may be homosexually oriented, this is no justification for treating them with the utmost suspicion. Many clergymen, for example, do not dare to acknowledge their basic homosex-uality because it may instantly be assumed that no choirboy, no teenage male confirmation candidate, is safe in their company.

Of course there are temptations for the single, homosexually-inclined person. There are just as many temptations for the single, heterosexually-inclined person, and I would suspect that these are far more frequently succumbed to than the homosexual's temptations. There are also temptations for the married person, whatever his or her sexual orientation. All these temptations are to be recognised and guarded against. Christians, as well as non-Christians, will not conquer them on every occasion. But none of this is any justification for treating the single person with suspicion and for imagining that he or she is odd, inadequate in a pronounced way (we are all inadequate in some way) and not to be trusted.

If, on the other hand, you have been married and are now single, the great consolation is that you can get remarried. Many a divorcee or young widow has been told: 'You're still young. Attractive. There'll be plenty of men after you.' And many friends and family members, who have not said this, have nevertheless thought it. Their friend's divorce or bereavement is a terrible, terrible event but they console themselves with the thought: 'At least when he's got over it, he can get married again. There are lots of women who would be only too pleased to be married to a man like that.' Indeed while most people do not want to think of marriage (though they may well seek sexual relationships) for some time after a divorce, some do search instantly for a new marriage partner. A man whose marriage broke up after 18 years determined: 'I will get married within two years.'

With this view of singleness, it is not surprising that any block put in the way of remarriage is perceived as cruel, because singleness is seen as cruel. As one example, a clergyman felt unable to conduct the marriage of a woman in his congregation to a divorcee (cf Matt. 5:32; Luke 16:18). A friend of the woman wrote: 'In effect aren't you condemning the already divorced members of your congregation to a solitary lifestyle? . . . What hope can you offer [divorced persons] individually for future happiness if you refuse to marry them?' The language is very expressive of the attitude: to withhold marriage is to 'condemn' people, singleness is a 'solitary lifestyle' ('solitary' is obviously used pejoratively) in which there can be no 'future happiness'.

All this leads us back to the New Testament. What does it have to say about a return to singleness for those who have been married?

## Singleness after the Death of a Spouse

Widows were people whom Old Testament Israelites and New Testament Christians were especially commanded to care for. It is not surprising, therefore, that a fair amount is written not only about how to help them but about their singleness.

### 1. Freedom to remarry

> A woman is bound to her husband as long as he lives. But if her husband dies, she is free to marry anyone she wishes, but he must belong to the Lord (1 Cor. 7:39).

This is the clearest, and most straightforward, statement in the New Testament about the options open to a person after the death of her or his partner. Before drawing out its implications, it may be as well to remind ourselves (the question was discussed in chapter 3) why only the woman is mentioned. The principal reason is probably because in Corinth, as in almost every society and every age, it was more often the case that wives outlived their husbands than that men outlived their wives (cf also 8; 1 Tim. 5:3-16). Fee suggests as a further reason that, in a chapter where statements about women consistently balance those about men, 39f speak to the women after 36–38 which was addressed to men.

But in any case we can be quite sure that Paul would have said the same to widowers. The point of departure here is the thought that a woman is 'bound' to her husband during his lifetime. Barrett points out that Paul has said a man is equally 'bound' to his wife (27 literally, cf 11). Barrett also suggests that the reason for not mentioning men here (in 39f) is 'because he was answering a specific question' put to him by the Corinthians.

Whatever the exact reason or reasons for only mentioning women here, we must clearly apply the teaching to either sex. The marriage bond exists while one's partner is alive. Consequently the wife (or husband) is 'bound' and not able to marry another. Death, however, breaks the marriage bond; she (or he) is then free to remarry. Paul lays only one restriction on the widow. She must marry 'in the Lord' (39 literally). In the context, the primary meaning must be 'with a member of the Christian society' (Godet, cf NIV), but Barrett, following Lightfoot, believes that it has a broader meaning as well: 'She must remember that she is a member of Christ's body, and not forget her Christian duties and responsibilities.' In other words, she must marry a Christian certainly, but her courtship and married life must also be thoroughly Christian.

Closely similar to 39f is Romans 7:1–3:

(1) Do you not know, brothers – for I am speaking to men who know the law – that the law has authority over a man only as long as he lives? (2) For example, by law a married woman is bound to her husband as long as he is alive, but if her husband dies, she is released from the law of marriage. (3) So then, if she marries another man while her husband is still alive, she is called an adulteress. But if her husband dies, she is released from that law and is not an adulteress, even though she marries another man.

Here Paul again says that a woman is 'bound' to her husband as long as he lives; he uses precisely the same Greek word (*dedetai*). For her to enter a second marriage during her husband's lifetime would be adultery (3a), but for her to enter a second marriage after her husband's death is not adultery (3b). Dunn well brings out the striking contrast in 3. The woman is named 'adulteress, with all the opprobrium, guilt and liability to the penalty of death which that word then carried, if she consorts with another man while her husband is still alive . . . Once her husband is dead, the same woman can do precisely the same thing without incurring any name or blame of adultery.' Why? What makes the enormous difference? Simply that she is 'bound by law to her husband' (2) while he is alive and 'released from the law of marriage (literally: from the law of the husband)' (2, cf 3: 'free from the law') when he dies. In other words, the law says that a marriage bond exists during her partner's lifetime which can only be dissolved by his death.

Here then, in both 1 Corinthians 7:39f and Romans 7:1–3 is a clear charter for the widow or – by extension – the widower.

They are free to remarry after the death of their partner and must only take care to marry 'in the Lord'.

## 2.  *Encouragement to marry*

So I counsel younger widows to marry, to have children, to manage their homes and to give the enemy no opportunity for slander. (1 Tim. 5:14).

Freedom to remarry was open to all who had been widowed but while – as we shall see – the New Testament gently suggests that it may be better for most widows not to remarry, the advice here to younger widows is very definitely to marry.

The situation envisaged in 1 Timothy 5 (discussed much more fully below) is that some widows took special vows and were enrolled on a list of 'official' widows who both received financial help and engaged in practical service and more directly spiritual ministry (3–16). Part of their vow was not to remarry (cf 11f). Paul had experienced the situation where some younger widows had been enrolled on the list (11). 'Younger' in 11–15 seems not just to envisage those 'under 60' (the only specific age mentioned in this passage: 9) but rather to have in mind those of child-bearing age, since Paul counsels these 'younger widows' to 'marry and bear children' (14).

In any case, enrolling younger widows, getting them to take vows and engage in ministry, had not worked (11–13). In particular, red blood was still coursing through their veins. Paul uses the verb *katastrēniaō* (11), the root of which (*strēniaō*) Arndt and Gingrich translate as 'feel sensuous impulses'; and as a result, they want to get married (11).

Paul's advice is that it is not appropriate to enrol such younger widows, and he positively encourages them to get married, to bear children (which is always seen as a fundamental part of marriage in Scripture), to manage (or better: rule, the Greek is *despoteō*) their households and not to play into the hands of the devil (because it is obvious to all if they take vows and then do not live up to them) (14).

The argument that rather than be dogged by unfulfilled desire in enforced singleness, it is far better to marry is closely similar to 1 Corinthians 7:8f, 36. Paul adds to this a characteristic idea of his – especially in the Pastoral Epistles – that he does not want the outside world, egged on by the devil, to have any opportunity to slander these Christian women (cf 1 Tim. 3:7).

Yet once again we should not think that Paul's only reason for marriage was to channel sexual passion and avoid an unnecessarily bad press. He sees marriage itself as God-given (cf 4:1–3), child-bearing as tremendously important (cf 2:15) and ruling a house as noble (cf Titus 2:3–5 – *oikourgos* (5) means 'working at home'). It is only because he sees the tremendous advantages which God has given to singleness that he sometimes appears to downgrade marriage. The truth is that he does indeed downgrade it from the position of undisputed pre-eminence which it holds today, but still he regards it as a gift from God, which is to mirror the relationship between Christ and his Church. And here (in 1 Tim. 5) he specifically encourages younger widows to remarry.

## 3. The happiness of singleness

> (39) A woman is bound to her husband as long as he lives. But if her husband dies, she is free to marry anyone she wishes, but he must belong to the Lord. (40) In my judgment, she is happier if she stays as she is – and I think that I too have the Spirit of God (1 Cor. 7).

We have already discussed the question of the authority with which Paul claims to speak in 1 Corinthians 7 (see chapter 3). The last phrase (40b) is almost certainly gently ironic; the emphatic 'I too' gives that away. Undoubtedly the Corinthians were claiming to have a special endowment of the Spirit; some of them were perhaps hinting that Paul was not Spirit-filled. Here, with a touch of irony, Paul says he thinks that he also has been given God's Spirit. It is a way of saying that he knows he has.

Yet he also says that 40 is 'my judgment'. This is not, then, a pronouncement given with full apostolic authority. In part this is because Paul sees the issue as a matter of quite fine judgment. Certainly there are troubles in marriage (28) and advantages in singleness (25–40), but the implication is that there are also troubles in singleness (36 mentions only one kind) and advantages in marriage (2–5, 7, 14, 16 are just some). The decision between marriage and singleness is therefore one of fine balance. In addition, Paul is well aware that for different individuals different courses of action will be best (7, 8f). We have already seen that his *general* advice to younger widows is to marry (1 Tim. 5:14); so here it can only be *general* advice to widows that it will be better for them not to marry.

However, while taking due note of the fact that this is advice ('my judgment') rather than a command, we should not dilute this teaching to the point where we dismiss it. Paul claims, specifically in this context, to have – and therefore to be writing by – the Spirit of God. The Christian may well feel that this claim has been vindicated by the inclusion of this chapter in Scripture, and therefore we listen to what Paul says in 40 with considerably more attention than just to the advice of a wise old Christian.

Paul says clearly that the widow may get married again or she may remain single. But his opinion is that she will be 'happier' remaining single. This word, placed first in the sentence for emphasis, is *makariōtera*. It means: 'blessed, fortunate, happy, usually in the sense: privileged recipient of divine favour' (Arndt and Gingrich). In the New Testament, it normally has a distinctly religious flavour: blessed by God. With this meaning it is the first word in all the Beatitudes (Matt. 5:3–11). But it can have 'less obvious religious colouring' according to Arndt and Gingrich who cite 1 Corinthians 7:40 as an example: 'happy'. This is, in essence, what Paul has said about singleness in general in 32–35: a single person can be 'free from concern' (32) because his 'undivided interest' (cf 34) can be devoted to pleasing the Lord.

Whatever the precise meaning of *makariōtera* – whether it means that she is more blessed by the Lord, or, simply, more happy – it is a revolutionary concept for people today. Compare the letter quoted at the beginning of this chapter: 'What hope can you offer [divorced persons] individually for future happiness if you refuse to marry them?' Yet this is Paul's Christian conviction.

And not only his conviction, but very likely his experience too. In 8 he has said: 'Now to the unmarried and widows I say: It is good for them to stay as I am' (the word 'unmarried' (so NIV) is clearly implied but is not in Paul's Greek). Paul was very likely a rabbi and it was almost obligatory for rabbis to be married. Since the clear implication of 7f is that he is not married at the time of writing, the probability is that he is a widower. He has known what marriage is, and he now knows singleness after marriage and he is able to make the comparison. Both his own experience (7f) and his experience of others (32–35) as well as his experience of the world (26–31) convince him that to remain single after the death of a partner is both happier (40) and better (Conzelmann rightly points out that good (*kalon*) in 8 is in fact a synonym for better (*kreitton*) in 9).

## 4.  A vow of singleness

We have already referred to the special order of 'official' widows described in 1 Timothy 5. We must now return to study this order in greater detail:

(3) Give proper recognition to those widows who are really in need. (4) But if a widow has children or grandchildren, these should learn first of all to put their religion into practice by caring for their own family and so repaying their parents and grandparents, for this is pleasing to God. (5) The widow who is really in need and left all alone puts her hope in God and continues night and day to pray and to ask God for help. (6) But the widow who lives for pleasure is dead even while she lives. (7) Give the people these instructions, too, so that no one may be open to blame. (8) If anyone does not provide for his relatives, and especially for his immediate family, he has denied the faith and is worse than an unbeliever.

(9) No widow may be put on the list of widows unless she is over sixty, has had but one husband, (10) and is well known for her good deeds, such as bringing up children, showing hospitality, washing the feet of the saints, helping those in trouble and devoting herself to all kinds of good deeds.

(11) As for younger widows, do not put them on such a list. For when their sensual desires overcome their dedication to

Christ, they want to marry. (12) Thus they bring judgment on themselves, because they have broken their first pledge. (13) Besides, they get into the habit of being idle and going about from house to house. And not only do they become idlers, but also gossips and busybodies, saying things they ought not to. (14) So I counsel younger widows to marry, to have children, to manage their homes and to give the enemy no opportunity for slander. (15) Some have in fact already turned away to follow Satan.

(16) If any woman who is a believer has widows in her family, she should help them and not let the church be burdened with them, so that the church can help those widows who are really in need (1 Tim. 5).

In this passage, Paul distinguishes between three types of widows: widows with families still living or others on whom they can be dependent (4, 8, 16); younger widows (11–15: see the discussion earlier in this chapter); and 'widows who are really in need' (this is the NIV translation of *hai ontōs chērai* (3. 5, 16), literally: 'real widows' (so RSV)). It is this third group with which we are now concerned.

The responsibility of the Church towards these 'official' widows was to 'give them proper recognition' (3). In the Greek this is simply: 'honour' (*tima*), a word which can mean 'support financially' as 17f makes clear. The immediately following context in 4 shows that 'honour' has the same meaning in 3. The church was to provide for the financial needs of these widows. In doing so, it was merely following the frequent Old Testament commands to care for widows in their need, a practice which was continued right from the earliest days in the Christian Church (Acts 6:1–3, cf Jas 1:27).

The Church was also to 'enrol' these widows (NIV: 'put them on the list' – 9, cf 11). On the one hand this meant that they would receive a regular distribution of food and other supplies (cf Acts 6:1); on the other hand, it meant that they received a place of special standing within the Christian community (hence my phrase 'official widows'). They were not quite officers within the Church and thus do not figure in the list of officers: overseers (3:1–7), deacons (3:8–13) and perhaps deaconesses (3:11). But they were also not what we might call 'ordinary

Church members'. In this respect, it is significant that immediately following the discussion of official widows (5:3–16), Paul mentions elders (5:17–20); elders were the same as overseers/bishops (cp Titus 1:5f with Titus 1:7).

We may say, then, that they had a recognised, and highly regarded, ministry and were honoured for their work (cf 1 Thess. 5:12). What then were their responsibilities? These are not laid out in detail for us, but Kelly is probably right in suggesting that the duties of a member of the widows' order were the same as the good works of which she had to give evidence before being admitted; 'so the best testimonial a newcomer could produce was to point to zeal and efficiency in carrying out these tasks voluntarily' (Kelly).

These responsibilities would, then, be: spending much time in prayer (5: the Greek – literally: continues in *the* supplications and *the* prayers – may suggest very regular attendance at the church's meetings for worship, cf Luke 2:37), engaging in good works (10a, cf the last phrase in 10), such as bringing up children, which may be a reference to the care of orphans, especially since she has no children or grandchildren now and may never have had any (10b, cf 3f), practising hospitality which would include the humble task of washing visitors' feet (10c,d, cf John 13:14) and helping those in trouble (10e).

In addition to these duties in which widows should already have been engaged before being officially enrolled, one seems to be mentioned which may only have begun after enrolment: going from house to house. Paul says that younger widows, who had been misguidedly added to the official list, 'learn to be idle as they go about the houses' (13 literally). NIV and RSV treat this 'going from house to house' as further evidence of their degeneracy, but I think it is much more likely that it was a form of pastoral visiting and informal teaching which formed part of their duties (cf Acts 20:20). Their mistake was not to visit people's houses but to be spiritually idle as they did so, and to use their time merely for gossip (13).

What then were the qualifications needed before widows could be put on the official list? 'The conditions for admission are extremely stringent' (Spicq). They include of course already practising all the duties (with the possible exception of the pastoral visiting) mentioned above; indeed, not only must they be engaged in these acts of service, they must be 'well known' for them (10).

In addition, they must be 'left all alone' (5) which in context clearly means that they have no family or other friends on whom they can be dependent (cf 4, 8, 16). They should have no other means of support. Moreover, they must be over 60 (9), 'the recognised age in antiquity when one became an "old" man or woman' (Kelly).

And then we come to two statements by Paul about marital qualifications. An 'official' widow must be 'the wife of one husband' (RSV), 'have had but one husband' (NIV footnote; NIV text: 'been faithful to her husband' is clearly wrong). This means that she must only ever have been married once, and that she should not have remarried after divorce or after the death of her husband (for further discussion of this phrase, see below).

Secondly, it is clear that she has taken a 'vow' or 'pledge' (NIV, RSV). This comes to light in a discussion of the younger widows who were enrolled but 'have broken their first pledge' (12). The context – which mentions their falling down on 'their dedication to Christ' and 'wanting to marry' (11) – makes it clear that theirs was a vow of singleness. Or rather: it was perhaps a vow of marriage to Christ, since the Greek expression in 11 – *katastrēniasōsin tou Christou* – means 'become wanton against Christ, feel sensuous impulses that alienate them from Christ' (Arndt and Gingrich). 'The language suggests that Christ is thought of as a spiritual bridegroom (cf 2 Cor. 11:2)' (Kelly). To give in to these sensuous desires is 'a sort of spiritual adultery . . . towards Christ who is their only husband' (Spicq).

These widows, then, whom Paul commends to be put on the official roll have not only never remarried, even after the death of their husband, but have taken a vow to remain single because they think of themselves as being married to Christ.

I cannot refrain from reporting a conversation I had recently, because it seems to me so exactly to capture the spirit of what Paul is writing about here. I met a woman in, I suppose, her mid to late 30s. She was divorced and, as it happens, believed that for some people it is legitimate to remarry after divorce. She told me her own story: 'I was deserted by an unbeliever, so I suppose if anyone may remarry, I come into that category. But I don't want to, because of the *freedom* I have found [I asked her what she meant and she talked about the freedom which she would not otherwise have had: she was studying at Bible College, she was also working in a handicapped children's home, she was helping lead at young people's Christian holiday parties]. And because I have come to see that the Lord the Creator is *my husband*, and if I married someone else, I'd have another husband. Of course God would still be my husband [if I got married] but I don't want to dilute that.' I asked her what would happen if she felt attracted to a man. She replied: 'I would break the bond before it got too far, just as you would do if you were attracted to a married woman.' She didn't actually quote 1 Corinthians 7 or 1 Timothy 5, but she was surely living by them.

Of course Paul recognises that it is possible to react to a new experience of singleness (after bereavement) in a quite different way. In his experience some younger widows – presumably after they had got over their initial grief – had become idlers and gossips, taking advantage of the financial support they were getting from the Church and then beginning to look for another marriage partner (11–13). As we have seen, he urged these younger widows to follow their natural inclination to marry and channel their energy in more productive directions (14). Earlier he had said that some widows had reacted to their being alone by throwing themselves into all kinds of self-indulgent pleasures (6). And these are only some of the less positive ways that human beings react to bereavement. He could have added that people respond, for example, by shutting themselves away or by immersing themselves in self-pity (on this whole subject see: Parkes: *Bereavement*).

Nor should it be imagined that Paul considers that taking a vow of singleness – or simply determining to remain single – is the only right reaction to widowhood. On the contrary, we have already seen that he says widows are quite free to remarry (1 Cor. 7:39; Rom. 7:2f) and that he positively encourages younger widows to remarry (1 Tim. 5:14). These are perfectly legitimate responses in a widow (or widower) to their singleness. Nevertheless, Paul clearly commends the decision that the 'official' widow makes. She finds herself 'left all alone' (5) and has decided to 'put her hope in God' (5. The verb is perfect: 'she *has* set her hope on God' – so RSV. 'Her attitude of mind is a settled and continuous one' (Kelly)). This is a mindset which 1 Timothy especially prizes (cf 4:10; 6:17). She has therefore vowed to remain single, and she has done so not because singleness in itself is inherently valuable but in order to draw closer to – to be married to – Christ (cf 11).

## 5.   A requirement for church leaders

In the Pastoral Epistles, Paul gives several lists of require-ments in church leaders. One of the phrases that recurs is (literally) 'husband of one wife':

> (1) Here is a trustworthy saying: If anyone sets his heart on being an overseer, he desires a noble task.
> (2) Now the overseer must be above reproach, the husband of but one wife . . . (1 Tim. 3).
> (12) A deacon must be the husband of but one wife and must manage his children and his household well (1 Tim. 3).
> (5) The reason I left you in Crete was that you might straighten out what was left unfinished and appoint elders in every town, as I directed you. (6) An elder must be blameless, the husband of but one wife . . . (Titus 1).

An identical phrase, with only the sexes reversed, is amongst the requirements for an 'official' widow: she must be 'the wife of one husband' (1 Tim. 5:9).

Paul clearly considered this requirement important. It is the first *specific* qualification he mentions in both lists for overseers/ elders (after the general terms 'above reproach' in 1 Timothy 3:2 and 'blameless' in Titus 1:6) and it is also required of both deacons and widows on the official roll. What does it mean? Three main possibilities have been suggested:

a) Faithful to his wife. This is the interpretation (it can-not be called a translation) which the NIV text chooses in 1 Timothy 5:9, though NIV is not consistent as it translates it in the other three places: 'the husband of but one wife'. But Kelly rightly insists that to interpret the phrase to mean 'not lusting after other women than his wife . . . is to squeeze more out of the Greek than it will bear'; Paul would have needed a fuller phrase to convey this.

The great stumbling block to this interpretation, however, is the word 'one'. In all four instances it is placed in the emphatic position as the first word. This interpretation takes no account of that fact and is therefore 'clearly too undefined' (Ellicott). The emphatic 'one' demands a more specific meaning than general marital faithfulness.

b) Monogamous. This seems to be the interpretation of GNB text: 'he must have only one wife', though again it is not consistent as the GNB text for 1 Timothy 5:9 has: 'She must have been married only once.' This interpretation is certainly grammatically possible, giving full weight to the emphatic 'one', but it is culturally unlikely in the extreme. Polygamy was virtually unknown among the Jews in the first century. It is true that Josephus, for example, twice mentions, without condemning it, that Herod the Great had several wives (*Ant.* 17, 1.2; *War* 1.24.2). In fact he had ten wives in all, some of them at the same time, but he was despised for it. And while polygamy was discussed by rabbis – for most people as theory rather than as fact – it was roundly condemned by Christians (Justin Martyr, *Dialogue with Trypho*, 134).

In the Roman world, polygamy was actually illegal. Roman law treated a second marriage (before divorce) 'not only as null and void but infamous. Where it was practised, it must have been practised secretly. It is probable that when St Paul wrote to Timothy and Titus not a single polygamist had been converted to the Christian faith' (Plummer). This interpretation is therefore highly implausible. It would be like proposing that a central requirement for twentieth-century clergy should be: 'A clergyman must only be chosen if he does not worship Baal' or 'A clergyman must only be chosen who does not practise sex with animals.'

But the final nail in the coffin of this interpretation is 1 Timothy 5:9 because 'whatever evidence there might be for polygamy in Jewish or pagan society at the end of the first century, there is none at all for polyandry' (Hanson). 'Even among the barbarians outside the Empire, such a thing as a plurality of husbands was regarded as monstrous' (Plummer).

c) Only ever married once. This is the interpretation of NIV (except, accountably, at 1 Tim. 5:9) and NRSV and of the marginal notes in GNB (and of GNB text at 1 Tim. 5:9) and NEB. It is also the interpretation of most modern commentators as it fits at both the grammatical and the cultural level.

We know, for example, that those who remained single after the death of their husband were much admired in Judaism. Judith's husband, Manasseh, died when she was still young. 'She was beautiful in appearance and had a very lovely face' but she went into strict mourning for almost three and a half years after her husband's death (Judith 8:2–8). When that period was over, she still refused to marry. She 'was honoured in her time throughout the whole country. Many desired to marry her, but she remained a widow all the days of her life after Manasseh her husband died and was gathered to his people. She became more and more famous, and grew old in her husband's house, until she was 105 years old' when she died (16:21–23).

The New Testament speaks in similar honorific terms of Anna who 'had lived with her husband seven years after her marriage, and then was a widow until she was 84 [or: for 84 years]. She never left the temple but worshipped night and day [cf 1 Tim. 5:5], fasting and praying' (Luke 2:36f).

We also know that the Greeks and Romans admired women who remained single after the death of their husbands. The Greek term for such a woman is *monandros*; the Latin is *univira*. This term occurs quite frequently in first-century pagan, Jewish and Christian funerary inscriptions. 'The adjective always constitutes a word of praise' (Spicq). Dibelius and Conzelmann also mention Livy 10.23.9 where service at the altar of Pudicitia was permitted only to matrons who had been wedded to one man alone.

Further, we have already seen that those who only married once, even though their marriage partner had died, were praised in the New Testament, and said to be 'happier' (1 Cor. 7:8, 39f).

And we find precisely the same teaching from the earliest days of the post-New Testament church. Thus in Hermas (writing before AD 150): 'And again I asked him [the shepherd-angel],

saying: "Sir . . . if a wife or husband die, and the widower or
widow marry, does he or she commit sin?" "There is no sin in
marrying again," said he, "but if they remain unmarried, they
gain greater honour and glory with the Lord; but if they marry,
they do not sin"' (*Mandate*, 14.4.1ff). Or again in Clement of
Alexandria (c. AD 150–215): If a widower remarries, he 'does
not commit any sin according to the Old Testament (for it
was not forbidden by the Law), but he does not fulfil the
heightened perfection of the gospel ethic. But he gains heavenly
glory for himself if he remains as he is, and keeps undefiled the
marriage yoke broken by death, and willingly accepts God's
purposes for him, by which he has become free from distraction
for the service of the Lord' (*Stromata* 3.12.88). As one more
example, St Jerome (died 420) wrote to a lady: 'You possess
this great privilege . . . Since Camilla, no woman, or almost
no woman, in your family has been married a second time';
and Jerome also said: 'We do not blame second marriages but
we only praise first marriages.'

Examples could be multiplied from the early Church. Suffice
to say that those who refrained from a second marriage after the
death of a partner were especially admired and that a bishop,
presbyter or deacon could not have been twice married and
could not be married to a woman who had been widowed
(Apostolic Canons XVII and XVIII).

Kelly sums up the evidence from all sources: 'There is abun-
dant evidence, from both literature and funerary inscriptions,
pagan and Jewish [and, one might add, Christian], that to
remain unmarried after the death of one's spouse or after divorce
was considered meritorious, while to marry again was taken as a
sign of self-indulgence.' This last point – that remarriage after
the death of one's partner was self-indulgent – certainly goes
beyond the New Testament, but the accumulated evidence
shows that 'husband of one wife' does almost certainly mean
'only ever once married'. It is also how the early Fathers clearly
understood the phrase in the Pastoral Epistles.

To sum up: 'ordinary' Christians could get married after the
death of their partner. Paul made it clear – very likely against
opposing ideas at Corinth (cf 1 Cor. 7:1) – that there was nothing
wrong in that (1 Cor. 7:39; Rom. 7:2f). But there were more

stringent requirements for overseers/elders, deacons and those women enrolled in the order of widows: for them there was to be no second marriage even after the death of their partner. This should not be surprising when the Old Testament high priest was also forbidden to marry a widow (Lev. 21:14). 'It was natural to expect the church's ministers to be examples to other people and to content themselves with a single marriage' (Kelly).

## Singleness after Divorce of or by a Spouse

So far in this chapter we have looked at what the Bible has to say about the single state which a person experiences in a new way after the death of his or her partner. We turn now to the subject of singleness after divorcing, or being divorced by, one's partner.

### 1.   In the teaching of the Old Testament

It is often assumed that the Old Testament simply could not imagine singleness (after a certain age) and that a divorcee would remarry immediately, especially if she was a woman. This is by no means a wholly false assumption. We have already seen that Jesus assumes a divorced woman will remarry, even though he does not approve of it since he calls it adultery (Matt. 5:32). We have also seen that it was Christ himself who brought in the revolutionary new view of the value and advantages of singleness.

Nevertheless, the Old Testament knows full well that some women will remain single after divorce:

> (12) If a priest's daughter marries anyone other than a priest, she may not eat any of the sacred contributions. (13) But if a priest's daughter becomes a widow or is divorced, yet has no children, and she returns to live in her father's house as in her youth, she may eat of her father's food (Lev. 22).

This comes in a section which discusses who may, and who may not, eat the parts of the sacrifices assigned to the priests (22:10-16). A priest's daughter is part of his family until she marries and may therefore eat from the sacred offerings (10). When she marries, she transfers into the family of her husband,

and unless he is also a priest, she thereby becomes ineligible to eat of the sacred offerings (12). But if she is divorced and moves back in with her father, she is again regarded as part of his family and able again to eat the holy food (13). The only restriction on this is if she has children (13). This is either because the children would then be expected to support her (so G. J. Wenham: *The Book of Leviticus*) or, more likely, because then she would remain tied to her husband's family through the child. In any case, the situation envisaged is that a woman is divorced, returns to her father's house and does not remarry (at least for some time).

Numbers 30 is another interesting chapter. It is entirely taken up with vows and whether they can be broken or nullified. Mostly it has to do with vows made by women and whether the man under whose authority they come (father or husband) can nullify their vows. It is because of this that the chapter can conclude: 'These are the regulations the LORD gave Moses concerning relationships between a man and his wife, and between a father and his young daughter living in his house' (16).

The chapter begins by saying that 'when a man makes a vow to the LORD', it is irrevocable (1f). However, if a woman makes a vow, it may be nullified: by her father if she is 'a young [unmarried] woman still living in her father's house' (3–5) and by her husband if she makes the vow before her marriage and he nullifies it immediately he hears of it after their marriage (6–8) or if she makes a vow while 'living with her husband' after marriage (10–15). In the midst of this discussion, a different situation is envisaged:

> Any vow or obligation taken by a widow or divorced woman will be binding on her (Num. 30:9).

No information is given on where she is living: whether she has gone back to be with her father (cf Lev. 22:13; but would she then be back under his authority so that he could nullify her vow?), or to live with her adult children, or elsewhere. But the significant feature is that these two types of women are the only ones mentioned whose vows are, like men's (2), irrevocable. They have full responsibility for the promises that they make to God. This, then, is further evidence that not all divorced women – nor, presumably, divorced men – married again. Some doubtless waited before remarriage; others will never have remarried at all.

## 2.  *In the teaching of Jesus*

> ... (9) [Jesus said:] 'I tell you that anyone who divorces his wife, except for marital unfaithfulness, and marries another woman commits adultery.' (10) The disciples said to him, 'If this is the situation between a husband and wife, it is better not to marry.'
>
> (11) Jesus replied: 'Not everyone accepts [not: 'can accept] as in NIV] this teaching, but only those to whom it has been given. (12) For some are eunuchs because they were born that way; others were made that way by men; and others have renounced marriage (literally: have made themselves eunuchs) because of the kingdom of heaven. The one who can accept this should accept it' (Matt. 19).

We have seen in chapter 3 that verses 11f constitute by far the most important teaching of Jesus on the subject of singleness. He uses the image of a eunuch to speak of those who are not able or willing to get married, and he distinguishes between three types of people for whom marriage is not a possibility and to whom singleness is what God has 'given' (11): those who are congenitally unable to contemplate full marriage (whether because their sexual organs never develop or – by extension – because they are emotionally, sexually or psychologically not equipped for heterosexual marriage), those who have been rendered incapable of full marriage (whether by castration or by influences which make them emotionally, sexually or psychologically unable to enter heterosexual marriage) and those who have chosen the single life and decided not to marry 'because of the kingdom of heaven'. It is this third group which, in the context, is clearly Jesus' principal concern; these are the only ones who have taken the decision themselves (though the other two groups also have a decision to take: to 'accept' what God has 'given').

Verses 11f, when they are discussed at all, are often seen in isolation, yet it is vital to see them in their context. Jesus was asked a question about divorce: 'Is it lawful for a man to divorce his wife for any and every reason?' (3). Having insisted on starting from God's creation ordinance of marriage (4–6) and answered an objection that arose from the Mosaic law (7f), he gives his answer to their original question, broadening it out to speak about remarriage as well (9).

The disciples are appalled by what they have just heard (10). They are appalled, as we have seen (chapter 5), because they realise that this is much tougher than the teaching of the school of Shammai. Shammai may have greatly restricted the legitimate grounds for divorce, but he did at least allow remarriage after divorce for adultery. What Jesus is saying is that there should be no remarriage after divorce under any circumstances (while the original partner is still living). So they blurt out that in that case it is better not to get married in the first place.

Now it is in this context that Jesus makes his famous statement about singleness. It must be, therefore, that the people he principally has in mind when speaking of those who 'have renounced marriage because of the kingdom of heaven' are those who, out of obedience to God their king, have determined to remain single after their divorce. Gundry draws attention to the parallel between 'because of the kingdom of heaven' (12) and Jesus' challenging standard in 5:20 'I tell you that unless your righteousness surpasses that of the Pharisees and the teachers of the law, you will certainly not enter the kingdom of heaven.' And he adds: 'Matthew stresses [in 19:10–12] that just as some men live as eunuchs because of congenital incapacity and some because of others' castration of them, so also Jesus' true disciples live as eunuchs after they have had to divorce their wives for immorality; i.e. in obedience to the law of the kingdom taught by Jesus, they do not remarry.'

## 3. In the teaching of Jesus and of Paul

In 1 Corinthians 7, as we have also seen, Paul – in part drawing directly on the teaching of Jesus (11) – has a great deal to say about singleness (7–9, 11, 25–38, 39f). Again, it is vital to see this teaching in its context.

It all stemmed from the fact that some Corinthians believed that all sexual intercourse was wrong (1). This meant that, in their view, one should not have intercourse with one's marriage partner (cf 2–6), that one should divorce one's partner (cf 10f) or at least that one should divorce an unbelieving marriage partner (cf 12–16).

While Paul is not entirely unsympathetic to some of their views (though for quite different reasons), he says *no* to all of these suggestions. Contrary to their views, sexual intercourse should continue between married couples (2–6) and one should not divorce one's partner (10f), even if he or she is a pagan (12–16). Yet Paul does acknowledge that in a particular circumstance divorce may be legitimate. Christ himself gave an exception to his own rule (11a, echoing Matt. 5:32 and 19:9). In this case – the case of legitimate divorce – the two options open to the Christian are reconciliation or singleness.

After a paragraph (17–24) in which he sets out the general principle – 'each one should remain in the situation which he was in when God called him' (20) – which governs the whole chapter, Paul goes on to a new question which they have raised ('Now about' – *peri de* – in 25 cf 1 is the tell-tale sign). This is the question of 'virgins', that is: the betrothed, though in the following verses Paul widens this out to speak about all single people (see especially 34).

But in fact this is a closely related subject. Both verses 1–16 (see 7–9, 11) and verses 25–38 treat the subject of singleness. And it may well be that both Corinthian questions – about marriage and about 'virgins' – stemmed from the same misconception: that the body was evil and sexual intercourse wrong. They were therefore also advocating the breaking of engagements (cf 25–38) and that widows should not remarry (cf 39f). Here Paul more nearly agrees with their conclusions, though again his reasons have nothing whatsoever to do with the alleged evil of the body (which he entirely denied cf, 2–6) and everything to do with the spiritual advantages of the single life (25–38) and its greater happiness (28, 40).

If, then, the two parts of chapter 7 are closely linked because both are dealing with questions arising from a basic Corinthian misunderstanding, both speak about singleness and both are governed by an axiomatic principle (spelled out in 17–24), then we must keep the material from both halves of the chapter together. In particular, all the advantages of singleness for 'virgins' and for the 'unmarried' which Paul spells out in 25–38 will equally apply to those who are single again after divorce (11) and after widowhood (8). They too will be able to disengage themselves far more fully from this passing world and prepare for God's new order (26, 29–31), they too can be spared suffering (28) and above all they too can live in undivided devotion to the Lord (32–35).

The final two verses (39f) come as something of a surprise. In a chapter where Paul has carefully spoken to men and women equally in each situation which he has discussed, one might expect a word to the 'virgins' after Paul has instructed the men betrothed to them (36–38). Paul does indeed turn to the women but he imagines them not single ('virgins'), nor even – in the first statement he makes – widowed, but married ('bound to her husband': 39a). He does indeed go on to speak about widows (39b–40) but he begins by repeating, in a different way, his teaching in verses 1–24 (especially 10–16) that marriage partners should not separate. There (10–16) he said that there was to be no divorce and, where there is even legitimate divorce, no remarriage. Here (39a) he says that the marriage bond lasts throughout life.

In other words, here is a further tie-up between the different parts of the chapter. Paul, in his last remark on the subject of marriage, reminds women (the whole chapter shouts that men should take notice too) that marriage is for life and that there should be no divorce. However, if marriage is broken by death (39, taking up the theme of 8) or disrupted by divorce, singleness must be seriously considered. It is in fact mandatory for the divorcee unless there is reconciliation (11) and is optional for the widow (8f, 39f), but the divorced person should not be disheartened or bitter, because Paul is convinced that he, like the widow, will be 'happier' remaining single (40, cf 25–38). This conviction, Paul believes, comes from the Spirit of God (40) but it needs of course to be accepted and personally assimilated by each divorced man or woman (cf Matt. 19:10–12).

## Conclusions

We constantly need to remember that this was not a piece of abstract theology that Jesus and Paul dreamed up in professional armchairs. It is true that Jesus was replying to a test question (Mark 10:2//Matt. 19:3) but it was one that was very much a live issue in his day and he must have been aware that it affected many lives. Moreover, Matthew 5:31f and Luke 16:18 are presented to us as being given in the context of his pastoral teaching. And certainly Paul was responding to very real practical questions in 1 Corinthians, and was giving instructions for the appointment of real elders, deacons and 'official' widows in 1 Timothy 3 and 5. What then are the conclusions that we should draw for the widowed and the divorced today?

### 1.  Remarriage after the death of a partner is good

We should never forget that this is part of the New Testament teaching. Marriage – if one is morally and emotionally free to get married – is good; the person who gets married 'does well' (1 Cor. 7:38). It is a 'doctrine of demons' to forbid marriage (1 Tim. 4:1–3) and not at all part of authentic Christianity which, on the contrary, recognises marriage as something 'good' and to be 'received with thanksgiving' (1 Tim. 4:3–5). In 1 Corinthians 7, Paul's whole approach is to argue against those who believe that even marital sex – and therefore marriage itself – is bad.

So, in turn, remarriage after the death of a partner is good. Every widow or widower is entirely free to remarry (1 Cor. 7:39; Rom. 7:2f). Indeed, Paul positively recommends it for some (1 Tim. 5:14; 1 Cor. 7:9). So when a young mother, left alone with young children through a fatal car crash in which her husband was involved, falls in love with another man and remarries, of course the church rejoices. When an older widower, feeling his loneliness intensely, finds a new wife and remarries, of course his Christian friends and family are delighted (though perhaps they are also wise enough to know that the adjustment and 'settling down together' within this new marriage may well not be easy, and that the couple will need as much, or more, loving support as any newly weds).

In all this, Christians are basically in step with the reactions of the world around them, with this single – and highly significant – difference: that we do not see remarriage as a merciful rescue from the appalling fate of prolonged singleness.

## 2. *Singleness after the death of a partner is better*

This is not true for all Christians, but it is for many. Paul can say as a general principle: a widow – or widower – is happier if she stays as she is (1 Cor. 7:40). We have seen that the exact meaning of *makariōtera* is not certain; it means either 'happier within herself' or 'more blessed by God', but in either case singleness is quite clearly regarded as the preferable state (cf 1 Cor. 7:38 where 'better' means 'what is preferable', not 'what is morally better'). Indeed, so much is this the general biblical view, not just some odd quirk of St Paul's mind, that in the Old Testament the high priest is not to marry a widow, in the New Testament elders and deacons should not remarry after the death of a partner (it is very likely that the qualifications in 1 Timothy 3 and Titus 1 were widely accepted in the churches (cf 1 Tim. 3:14–16) and were not just new ideas dreamed up by Paul), and those enrolled in the 'order of widows' must make a pledge not to remarry.

Why is singleness preferable? Partly, perhaps, because by so doing widows and widowers remain true to the one marriage commitment they made (even though the marriage bond is now broken and they are technically free to remarry). This is both explicitly stated in some early Christian writings (e.g. Clement of Alexandria, *Stromata*, 3.12.88 quoted above) and is true to how many widowed men and women feel until their dying day. It is very rarely appropriate, and normally impossible, to seek to persuade them otherwise.

But the main reason why the Christian widower sees singleness as preferable is because he sees himself as married to Christ (cf 1 Tim. 5:11), as able to give himself in undivided devotion to Christ (1 Cor. 7:32–35); and his appreciation of what that means will almost certainly be all the richer because he has known – as Paul probably knew – what human marriage is.

This Christian conviction – that for Christian widows and widowers singleness is to be preferred – is in complete contrast with the generally accepted view in the non-Christian world. There death is seen, rightly, as an awful thing in itself. But it is compounded by the fact that it leaves the widowed person single, 'all alone' (cp 1 Tim. 5:5); it is not just that the widower is bereft of the person he loved, but he is also – to make matters worse – now single.

The Christian view is quite different from this. Of course Christians acknowledge that there are disadvantages to singleness, all the more if you have known rich companionship in marriage, 1 Corinthians 9:5 is just one example of this and has added poignancy if Paul was indeed a widower. But there are also both disadvantages to marriage (e.g. 1 Cor. 7:28) and advantages to singleness (e.g. 1 Cor. 7:25–38). And the New Testament is convinced that, as a general rule, the advantages of singleness – perhaps particularly, though not only, after the death of a partner – outweigh the advantages of marriage.

## 3. Singleness after divorce is mandatory (during the partner's lifetime)

St Paul, quoting Jesus, says that only two options are open to the divorcee. One is reconciliation (1 Cor. 7:11). This should never be forgotten. Divorce is a wrong; it is a breaking of God's intention for every marriage and any marriage. It may of course be legitimate in the case of adultery but in that case too, very obviously, the whole relationship has gone wrong. Therefore the ultimate aim of everyone concerned with a divorce must be to set the wrong(s) of divorce right and bring about reconciliation if at all possible.

But it is not always possible; not in the short term, or the foreseeable future, anyway. In that case, singleness is the only other possibility (1 Cor. 7:11). Why? Because the marriage bond still exists (1 Cor. 7:39; Rom. 7:2f) and that is why any remarriage after divorce – during the lifetime of one's partner – is consistently called adultery (Matt. 5:27–32; 19:9; Mark 10:10–12; Luke 16:18, cf Rom. 7:3).

Needless to say the late twentieth-century Western world finds this extraordinarily hard to accept. And, at least for the next decades, it is going to get harder and harder to accept this teaching. Increasing numbers will either themselves be divorced and remarried, or have others whom they hold very dear who are divorced and remarried. It is inevitably extremely difficult for such people to accept Christ's teaching that divorced people should be reconciled to their original partners or remain single.

Moreover, an increasing number of people will find happiness in a second marriage after divorce or will know those who have found happiness in remarriage after divorce. This is bound to be the case, even though the statistics show clearly that this is not true for the majority, since the majority of second marriages end in divorce. But for those who do experience – at first hand or by watching others – happiness in a second marriage, it is hard to accept that reconciliation or singleness are the only options open to those who divorce.

The sad fact is that, in many countries and many denominations, the churches are actually accelerating this trend to reject the biblical teaching. I can speak most intimately of my own denomination, the Anglican Church, and of the two countries where I have ministered, Britain and the United States. In both countries until recently the Anglican Church upheld through canon law the understanding that the marriage bond continued until the death of one partner, that legal divorce could not dissolve it, and therefore it was morally wrong to remarry after divorce while one's partner was alive. As I write, this is still the position within the Church of England (though many are seeking to get the canon law changed), and as a result the New Testament position on remarriage after divorce is widely seen within the community as valid, even when it is not agreed with. In that sense (and in that sense only because the underlying reasons are rarely appreciated), a clergyman or lay Christian maintaining that a divorcee may not remarry is 'understood'.

In America, by contrast, the canon law was changed in 1976. In an astonishingly short period of time even loyal members of the Episcopal (= Anglican) Church could not even imagine that remarriage after divorce could be wrong. The teaching of Christ and of the apostle Paul on this subject is not only ignored; when it is put forward, it is simply not understood and not considered a view that any twentieth-century Christian could hold.

To maintain the contrary is, therefore, unpopular. Yet we have no liberty to excise New Testament teaching that we find uncomfortable. All Christians, and especially Christian leaders, must not only maintain that singleness after divorce is the only option (other than reconciliation) for the follower of Christ, but must explain the reasons why. Jesus showed us the way: it is teaching about the permanence of marriage and of the marriage bond that is urgently needed.

## 4.  Singleness after divorce is good

That is of course precisely what the disciples could not believe. When they realised that Christ was saying a man must remain single after divorce, they were horror-struck; perhaps it would be better not to marry at all (Matt. 19:9f). Jesus replied that this action – staying single after divorce – is done 'for the sake of the kingdom of heaven' and therefore, obviously, is good (Matt. 19:12).

We have seen that exactly the same teaching is found in 1 Corinthians 7. Paul says that the divorced person must be reconciled to his partner or remain single (11) and then goes on to give the lengthiest passage in the entire New Testament on the blessings of singleness (25–40).

This again is a truth – a fact of New Testament experience and the experience of many Christians down the ages – which twentieth-century Western society finds very hard to accept. This is obvious in the language people use about singleness. One example: 'What if the innocent party refuses to be reconciled? Is the guilty party doomed to celibacy?' (Luck p.167). Or again, in the letter quoted at the beginning of this chapter: 'Aren't you condemning the already divorced members of your congregation to a solitary lifestyle?' It is not only the words 'doomed' and 'condemning' that are significant; the single life itself has become 'celibacy' (obviously, in context, used pejoratively) and 'a solitary lifestyle'.

Of course Christians must recognise that people can be extremely unhappy in singleness (as they can in marriage) and indeed many are: some kick against it, they seek – sometimes desperately – to get out of it, they refuse to accept it. This is precisely where Jesus' concluding words in Matthew 19:12 are so important. Speaking specifically in the context of remaining unmarried after divorce, he says: 'The one who can accept this should accept it.' We saw in chapter 3, that this is equivalent to Christ's saying: 'He who has ears to hear, let him hear.' It is not a concession: 'You can take this or leave it, according to your inclination.' It is a challenge: 'Those to whom God has "given" (11) singleness – specifically those who have divorced, even if legitimately – must accept singleness.'

It is not only the divorced who need to hear Christ's challenge to accept this teaching of his, it is the whole Church. All of us need to accept this teaching – that it is not only right, but better, to remain single after divorce – intellectually; the very word Jesus uses here (*chōreō*) means primarily 'grasp (mentally), comprehend, understand' (so Arndt and Gingrich). But the word has a broader meaning: 'to grasp with a view to acting on it' (Lagrange). It is therefore part of Jesus' challenge, both to the divorced and to the whole Church, to so accept this teaching of his that it becomes the determining factor not only in their thought but in their action. Christ's teaching about the good of singleness after divorce needs to determine what we do and say, and what we refrain from doing and saying.

# 8

# Biblical Conclusions

Four questions have dominated the first part of this book:
- What happens at marriage?
- How does God view singleness?
- Is it ever right to divorce?
- Is it ever right to remarry?

This chapter is an attempt to take one more look at those questions and summarise the ways in which the New Testament answers them.

## What Happens at Marriage?

It is absolutely essential to begin with this question. It is essential, in the first place, because this is where Jesus began. His questioners were eager to have his views on divorce (Mark 10:2//Matt. 19:3), but Jesus would not answer their question until first he had made them understand what God does – what God's involvement is, what changes he brings about – at the moment when a couple are married.

It is also essential to begin at this point because without it the rest is incomprehensible. People today do not understand the New Testament position on divorce and remarriage because they have never understood what, according to the Bible, happens at marriage. When, however, this is understood, it certainly does not remove the enormous difficulties in putting the New Testament teaching into practice, but it does remove the objections to, and the sheer incomprehension of, what is viewed by increasing numbers as an intolerably harsh and inhumane position.

## 1.  In the teaching of Jesus

a) God joins the couple together.
This is absolutely central to Christ's thinking. The concept of
a marriage bond was widely held in the ancient world. What
was new in Jesus' teaching was that it is God who joins a
couple together (Mark 10:9//Matt. 19:6). What is more, God
joins together not just Christians who have prayed long and hard
about their decision, nor only those who belong to the people of
God; God joins together all human couples. Jesus makes this
clear by going back to 'the beginning' (Mark 10:6//Matt. 19:4,
cf 8), to God's creation ordinance.

This does not mean of course that there are no foolish marriages, which should never have been entered into in the first
place. But it does mean that, even in these cases, God recognises
these marriages; indeed he validates them. He is the ultimate
minister, magistrate or judge joining the couple together. They
of course take the decision to marry, and this particular marriage may be contrary to God's will. Nevertheless, he joins
them together: he accepts, and indeed effects their marriage
(he 'yokes them together') – just as the clergyman plays his
part in bringing about the marriage even when he thinks the
couple are mismatched – and from then on he forbids anyone
to destroy the marriage ('let man not separate them').

b) They become one flesh.
This equally crucial idea is first introduced by Jesus as a quotation of Genesis 2:24 (Mark 10:8//Matt. 19:5). But he then
draws an important conclusion of his own, not explicit in the
Genesis text: 'So they are no longer two but one [literally: one
flesh]' (Mark 10:8//Matt. 19:6). So Jesus denies that, at the
most fundamental level, they are any longer two individuals,
and affirms that, at this same fundamental level, they have
become a 'couple', one joint entity.

Of course it takes time before a newly married couple think
in this way and act in accordance with their new understanding. Some couples hardly even begin to do so. And the most
harmonious couples have not wholly succeeded in thinking and
acting in this way by the end of a married lifetime. But that is not

Jesus' point. He is not talking about what we become (after years of marriage) in our own eyes or even in the eyes of other people. He is talking about what we become (at the very moment of our marriage) in the eyes of God. Sexual union – what we often call the 'consummation' of a marriage – is certainly part of this being 'one flesh', and it is of course something that we do. But much more important in Jesus' eyes is what God does: he not only 'joins us together', he makes us into (this is the sense of Genesis 2:24's Hebrew: *hāyâh lᵉ*) one flesh, one entity.

## 2.   In the teaching of Paul

Paul clearly knew the teaching of Jesus now recorded in Mark 10//Matthew 19. He specifically quotes Jesus' teaching on marriage and divorce in 1 Corinthians 7:10f. He also takes over Jesus' understanding of the couple as being one flesh. In fact, he makes an interesting distinction between the genuine but dissoluble becoming one flesh and the far more profound and indissoluble becoming one flesh.

Some Corinthian Christians were visiting prostitutes. By having intercourse with them, they were creating a psychological bond with the prostitute much greater than they imagined. Paul says that the prostitute and her client become 'one body' and then immediately quotes Genesis 2:24: 'The two will become one flesh' (1 Cor. 6:16). This bonding is real, but it is possible, in large measure, to extricate oneself from it. There is no marriage either intended or effected, God has in no sense yoked these two together, and therefore Paul tells his readers to 'flee from' the prostitution they have become involved in (18).

But Paul also recognises that there is an entirely objective and inextricable union established in marriage. In Ephesians 5:22–33, he again quotes Genesis 2:24. He sees this as applying to the marriage between Christ and his Church (32) but also to human marriage (28f, 33). Far from encouraging the couple to 'flee from' difficult relationships, he draws the conclusion (for the husband) that he 'must love his wife as he loves himself' (33) because his wife *is* himself (28).

Paul's teaching in this area is dependent on Jesus' understanding of what happens at marriage. It is possible also that his command: 'Do not be yoked together with unbelievers' (2 Cor. 6:14) is an echo of Jesus' view of marriage in which God 'yokes together' the partners (so Mark 10:9//Matt. 19:6 literally). It is true that 2 Corinthians 6:14–7:1 may be prohibiting a wider range of relationships with unbelievers than simply marriage, but it would seem that only intimate relationships are involved (cf 1 Cor. 5:9f) and that marriage is almost certainly included (cf 1 Cor. 7:39). It may well be, then, that Paul is saying: 'You know how people are "yoked together" in marriage? Do not be so "yoked", whether in marriage or in other intimate relationships.' Paul would then be quoting Jesus' teaching on marriage and applying it – by analogy – to other close relationships.

But Paul does not simply quote Jesus in his teaching about marriage. He also has his own ways – and his own language – for putting across the same ideas as those of Jesus. Most important of these is his idea of the marriage bond, mentioned in 1 Corinthians 7:27 (literally: are you bound to a wife?), 1 Corinthians 7:39 and Romans 7:2. Paul teaches clearly that this bond is established at marriage and is broken only by the death of one partner (1 Cor. 7:39: Rom. 7:2f).

This, then, is the New Testament's view of what happens at marriage: God himself joins every couple together and forbids anyone from tampering with this yoking he has made; in God's eyes, the couple cease to be primarily two individuals and are made fundamentally one; and a marriage bond is established which only death can destroy.

## How Does God View Singleness?

If, then, marriage is spoken of so highly (as it is especially in the Old Testament), where does that leave the single person, particularly the person who is not single by choice? This also is an essential question to face, especially if Jesus forbids re-marriage after divorce to some (as he indisputably does) and perhaps to all. Again, a great deal of misunderstanding of the New Testament prohibition of remarriage has been caused by a failure to understand, and by the Church's failure to explain, the Christian view of singleness.

## 1. In the teaching of Jesus

a) Singleness is a life 'given' by God to some people.
This is the teaching of Matthew 19:11, and in the following verse Jesus speaks of three groups of people to whom singleness has been given. Some are given their singleness by God at birth: because they are incapable physically of consummating any marriage or perhaps because they are congenitally homosexual. Some are given their singleness by God in some event subsequent to birth: they are 'made that way by men'. Of course castration is an evil – a horrific evil – but it is important to realise that the resultant singleness is given by God (for this pastorally vital distinction between something that can be at one and the same time 'a messenger of Satan' and the will of God (indeed: something to be 'delighted in'), see 2 Cor. 12:7–10). And some are given their singleness by God as a moral demand. He asks them to embrace it 'because of the kingdom of heaven', because the requirements of the kingdom of heaven demand it in their case.

Yet in this last case, singleness is not imposed on them, whether they accept it or not. Rather, they must respond freely to the demand of the kingdom of heaven. This is why, while the other two verbs are passive (were born, were made eunuchs), the third verb is active (made eunuchs of themselves). So God 'gives' singleness to this third group, but they must accept or reject it.

Under what circumstances might a person conclude that God was giving him singleness, and that this was what the kingdom of heaven required? The context (1–12) makes it clear that Jesus has principally in mind the person who has been through a divorce (especially 9), but it is quite possible that Jesus has, in addition, a wider application in mind.

b) Singleness is the life we will all have in heaven.
Jesus was asked a trick question about marriage in the afterlife (Mark 12:18–23//Matt. 22:23–28//Luke 20:27–33). He must have shocked every single one of his listeners – whether from the Sadducean party or not – by saying that there would be no marriage in the post-resurrection age (Mark 12:25//Matt. 22:30//Luke 20:34–36).

Happily married couples often find this hard to accept. This is partly because they swing to the opposite extreme and think Jesus is saying that their present partners will mean nothing to them. In fact – though the New Testament does not speak directly on this and therefore we need to be cautious – there is every reason to believe that much of what is good in our relationship with our marriage partner will be not only retained but enhanced. Heaven is a place of bliss; there is no need to fear any loss as compared with our life on earth.

But much of the inability to accept Christ's teaching about there being no marriage in heaven stems from an antipathy towards singleness. Singleness is seen as a loss, a diminishment, a state to be pitied. This is clearly both far from Christ's own experience (as a single man) and far from his teaching here. The single life is in fact an essential element in the full life of a child of God in heaven (Luke 20:35f).

This does not of course for a moment mean that we will have no other relationships in heaven. On the contrary, 'the marriage relationship is transcended in a new level of personal relationships' (Marshall on Luke 20:35). But undoubtedly the greatest relationship is with God himself.

c) Singleness is a life to be accepted.

If singleness is given by God to some during their earthly life, and if it is God's gift to all of us in heaven, then – rather than struggle against it – we must accept it. This is the basic message of Matthew 19:12: 'The one who can accept this should accept it.' We have seen that this is not an invitation to 'take it or leave it' as far as Christ's teaching on singleness is concerned. Rather, it is a challenge for those to whom God has given singleness – especially, in context, the divorced – to accept it.

The very context of Jesus' teaching here, and particularly the disciples' surprised outburst (10), shows that Jesus is well aware that this teaching is difficult. Nevertheless, it needs first to be grasped intellectually (the principal meaning of *chōreō* – 'accept' – in 11f). As far as we can, we are to grapple with what Christ is teaching here and why he is saying it: our minds are to get to grips with this (perhaps alien) teaching, to understand it and to submit to it. And then secondly we are to act on his word and live it out (an idea also present in *chōreō*). His teaching on singleness is to affect our life profoundly – our own life if we are single, and our behaviour towards the single if we are married – as well as our mind.

## 2. In the teaching of Paul

It is almost certain that Paul knew the tradition that lay behind Matthew 19:3–9 because i) he seems to know how Jesus used Genesis 2:24 (Matt. 19:5f, cf Eph. 5:28–33; 1 Cor. 6:15–17) and ii) he clearly knows of a saying/sayings of Jesus on divorce (1 Cor. 7:10f) and iii) he knows an exception that Jesus made to his command forbidding divorce (Matt. 19:9 but not in the Markan parallel, nor in Luke, cf 1 Cor. 7:11). In these circumstances, it is quite likely that he also knew the tradition which lay behind Matthew 19:10–12, especially as this is closely tied to verses 3–9 in Matthew.

So it is not surprising that he too sees singleness as given by God (1 Cor. 7:7), and that he too knows that marriage belongs only to this 'passing' age (1 Cor. 7:31). Indeed he urges married people, in the light of this, to live as if they were unmarried (29), by which he certainly does not mean to neglect their partners (cf 2–6) but rather that they should not put an absolute value on marriage or cling to it as essential to their happiness. This cannot be so as marriage belongs only to 'this world' (31).

But again, in addition to repeating Christ's teaching on singleness, Paul gives us further teaching as his own contribution to the New Testament picture:

a) Singleness is a life free from the 'troubles' of 'this present distress'.
This is especially the argument of 1 Corinthians 7:25–8. The present age – that stretches from Pentecost to the Second Coming – is one of 'distress' (RSV. A better translation for *ananke* than NIV's crisis). This is true for all humans, and especially for all Christians. But these 'troubles' are greatly compounded for the married person who suffers not only on his (or her) own behalf, but on behalf of his partner and children. Paul

is not of course denying that single people also have troubles (his whole point is that we have troubles enough already in this 'present distress') nor that a marriage partner can lessen, by sharing, the weight of troubles. He also fully realises that different circumstances may tip the balance of advantage in a different direction (28a, cf 36–38). But with all these provisos, we must come back to what Paul's teaching actually is, borne out by the experience of many couples (including happily married couples): we live in a time of distress (especially for Christians) and marriage increases the stress and trouble in most people's lives.

b) Singleness is a life of undivided devotion to the Lord.
Certainly it can be, and will be, if accepted and used aright. This is the argument of 1 Corinthians 7:32–35. Marriage brings a whole range of new 'concerns' into a person's life. These concerns – unlike the 'distress' and 'troubles' of 25–28 – can be very good. It is good for 'a married man to be concerned about . . . how he can please his wife' (33, cf 34d). Nevertheless they tie our thoughts still further to 'this world' (33, 34) and above all they divide our attention and devotion (34, 35). We cannot give our whole attention to the Lord 'without distraction' (*aperispastōs* 35; NIV: undivided).

All here depends on acceptance. It is a common fact of Christian experience that some find their singleness extremely difficult to accept; they go through periods of resenting it, they hanker after marriage, and so they may actually be less, rather than more devoted to the Lord. But this is not due to their singleness itself, but rather to their reaction to the single life. It is also a common fact of Christian experience that single men and women who have been able to accept their singleness are indeed set free to draw especially close to Christ, in undivided devotion to him.

c) Singleness is more blessed than marriage.
This is Paul's conviction in 1 Corinthians 7:40: 'In my judgment, she is *makariōtera* if she stays as she is.' In the context Paul is talking about singleness after bereavement (39), but

1 Corinthians 7 as a whole shows that Paul believes much the same is true for all those who are single (e.g. 7f, 25–38). We have seen that the word he uses (*makarios*) normally in the New Testament means 'blessed by the Lord' but may have the weaker meaning of 'happy in herself'.

Paul is aware that singleness is not the more blessed/happier state for all. For some, marriage is God's gift (7). Paul positively recommends marriage for those who are sexually very awake and for younger widows (9, 36; 1 Tim. 5:14). Nevertheless, he is convinced that as a general rule – and for many people – it is better (1 Cor. 7:38) and happier/more blessed to remain single.

So, as we take the New Testament teaching as a whole, we find that God gives a single life to some on this earth and to all Christians in heaven. We need therefore to consider carefully whether – for the time being or for all of our life – singleness is God's gift for us. If so, we will avoid many troubles inevitably tied up with being a married Christian in this world and, positively, we will be free to give ourselves in undivided devotion to Christ; we will find it a better and happier state than marriage. And to find these treasures in the single life, we need to respond to Christ's challenge: to accept God's gift and build on it.

## Is It Ever Right to Divorce?

### 1.   *In the teaching of Jesus*

Jesus' answer to this question is very clear: almost never. The whole weight of Jesus' argument, in Matthew just as much as in Mark, is against divorce. In Mark of course divorce is prohibited absolutely; no exceptions are made (10:1–12). Luke's saying is actually about remarriage and not, in the first instance, about divorce (16:18). But in Matthew 5:31f and Matthew 19:1–12 Christ's teaching is also given precisely in order to forbid divorce. The prohibition of divorce and remarriage is part of what it means when God says: 'Do not commit adultery' (Matt. 5:27–32). A couple becomes one flesh in marriage; God joins them together; they are not to be put asunder: this is the answer to the question Christ faced about whether and when it is right to divorce (Matt. 19:1–9). When we get impatient with the answer and ask: 'Yes, but when is it all right to divorce?', we are asking the question in much the same way as the Pharisees: we want to know when we *may* divorce, not when we may not. Yet the entire drift of Christ's teaching is to prohibit divorce.

Nevertheless, an exception is given in both Matthew 5:32 and 19:9. In both cases, the exception is the case of *porneia*. We have seen that this is a very general word for illicit sexual intercourse, and that while adultery is principally in mind, it includes homosexual relationships, incest and bestiality. In the case of adultery, divorce was mandatory both in Judaism and in Roman law. Jesus however did not mandate it; he merely permitted it – and the change of verb from the Pharisees' 'command' to Jesus' 'permit' is probably deliberate and significant (19:7f). So even in his exception, Jesus leaves the way open for the couple to continue living together as man and wife.

## 2. *In the teaching of Paul*

Paul very specifically quoted Jesus (1 Cor. 7:10f). It is rare for him to refer directly to the teaching of Jesus, but on this issue he does so, referring not only to Jesus' general prohibition of divorce but also to his specific exception. We have seen that it is impossible to understand the exception of verse 11a ('But if she does . . .') in any other way.

It is often said that Paul adds a second exception: the case of mixed marriages. This is precisely what he did not do. It was the Corinthians who were (almost certainly) saying: a Christian should divorce his pagan partner (cf 1 Cor. 7:1). Paul answers this with an emphatic *no* (12–14).

What he does add is that if a pagan partner insists on leaving, the Christian may let him (or her) go. The Christian does not have to feel enslaved to the promises made in marriage so that the Christian pursues the pagan partner at all costs and refuses in any way to acquiesce in the separation. On the contrary, the Christian may 'let him leave' (15). But again we must not imagine that this is a further exception, added to the one (illicit sexual intercourse) mentioned by Jesus. The New Testament only mentions one situation in which a Christian may (not: must) divorce his partner.

## 3.  May we add other exceptions?

But could there be other legitimate exceptions? Murray (pp.76–8) and Bromiley (p.68) both warn against going beyond the clear statements of Scripture. The great value of their approach is that churches have in fact found it easy to make more and more exceptions, until they end up (in practice if not always in theory) accepting divorce and remarriage in almost every circumstance. Experience shows that a firm opposition to divorce quickly becomes the exception, in stark contrast with the teaching of Christ and Paul whose clear basic stance is that divorce is prohibited and that the exception is very much an unusual deviation from the norm.

Others, however, have been prepared to admit a few further exceptions to the prohibition of divorce. At the time of the Reformation, the Continental Reformer Martin Bucer suggested that serious crime, impotence, leprosy and insanity were legitimate grounds for divorce (Winnett p.1). In England, Cranmer clearly agonised over the issue of divorce and remarriage but he was part of the Commission that drew up, during Edward VI's reign, draft canons known collectively as *Reformatio Legum Ecclesiasticarum*. These were never in fact ratified as canon law but they do allow divorce not only for adultery but for malicious desertion, prolonged absence without news, attempts against the partner's life and cruelty (Atkinson p.60).

Several of these suggested grounds are open to very serious objections. It is doubtful, for example, whether a Christian can subscribe to any of Bucer's additional grounds, unless perhaps the individual was well aware of his crime, sexual incapacity or disease before marriage and deliberately concealed it from his marriage partner. Even then, there would be a strong case for saying that the original marriage was invalid rather than that a valid marriage should now be legally brought to an end; in other words, it would be a case of nullity rather than divorce (see Kirk, *Marriage and Divorce*).

However, my own opinion is that it is legitimate – with great caution – to add further exceptions to the one (illicit sexual intercourse) explicitly mentioned in the New Testament. These may be grouped under two headings:

a) Occasions when a Christian may acquiesce in a divorce.

These, like the situation in 1 Corinthians 7:15f, would not in fact be exceptions to the prohibition of divorce, since they do not legitimise an instigating of divorce proceedings. They would merely allow the Christian to agree to a divorce on which his partner is insisting.

Paul mentions one such instance: where a Christian is married to an unbeliever and the unbeliever insists on leaving because (it is implied) he cannot stand his partner's new-found faith (1 Cor. 7:12–16). There is every reason to believe that Paul mentions this particular case (the marriage of believer and unbeliever) because it was an issue raised by the Corinthians themselves in their letter (cf 7:1). We do not need to conclude, then, that this is the only circumstance in which Paul would have allowed a Christian to acquiesce in a divorce initiated by his partner. On the contrary Paul's reason – 'God has called us to peace' (15) – would apply in many other similar circumstances.

It is not uncommon for a Christian to be concerned about how he should behave when his partner wants to divorce him. He believes divorce is wrong, he is (in many instances) still in love with his partner, he doesn't want to go against the commands of God, yet his partner is putting all sorts of pressure on him not to contest the divorce and to let it go through as quickly as possible. What should he do? If he is convinced that nothing will change his partner's mind, that opposition on his part will only lead to bitterness and anger in his partner and indeed a turning away from the Christian faith (cf 16), if the interests of 'peace' (15) are clearly served by agreeing, then in my opinion the Christian has nothing to feel guilty about if he acquiesces in the divorce process.

Of course this concession can be misused. The Christian, for example, should never be bullied by his partner into initiating divorce, even for adultery; the Christian who wants a divorce must never goad his partner into starting divorce proceedings and then say that he is only acquiescing in his partner's wishes; the Christian who has 'let his partner go' (15) should nevertheless continue to be open to reconciliation (1 Cor. 7:11) even after the divorce has gone through. However, it is my opinion that where one partner (whether a Christian or an unbeliever) insists on divorce on grounds other than adultery, the other partner is 'not enslaved' (15) and may accept the divorce, even to the extent of signing legal papers that make the divorce go through more quickly.

b) Occasions when a Christian may initiate separation.
Almost all writers are forced to admit that there are grounds other than adultery for a Christian separating from his partner. Even Bromiley writes: 'Naturally, circumstances arise when separation may be advisable and even necessary. Christians, too, can be or become cruel and vindictive and physically or mentally dangerous' (p.69). It seems to me that 'dangerous' is the operative word here. Where one partner becomes dangerous – either through physical maltreatment or mental cruelty – then it may be legitimate for the other partner to separate. It cannot be right, for example, for a wife to have to accept beatings week after week.

Yet immediately I have said that, I want to qualify it. Suffering is inherent in human relationships, even intense suffering. This is certainly not a mandate to leave a marriage immediately it runs into serious difficulties. What is more, human beings frequently inflict deliberate suffering on those closest to them. Often this suffering has to be accepted and forgiven. It would not be legitimate for a Christian, who has long wanted to be out of a marriage, to seize on a single example of beating or mental cruelty (even if largely unprovoked) as justification for a separation. In the same way, a Christian who has grown tired of a marriage may not seize on one isolated case of sexual infidelity as the reason for divorce when in fact the adultery is only a small contributory factor.

Indeed, a Christian should never separate without careful and prolonged consideration. He (or she) knows that the whole force of the New Testament teaching is against divorce; he knows he should do everything in his power to sustain the marriage. He will therefore only leave after dangerous behaviour (or adultery) by his partner has become habitual and his tentative decision has been confirmed by some godly person whose confidential advice he seeks.

I have deliberately used the word 'separation' throughout this section and reserved 'divorce' for the case specifically mentioned by Christ: adultery. We have seen that this distinction would probably not have been clearly recognised by the New Testament writers. Paul, in 1 Corinthians 7:10–16, does indeed use two words – *chōrizomai* (to separate oneself) and *aphiēmi* (to send away) – but he seems to use them interchangeably. To leave your wife was – in Paul's day – to divorce her.

Nevertheless, the distinction may be helpful for us today. Christ clearly permitted his followers to divorce their partners on the grounds of adultery. They would not then be obliged to seek reconciliation; they might remain unmarried (1 Cor. 7:11). In the case of dangerous maltreatment, we have no explicit New Testament justification for divorce. It may be wise, then, to suggest separation only. This leaves the way open more easily for reconciliation and for resumption of married life.

The New Testament, then, only allows one ground for divorce: illicit sexual intercourse. It also mentions one specific instance in which a divorce initiated by one's partner need not be contested: an unbeliever insisting on a divorce from a newly converted Christian. There are good reasons for extending this latter permission (to acquiesce in a divorce) to other cases. We are on much shakier ground when extending the grounds for initiating divorce and should always lean in the direction favoured by the New Testament: prohibition of divorce.

## Is It Ever Right to Remarry?

If this question arises after the death of a partner, the New Testament answer is most certainly: yes. The marriage bond is broken by death, so that the surviving partner is free to remarry (1 Cor. 7:39; Rom. 7:2f). We have seen that in 1 Timothy 5:14 women who are widowed at a young age are positively encouraged to remarry.

However, although there is no question that it is legitimate for the widowed to remarry, Paul (who may well have been a widower himself) says that it is 'good' for them to remain unmarried (1 Cor. 7:8). In context, this clearly means 'better' than remarrying. Moreover the widow who remains unmarried is happier/more blessed (1 Cor. 7:40). It is also a requirement for elders and deacons (if widowed) and for those enrolled as 'official' widows within the church to remain unmarried after the death of their partner (1 Tim. 3:2, 12; Titus 1:6; 1 Tim. 5:9).

But what about remarriage after divorce? All here hinges on the teaching of Jesus. In Mark, Jesus clearly answers no. Remarriage after divorce, whether it is the man or the woman who has initiated the divorce, is described as adultery; no exceptions are given (Mark 10:10–12). The saying in Luke is really all about remarriage and not primarily about divorce at all. Here not only remarriage after divorce but a first marriage to a divorcee are prohibited; they are both adulterous (Luke 16:18).

In Matthew 5, divorce is allowed in the case of *porneia* (illicit sexual intercourse). The question inevitably arises: if divorce is permitted in this situation, is remarriage also permitted? It is a question we very much want answered but we cannot 'wring' (Davies and Allison's phrase) an answer from a saying of Christ's which did not have the question in mind. His concern was to show that remarriage after divorce or marrying a divorcee come under the prohibition of the seventh commandment: 'Do not commit adultery' (Matt. 5:27–32). In this his teaching is precisely the same as that recorded in Luke and Mark. To this, an exception was added: it is not wrong to divorce your wife for sexual infidelity (32a). We have seen that this may have been included because contemporary law – both Jewish and Roman – insisted on divorce in the case of adultery, and it needed to be made clear to Jesus' followers that it was permissible in this case to follow the law. This says nothing about the rights or wrongs of remarriage after divorce for adultery and the continuation of the verse (32b) makes no mention of the exception (the word 'so' is gratuitously introduced by NIV and is not present in any Greek manuscript); it simply prohibits all remarriage of divorcees.

If we had only Matthew 5, and especially in the light of 32b, we would have to conclude that no remarriage is permitted after divorce; it is always adultery while one's partner is still living. However, we must repeat that Matthew 5 does not address the question directly and so no definitive answer is possible from this passage.

But how about Matthew 19? Does Christ in this passage allow remarriage after divorce in some circumstances? Before we discuss this question in detail, it would be wise to stress what virtually all are agreed on, since these fundamental and important areas of agreement can be obscured in the heat of debate:

a) This is the only saying of Jesus which *could* lead us to believe in *any* remarriage after divorce.
Mark clearly forbids remarriage after divorce during the lifetime of one's partner. Luke equally emphatically does the same. No exception is given in either case. Matthew 5 if anything suggests that remarriage after divorce is not permitted in any circumstances (32b). Matthew 19 is, therefore, the only part of Christ's teaching on which a case for remarriage after divorce could possibly be built. If it can be established here, then Matthew 5 could be read in such a way as not to contradict – perhaps even to support – this; but if it cannot be established here, it cannot be established anywhere within the sayings of Jesus.

b) Jesus prohibits most remarriages after divorce.
In Mark and Luke, he seems to prohibit all remarriage after divorce; no exception is given. In Matthew – both in chapters 5 and 19 – Jesus prohibits remarriage at least where divorce is not for sexual infidelity. This is the whole thrust of 5:32 and 19:9. It is not to *allow* remarriage. Jesus is specifically prohibiting remarriage. He nowhere says that remarriage is permitted. Everywhere his concern is to show that remarriage (at least in most circumstances) is adultery.

Furthermore, remarriage is prohibited to the adulterer where the divorce is for adultery. He may not commit adultery, thereby engineering his own divorce and reward himself by marrying the person with whom he committed adultery. He is not free to remarry. It is his duty to repent and to seek reconciliation and full restoration of the marriage.

Since Jesus clearly teaches that in most cases remarriage after divorce is adultery, there is no justification for churches to say: 'Yes we remarry divorcees' or 'Yes we bless second marriages.' No such blanket statement is possible, if we are to remain true to Christ's teaching. Indeed, even for those churches that believe remarriage after divorce for adultery is permitted, the general policy must – in line with the whole trend of Jesus' teaching – be: 'We do not feel able to remarry divorcees (except in certain limited circumstances)' or 'We are not able to conduct a service of blessing for second marriages (except in certain limited circumstances).' This should be common ground between all churches.

c) From a purely grammatical point of view, Matthew 19:9 could allow or prohibit remarriage after divorce for adultery.
It could mean: 'Anyone who divorces his wife and marries another woman commits adultery, except that a man may divorce his wife for marital unfaithfulness (without the right to remarry)' or: 'Anyone who divorces his wife and marries another woman commits adultery, except that a man who divorces his wife because of her marital unfaithfulness and marries another woman does not commit adultery (because remarriage in this case is permitted).' Some would say that Matthew 19:9, taken by itself, is more likely to have the first of these meanings; others would say that, taken by itself, it is more likely to have the second of these meanings. But grammatically – with the exception placed where it is in the sentence – it could mean either.

Let me again repeat that these three statements – that Matthew 19:9 is the only saying of Jesus which could lead us to believe in any remarriage after divorce; that Jesus intends to prohibit most remarriages after divorce even in Matthew 19:9; and that grammatically Matthew 19:9 could allow or prohibit remarriage after divorce for adultery – are agreed by virtually all who have studied this subject.

However, we cannot – and churches cannot – leave it at that. We must work through to a full understanding of Christ's vital teaching in Matthew 19:9. Since grammatically the meaning is open to two rival interpretations, the context must decide which interpretation is correct. This book is convinced that in Matthew 19:9 – as in Mark 10:10–12, Luke 16:18 and Matthew 5:27–32 – Christ prohibits remarriage even in the case of divorce for adultery, and that we are driven to this conclusion by four facts:

## 1. The surprise of the disciples

The disciples immediately respond to what they have heard Christ say in Matthew 19:9. If even his enemies knew that Jesus had strict views on divorce (cf 3), we can be quite certain that his disciples knew. It would not have surprised them if he had sided with the School of Shammai and allowed divorce only where there had been marital infidelity, in which case remarriage would also be permitted. The fact that they are so obviously taken aback (10) shows that they realise Christ is teaching something much stricter than the Shammaites. Since Christ clearly does allow divorce in the case of adultery (in line with the Shammaites), this must mean that he forbids marriage in this instance (in contradistinction to the Shammaites).

## 2. Jesus' reply to their outburst

Jesus responds to 'this word' (NIV: teaching) of theirs (11). They hope he will vehemently deny the conclusion they draw from his teaching about divorce and remarriage. But he does not rebuke them for what they have said. His only correction is that singleness (which he discusses under the image of being a 'eunuch' i.e. incapable of marriage) is not for everyone (their suggestion in 10) but for those 'to whom it has been given' (11). God 'gives' singleness to people in a variety of ways: it may be from birth, it may be imposed unwelcomely by men (which refers primarily to physical castration but may, in context, include those who are divorced against their will) or it may be self-imposed because of the known demands of the kingdom of heaven (12).

Once more, it is essential to grasp the context of this discussion. The context is that Jesus has answered a question about divorce and has enlarged it to include the subject of remarriage (1–9). The disciples have expressed amazement because Jesus' teaching seems so much tougher even than the

well-known position of Shammai. And Jesus agrees that it is
tough, but states that God gives singleness to some – in context, he clearly has in mind those who are divorced – and the
challenge is for them to 'accept' it (11, 12). Far from correcting
a possible misunderstanding by the disciples of his teaching,
he effectively says: 'You have correctly grasped my teaching.
Singleness is indeed given by God to those who have divorced
even after their partner's adultery. They must now accept that
God has given them a single life.'

## 3.   The interpretation of Christ's teaching by St Paul

The passage 1 Corinthians 7:10f is tremendously important for
our understanding of Matthew 19:9. In these verses Paul does
something which is rare in his writings: he directly quotes, or
paraphrases, Christ's teaching (10f, cf 12ff). He quotes Christ
as denying divorce to both partners. He also quotes Christ
as allowing an exception; we have seen that 11a is part of
his quotation of 'the Lord' and it is quite impossible that he
would interrupt his quotation of Christ's 'command' to say:
'But if you disobey Christ . . .'.
   The exception, then, must refer to the only exception Christ
allows: marital unfaithfulness. This means that Paul must know
the tradition that lies behind Matthew 5:32 or 19:9 or both. In
this situation of marital unfaithfulness which is Christ's own
exception to his prohibition of divorce, the wife (and, by implication, the husband too, since all the teaching on marriage
in 1 Corinthians 7 is said again and again to apply to both
partners) must 'remain unmarried or else be reconciled to her
partner' (11). These are the only two options for the Christian.
Paul clearly understood Christ to forbid remarriage even in the
exception: after divorce for adultery.

## 4.   The interpretation of Christ's teaching by the early Church

The Fathers are almost unanimous in understanding Christ's
exception in the same way. They often write about divorce and

remarriage, and concentrate more on the issue of remarriage than that of divorce. When they speak of divorce, they frequently mention the Matthean exception. When, however, they speak of remarriage, they never mention any exception (Ambrosiaster is the only clear exception up to the end of the fifth century). Their normal practice is simply to prohibit remarriage absolutely (as in Mark and Luke) but significantly they often do this in a context of quoting Jesus' divorce sayings in their Matthean form or in the course of a commentary on Matthew's gospel. Where they do raise the specific question of whether remarriage may be legitimate in the case of divorce for adultery, they prohibit it.

These, together with Paul, are the earliest interpreters of Christ's teaching. Most of them spoke the language of the New Testament (some of them, of course, wrote in Latin but a large number of these would have understood Greek). It is true that they were in some ways more ascetic than the writers of the New Testament. Nevertheless, they clearly sought to base their teaching about remarriage on the words of Jesus – they quote him on this subject frequently – and they clearly understood him to prohibit remarriage after divorce. They either make no exception to this rule or explicitly deny there is any exception, while faithfully recording the exception to the prohibition of divorce.

These are the reasons, then, for believing that both the Gospels and Paul (the other New Testament writers do not discuss the issue) prohibit remarriage under any circumstances during the lifetime of one's partner. The response of many Christians today – perhaps of us all – is to say: 'Yes, I see it is biblical, but it is also very hard.'

It is hard. And for that very reason it is vital to see *why* the New Testament forbids remarriage. So many people think Christ is saying: 'You cannot be forgiven. Your divorce is such a serious sin that it stains your whole life and your record cannot be wiped clean. That is why remarriage is not a possibility for you.'

It is probably the Church's fault that this is the message which has come across, but it has nothing to do with the teaching of Christ or his apostle Paul. Remarriage is not open to the divorcee not because he is divorced but because he is still married. It is because God yoked him and his original partner together. It is because in God's eyes they became, in marriage, no longer two but one. It is because God joined them together in a marriage bond that can only be broken by death. It is because of the nature of marriage that taking a second wife is impossible, not because of the nature of divorce.

Calvin, who would not agree with everything written in this book, is nevertheless magnificent on this subject and is worth quoting at length. He comments on 1 Corinthians 7 :11:

> [Paul says that] marriage . . . is a covenant consecrated in the name of God, which does not stand or fall according to the whim of man, so as to be made invalid at our pleasure. The point is this: since other agreements depend merely on the consent of men, they can similarly be dissolved by their consent. But, if those who have been bound together in marriage now regret what they have done, they are no longer free to 'break the bond' (as the saying goes) and go their own ways in search of a new arrangement with someone else. For if natural rights cannot be destroyed, much less can this, which, as we have already said, takes precedence over the principal natural bond that there is.
>
> But [as to Paul's] commanding the wife, who is separated from her husband, to remain unmarried . . . if she has been put out of the house, or if she has been rejected, she must not think that even in those circumstances she is free from his power; for a husband has no power to render a marriage invalid. Therefore, Paul is not here giving permission to wives to separate from their husbands of their own free will, or to live away from their common home, as if they were widows. But he declares that even those who are not taken back by their husbands remain bound, so that they cannot go to other husbands (translation: D.W. and T.F. Torrance, Oliver and Boyd, 1960).

It is really impossible to understand Christ's (and Paul's) prohibition of remarriage unless we have first understood Christ's (and Paul's) understanding of marriage. Even then, it is impossible not to think this position extremely hard unless we have also understood the very positive value that Christ (and Paul) give to singleness. But once we have understood both that in marriage God joins together every couple in a marriage bond that only death can break and that the single life gives unparalleled freedom to devote oneself to the Lord, then Christ's (and Paul's) prohibition of remarriage becomes something we can not only understand but embrace.

# PASTORAL PRACTICE

# 9

# Educating

Many Christians reading this book – or others like it which explore the New Testament teaching on divorce and remarriage – may feel a certain despondency at this stage. Pastors of churches may especially feel their heart sink. They have grappled with the teaching of Scripture, and in particular the teaching of Christ himself, but they are very unhopeful that it will be accepted even within their churches, let alone society at large. Why? Because the teaching of the New Testament on this subject seems so completely at odds with the spirit of the age.

There is certainly a great measure of truth in that last assertion – we have seen evidence for it in chapter one – but it is only part of the truth. The 1971 Church of England Report: *Marriage, Divorce and the Church* puts this very clearly. The Church, it says, stands for what many people instinctively acknowledge as true about marriage 'because to accept [these Christian truths] is to go along with the grain of human nature, and to reject them is to cross that grain'. But it also stands for these truths against 'forces, whether in the mind or in the exercise of political or other power, which imperil these truths, or make it excessively difficult for people to perceive them and to live by them. There is an inevitable tension between the Church and society, as well as a natural accord' (p.58f). In other words, because human beings are made in the image of God and have a conscience which, however imperfectly, relays the demands of God, and because human experience, for all its mixed signals, does actually bear out that it is best to live in obedience to God, we should not be surprised that many people instinctively recognise the rightness of the New Testament teaching on marriage. But because human beings are also fallen, and seek often to suppress what their consciences tell them, and because human experience seems to suggest that, at least in the short run, it is advantageous to disobey God, there is a great deal of antagonism to the New Testament teaching on marriage.

This explains the fact that people often admire, and even applaud, Christian leaders and churches who take a firm stand about the permanence of marriage, but at the same time want a lower standard, and a more flexible approach, for themselves and their friends. In other cases, the ambivalence is expressed in their attitude towards their own situation. A woman wrote to me: 'I don't think I've ever thought of remarriage as wrong from a biblical point of view. Let's face it, so many Vicars *do* marry divorcees or bless their marriages . . . [However,] I feel I wouldn't want to marry in church. Despite what has happened, I still feel that my first marriage in church (when I *wasn't* a Christian) is sacred to me and I would *not* like a "repeat performance". I would feel uncomfortable.'

Nevertheless, the Church's task should not be underestimated. Robert Bellah, a sociologist at Berkeley, gathered together a team of American academics, mostly in the field of the social sciences, and wrote a justly famous book, *Habits of the Heart*, which sought to analyse American society. The research was conducted between 1979 and 1981, largely through extensive interviews, and the book was published in 1985. One of their conclusions is that lifelong marriage is no longer what most Americans expect. 'Two people sharing a life and a home together' is what 96% of Americans recognise as the ideal (according to surveys in 1970 and 1980), yet when people were asked in 1978 'whether "most couples getting married today expect to remain married for the rest of their lives", 60% said no'. Bellah believes he knows the reason: 'In addition to believing in love, we Americans believe in the self' (p.90).

Almost all, even of the happily married, interviewees 'resisted the notion that such [enduring] relationships might involve obligations that went beyond the wishes of the partners . . . [They were] uncomfortable with the idea . . . of sacrifice . . . Love might require hard work but could never create real costs to the self' (p.109f). The sad fact is that while Bellah and his fellow researchers did notice a difference of attitude between committed Christians and those who were not Christians, it was only a difference of emphasis. Christians too were very reluctant to think in terms of duty or moral obligations within marriage.

This is just as true in Britain. Phypers writes: 'Christians often come to marriage with the same secular presuppositions as their non-Christian contemporaries . . . Beyond a vague notion that God will bless them because they love him, even Christians are largely unaware of the divine dimension in their marriages; for them, like their contemporaries, marriage is a means to happiness and little more' (pp.4f).

It is largely the Church, and in particular Christian leaders, who are to blame for this. Sexual mores have changed radically in the West during the second half of this century, and the Church has all too often simply tagged along behind: giving ground all the time, assimilating the new ethics, often baulking at the more extreme examples of sexual theory and practice but still much closer to the contemporary 'norm' (which is, of course, constantly shifting) than to the teaching of Jesus.

Yet the Church's calling is to stand firm by the will of God and to proclaim it unapologetically, advocating positively what God has said about the single life, about marriage, about divorce and remarriage and standing out against every divergence from God's revealed will. This is the calling not only of Christian leaders, but of all Christians.

What then can we do? What should we do? How can we affect and change society? And how can we help and care for the many within our own Christian family whose lives have been deeply affected by divorce and remarriage, and by society's often unChristian attitudes towards the single life and towards marriage? It is these questions with which the final four chapters seek to grapple.

This current chapter focuses on the Church's responsibility to educate: to teach and argue for the New Testament view of singleness and of marriage. Or rather, to re-educate. Because it is not as if the world – more particularly the 'Christian' world – never accepted this. It is helpful to have a historical perspective on this subject. Jesus' teaching about marriage and singleness was revolutionary in his day but it spread rapidly and became very widely accepted in the Western world. There is no reason why, with God's help, the Church should not turn the tide again today.

But this will need a sustained effort in education. In his book *Issues Facing Christians Today*, John Stott concludes a chapter on Marriage and Divorce with four pastoral conclusions. The first is: 'The need for thorough biblical teaching about marriage and reconciliation' (p.275). Jack Dominian says the same in the language of the social scientist: 'Since the welfare of societies and nations depends on the well-being of the individual marriage and family, we have to learn how best they can be achieved. It can only be done by widespread education and preparation for marriage, the identification through research of its intrinsic destructive forces and the provision of readily available and effective help for those who need it' (p.14).

## 1. *The family*

In the Bible, the family is the primary place of education and instruction.

> The careful upbringing and education of . . . children [was] considered . . . one of the most important functions of parent- hood and . . . wisdom, which was the means of acquiring fear of the Lord and its consequent righteousness which would result in the Lord's earthly blessing for one's children, was held in the greatest esteem and regarded as the optimum of human attainment . . . According to the Old Testament, it was incumbent primarily upon every father of a family to impart instruction to his children (Kaster pp.29f).

This can be seen from the earliest patriarchal times, where God says of Abraham: 'I have chosen him, so that he will direct his children and his household after him to keep the way of the LORD by doing what is right and just' (Gen. 18:19). It is a particularly strong emphasis in the book of Deuteronomy: 'Only be careful, and watch yourselves closely so that you do not forget the things your eyes have seen or let them slip from your heart as long as you live. Teach them to your children and to their children after them' (4:9; see also 4:10). 'Impress them on your children' (6:7; see also 6:4–9, 20–25). 'Teach them to your children, talking about them when you sit at home and when you walk along the road, when you lie down and when you get up' (11:19; see 11:18–21, cf 32:7). In fact, it is the teaching of parents that keeps their children from going astray morally and spiritually (Ps. 78:1–8 cf, Prov. 22:6).

The New Testament has precisely the same view of the importance of the family in Christian education: 'Fathers, do not exasperate your children; instead, bring them up in the training and instruction of the Lord' (Eph. 6:4).

The father has a special responsibility, as we have seen, for spiritual leadership and education within the family. But the mother has a vital role, alongside her husband, in religious/Christian education. After its prologue, the first words in Proverbs are: 'Listen, my son, to your father's instruction and do not forsake your mother's teaching. They will be a garland to grace your head . . .' (1:8f, cf 6:20–22). Proverbs 31:1–9 contain 'The sayings of King Lemuel' which, we are expressly told, 'his mother taught him' (1). And 1 Timothy 5:10 lists among the requirements for those who may be enrolled as an 'official' church widow that she should be 'well known for her good deeds, such as bringing up children . . .'. The Greek here is *teknotropheō* which Arndt and Gingrich define as to 'bring up children i.e. care for them physically and spiritually'.

Of all aspects of Christian education, it is this which today needs most to be stressed. Many families see school and church as the places of religious instruction. This is not only so among those who 'send their children off to Sunday school' but among regular church-going parents as well. Few have realised that the primary responsibility for Christian education lies with them or thought out what in practice that might mean. It is also striking that many fathers are content – and relieved – to hand over this responsibility entirely to their wives, when the biblical picture is not only that both parents are called by God deliberately to educate their children as followers of God but that the principal responsibility in this area lies with the father.

a) Teaching
Direct teaching is certainly expected to be the prime means
of instruction, both in answer to a child's question (Exod. 13:14f;
Deut. 6:20–25; Josh. 4:21–24) and in a more premeditated,
though natural, way (e.g. Deut. 11:18–21). Instruction certainly
includes explaining God's mind on sexual issues (e.g. Prov.
5).

*i) Teaching about marriage*
One mark of Christian parents' teaching about marriage will
be *realism*. Children are so constantly fed on unreality when
marriage is discussed. So many of their stories end: 'They got
married and lived happily ever after', as if marriage were the
ultimate happiness and no problems need be expected once
we are married. Hollywood has traditionally reinforced this:
the last reel ends with the couple marrying and driving off
into the sunset. Even a modern film like *The War of the Roses*,
which is entirely concerned with marital disharmony, turns
the subject into farce and therefore fails completely to help
people think with any seriousness about separation and divorce. Romantic novels only add to the unreality with which
love and marriage is perceived.

   Christian parents need to bring realism into their children's
perceptions of marriage. Children come up against real-life and
television marriages all the time and these need deliberately
(though tactfully) to be brought in to family conversations.
Families can talk about the realities of marriage: for example,
how marriages entered into when very young are much harder
to sustain ('Every major study in the last 30 years and all
the official statistics have found that age at marriage is associated with success . . . Marriages below this age [18–19]
run a considerably higher risk of breaking down' Dominian
pp.130f) and that serious incompatibilities are often far more
obvious to their friends than to the two people who are in
love.

   Children see other marriages at first hand when they visit the
homes of their friends or when their whole family stay with
others. These marriages too can be sensitively and naturally
discussed, not being indiscreet or encouraging children to judge

others, but simply encouraging realism in their appraisal of marriage.

And then every couple speaks to their children about their own marriage. It is understandable, and right, that parents should speak principally about the stability of their marriage and not be too open about the difficulties they encounter. Children today are very aware that their friends' parents' marriages have broken up and need to be reassured about the security of their own home. Nevertheless, we only reinforce unreal expectations of marriage if we give the impression that there are no problems to be worked through.

One man said to his child, after more than 50 years of marriage: 'I have never had to forgive your mother anything, as far as I can remember.' This is not only manifestly untrue; it completely fails in the task of educating the child about the realities of marriage.

And a second feature which will mark out Christian parental education about marriage is the emphasis on *permanence*. For the Christian, marriage really is for life. This repeated emphasis will of course itself greatly reassure children about their own parents' marriage. They know that both father and mother are utterly convinced that marriage is for life and are assured that their parents will live by this conviction. This combination of (not overdone) realism about Dad's and Mum's marriage and an unwavering stress on the permanence of marriage is the best possible education *about* marriage and preparation *for* marriage.

Within this teaching, the parents will certainly want to underline the importance of the vows: husbands and wives tell each other right at the outset that there will be 'worse' times as well as 'better', 'poorer' as well as 'richer', times of 'sickness' as well as 'health', but they promise that they are taking each other 'till death do us part'. These are the promises they have made, and they must stick by them. But Christians will want to set even greater importance on God's act: God joins husband and wife together – whether they are married in church or not – and God makes them, on their wedding day, one flesh.

Christ's conclusion from this – which again needs specifically to be taught, especially since it is so little understood today – is not only that man *must* not separate what God has joined together but man *cannot* separate a man from his wife. God forges a marriage bond which only death can sever. Parents may well point out the psychological evidence for this; frequently couples divorce yet find they are much more 'tied' to their partner than they ever imagined. A typical comment is that of one woman about the possibility of her divorced husband remarrying: 'On the one hand, I couldn't bear the thought of it. To be honest, after all he'd put me through, I didn't want him to be happy . . . But on the other hand, if he had married I would have felt some finality and purpose to what had happened . . . Although I don't feel married to him, I don't feel totally divorced either.'

That is evidence, frequently echoed in others' experience, of what Christ taught. Yet even when that continuing tie is not felt or not acknowledged, Christ says that it is still there. Marriage is permanent (until broken by death) whether marriage partners recognise it or not, and therefore Christian parents will want to make this very clear in their teaching about marriage.

*ii) Teaching about divorce and remarriage*
Here again the need for careful parental education is paramount. Our silence on the subject can sound to our children like our acceptance of, and indifference to, divorce in the world around us. Certainly our children will be picking up ideas about divorce, and many of them will be far from Christian. Stott quotes an article from the June 1982 issue of *New Woman*: 'Letting go of your marriage – if it is no longer good for you – can be the most successful thing you have ever done. Getting a divorce can be a positive, problem-solving, growth-orientated step. It can be a personal triumph.' Stott comments: 'Here is the secular mind in all its shameless perversity. It celebrates failure as success, disintegration as growth, and disaster as triumph' (Stott, *Issues* p.260). 'Today . . . divorce is regarded as more normal than never having been married at all' (Freeman p.196).

Against this attitude, Christian parents will want to show that divorce is *always* a tragedy. But Christ's teaching goes further than that. Despite the unpopularity of the thought, Christian parents need to teach that divorce is *often* a moral wrong, a sin. This is of course not always the case. We have seen that

Christ clearly did allow – though not command – divorce in the case of adultery. We have also said that in some other, very limited cases divorce may also be open to the Christian, for instance where there is repeated physical brutality. But in all other cases Jesus specifically forbids divorce; and to divorce on other grounds – or even to use adultery as one's justification when the real ground is unbearable tensions within the marriage – is to go against an express command of God. It is not just a tragedy; it is a sin. There may indeed be very strong pastoral reasons for not pointing this out immediately (or, in some cases, ever) to a divorcee, but there can be no justification for omitting this essential part of Christ's teaching as we seek to bring up our children 'in the training and instruction of the Lord' (Eph. 6:4).

Of course, like all teaching of children, this will need to be handled with care. Children do need to know that many divorces are sinful in God's eyes, but they also need to learn the tremendous pain involved in divorce and learn compassion for all involved (cf John 8:10f), including the children. Certainly they must be taught to guard against any insensitivity towards the children of divorce whom they will meet at school and against being judgmental towards one or both parents. Equally, children must see their own parents' compassion for those caught up in divorce; otherwise when they themselves are adults and their marriages perhaps run into serious difficulties, their parents will be the last people they will want to turn to. But all these considerations only urge us to show sensitivity and to a realisation of the relationships our children do and will find themselves in. None of these factors should lead us to hush up Jesus' teaching or suppress the fact that he taught that many divorces are rebellion against the will of God and should never even have been considered.

When we turn to the question of marriage, most children learn from their parents precisely the opposite of Christ's view. A family member or friend announces his engagement (having been divorced) and the child hears his parents saying: 'Oh, I'm so glad he's getting married again!' Christians need to think carefully what a truly Christian reaction might be to the news of remarriage, and communicate that to their children.

There is no getting away from the fact that the main truth to explain to our children is that remarriage during the lifetime of our partner is disobedience to God. Christ calls it adultery, and this is hardly, therefore, news that we can be joyful about. But what is essential is that we explain the reason for Christ's forbidding of remarriage. Most Christians conveniently ignore Christian teaching on remarriage. Those who are aware of it tend to ascribe it to 'some (hardline) churches', 'some vicars' rather than Christ himself. And they also tend to think that the only possible reason for disallowing remarriage must be the sin of divorce.

Other Christians are uneasy about remarriage but think that prayer – and especially the peace that God may give or withhold – will show whether it is right in their case. I have on many occasions had discussions even with otherwise mature Christians along these lines; as one woman who was engaged to a divorced man put it to me: 'I said to God: "If this is wrong, you are going to have to get me out of it. I haven't the strength".' To her the relationship was obviously right because 'I've been so much happier . . . I've been in wrong relationships before and God has . . . always put up road blocks.' The implication was: because there were no road blocks this time, the relationship must be right. Had a friend of hers said the same thing about an adulterous relationship, basing the rights and wrongs on whether she felt 'so much happier', this woman would have been appalled. Yet that is exactly what Jesus calls marriage to a divorcee: adultery (Matt. 5:32; Luke 16:18).

What this shows is that the reason for Christ's prohibition of remarriage has never been grasped; and part of the fault for that must lie in the lack of parental teaching. Why is the divorced man or woman not free to remarry? Why would such a remarriage be adultery? It is because, according to Christ, the divorce has not affected the marriage bond, because the original marriage still exists in God's eyes. This needs to be made clear. Thielicke has a splendid analogy: he makes a comparison between the divorcer's – and remarrier's – relationship to 'the continuance of the original order of creation' (he means in effect: the permanence of the marriage bond) and the atheist's relationship to God. The atheist denies the existence of God but that does not stop God being God and in fact influencing the atheist. Similarly, the divorcer – and remarrier – may deny the existence of the order of creation [the marriage bond], but it still exists and influences him (p.114).

All this will need to be explained when, for example, a family member gets remarried after divorce. Of course this puts the Christian in an embarrassing and difficult position. It is surely clear that – except in very unusual circumstances – he cannot attend the service. Yet he must explain to his children why they will not be going as a family, even though their refusal may well be hurtful to the couple getting married.

And it may also be right to find some sensitive but clear way to explain the reason to the couple themselves. This will not always be appropriate – our natural reaction to look for some excuse to explain our not attending may sometimes be right – but too often our silence conveys that we are sitting in judgment or that we consider the divorce to have been an unpardonable sin. So, sometimes it will be right to offer a sensitive yet unapologetic explanation to the couple; but almost always it will be right to use this as an opportunity for teaching our children the reasons for Christ's prohibition.

### iii) Teaching about singleness

Once more the Christian parent needs to start teaching about singleness at an early age, because from our earliest years we are taught to think that happiness can only be found in marriage. I have already referred to the endings of so many children's stories with their 'happily-ever-after' marriages. A favourite for a time with my elder daughter was an Edwardian story, *Ameliaranne and the Green Umbrella*. In this the villain of the piece was the Squire's unmarried sister, Miss Josephine. Our daughter could frequently be heard describing her (and, occasionally, real-life people too) in the words of the book as 'a cross old maid'.

If anything, attitudes towards the single life have grown worse since Edwardian days. 'Society has stereotyped the unmarried as sick, queer, misfit, frigid, homosexual, abnormal, maladjusted or coming from a broken home or a home where love was not modeled' (Hensley p.28). In a seminar for those who have been divorced, Tom Jones counsels divorcees to deal with the 'myths of "fulfilment" . . . and "normalcy" that surround marriage'.

We tend to think of singleness as a disease and marriage as a cure, of singleness as abnormal and marriage as normal, of singleness as unfulfilled and marriage as fulfilled. Jones says that these are all myths and adds that the last people who should fall for these myths are those who have known marriage and then been divorced (*Second Wind* – tape by Tom Jones).

But this attitude towards singleness is deeply ingrained in the Church also. Commenting on 1 Corinthians 7:35 – 'not to restrict you', literally 'not to throw a noose around your neck' – Fee says that the irony is that we have made this subject (Paul is discussing singleness in 7:35) precisely into a restricting noose: 'Roman Catholicism has insisted on celibacy for its clergy even though not all are gifted to be so; on the other hand, many Protestant groups will not ordain the single because marriage is the norm, and single people are not quite trusted.'

Again, a historical perspective is helpful here. It has not always been so. 'Attitudes to the single life have varied very sharply in Christian history, the Middle Ages (and to a lesser extent the nineteenth century) tending to romanticise it, our own age inclining to pity it' (O'Donovan, *Marriage and the Family*, p.105). So there is no reason to believe that they cannot be changed again. Indeed, I think they must change. An article in *US News and World Report* (3 August, 1987) states that the number of 'live-alones' in the United States aged 25–34 went up by 346% between 1970 and 1986; the figure for the 35–44 age bracket increased 258% in the same period. In 1986 4.7 million divorced Americans were living alone, a threefold increase since 1970. The Report goes on 'Society still considers them [singles] an eddy in the married mainstream' but the implication is that this cannot long continue. Attitudes must change towards a substantial, and fast growing, minority in the population. Here is an opportunity for Christians to lead the way in reappraising singleness.

Parents have a vital role to play in this. We need to talk to our children about singleness as well as marriage, about the advantages and disadvantages of each. Of course, in discussing marriage and being realistic about its problems and difficulties, we will also point out the joys and comforts of being married. Similarly we will talk about the difficulties and loneliness that can be associated with singleness, but we will also point out its very real advantages. The test of our education, our Christian communication about the single life with our children, is if they come to accept that while marriage is very 'good', singleness is 'better', and while marriage can bring much joy, singleness can be 'happier' (1 Cor. 7:38, 40).

In talking to our children about singleness as well as marriage, we will not only be discussing it in general, but specifically as it relates to their own future. The constant assumption implied in: 'When you get married . . .' is neither very helpful nor very Christian. Children should grow up feeling that it is a very viable option to remain single, either for many years or for life, and that they can be the more peaceful, the more useful and the closer to Christ, for remaining single. They should know that we as their parents would not be at all disappointed, but rather proud, if their 'gift' was to remain single 'for the sake of the kingdom of heaven' (1 Cor. 7:7; Matt. 19:12).

One significant way in which we convey messages about singleness to our children is how we discuss the lives of friends or relatives who are single. Of course singleness for some is a very sad experience, and we must acknowledge that. But we also want to point out how the many advantages of singleness work out in practice. Children should hear much less from us: 'I do hope she will get married,' and much more: 'She could never do that if she were married.' 'Often [single people] have developed their minds and skills in a way married people have not had time to do' (Hurding p.62 quoting Gini Andrews: *Your Half of the Apple* p.155). Often too they have the time and freedom to spend longer in prayer and drawing close to Christ, and to devote themselves to unstinting Christian service.

In the context of this book, children should recognise that there are also distinct advantages in singleness after divorce. At the time of separation or divorce, most people immediately feel all the losses (which are, of course, real) of the single life; that is why so many rush into a remarriage at a time when they are quite unready for it emotionally. But 'the longer you live alone, the more you realise there are distinct advantages in singleness', so writes Helen Hosier, herself a divorcee (p.134). For some this is the renewed, and much-enhanced, self-esteem that comes from thinking and planning for yourself having been in a marriage where all decisions were taken for you, or of finding you are capable of handling a responsible job when you thought you had lost that ability. For many, it is a precious growing close to your children, which a remarriage might well imperil. And for many more, it is growing close to Christ through having to depend still more deeply on him.

b) Example

If parental teaching is vital, and many children fall into un-Christian attitudes because parents are not in the habit of having family conversations about singleness and marriage, parental example is still more essential. 'Marriage instruction begins in the home . . . Education by example is the most powerful form of marriage instruction a child will receive. It will far outweigh any subsequent teaching he may receive' (Phypers p.138).

Putting it very simply: if we want our children to have good marriages, the best possible preparation for them is for us – their parents – to have a good marriage. Dominian puts this very clearly:

> It is at home above all that children will experience their first and most vital contact with marriage in the relationship of the parents. What they see, experience and feel about this exchange will influence their own potential roles and expectations. It is the marriage of the parents that will give meaning and shape to the goals of their own future marriage, hence the vital importance of preventing marital disharmony between the parents (p.138).

A Church of England Report concluded: 'Marriage preparation is a long-term process. It starts from a child's impression of the quality of his parents' marriage' (*Marriage and the Church's Task*, p.71).

Study after study has shown that children of divorced parents are much more likely themselves to divorce. But the converse is also true: children of good, healthy marriages are much more likely themselves to form, and maintain, good marriages. This is not to advocate an attitude of: 'We must stay together for the sake of the children' when a marriage runs into difficulties. Rather, it is to advocate the attitude: 'We must make our marriage work for the sake of the children.' It is true that it is almost always better for the children if the parents stay together rather than separating; but a hollow shell of a marriage will not provide a good pattern for the children to follow. Rather, even if a couple will not seek help and healing for their own sake, they may be impelled to do it for the children's present welfare and future marriage prospects.

## 2.   The youth group

The family is of primary importance, but the Christian youth group can often be the second greatest influence on the child's – and especially the teenager's – life. From the earliest days, the youth group should be consciously preparing its members for lifelong marriage or singleness.

a) 'From the earliest days'
By the 'youth group', I mean any organisation within the church which is catering for children or young people. This certainly includes the later teenage group (Senior High in American terms), but it also encompasses the Sunday School classes, Junior Church and young teens. As early as we start giving any Christian instruction at all – once a child has graduated from the crèche – we should start teaching about marriage and singleness.

The first series of sermons I preached at my present church happened to be on Genesis 1–3 and we discovered that Genesis 2:24 would fall on a Family Service Sunday. We decided not to break the series but to preach on this to the children. Afterwards, some questions were raised as to the appropriateness of this text for a Family Service, and one member of staff replied that it was absolutely appropriate because we are charged to teach 'the whole will of God' (Acts 20:27). But there is a still more pertinent reason: we want children to develop a Christian view of marriage from their earliest days.

The fact is that they do have ideas about marriage certainly by age two or three. This is picked up partly from stories, partly from what their parents tell them, partly from what they see in their parents about how 'Mummies and Daddies' relate. The only question is whether this view, as it develops, will be a realistic and Christian view or not.

b) 'Consciously preparing for marriage'
Sex, love and boy-girl relationships are constantly on many young people's minds – and at an increasingly early age. I was listening again recently to the music of my youth (early '60s) and it is almost all about love and relationships. It is however, for the most part, remarkably 'tame' compared with the lyrics of the day. I think of the part in the Beatles' 'Norwegian Wood' where the singing stops, the guitars play and I have always imagined this was to suggest that the singer slept with his girlfriend. That reticence has long since passed, and the most explicit promiscuity invades the lyrics and music videos of today.

Teenage magazines, of which there are a plethora, constantly discuss sex and boy-girl or homosexual relationships. Teenagers find friends with whom they can discuss these questions freely and frankly.

Not all of this openness is unhelpful of course, but the vast majority of the material with which teenagers and even children are bombarded is profoundly unChristian, and often deeply inimical to, and subversive of, a Christian view of marriage.

We need to ask ourselves, therefore, whether this subject is sufficiently often on our youth group programme. There was a time when these issues were hardly discussed at all within Christian young people's groups; or, if they were referred to, it was with the utmost coyness. It is good that now most teenage groups, at least, have talks or discussions on sex, on boy-girl relationships, on masturbation. These issues of course need to be discussed from a Christian perspective. Tony Rees writes: 'The trouble with our world is not that it makes too much of sex but too little. Sex has such deep psychological implications for the total personality' (private communication; cf I Cor. 6:12–20).

But we also need talks specifically on the Christian view of marriage. I remember once on a young people's holiday party leading a Bible study on I Thessalonians 4:1–8. In my desire to be relevant, I asked questions entirely about what this passage taught the group about boy-girl relationships. My fellow leader protested that the passage was not about teenage relationships at all but about marriage (so, rightly I believe, RSV at 4:4, cf NIV footnote) and that this is what we should have been discussing. I believe he was right, and that it is just as valuable for a teenager to gain a Christian view of marriage as it is for him to think Christianly about the relationship he may currently be in.

The RSV of 1 Thessalonians 4:4 speaks about 'knowing how to take a wife for oneself'. This too can be a very important part of the youth group's instruction. Dominian, in a chapter entitled 'Prevention', writes of what factors, present before a marriage takes place, make a happy marriage less likely (pp.129–39). First on his list of four is the young age at which some people marry – divorce being much more likely for those who marry under age twenty – and the last is in security and in stability of character. Dominian urges friends and family to help prevent marriages where these factors are present.

Of course prevention of ill-considered marriages is only part of the help that can be given in 'knowing how to take a wife/husband for oneself'. It is equally important to show what positive ingredients make for a healthy marriage relationship. A friend of ours works among university students in the USA and wrote recently: 'My darling Jane and I have been married 15 years now. As my life still has so much to do with young people – who often are not married but want to be – and as I watch many in my generation disconnecting from their marriage vows, I have found myself wondering more and more why we don't teach our children to be friends, rather than dates. Since marriage seems much more a long friendship than a long date, our failure to teach the virtues of friendship seems not a small thing in the well-being of marriages.' Christian youth groups can seek to instil these considerations from an early age in a conscious attempt to prepare their young people for marriage.

c) 'Preparing for lifelong marriage'
It is not only courtship and preparation for marriage that needs to be taught from a Christian point of view. It is still more important that the youth group should teach about the nature, the essence, of marriage. Central to this teaching will be the

truth that, in God's eyes and therefore in reality, it is lifelong. Many children, and especially teenagers, will be experiencing difficulties with their parents. There will be times when they wish they could break free from their parents. Yet they know this is impossible. And not merely from a financial or legal point of view. Long after they become financially independent and have left home, they know that they will still be their parents' child; the relationship, for all the pain it may cause, is indestructible.

Since young people understand this clearly, it is an excellent springboard from which to teach the permanence of marriage. There may be very major difficulties in a marriage, the parents may even live apart or go through a legal divorce, but the relationship itself is indestructible. Whether they realise it or not, only death can break the marriage.

This will inevitably lead on to Christian teaching within the youth group about divorce and about remarriage. Indeed, it is essential. Many children not only in teenage, but in pre-teenage, church groups will have divorced parents. Almost all will have friends whose parents are divorced and will be used to going into homes where a divorced parent is single-handedly bringing up the children or where there has been a remarriage. Since this is very much part of most children's everyday experience, it is of course important that they should learn to see divorce and remarriage from a Christian point of view.

Obviously great care will be needed in how this teaching is given. It will be important to speak with the utmost sympathy and understanding for those who have been unaware of, or have not felt able to follow, the teaching of Christ. We must guard carefully against any sitting in judgment by the children on their own parents or the parents of their friends. Rather, they must be helped to gain a compassionate understanding of what drives people to separate and what makes many long for remarriage. Nevertheless, we cannot shirk, especially with older teenage groups, helping our young people to know and understand the teaching of Jesus.

Again, it may be helpful to point out that what Jesus says about the permanence of marriage even after divorce is often echoed in the experience of those who are divorced. A poem puts this clearly:

It doesn't make sense
that I should care
when you are dating someone else.
Our decision is firm
and I would not return . . .
This is one of those complications
of never being able to neatly segment
life relationships . . .
[I feel] a mixture of anger and regret,
with an edge of love,
like ink running on wet paper,
fingering its way across the page.
We do not separate ourselves from love
as neatly as we might wish we could. (Mattison p.34)

But again we need to pass on Jesus' teaching that the marriage tie does continue to exist, whether this is grasped at the emotional level or not.

It is also necessary to teach about the permanence of marriage so as to communicate what an enormous step marriage is. The fact that the commitment really is lifelong needs to be carefully weighed before seriously considering marriage. When the disciples heard Jesus' teaching about divorce and especially about remarriage and blurted out: 'If this is the situation between a husband and wife, it is better not to marry' (Matt. 19:10), they were at least partly right. As the Church of England marriage service puts it: Marriage 'must not be undertaken carelessly, lightly, or selfishly, but reverently, responsibly and after serious thought'.

Another very important educational influence will be the example of the leaders. Clergy need to be especially careful in choosing Sunday School and teenage group leaders. They need not be people whose marriages are perfect in every way – again, a certain realism about the problems and struggles of marriage can be very helpful – but they should be people who are utterly committed, in theory and in practice, to the permanence of marriage.

d) 'Preparing for lifelong singleness'
It is very unhelpful if the youth group teaching assumes that one

day all its members will be married. This is in fact unlikely to be the case and it can also lead to, or increase, unhappiness in those who reach an age when they feel they should be married and yet are still single. We fail our group members, therefore, if we do not give Christian teaching about making the most both of a prolonged period of adult singleness and of lifelong singleness. When I ran teenage youth groups and holiday parties, I made it a rule never to have a talk on marriage without an accompanying talk on the single life.

It is very important that this teaching, if it is to be fully Christian, should be both realistic and positive. Certainly it must be realistic about the struggles and difficulties, the loneliness and longings that many people experience in being single. But the dominant note should certainly be positive, and positive about the specifically Christian advantages of the single life.

The advantages of singleness are often seen in their purely secular form. M. Evening has a considerable list: from being able to travel widely and having a wide circle of friends to being able to develop and expand one's personal interests (p.218). These gains are real but they are not the reasons for preferring singleness on which the New Testament dwells (Matt. 19:11f, 1 Cor. 7). O'Donovan is much closer to the mark. He describes marriage as having an 'I-We-They structure': 'I' because marriage 'meets personal need', 'We' because it is 'a reciprocal partnership of mutual trust and love', and 'They' because within marriage 'children are born and . . . cared for'. O'Donovan says that in the single life 'We' is lost – I would prefer to say: it becomes less dominant – but by contrast both 'I' and 'They' may gain: 'I' because singleness can become 'the door into a fuller exploration and discovery of the self in its relation to God. Freedom from marriage becomes freedom for the inner life'; 'They' because there is 'a greater availability for a wider range of relationships, more involvement with the needs of society and the Church, more freedom to move in response to a call for help or a summons from the Spirit of God'. O'Donovan concludes that the single life can be just as 'emotionally demanding and fulfilling' as marriage (*Marriage and the Family* pp.97, 104f).

For many members of the youth group a period of adult singleness will be a temporary phase (which still needs to be understood and experienced as a Christian); for others it will be lifelong; for others still it will be a new experience after the death of their partner, or after divorce. While a youth group cannot teach on every subject, this possibility also needs to be recognised and touched on.

Once again, the example of the leaders is vital. It is often the case that some youth group leaders are single, and indeed this should be positively encouraged; it is very helpful to have a mixture of both married and unmarried as role models for the youth group members. It is not necessary for single leaders to conceal the struggles they sometimes go through but it is inappropriate to appoint youth leaders who are not at all at peace with their singleness. Rather, the teaching of all leaders and the example of the single leaders should show the group members that singleness may well be God's 'gift' to them (1 Cor. 7:7) at least for some years to come, and that contentment (Phil. 4:10–13) does not mean a wistful (or even bitter) resignation but a joyful acceptance of God's good purpose in giving us (perhaps temporary, perhaps lifelong) singleness.

## 3.   The church

Of course the children and young people are very much members of the church, but I turn now to the education of the adult membership of the church.

### a) Preaching
Time and again I come up against a reluctance to preach on the subject of singleness and especially of divorce and remarriage. In the Episcopal Church of the USA it is the almost universal practice to preach from the set Lectionary passages, normally from the Gospel. While I was serving in the Diocese of Pittsburgh, I was part of a discussion group for evangelical clergy in the Diocese and we happened to meet when the following Sunday's gospel was Mark 10:2–9. As evangelicals we might have been expected to respect the Bible and preach directly on the theme of this passage, but in discussion it emerged that one rector had decided not to preach on the gospel on this occasion as all his congregation were in their 60s and 70s

(did this mean that they never came across divorce?). Another said he would be speaking on the gospel but would preach about the importance of relationships and hardly mention divorce (let alone remarriage). Another said much the same. Not one said that he or she would be preaching on divorce. I was reminded immediately of a conversation I had in South Africa with an intelligent white ordinand in the Dutch Reformed Church. He had preached the previous Sunday on the Good Samaritan. Though he had seen that Christ's story had implications for the South African racial situation, he had preached instead on the need for compassion amongst the members of the (white) congregation. When I asked him why, he said that he did not want to create a stir or get into the local press.

By contrast, Martyn Lloyd-Jones begins his sermon (incorporated into his commentary) on Matthew 5:31f by saying:

> How often do we hear an address on a text such as this? Is it not true to say that this is the kind of subject that preachers tend to avoid? And thereby, of course, we are guilty of sin. It is not for us to study some parts of the Word of God and to ignore others; it is not for us to shy at difficulties . . . Because of our failure to expound the Bible systematically, because of our tendency . . . to choose what interests and pleases us, and to ignore and forget the rest, we become guilty of an unbalanced Christian life. That in turn leads, of course, to failure in actual practice . . . One can easily understand why people tend to avoid a subject like this; but that is no excuse for them. The gospel of Jesus Christ concerns every part and portion of our life, and we have no right to say that any part of our life is outside its scope.

Our preaching will not of course only be on divorce and remarriage. Indeed it will be impossible to preach on these subjects without preaching first on the Christian understanding of marriage. The Church of England Report *Marriage and the Church's Task* mentions as one way in which marriage can be sustained by the Church: 'reflecting upon and celebrating marriage and family life . . . through preaching' and 'through imaginative use of the liturgy' (p.72). Similarly the Free Church of Scotland Report *Marriage and Divorce* gives as its first recommendation under a heading 'Pastoral Responsibility': 'The biblical doctrine of marriage as between one man and one woman for life should be given due prominence in preaching. There is a tendency to assume that people know this, but it needs regular reinforcement. We have to arm conscience against lax views of marriage' (p.51).

As I write this chapter, we have just finished a series of sermons on singleness and marriage at our church. I list below the titles and principal passages expounded. I have also shown which were preached at Family Services, with even young children present, to demonstrate my conviction that we must begin as soon as possible teaching children a Christian perspective on marriage:

*For better, for worse*

| | |
|---|---|
| 1. Marriage – a fit helper | Genesis 2:18–23 (Tape 27)[1] |
| 2. Marriage – leaving | Genesis 2:21 (Tape 27. John Hobbs)[2] |
| 3. Marriage – cleaving | Genesis 2:24 (Family Service. Tape 28 John Eddison) |
| 4. Marriage – one flesh | Matthew 19:4–6 (Tape 28. Tom Jardine) |
| 5. Marriage – having children | Genesis 1:28 (Mothering Sunday Family Service. Tape 31. Keith Dyde) |

---

[1] Some readers may like to listen to these tapes to see how one church has tried to preach biblically and relevantly on these subjects. Each tape has two sermons on it and can be obtained from: All Saints Tape Library, The Parish Office, Chapel Green, Crowborough, East Sussex, TN6 1ED. The current price is £3 per tape (cheques: 'All Saints Church') including postage.

[2] I have included the names of preachers where I did not preach the sermon.

6. The single life                 1 Corinthians 7:25–38
                                    (Tape 29)

7. Sex is for marriage             1 Thessalonians 4:1–8
                                    (Family Service. Tape 30.
                                    Tom Jardine)

8. Divorce                          Matthew 19:1–9
                                    (Tape 29)

9. Remarriage after divorce        1 Corinthians 7:10f
                                    (Tape 30)

10. Singleness after divorce        Matthew 19:9–12
                                    (Tape 31)

11. Reconciliation                  Hosea 1–3 (Tape 33)

12. Marriage to an unbeliever       1 Corinthians 7:12–16
                                    (Tape 32)

13. Winning your partner for        1 Peter 3:1–6 (Tape 32.
    Christ                          John Hobbs)

14. The riches of married love      Song of Solomon 8:6f
                                    (Family Service. Tape 33.
                                    Chris Gale)

To help me prepare especially for the more difficult sermons, I invited a group of divorced members of the church, about half of whom were remarried, to meet with me on five occasions, in order to help me understand, and speak relevantly to, the real pastoral issues. Before each evening, they wrote notes for me in response to four or five questions which I put to them. For the two hours that we then met together, we discussed other related questions. This was of the utmost benefit to me. The areas discussed on the five occasions were: 1. The story of your marriage, divorce (and remarriage). 2. Your experience and needs at the time your marriage was breaking up.

3. Your experience and needs immediately after the break-up of your marriage. 4. Being single again. 5. Thoughts about and/or experience of remarriage.

Throughout the series – right from the very first sermon – we tried to preach with both firmness and compassion: firmness in that we would not waver from what we believe Christ taught, even though his message in this area was tough for his contemporaries and is tough for us; compassion in that we were well aware that this is a most painful subject for several in our congregation. We sought to be honest and realistic both about the struggles in our own marriages and in those which we encounter in pastoral ministry (while, of course, preserving complete confidentiality).

As a series, it has provoked more discussion and thought than any other within living memory. Some have been profoundly grateful for the teaching, some have been deeply disturbed, a few have been angry, at least one has come to faith in Christ as a result of this preaching. All staff members have found their pastoral load increasing very considerably, sometimes because people have taken the initiative to come to talk to us (and then, on occasion, encouraged their friends to talk to us as well), sometimes because we have taken the initiative in speaking, especially where we know the personal circumstances are very painful or where (in a few cases) people have walked out of a service in obvious distress. We have also held talk-back sessions/question times after these services about once a month, and these were often very constructive times at which the people most affected (e.g. the remarried after divorce) were often present.

The hardest truth to get across was that there can be complete forgiveness for any sin involved in divorce and that Christ's prohibition of remarriage is because the original marriage still exists and not at all because of the sin of divorce. One member of our discussion group, herself remarried, wrote: 'I felt that to say remarriage was out of the question was to suggest that I was worse than a murderer – after all, a murderer has been forgiven, you don't banish him from ever being with other people . . . I felt . . . that true forgiveness did not involve punishment.' We had, therefore, to say again and again in these sermons that, in this area as in every other, Christ brings complete forgiveness of sins to those who repent. I think in retrospect it would have been good to have included in the series, perhaps at the end, a sermon on I Corinthians 6:9–11.

A sermon series like this will need a great deal of prayer and more than usual care in preparing what to say. Opportunities for various kinds of comeback and of pastoral ministry will be essential. Another member of our discussion group wrote: 'I realise that the Church has to take a stand on such issues [divorce] and, to be honest, feel that the Church has sat on the fence for too long . . . but you should never, never forget that you are talking to people who, for the most part, are undergoing a terrible time of stress and strain, guilt, sadness and fear, and there has to be . . . understanding and compassion for them – as well as a very real offer of help in whatever form that might be required.' Again, what is needed is both boldness in tackling this part of Christ's teaching and sympathetic understanding of the pain that people will inevitably feel.

John Stott writes most movingly about this at the beginning of his commentary on Matthew 5:31f:

> I confess to a basic reluctance to attempt an exposition of these verses. This is partly because divorce is a controversial and complex subject, but even more because it is a subject which touches people's emotions at a deep level. There is almost no unhappiness so poignant as the unhappiness of an unhappy marriage, and almost no tragedy so great as the degeneration of what God meant for love and fulfilment into a non-relationship of bitterness, discord and despair. Although I believe that God's way in most cases is not divorce, I hope I shall write with sensitivity, for I know the pain which many suffer, and I have no wish to add to their distress. Yet it is because I am convinced that the teaching of Jesus on this and every subject is good – intrinsically good, good for individuals, good for society – that I take my courage in both hands and write on.

And of course we will not only preach on these subjects in a set series on singleness and marriage. Sometimes the subject will come up in the normal course of preaching – as it should have done in those American churches when they came to Mark 10:2–9 in the Lectionary; and as it did with us recently when we were preaching through the Sermon on the Mount and had a whole sermon on Matthew 5:31f – sometimes it will simply form a part of our teaching, perhaps an application of some general biblical teaching about relationships. Here too, especially if the preacher is married, he will need to beware of presenting marriage as the only 'normal' way of life and will need also constantly to speak about the experience of singleness: what it is and what it can be, both for the never married and for those who are single again after bereavement or divorce.

b) Marriage preparation

'In our society there's more time taken in learning how to drive a car than in learning to prepare for marriage' (*Second Wind* – tape by Bob Burns). Much of the blame for this can be laid at the door of the Church. In England, the large majority of first marriages still take place in church. The Church therefore has a specific, and highly important, responsibility to prepare couples for marriage.

In fact, considerable progress has been made in this area in the last 10–20 years. The parents of today's wedding couples for the most part received minimal marriage preparation from the vicar or minister. He perhaps met with them once, made some rather general remarks about marriage, passed on what had become one or two well-worn 'tips' and briefly explained what would happen in the service. Today couples are often required to meet on three or more occasions with those – frequently a lay couple – who are preparing them for marriage. There is a real attempt to understand the circumstances of their particular relationship, and questions of finance, relationships with in-laws, sex, etc. are frankly discussed in detail. Others feel that these issues, while important, are not the key to marital success and therefore concentrate almost entirely on the development of communication between marriage partners.

All this is healthy, yet we also need to make absolutely clear what is at the heart of Christ's teaching about marriage: that marriage is lifelong. He does not teach merely that this should be the case, but that it *is* the case. marriage lasts for life. Canon

B30 of the Church of England states: 'The Church of England affirms, according to our Lord's teaching, that marriage is *in its nature* a union permanent and lifelong, for better for worse, till death them do part, of one man and one woman, to the exclusion of all others on either side . . .' (my emphasis). The Canon goes on: 'It shall be the duty of the Minister, when application is made to him for matrimony . . . to explain to the two persons . . . the Church's doctrine of marriage as herein set forth, and the need of God's grace in order that they may discharge aright their obligations as married persons.'

This message needs to come across loud and clear. In practice, it means that conflict resolution will form an important part of marriage preparation and that there will also be, even at this stage, a discussion of the Christian view of divorce and remarriage. It is essential that the couple should understand, from God's point of view, which options are open to them and which are not, when/if their relationship runs into difficulties.

The Canons of the American Episcopal Church forbid any marriage until the couple have signed the following declaration: 'We, A.B and C.D., . . . do solemnly declare that we hold marriage to be a lifelong union of husband and wife . . . We do engage ourselves, so far as in us lies, to make our utmost effort to establish this relationship and to seek God's help thereto.' (1985 Canons I.18.3). This declaration, which – using a more modern form of words – we are going to ask couples in our church to sign, provides an excellent means for teaching the permanence of marriage and its implications for the possibility of divorce. Signing it should only take place at the end of a course of marriage preparation and should be taken with the utmost seriousness.

We have already mentioned that many marriage preparation courses are today led by lay couples. This can be very helpful, but far more important than whether the leaders are clerical or lay is the issue of what mood/atmosphere they are able to create. They must themselves be relaxed and able to make the engaged couples relax (a home is normally far more conducive to this than a hall). The time must be unhurried – a whole evening with opportunity to chat and to have something to drink, rather than a 'meeting' of an hour or so. The leaders must be able to understand the thoughts and feelings of those getting married today (e.g. how it does and does not alter their view of marriage that they are very probably sleeping or living together already) and must be prepared to be frank about their own marital difficulties, especially those they encountered in the early months of married life. And they need to leave plenty of time for the couples to talk privately about the issues raised, preferably during the marriage preparation evenings (perhaps giving each couple the privacy of a room to themselves) or/and as work to be done by the couple between preparation sessions.

If this careful preparation and emphasis on the permanence of marriage means that some decide not to get married, this should not in any way be seen as a disaster; frequently it will be a very positive development. Bob Burns explains that in his church the policy is that if you are not a member, you must go through the church's pre-marital course before the church will agree a date with you. The reason is that it gives couples time to think about what they are doing. The result is that as many as 25% of those who have been through the course decide not to proceed with their marriage (*Second Wind* – tape by Bob Burns).

One of the most important factors leading to marriage breakdown is young people who, despite serious doubts during courtship and engagement, go ahead with their marriage (Green p.10). This means that friends and clergy must listen carefully to any hesitations that are expressed and must have the courage to say so when they consider a match unsuitable, even after the couple have become engaged. This is not of course to take any pleasure in the pain that will inevitably be caused, nor to offer insensitive advice when we are not in possession of the facts, but it is far better to help a couple think again carefully and perhaps break off their engagement, than to suppress our real and serious hesitations and say nothing, so that a couple are swept along into a disastrous marriage. As a Church of England Report says: 'Some [couples], perhaps, need help [from the clergy] not to marry, or not to make this marriage, at all' (*Marriage, Divorce and the Church* p.53).

The trouble of course is that the engaged couple are often not in any mood to hear danger signals or heed advice. They frequently believe that there are no, or only minimal, problems in their relationship and are sceptical about their need of marriage preparation. Churches therefore should seek opportunities to continue supporting marriages – both of church members and of those outside – after the wedding service. 'Counselling one year into marriage can do a lot to avert potential crises, for it is then that couples are beginning to face up to areas of conflict' (Green p.35f). As a church, we hold a dinner one year later for all those who have been married in the previous year; it is here that we can invite couples to join a monthly discussion group where they can thrash out issues and questions which their experience of marriage has thrown up.

The arrival of the first – or the second – child can also prove a serious tension point in a marriage. There are far more divorces in the first ten years of married life than thereafter. In 1985, 27% of all the divorces granted in Britain were to people who had been married for 4 years or less; 26% were for those married for 5–9 years. The figure for the next bracket (10–14 years) dropped sharply to 17% (Stone p.442). The Falls (Episcopal) Church in Virginia has developed a highly successful programme called FLAG (Family Life and Action Groups). Couples meet together in a home to work through a course that deals from a Christian perspective with marriage and family issues. Many have found their marriages strengthened as a result.

There are also Marriage Encounter and Marriage Enrichment weekends. The methods vary. The important goal is to get couples talking together and/or with other couples about their marriages, and for the Church to be ready for pastoral counselling ministry if a couple, or even one of a couple, wants to talk further and in confidence.

c) Example
One of the most important contributions that the Church can give to the strengthening of marriages and of Christian standards is the example of the clergy and lay leaders. If single, they should be content and fulfilled in their singleness, even if this basic contentment is not without struggles. If married, they should clearly be utterly committed to their marriage partners and give high priority to the nurturing of their marriage. If divorced, they should not be remarried, nor should they be married to a divorcee (cf Luke 16:18).

The report *Marriage and the Church's Task* recognised that great strains are put on clergy marriages by the nature of their job. It recommended therefore that selectors of ordination candidates should 'consider carefully . . . the quality of the marriage relationship of candidates' (which is, of course, only possible if wives/husbands and fiancé(e)s are present at selection interviews and conferences) and that the clergyman's family life should be a subject on both ordination and post-ordination training (p.74).

The clergyman himself must carve out time for his family. This is often extraordinarily difficult but must be fought for and insisted on with the parish, even if it meets with some opposition. Parishes have for the most part accepted that a clergyman's day off should not (normally!) be disturbed. They need to learn that a minister also needs some time each day with his family. One minister of a large church refuses any interruption between 5 and 7 p.m. each day and will not even answer the telephone for friends of his. He considers this to be essential if he is to give his family proper attention.

Probably every Vicarage and Manse needs an answerphone, and the clergyman must have the discipline to let the machine take the message rather than picking up the handset during 'family time'. This not only allows us to fulfil marital and parental responsibilities, it also teaches the rest of the church by example. And the minister must then be careful that he does not so overwork his lay leaders that time with their own families becomes impossible for them.

It is also important that both minister and lay leaders should be seen with their families in public. I was at a conference recently at which some parishioners, seeing their vicar playing with his family, remarked: 'We don't see him very often with his children.' Clergy should never think that time with their children in a public place or while having coffee after church is wasted. Of course time with one's family is not wasted in any case, but it is also a powerful, if unobtrusive, means of emphasising to the congregation the importance of family life.

Yet another way in which married clergy can teach is by the way we speak of our partner in public: both in sermons and in conversation. Certainly there should be realism: the pastor will help no one by pretending, or encouraging others to believe, that there are no problems in his marriage. Yet all references to his partner should show clear love and respect and an unshakeable commitment to her.

## 4. The school

Archaeological evidence reveals that schools were widespread in Egypt and the Fertile Crescent from very early times. 'School texts' have been discovered in ancient Sumer from as early as 2500 BC. A much later example of such a foreign school, training young men to be servants of the king, is found in Daniel 1:3–5.

Within Israel, different groups were involved in education. The Levites taught the law of Yahweh (Deut. 33:10), prophets had their disciples (Isa. 8:16). But it was especially the wise men who trained young men for life in the world and who called their pupils 'sons'. The most important compendium of the wise men's education is of course the book of Proverbs and, significantly, instruction in a wise sex life is very much included (especially Prov. 5).

The modern school cannot of course exactly reproduce the aims and methods of an Israelite school. Within government education, it cannot be as prescriptive as in ancient Israel, nor can it concentrate so determinedly on moral directives, but it can and should see its mandate as much wider than merely imparting information or developing the capacity of the mind. Like the Israelite school, it can seek to train a child for life (cf Prov. 22:6).

a) Teaching
It is good that sex education is now widely given in schools, although it is essential that sex education should begin and continue in the home. Parents cannot heave a sigh of relief and pass all the responsibility to the schools. Talking about sexual matters should begin early as children see their parents naked and as the 'facts of life' are naturally discussed, for example, when another baby is due in one's own, or a friend's, family. There are several excellent books available for young children. My particular favourite is P. Mayle: *Where did I come from?*

This teaching in the home needs also to continue. As a teenager I asked my mother: 'Why did you never tell us about the facts of life?' I have frequently since teased her for her reply: 'But I did! I remember distinctly telling you when you were three. You thought it rather disgusting!'

But sex education by itself is not enough, nor even what is most needed. School, as well as home, needs to provide continuous education in relationships. Tom Jones, having made the point that sexuality 'involves your whole nature [/personality], not just your genitals' describes the education he received as a young adult in the '50s and early '60s: 'The doctors talked only about biological facts, the social organisations talked only about diseases and unwanted pregnancies, and the church just didn't talk. Any thinking you did concerning sexuality, you did *all alone*' (*Fresh Start*, p.60).

Schools must be careful that they do not fall into this trap of teaching only about the biological facts and methods of contraception. This so-called 'neutral' approach gives the impression that the moral issues are not really important, and above all removes the vital element of human relationship from sexual issues. The report *Marriage and the Church's Task* concludes: 'We consider that Personal Relationships – by which we do not mean merely Sex Education – should be a normal part of an educational curriculum in schools and colleges of Further Education since it represents another essential element in the long-term process of preparation for marriage' (p.71).

It is very important that this teaching should not merely take place in set-piece discussions – for example in R.E. lessons – but should be woven into the whole curriculum. For example, teachers and pupils should be encouraged to comment on and discuss the quality of the relationships, and especially the marital relationships, in literature, whether they are reading Jane Austen or D. H. Lawrence, Racine or Flaubert. 'What are the consequences of adultery in this novel?', 'Do you think the happiness experienced in this clandestine affair is true to life?' A play or novel easily sucks us into its own world and its own set of values. Teachers need to help pupils question these attitudes and values, both for their accuracy in reflecting common human experience and for their morality.

Within Religious Education, schools should not only encourage discussions of boy-girl relationships, but also of marriage, singleness and divorce. As in other subjects teachers should not shy away from direct teaching, from explaining the Christian view of marriage: that it is God who joins husband and wife together, and that he does so for life. Of course pupils should be enabled to interact with this Christian view and indeed to disagree with it, but they should have the opportunity of hearing it clearly explained rather than only hearing their own views and those of other pupils.

Marriage could also well form the subject for a series of school assemblies. Singleness and divorce, while of course they need to be handled with care, can and should come into such a series. With some imagination, it will be seen that schools have many opportunities to teach in this vital area of personal and marital relationships.

b) Pastoral care

All schools are aware that an increasing number of their pupils come from homes where there has been a divorce. Often they notice distinct changes in the children's behaviour or academic performance after the parents have separated, and this can manifest itself again where the custodial parent (usually the mother) remarries and problems arise with the new step-parent.

Teachers need not only to be aware of difficulties in the home but to help children both individually and together with others. One mother wrote: 'The head of Infants . . . got a group together and had a chat about various situations where Mum and Dad don't live together, and one day Christopher came home feeling so much better because he knew he wasn't alone in this problem.'

c) Example

Many teachers feel: 'Our private lives are our own affair.' This reveals a very understandable desire to protect one's privacy, but it is utterly untrue. Teachers' personal lives, and the values on which they are based, will inevitably affect the values which they impart to the children; and in any case children are almost certain to find out much about a teacher's private life, sooner or later. The moral judgments imparted – both by teaching and example – will affect the children in the most import- ant areas of their training for life; and, as we have already said, so-called moral neutrality will come across as moral in- difference, even as amorality.

Of course it is important to employ educationally competent teachers, so that children grow up with a good working knowl- edge of the subjects that they are taught. It is just as important to employ morally exemplary teachers, so that children grow up with a standard of personal life and marital relationships to learn from and emulate. A school should be just as proud that most of its pupils have gone on to form stable marital relationships as that they have achieved good GCSE or A level results. Conversely, if many of its ex-pupils are clearly unable to sustain good marriage relationships, the school should be asking serious questions about what more it can do – by teaching and example – to prepare its pupils for life.

## 5. *The media*

Writers, film-makers, journalists and producers of radio and TV programmes have an enormous influence on us all, and it has to be said that a great deal of their influence runs directly against the Christian view of relationships and marriages. Broadcasting in the early '40s, C. S. Lewis could say: 'We grow up surrounded by propaganda in favour of unchastity' (p.88).

Moral issues are frequently not discussed at all. When they are, or when they are merely implicit, the attitude is frequently that of one marriage counsellor who describes how she helped a divorced man to start dating women: 'Ego-building procedures and the right to personal pleasure were emphasised' (Freeman p.201).

Sadly, this is even the case where the subject is overtly Chris- tian and the writer is clearly sympathetic to the Christian faith. Notable recent examples are the TV film, and the play, both called *Shadowlands* and both discussing C. S. Lewis' marriage. He married a divorcee and clearly wrestled with the question of whether he was able to do so as a Christian. This moral dilemma is hardly touched upon by the TV film or play, and the questions and moral arguments involved are never really explored. The opportunity for a serious discussion of the Christian view of marriage is entirely lost.

If these issues are to be discussed, and if the media's influence is to become more wholesome, Christians must see it as a vocation to write or to produce programmes. Phypers says that TV throughout the world 'must represent one of the most insidious and persistent attacks on the sanctity of sex and marriage in the world today . . . We need a positive response. In our entertainment-orientated society, we need Christian writers producing material of the highest quality which wins its place in the ratings on sheer merit, yet which reflects Christian values instead of the shifting sands of secularism. This is not to deny that adultery and divorce are proper subjects for TV drama, but it is to plead that they receive honest treatment instead of being glamorised and portrayed as [morally] normal' (p.152).

Christian writers protest that they should not always be expected to write evangelistic tracts. This is absolutely true, but their writing should always be compatible with, indeed advocate, a Christian worldview. In the context of this book, I would love to see Christian writers and programmers explore the human experience of continuing to be 'one flesh' with your partner even after divorce. As one divorcee wrote: 'I felt like a branch torn off a tree – that I wasn't a whole person, but still had the need to be part of the unit.'

## 6.  Society

In January 1990 Margaret Thatcher gave a major speech in which she presented the Conservatives as the party of the family. In 1991 Labour followed suit, maintaining that it was the party which really cared for the family. But what does this amount to? The only new initiative that the government has taken so far is to ensure that alimony is more regularly paid and that therefore the financial burden on the state is lessened. This has done almost nothing to strengthen the family and indeed has, if anything, increased acrimony between the separated partners. The act itself is probably necessary but it is no evidence that the Conservatives have thought seriously or deeply about the family.

Time and again the fundamental issues are not faced. In the 1980s the Lord Chancellor set up a review body to look into conciliation services. A committee was formed by the Order of Christian Unity to submit material to this review body. While recognising that 'conciliation has a useful subsidiary function', the first words of the OCU's report are:

> Our Committee convened to submit recommendations to the Committee appointed by the Lord Chancellor to review current arrangements for conciliation . . . We consider that these terms of reference are too restricted . . . The basic problem [is] the acute problem of the high divorce rate. Changes which simply relate to attempts at conciliation are likely to do little to reduce the enormous cost in terms of human misery and financial resources. There is little point in painting the house while the foundations are collapsing. We therefore believe that the main emphasis should be the need to preserve marriages, or reconciliation (p.3).

Lip service is sometimes paid to these basic questions. The preamble to the 1969 Divorce Reform Act describes it as 'An Act . . . to facilitate reconciliation in matrimonial causes'. In fact, the divorce rate more than doubled in the two years following the introduction of the act and has grown steadily since then. In America they are at least more honest. In the past, most US states had a legal requirement that attempts at reconciliation should be made before a divorce is granted; by 1982 only two states continued to insist on this where the alleged grounds were 'irreconcilable differences' (Chapman: *Hope* p.98). As a Church of England Report commented: 'There is a curious discrepancy, at the level of public policy-making, between an increasing awareness of the need for concerted policies for the *family* and an almost total lack of interest in sustaining *marriages*' (*Marriage and the Church's Task*, p.69).

Changes need to take place both at the level of society's attitudes and at the level of the law. The two are linked and neither can be neglected. Certainly our legislators, faced with the enormous human tragedy of marital breakdown, cannot simply wash their hands of moral responsibility and claim that they have no power to do anything except to follow public opinion, nor can they say that legal enactment will fundamentally alter nothing. William Temple wrote: 'To say that you cannot make folk good by Act of Parliament is . . . a dangerous half truth. You cannot by Act of Parliament make men morally good, but you can by Act of Parliament supply conditions which facilitate the growth of moral goodness and remove conditions which obstruct it' (quoted in Atkinson p.177).

This is not the place to suggest detailed new legislation but Atkinson describes the three goals which the civil law should set out to achieve:

1. To provide a context in which covenanted love-faithfulness (he is deliberately using Christian language; a secularist might say: committed marital relationships) can flourish and be maintained – and therefore to minimise the opportunities in which the temptation to 'threaten to apply for divorce' can arise and to provide barriers also against easy divorce.
2. To maximise opportunities – and agencies – for recon ciliation and support when marriages are in trouble.
3. To regulate the ways in which society will tolerate the termination of marriage covenants so as to maximise justice and social stability (p.158).

It is so easy for all the attention to fall on the third of the above aims, with the result that all legislation becomes – in practice if not in theory – legislation for divorce. Legislators need to give just as much thought, perhaps more, as to how the first two aims can also be encouraged by legislation.

It is on the second aim that the Order of Christian Unity's Report concentrates. It is convinced that a Welfare State which cares for so many of our physical, social and educational needs should also be providing widely available reconciliation services. In particular, it recommends that most marital cases should be shifted from the Divorce Courts to Magistrates' Courts whose 'principal aim [should be] to encourage reconciliation and conciliation. Affiliated to these courts should be a National Reconciliation and Conciliation Service . . . largely staffed by voluntary workers . . . The aim is not to make divorce more difficult, but to ensure that it is really necessary' (pp.22f).

There is enormous value, then, in those organisations and pressure groups, such as Care for the Family and FLAME, which, by research and publications, conferences and rallies, open letters and political lobbying are seeking to influence government legislation and priorities in favour of supporting marriages. Much more still needs to be done. The Tavistock Institute of Marital Studies writes in its prospectus: 'Despite high divorce rates, the marriage relationship is still the mainspring of most families. Yet there is less research about marriage than about other relationships and issues which impinge on family life. Even more neglected is the investigation of ways in which troubled marriages can be helped.' Further research and political pressure will eventually lead to legislation that is more supportive of marriage.

But it is essential that society's attitudes are also changed. We need a crusade – just as dogged and patient as Wilberforce's as he sought to change entrenched attitudes towards slavery – which will explode myths and radically alter public opinion. Despite so much human evidence to the contrary, it is extraordinary what myths have taken hold of the popular imagination and will not easily be dislodged. I mention five of the most common:

1. *'You are more likely to make a good marriage if you sleep together regularly beforehand.'* This idea is not only firmly ensconced in the mind of the young but frequently in the mind of their parents also. Young people seriously considering marriage, it is believed, are not only following pleasure in sleeping together; they are acting responsibly in discovering whether they are sexually compatible. The facts point in precisely the opposite direction. In the early '70s, 7% of women who married had lived with their husbands before the wedding. By the late '70s this figure had risen to 20% (Order of Christian Unity p.6). I have no current figures but would imagine, from my experience of engaged couples, that the figure is now well over 50%. Phypers comments: 'If the argument of the humanists is correct, we should therefore be enjoying a higher degree of marital happiness

than ever before. In fact the opposite is the case' (p.73). And there is a distinct correlation between living together before marriage and a higher failure rate in marriage. An extensive study of young couples in Columbus, Ohio, revealed that those who had lived together before marriage had markedly more marital problems especially 'in the areas of adjustment, happiness and respect' and, significantly, of sex (quoted in Phypers pp.72f).

2. *'When love dies, it's best to be honest and separate.'* This is highly questionable from a moral point of view: it prizes honesty but ignores pledged commitment, and it assumes that honesty can only lead to separation and does not enquire whether honesty may lead to a recognition that help is needed and a new determination to work at and rebuild the marriage.

But 'best' in this common attitude probably does not mean 'morally best' but 'most advantageous', 'happier in the long run for all concerned'. This too runs right against common experience: 'It is not yet generally realised that for most people divorce is a miserable condition and that for many there would be less unhappiness in working to preserve a marriage than to dissolve it' (Order of Christian Unity p.13). M. D. A. Freeman, Professor of English Law at University College, London writes: 'When we knew very little, we could believe in myths like divorce being better than bad marriage and time as a great healer' (in Wallerstein and Blakeslee p.7).

3. *'Divorce is often better for the children than living in a loveless home.'* This is certainly not what the vast majority of children themselves think. Most dream, beg and even plot and scheme to bring their parents back together again, often even after one or both parents have remarried. Although some children later on tell their parents they did the right thing, almost none believe at the time it is for the best. The children normally suffer far more after divorce than they ever did while the parents were together, however poor the relationship.

4. *'There is no fulfilment without marriage/marrying again.'* This is a very widespread view and was put bluntly by one pastor whom Laney reports: 'God wants Christians to be fulfilled, and divorced people who desire marriage will not be fulfilled and satisfied apart from having a husband or wife and a family' (p.110). This is true neither to human experience nor to the Christian

gospel. We have seen both from New Testament teaching and Christian experience that there can be enormous fulfilment in the single life, though of course there can be difficulties too. Similarly within marriage there can be enormous joys and there can also be great frustrations and unhappiness. 'People who say "I would be fulfilled if only I were married" are precisely those not ready for marriage. You simply bring your own lack of fulfilment into your marriage' (*Second Wind* – tape by Tom Jones).

5. *'People normally learn from their mistakes and make a greater success of their second marriage.'* It seems to stand to reason: people live and learn. Sadly, the facts do not bear this view out. In the USA 57% of second marriages end in divorce; the figure is higher (60–65%) where both partners are divorced (Hosier p.185, *Second Wind* – tape by Tom Jones). In Britain 4–5 out of 10 second and subsequent marriages end in divorce, whereas the figure for first marriages is 3 out of 10 (Phypers p.120). Tom Jones suggests three reasons for this higher incidence of marital breakdown: 1. 'In remarriage, you bring baggage with you' – you bring many ideas about marriage and a lot of marriage-related hurts, fears and insecurities into your new marriage. 2. 'In remarriage you (often) bring children with you' and therefore a whole network of highly important and potentially difficult relationships. 3. 'In remarriage, you bring financial baggage with you' – financial commitments and established ways of handling money which frequently are not adequately discussed before second marriage (*Second Wind* – tape).

All of these myths need to be exploded and to be seen for the hollow untruths that they are. The evidence is there before our eyes but we are very reluctant to examine it. Professor Anthony Clare writes in the preface to *Second Chances* that despite the prevalence of divorce:

there is an extraordinary disinclination to look closely at the phenomenon of divorce, examine its seriousness and quantify the enormity of its impact on our lives. Are we afraid of what we might find? . . . We do sometimes seem unduly eager to play down the potential adverse consequences of divorce and resort rapidly to the reassuring view that it is better for partners and their children to suffer the presumably short-term effects of marital dissolution than endure the long-term hardship of marriages that are dead in everything but name (in Wallerstein and Blakeslee p.11).

The book goes on to show how totally unfounded this 'reassuring view' normally proves to be.

We need therefore to draw public attention to the sheer devastation caused by divorce, in order that public attitudes may change in the direction of building up marriages, seeking to dissuade friends from divorce, being prepared to put effort into repairing and sustaining marriages, instead of simply accepting divorce as 'part of life'. One of the most important researchers into the effects of divorce is Judith Wallerstein. When she began her research in 1971 she imagined 'according to the prevailing view at the time [that] divorce was a brief crisis that would resolve itself'. She therefore expected her study of divorcing families to last about a year 'for we believed that normal, healthy people would be able to work out the problems following divorce in about that time'. In fact she found that 12–18 months later, 'their wounds were wide open. Turmoil and distress had not noticeably subsided. Many adults still felt angry, humiliated and rejected, and most had not got their lives together again. An unexpectedly large number of children . . . were worse [than in the early months of the divorce]' (Wallerstein and Blakeslee pp.16, 21, 22). She carried on her research into the same families ten and fifteen years later and found that many families' members were still deeply wounded and incapacitated by the original divorce.

Society needs to be made aware of the effects of divorce on the partners. At the time of separation, one or both are usually so aware of the intense pain within the marriage that anything else would appear preferable; and indeed the immediate reaction is often relief. But frequently the experience of separation and divorce proves much more painful than either party ever anticipated. The experience of divorce is often compared to bereavement and there are many similarities, but Green notes seven ways in which divorce is worse: the memories are more painful – often bereaved people know (or believe) that they were loved; the helpful rituals of bereavement, in particular the funeral, are missing; people rally round someone bereaved – they often avoid, or even accuse, a divorcee; both bereavement and divorce involve legal matters, but the legal affairs associated with divorce can go on and on; in divorce, bitterness over arrangements is often added to grief; widowhood has a measure of respectability, divorce has not; and one is more likely to be financially worse off after divorce than after bereavement – many have insurances against death, not against divorce (pp.12–14). To this we might add that divorcees much more often have to leave their home and perhaps their job as well. 'Divorce . . . is more like having both legs cut off than it is like dissolving a business partnership or . . . deserting a regiment' (Lewis p.93).

Society also needs to be made aware of the effects of divorce on the children. Almost all separations/divorces come as a complete shock to the children. They may have been aware of bitter rows, even of physical abuse, but they have rarely recognised the extent of the problem (cf Crispin p.203). And so their parents' separation comes to them as a crushing blow. Sometimes the devastation caused to them is immediately obvious in their changed behaviour – for example, regression in younger children, aggression in many boys, withdrawal in children of both sexes – but one of the prime conclusions of Wallerstein's research is that the harmful effects of divorce may not emerge until many years later. In others, the adverse results can be apparent from the beginning and then become more pronounced as time goes on. Of her study of families five years on from divorce, published as *Surviving the Breakup*, Wallerstein says: 'A large number of youngsters – well over a third of the whole group – . . . were significantly worse off than before [at 12–18 months]. Clinically depressed . . . they had deteriorated to the point that some early disturbances, such as sleep problems, poor learning or acting their problems out had become chronic' (Wallerstein and Blakeslee p.23). They were often very angry with their parents for divorcing and also insecure: half were intensely afraid of being abandoned by their (non-custodial) father, and a third were afraid that their mother might disappear as well (quoted in Parkinson p.2). Dominian quotes research which shows that later in life the problems persist: the statistics for crime, alcoholism, even suicide and – significantly – divorce are much higher in the children of divorcees (pp.122–7).

Remarriage is often thought to be the answer to this problem. 'My children need a new father/mother.' Sometimes, certainly, the new 'blended family' works well. But for the most part this is another myth. Frequently children find the new step-parent an intruder whom they resent, and the family problems – for the children and for the new marriage partners – are more often increased than resolved by a second marriage.

Thirdly, society needs to be made aware of the effects of divorce on society itself. The costs alone are gigantic. The Order of Christian Unity Report gives detailed figures to show that the cost of divorce in Britain is 'in excess of £1,000,000,000 per annum' (pp.8f). That was in 1980–1. The preliminary results of the 1990 General Household Survey show that in 1988–89 'the cost of all income-related benefits for lone-parent families [not, of course, all of them divorcees] was £3.2 billion . . . The survey figures suggest that the bill must now be approaching £5 billion' (*Guardian Weekly* 29 September, 1991). Economic self-interest alone should therefore wake society up to the need for a radical change of attitude and of action towards divorce. But much more importantly, the disintegration of the family means the destruction of the basic building block within society. The same Order of Christian Unity Report states its belief that 'the instability of family life and the high divorce rate are important contributory causes of a general moral decay' and gives as evidence of this moral decay sharply increased figures for illegitimate births, abortions, children in care and young offenders (pp.9f).

The question is: who will take up this challenge? Who will be the Wilberforce of today, devoting a whole life to changing society's attitudes to marriage, divorce and remarriage? Public opinion has been changed dramatically in the last decade over green issues and pollution. It has in past history been changed dramatically in the direction of a Christian view of marriage: 'the doctrine of the indissolubility of marriage was very much of a novelty in the world into which Christianity brought it' (Kirk p.33). So it can be changed again – as it needs to be radically changed – in the areas of sex, singleness and marriage.

It will not be an easy task, but then it was not for the early Church either. Fee comments on 1 Corinthians 5:1–13:

> In a culture where one could matter-of-factly say, 'Mistresses we keep for the sake of pleasure, concubines for the daily care of the body, but wives to bear us legitimate children' (Demosthenes *Or.* 59.122), the Judaeo-Christian moral restrictions on human sexuality were not easily absorbed by pagan converts . . . *Porneia* appears so often as the first item in the New Testament vice lists not because Christians were sexually 'hung-up', nor because they considered this the primary sin . . . It is the result of its prevalence in the culture, and the difficulty the early Church experienced with its Gentile converts breaking with their former ways, which they did not consider immoral.

Yet the Christian view did make remarkable headway: 'The rapid spread of Christianity and the acceptance of its norms of conduct [i.e. 'extra-marital chastity and fidelity in both partners to a marriage'] was proof of the Spirit's power behind the message. From that evidence we can take comfort and courage for the future as we face the widespread *porneia* of our own day'(*Marriage and Divorce*, pp.32f).

There are also developments in our contemporary society which can give us hope that the trend may be reversed. In West Germany, for example, while in 1960 the divorce rate was almost twice as high as in the United Kingdom, by 1986 it was 50% lower; and the divorce rate in several West European countries has remained static or even decreased during the second half of the 1980s (EEC Demographic Statistics, 1990). The AIDS epidemic is causing people to change drastically their sexual habits. It does not yet seem to have changed people's sexual attitudes very much but that may well follow as the world wakes up to the magnitude of the problem and that advocating 'safe [pre- and extra-marital] sex' is simply not enough.

To turn the tide will probably need several significant leaders who will see this as a lifetime's vocation, but it will also need an army of ordinary Christians and secular men and women who have come to see the gravity of the situation and are taking action to change it: teaching their own children, becoming youth leaders, teaching on moral and relational issues in schools, writing about marriage from a Christian perspective, becoming counsellors in Relate (the new name for the Marriage Guidance Council) and other counselling organisations.

'We've never had a greater need of Christ's teaching about marriage and divorce. To tackle the difficulties that arise in many marriages, and to avoid the damage inflicted by divorce, we need authentic and strong motivation. Christ's teaching is uniquely capable of giving us that' (Flood p.24). It is up to us to see that this teaching is disseminated, explained, understood and acted upon.

# 10

# Caring

Educating and seeking to change public perceptions are vitally important; but they are not enough. The Church has the responsibility to care for those who have been damaged or are in need. This care certainly extends to those who are not yet members of the Church but the problems of singleness, marriage, divorce and remarriage are not at all confined to those outside the Church. Phypers rightly points out: 'As a new generation begins to turn to Christ from non-church backgrounds, so a growing number of converts are bringing tangled sexual and marital relationships with them into the life of the Church' (p.2). Growing churches, especially those working in city centres among young adults, find that a significant percentage of those in groups for new Christians are still living with a boyfriend or girlfriend. Many join our churches already divorced and remarried. It was ever so. Paul says to the Corinthians: 'Neither the sexually immoral nor idolaters nor adulterers nor male prostitutes nor homosexual offenders . . . will inherit the kingdom of God. And that is what some of you were. But you were washed . . .' (1 Cor. 6:9–11).

Moreover, those who are already Christians are not exempt. Belief in Christ and a committed relationship with him is certainly an enormous help in sustaining marriage; of course we should expect to see, and do see, a marked difference between the stability of Christian and of non-Christian marriages. Nevertheless, Christians do find homosexual temptation too strong for them, their marriages do fall apart, they do remarry. This also was ever so. Paul writes to Christians in Corinth who have become involved in incest (1 Cor. 5:1-5), in prostitution (1 Cor. 6:12–20) and in sexual immorality more generally (1 Cor. 5:9–13; 10:8; 2 Cor. 12:21). The experience of divorce in particular can be worse precisely because one is a Christian. Guilt is almost always a problem in divorce but it may be heightened for the Christian, who feels he has done what God hates (Mal. 2:16). He may feel estrangement from God: 'Have you divorced me too, Lord?' He may feel that the two most important supports of his life – his wife/husband and his God – have both been removed from him.

So pastoral care, in its widest sense, is an inescapable responsibility for the Church. In 1937 it was proposed in the Lower House of Convocation in Canterbury that an instruction be put into the marriage service that a couple should go to their parish priest or bishop if they are in marriage difficulties (Atkinson p.186). This is in fact enshrined in the US Episcopal Canons: 'When marital unity is imperilled by dissension, it shall be the duty of either or both parties, before contemplating legal action, to lay the matter before a Minister of this Church, and it shall be the duty of such Minister to labor that the parties may be reconciled' (1985 Canons I.19.1). But of course words in Canon Law are not enough. These need to be translated into action and the Church needs to reach out to its bruised and troubled members with pastoral care.

This chapter would be inordinately long if it sought to address the issues of singleness as well as marriage, of homosexuality as well as heterosexuality, of ministry to those outside the Church as well as those within. So it will concentrate almost exclusively on pastoral ministry towards those who have some contact with Christians and whose marriages are in difficulty or who are separated, divorced or remarried. We will look in turn at the pastoral care which can be given by a Christian friend, by the Church as an organisation or family, and by the legal profession.

## 1.  The Christian friend

By this I mean the individual Christian. He or she may well be a clergyman, church staff member or lay pastor. But it is a great mistake of the US Episcopal Canon just referred to, and of many church members' expectations, to think that it will always, or even normally, be the minister to whom a person with marriage difficulties or a divorcee will open up. This will happen, of course; but far more often, the individual or couple in trouble will talk freely to a Christian (non-ordained) friend, and this friend is much more likely to have the time to listen and to 'be there' again and again which may well be required. Indeed 'ordinary' Christians, as friends and family members, are almost always involved at some level in every marriage breakdown. All Christians should, therefore, see it as part of their calling from God to listen and, where appropriate, give advice. Divorced Christians may particularly see this as a God-given ministry, because often those who have been through the agony and confusion of divorce are most able to help others going through a similar experience; this is in fact one of the ways in which God can bring good out of, and use, the experience of divorce, which at the time, seems all pain and pointless (cf 2 Cor. 1:3–7).

a) Taking the initiative

Taking the initiative is the great difference between a Christian friend and a counselling service like Relate. The latter will obviously never initiate help, counsel or even just listening; the former can and should. Of course this needs both courage and tact. Some Christians have well-meaningly but tactlessly blundered into a couple's marriage and merely succeeded in getting the couple's backs up and even making a difficult marriage worse. But far, far more often it is courage rather than tact that is lacking. Christian friends see a marriage running into problems but lack the necessary boldness, or fear that they would not know what to say, and so keep quiet. Many marriages could have been saved if friends or family had spoken up – or rather, encouraged those concerned to open up and themselves speak – much earlier on.

I write in a week when a parishioner has taken her courage in both hands and asked me whether she is right to have detected difficulties in my own marriage. She approached me very lovingly and tactfully, with hesitation and yet clearly, and I am grateful. We have all been made 'watchmen' for each other, not in the sense of prying inappropriately into other people's marriages but in the sense of caring enough to take the initiative and then listen – and perhaps advise – when we see, or think we see, that a marriage is in difficulties (cf Ezek. 3:16–21; 33:1–11).

### i) When a proposed marriage seems unsuitable

We have touched on this in the last chapter. Too many people who divorce say that their family and friends seemed to push them into the marriage ('When are you two going to get married? You've been going out long enough!') or brushed aside their hesitations, during courtship or after engagement, without taking them seriously.

On the other hand, when a marriage breaks down, friends often say (most unhelpfully): 'I never thought it would work,' 'It always seemed to me a strange partnership.' Some of this of course is being wise after the event. But far too often friends have real hesitations and do not voice them. At the risk of weakening our friendship, it is incumbent upon us to share any doubts that we have. Of course this will need to be done with great care, of course the decision remains with the couple themselves, of course a broken engagement leads to great hurt for both parties, but far, far better to help a couple see that a marriage is unlikely to work well than by our silence to let them go ahead and then find immense problems which we had largely foreseen.

### ii) When a marriage is in trouble

A man, now divorced, wrote to me recently: 'Most of our friends who recognised we were in serious trouble steered clear of us.' This is, sadly, very typical, and the result is that many more marriages break up than need to. A Government Report, *Marriage Matters,* states: 'Many people feel the need of help [with the decision about whether to preserve or break up their marriage] . . . Failure to get help when it is needed often leads to unnecessary break-up and to chronic unhappiness' (quoted in Order of Christian Unity p.13).

One encouragement to Christians, understandably hesitant about taking the initiative to talk, is that those whose marriages are in trouble would often like to talk if the person and the opportunity were right. One man wrote: 'For at least 18 months I realised my marriage was in trouble before I told anybody – or perhaps admitted to anybody that I had failed, as I saw it then. Upon receiving a solicitor's letter [from his wife's solicitor], I first told my father which at the time was a great relief to me.' Many divorcees say: 'If only someone had had the courage to talk to us.'

*iii) When there has been a separation or divorce*
Most people experience a loss of friends at the time of marriage break-up. Some side with the other partner, many stay away in embarrassment, not knowing what to say. Some see it as supportive to speak with vitriol about the other partner, which is almost always unhelpful, or to say 'I would never have thought it; you seemed such a happy couple', which is almost equally hurtful. In fact, this is a time when those who have lost their partners especially need friendship, friends who are prepared sometimes to spend hours on the phone or in their company, friends who do not need to know all the details of the break-up but are prepared to ask a simple question: 'What kind of week have you had?' and then *listen*.

Judith Mattison's piece, *Phone Calls*, sums this need up well:

> In the midst of bedlam
> or silence
> the phone rings
> and someone wonders,
> 'Are you all right?'
> This precious connection
> restores my sense of self
> and brushes aside the toil of thoughts
> which were churning inside me.
> Someone called.
> Someone cared.
> I'm not alone. (p.27)

Nor should it be imagined that because someone *seems* to be coping, he or she is. This is very often not the case, even – sometimes especially – where he has developed another relationship quickly, even – and again sometimes especially – where that is heading towards marriage. One woman wrote: 'It would have been nice if someone had asked me how [my experience of] divorce was going. Because I was coping, people tended not to offer help . . . I did not want people to think I was a failure and that I was struggling on my own, so I . . . put a brave face on things. It should not be assumed that people always feel confident . . . even if that is the appearance they give . . . I felt very lonely and afraid and would have loved a shoulder to cry on, but I was too proud to confide in anyone. Perhaps if someone had asked me how I felt, I would have found it easier to be honest with myself and them.' In fact this woman was realising she had made a mistake and wanted to get back with the husband whom she had divorced.

Another woman wrote: 'I didn't let anyone know I needed anything. I had to hold my head up high to show how strong and self-sufficient I was. Amanda [her daughter] and I were the happiest people in Penzance, and nobody was going to know the extent of the pain we had been through . . . I have never broken down in front of anyone. My parents . . . know nothing of our problems.' In fact, various Christians approached this woman with friendship and gentle, caring questions, and gradually she began to open up. Once again, the initiative had to come from others and might never have come from her.

*iv) Before a new relationship forms*
The assumption almost always is that remarriage is all right. Remarkably few, even among Christians, have ever considered the teaching of Jesus in this area, or even asked *why* the Anglican and Roman Catholic churches prohibit remarriage, or wondered whether their vows and what God did at their original marriage might make a second marriage an impossibility 'till death – not divorce – us do part'.

It is therefore essential for Christian friends to raise the question of the future with divorcees, to talk it through. Certainly this should not be done too soon; someone coming to terms with separation and divorce has enough to grapple with, without having this further issue to wrestle with as well, especially if – as, sadly, is the case with most – he has had no teaching on the subject in the past (see the previous chapter). But the subject should not be delayed too long either. Many friends – including, sadly, Christian friends – will be saying right from the beginning: 'You'll find a nice girl soon'; 'You're very attractive. There are bound to be men who would love and respect you.' So the issue is already a live one in many divorcees' minds. What is more, many, many engage in relationships very soon after divorce. Sometimes these are of a purely physical nature – in a search for sexual comfort or to prove oneself sexually (cf Abulafia pp.164–7) – sometimes they lead to marriage: more people get remarried in the first two years after divorce than at any subsequent period. So it is essential that the Christian friend takes the initiative in raising the subject at an early stage, first of course listening to what the divorcee is already thinking before considering together the teaching of Jesus Christ.

More difficult to anticipate is when a single Christian begins going out with a divorcee. However, in many cases there is an initial hesitation, whether based on the teaching of Christ or on more general considerations (e.g. where there are children involved). Here it is absolutely essential for Christian friends to raise the issue gently as soon as possible; it will almost certainly be too late once an engagement has been announced and undoubtedly will cause much more pain at that stage (whether the couple break off the engagement or go ahead with the marriage).

b) Non-judgmental

Almost every person caught up in divorce, or contemplating divorce, is plagued by guilt. This is just as true – sometimes more so – for the one who is abandoned as for the abandoner. The experience of two women, both abandoned without any warning whatsoever, is typical: 'I felt very, very guilty; that it must have been my fault . . . I felt I needed God's forgiveness for splitting the family, and his support that what had happened was right. I was constantly reminded that divorce and separation were not acceptable when reading the Bible but still felt guilty even though I'd not made the decision.' 'Emotionally I felt shellshocked. I was a failure. If I hadn't been able to keep my husband, what hope did I have? I swung from unnatural highs to the deepest lows . . . I don't remember feeling angry but I did feel a deep sense of injustice that Mike had not given me a chance to put right whatever he felt was wrong in our marriage. About 10–11 months later, I began to feel guilty and that I must be a wicked person . . . I didn't go to church because I felt evil and unclean.'

Guilt is often just as real in those who put on a brave face and pretend that there is nothing they are struggling with; and, as the two quotations above show, it can, if anything, be worse for the Christian. One of the biggest fears that many will have, as they venture to talk about what has happened, is that friends and family will disapprove. That is why many try to conceal the fact that they have separated and, after divorce, will often conceal the fact of their original marriage. Their longing, especially in the initial stages, is for acceptance and approval.

They are often plagued by self-doubt as well as guilt; they long to be told that they have done the right thing or reacted in the right way: 'Once I'd made the decision to go ahead with a divorce, I wanted to feel supported by friends and family in that decision. Most people realised I hadn't come to this decision lightly, and many said they were convinced I'd tried my best to save the marriage. This was helpful.'

Therefore it is imperative that we, as Christian friends, are open and accepting. 'Being accepted by other people is a vital part of the healing and rebuilding process' and can make all the difference between keeping going and giving up in despair (Green p.108). Clifford tells of a woman whom two things kept going after her divorce: her work and 'her vicar's complete acceptance of her as a person' (p.4).

Christian friends need to take this approach not because the experience of guilt is necessarily wrong – it may well be overstated, but there probably are faults and sins to be repented of – but because we will otherwise be no help. 'People in a broken marriage know they've failed. They don't need to be told' (Green p.21). Laney, in a section on counselling those considering divorce, gives as his first advice: 'Communicate unconditional love and acceptance.' People considering divorce frequently sense rejection from their friends and family. Our acceptance of them as people is vital and does not necessarily mean approval of all that they do. Laney cites Romans 5:8 to show that this is true of God in his relationships (p.135).

It is equally important not to appear judgmental in taking sides. It is essential not to take sides – or be thought to take sides – against the person, or one of the people, you are talking with. We must be studiedly even-handed. Recently, I threw away any possibility of being helpful within a very difficult marital relationship because my manner made it obvious that I considered one partner was contributing more to the marital difficulties than the other. The partner concerned immediately sensed this and was closed to any help I might bring from that point on.

It is equally important not to take sides *for* the person you are talking with. Certainly he should sense from us understanding and empathy. But immediately we take his or her side against his partner – which friends are often inclined to do and think will be supportive – we either (to our surprise) provoke a reaction in which the person we are talking with leaps, perhaps angrily, to his partner's defence, or we offer emotional support at the expense of doing anything constructive to heal the relationship. Both parties, whether present or absent, need compassion and understanding from us, but not our sitting in judgment on them or on their partner.

### c) Committed
But this unjudgmental attitude does *not* mean we are neutral: that we do not care whether the marriage stays together or breaks up, whether there has been a divorce or not. Not only do we care, but it should be apparent that we care.

Freeman, who, as far as I am aware, is not a Christian, is scathing about the 'neutral' approach and shows rightly what harm it can cause:

> The attitudes and values the marriage counselor holds in regard to divorce . . . may be crucial to the couple seeking help. Counselors will frequently say that they take a neutral position on divorce . . . 'It's entirely up to the couple.' For me this is an amoral position . . . We do have values . . . So-called lack of bias carries an implicit message not only of acceptance but even of permissiveness, which may prematurely move

the couple in the direction of divorce. In a first session I freely acknowledge . . . that the goal will be to help them maintain their marriage if possible . . . I may say: 'You have invested twelve years of your lives and three children in this relationship. This investment should be salvaged if it is at all possible.' I do add: 'If, however, divorce is inevitable, you will at least feel better for having made a serious effort to work things out' (p.194). Knowing the many pressures and stresses the couple will face as a broken family and the gravity of the issues involved in divorce, the responsible marriage counselor is justified, even required, to be biased in the direction of restoring and rebuilding the family (p.195).

This is the judgment of someone not writing from within the Christian tradition: she sees that a position which presents itself as 'neutral' actually increases the likelihood of divorce. From a Christian perspective – knowing that God has joined this man and this woman together – we will be all the more careful that our attitude and counsel do not separate them, against the express command of Christ (Mark 10:9//Matt. 19:6). And we will be just as committed to encouraging reconciliation or, if that is impossible, remaining single after divorce (1 Cor. 7:11). In fact, more so – because Christ does allow (not advocate) legal divorce in the case of adultery (Matt. 5:32; 19:9) whereas no such exception is allowed in the case of remarriage (Matt. 19:9–12; 1 Cor. 7:10f).

It is normally helpful, as Freeman advocates, to declare your stance at the beginning. This should not at all be done in such a way that you seem to consider the matter closed and to have made up your mind before you hear the facts; hence the value of Freeman's statement that if divorce does happen, they will know they have done their best to save the marriage. Rather, the purpose of declaring yourself is to show the positive and hopeful attitude with which you will listen and approach your discussion. You hope, and believe, it may be possible to save, or restore, this marriage and you want to join the individual or couple in working positively towards that. 'The dreams and hopes you shared when you got married are still worth fighting for' (Chapman, *Hope*, p.12).

It is interesting to hear two women, both of whom ended up divorcing their husbands, commending this approach. One writes that what people should have done at the time their marriage was breaking up was to 'give us the idea that it was never too late to change your mind *if* you wanted to'. The second says: 'I knew he [God] had brought me to Manchester to find him [God], as I had no one to talk to where I used to live – well, no one I felt I could talk to who wouldn't say: "Leave him". I needed someone to *help me to put things right.*'

The Order of Christian Unity Report devotes an entire chapter to a Bristol-based counselling organisation whose counsellors are chosen, amongst other things, for 'their commitment to trying to repair even the most difficult relationships'. Indeed, the whole service was set up because of a felt 'great need for an uncompromising reconciling approach to marriage counselling'. It is reported as having a very high success rate in bringing healing to marriages. 'We believe that "Marriage Repair" [the name of the organizstion] is an embryo which could and should be developed into a national service' (Order of Christian Unity pp.15–17).

In 1985 Marriage Repair changed its name to Network. In its 'Guidelines for Counsellors' it states:

> Marriage is ordained by God and intended as a lifelong partnership of unconditional commitment. Growth in the relationship comes in large part by the couple meeting problems and working through them. Divorce is not therefore an option that the Network Counsellor will suggest to the couple. Where one or both of the parties is looking for a divorce, the Counsellor will encourage them . . . to recommit themselves to the marriage and to work through the problems however hard they may be . . . The Counsellor will need to help the couple to see that they are not being asked to resume the bad marriage they have had but to start afresh and work towards a transformed relationship . . . It is not helpful if the client perceives himself . . . simply as an object whose marriage must be repaired at all costs. The first priority is an acceptance of that person in Christ, and whose ultimate good lies in a relationship with Him and in a renewed marriage.

There is a tension here, of course: between acceptance of the person as he is and an unwavering commitment to Christ's view and standards of marriage. If a person only wants to hear one thing (support of his determination to end the marriage or to marry a divorcee or to remarry), then a Christian friend's 'committed' stance may well be received as 'judgmental', however much the Christian has sought to avoid this. You see this very clearly in the following account: 'I discussed the biblical attitude [to divorce] with X [a close Christian friend] and found to my dismay that he was very black and white in his interpretation . . . I found it only added to the pressure I was under to be told that I should make every effort to keep my marriage intact. I felt guilty enough about wanting a divorce – I didn't need to be told that I was going against God's law. Unless you have been in the situation of an unhappy marriage, it is impossible to comprehend the depths of despair reached when living in those circumstances.'

This reaction is very understandable, and the Christian friend often sees the force of the argument: 'You can't possibly understand what I am going through.' This is why the most helpful friends are often those who have been through divorce themselves. But we cannot – whether we have been divorced ourselves or not – surrender our allegiance to Christ and his teaching. We must be as understanding, as unshockable, as gentle as possible but we must also hold true to Christ's teaching on marriage. In the long run, this must be the most caring approach, even if we are not always able to give the immediately reassuring response that people want to hear.

But what about remarriage? Is it really caring to refuse a young divorcee a second marriage? G. L. Archer faces this question especially where children are involved: what if the children need a two-parent home? Would it not be best for the children if the custodial partner remarried, especially when she has been deserted by her partner?

> The answer to this question is the same as in every other situation when it seems easier to solve a problem by doing what any unbeliever would do under the circumstances. The issue of full submission to the revealed will of God and complete trust in the faithfulness of God is really at stake here. God has not called us to be happy, but he called

us to follow him, with all integrity and devotion. Hebrews 11:35[ff] honours . . . Old Testament believers . . . None of them enjoyed what the world would call 'happiness' but they did obtain something far more important: the 'approval' of God [39] (quoted in Heth and Wenham p.96).

Calvin is also fine on this. Commenting on 1 Corinthians 7:11a, and therefore speaking from the woman's viewpoint, he asks whether a woman shouldn't be allowed to remarry if her sexual drive is strong, on the analogy of verses 8f.

Would it not be inhuman to refuse her the remedy when [she is] constantly burning with desire? I answer that . . . it is the Lord's part to bridle and restrain our affections by his Spirit though matters should not succeed according to our desire. For if a wife should fall into a protracted illness, the husband would, nevertheless not be justified in going to seek another wife . . . The sum is this: God having prescribed lawful marriage as a remedy for our incontinency, let us make use of it, that we may not, by tempting him, pay the penalty of our rashness. Having discharged this duty, let us hope that he will give us aid should matters go contrary to our expectations (Calvin Translation Society).

Both Archer and Calvin are making the same point. God has ordained that marriage is a lifelong union. Christ reaffirmed this and taught that neither divorce nor desertion breaks the union. Of course it can be extremely hard to live by these truths, just as (Calvin argues) it can be hard to live with a marriage partner who contracts an incurable, and perhaps disconcerting, illness. But God can only be feared (again Calvin argues) if we take the law into our own hands and act against his commandments; whereas God can be wholly trusted and will provide all the grace we need, if we steadfastly determine to obey him.

The Christian friend, then, is committed to the teaching of Christ and gently but firmly makes this clear. He listens hard before speaking (Jas. 1:19), but then he 'speaks the truth . . . with confidence, conviction and compassion' (Laney p.143).

d) Compassionate

Anyone going through severe marriage difficulties – still more those who have experienced separation or divorce – will almost certainly be going through tremendous pain. It may well have taken enormous courage to open up to you (if you as a friend have taken the initiative in carefully asking) or to come and see you. It is very important that we recognise this strength of feeling and in no way underestimate it. Chapman's approach is helpful when he says in his first chapter: 'The purpose of this chapter is not to minimize the hurt, pain, frustration, anger, resentment, loneliness and disappointment you may feel. Nor is it to take lightly your past efforts at marital adjustment' (Chapman: *Hope* p.17).

Unless the person or couple in difficulties senses this compassionate and understanding response, they are likely to clam up. St Paul, in one of his most moving passages, speaks of his pain when he is open and receives no corresponding openness and warmth from those he has spoken with: 'We have spoken freely to you, Corinthians, and opened wide our hearts to you. We are not withholding our affection from you, but you are withholding yours from us. As a fair exchange – I speak as to my children – open wide your hearts also' (2 Cor. 6:11–13). Paul speaks here not, of course, in a formal counselling situation but rather of his disappointment in his Christian friends. It is precisely within this context of Christian friendship that many of the most helpful discussions about marital difficulties, divorce and remarriage take place. And of course exactly the same quality of compassion is essential in the professional counsellor: 'Sympathy, empathy and infinite patience are the essential ingredients without which counselling is unlikely to succeed. Clients respond to men and women from whom they receive a sympathetic understanding' (Dominian p.142).

When we come to respond, whatever else we may say – and it may, as we have seen, be necessary to pass on and explain some 'hard teaching' (cf John 6:60) – we should always put forward, as a dominant note, the love of God for the individual, for the partner and for the family. This reassurance of God's love (and forgiveness) is almost always needed.

One of the most helpful ways of bringing this reassurance is by looking together at Scripture. One most fruitful area of the Bible is Isaiah 40ff because these chapters were given to comfort Israel after the devastating experiences of the Fall of Jerusalem and of exile. Some examples will show how immediately relevant they may be to those who are separated or divorced:

> Comfort, comfort my people, says your God. Speak tenderly to Jerusalem, and proclaim to her that her hard service has been completed, that her sin has been paid for, that she has received from the LORD's hand double for all her sins (40:1f).
> He tends his flock like a shepherd: He gathers the lambs in his arms and carries them close to his heart; he gently leads those that have young (40:11).
> He gives strength to the weary and increases the power of the weak . . . Those who hope in the LORD will renew their strength (40:29–31).
> When you pass through the waters, I will be with you; and when you pass through the rivers, they will not sweep over you. When you walk through the fire, you will not be burned; the flames will not set you ablaze (43:2).
> In all their distress he too was distressed, and the angel of his presence saved them. In his love and mercy he redeemed them; he lifted them up and carried them all the days of old (63:9).

One of these Scriptures – not a whole avalanche of them – may be just the comfort and encouragement needed, especially if it has also been necessary to say something 'hard' about the need to stay within the marriage and work patiently to improve it, or to continue considering oneself married in God's eyes even after a (perhaps justified) legal divorce.

Another area where reassurance may be especially necessary is in 'what we've done to the children'. Clifford writes: 'However deep the guilt and grief that parents may feel at having put a child in this position [of divorce], they and those around them should not lose sight of God's special love for these little ones and should not cease to invoke it' (pp.32f). She says that particularly helpful verses to pass on, which demonstrate this truth, may be: Psalm 10:14, Jeremiah 49:11 and Matthew 18:14.

Scripture will be helpful not only in discussion and sharing with a friend, but also when the individual in marital difficulties is on his or her own. Many, many have found the Psalms extraordinarily moving and strengthening at this time in their lives, precisely because of the pain and confusion, as well as the confidence in God, which echoes through them:

> The pages open to psalms easily,
> worn by frequent use,
> and following, as they do,
> the book of Job,
> who also longed to understand.
> I am revealed in these psalms, these songs.
> I lament,
> weep,
> cry out in anger,
> and confront God with my life.
> And I worship,
> praise,
> hope,
> believe, and trust.
> Wrapped in these ancient words
> are all those emotions and thoughts
> which pass in and out of my life daily.
> I turn to the timeworn wisdom of God
> and God's people
> to find my solace and hope. (Mattison p.51)

Yet another theme of Scripture to explore is the similarity between some of Christ's experience and the sufferer's. He understands. He has been through betrayal (Matt. 26:47–50; Luke 22:47f), rejection (Mark 14:71) and loneliness (John 6:66f; Matt. 26:40). We should never underestimate the power or importance of Scripture in our counselling. 'Sharing a single verse with someone who has never had occasion to apply it to his or her own suffering may be helping that person to re-establish communication with God' (Clifford p.19).

And in all the listening and talking and sharing of Scripture, if tears come naturally to you as a Christian friend, let them flow. It is good to take Romans 12:15 very literally: 'Rejoice with those who rejoice, weep with those who weep' (so, rightly, RSV), cf Job 30:25. 'Silence is more healing than artificial words, and sympathetic understanding a greater balm than pity.' Weeping with a friend can be better than a professional counselling session (Green p.20). And this can be, if natural, the vital factor which saves us from being, or seeming, condescending, which is so quickly picked up and so deeply resented by those in marital trouble.

Yet in all the compassion which we pray Christ will give us (cf Phil. 1:8), we can never, and must never, sacrifice a Christian understanding of the situation. When we come to respond, it is God's teaching we are to pass on, which is not always what we would like to say or our friend would like to hear. Jesus' dealing with the woman taken in adultery is tremendously instructive (John 8:1–11). He does not condemn her (11), he is remarkably sympathetic towards her (7–11), yet he has no hesitation in calling her adultery a sin or in telling her simply and clearly not to commit adultery again (11). Network Counselling Service sets out its basic approach: 'Our counselling in Network is modelled on the pattern of Jesus. We seek to let his love flow through us. That love is challenging yet accepting, disturbing yet creative, convicting yet restoring. Many people coming for counselling may have felt judged and rejected. That should not be our way. We accept each person in Christ where they are. Yet we understand that their Creator has a plan for that Client's life. We try to perceive that plan of God and work towards it' (Network Counselling: *Guidelines for Counsellors*). We are to 'treat the divorced person in the same way that Jesus Christ has treated us: redeeming us from our past failures, forgiving us for our present sin and challenging us to live and relate on the basis of the truth revealed in his Word' (*Fresh Start* p.48f).

Some are by temperament inclined to be lenient, flexible, prepared to make exceptions to Christ's teaching; others see very clearly what Christ has taught and find it very hard to be sympathetic to anyone who is plainly departing from this teaching. Chapman provides an excellent example of a true combination of compassionate understanding and clarity of principle. He speaks to a man whose marriage is unhappy and who is strongly attracted to another woman: 'I am deeply sympathetic with the dilemma an affair presents. You do not like the idea of divorce, but the affair is so much more meaningful than your marriage. In just a few weeks or months you have come to love this person more than you love your mate. You are able to communicate with such freedom and understanding. It seems that you were meant for each other. How could it be wrong when it seems so right? You know that it is a violation of your marriage vows. You know that such activity is condemned in Scripture. Yet, you reason, God will forgive and in time everything will work out all right . . . It is true that God will forgive if we genuinely confess and repent of our sin. Repentance, however, means to *turn from* sin. God will not forgive while we continue to sin' (*Hope*, pp.22f).

e) Patient

We should not imagine for a moment that everything is going to be sorted out after just one conversation. Indeed, it may very well be that you have only been told part of the story, more particularly if you have taken the initiative and encouraged a friend to talk, or if you are a professional (clergyman or counsellor) and are not already known and trusted, or if one of the marriage partners is unwilling, or reluctant, to talk to you as well.

But even where there is no reluctance to speak – perhaps especially then! – the Christian friend will need great patience. He will often need to listen and listen and listen again, frequently to the same stories and the same emotions as they are gone over a hundred times. This in itself is invaluable ministry. In less serious cases, all that is sometimes needed is a listening, sympathetic ear and this alone gives fresh courage to go back into the marriage and continue trying to make it work. In other cases, a person who is allowed to talk, and knows he is being listened to, is able, simply as he speaks, to sort out some of his own problems: 'Certain friends were able to just listen to my ramblings with the result that I would often answer my own queries in a logical and sensible manner with just the odd bit of comment or suggestion from them.'

But of course this needs time, and often availability – on the phone or in person – at all hours of the day and night. Clergy may well not be able to give this time. This is another reason why friends and lay pastors are frequently those who are able to give the greatest help.

### f) Enabling

Should counselling be directive or non-directive? It is nonsense as Freeman has pointed out (see above), for the counsellor or Christian friend to pretend, either to himself or to the person he is talking with, that he is entirely 'neutral' and that it makes no difference to him what his client or friend decides. And specifically as Christians, living under the authority of Christ and his teaching on marriage, there will normally be a direction in which we hope this individual or couple will go. Thus 1 Samuel 12:23 is a justly famous verse but is known only for its first half where Samuel says: 'As for me, far be it from me that I should sin against the LORD by failing to pray for you'. The verse continues: 'And I will teach you the way that is good and right'. We have no need to fear that this is arrogant, so long as what we say is, and is seen to be (hence the value of looking together at Scripture), the teaching of Christ which we are merely passing on.

Yet any decision must be theirs. We can enable them to make it, but it must be they who take the decision for themselves. The National Family Conciliation Council in Birmingham has a higher than usual success rate not in conciliation (sorting out joint decisions, e.g. over finance and access to children, without acrimony) but in reconciliation (bringing the partners together again). Staff member John Akers explained why:

> I might say, 'From what I'm hearing from you, I don't think you've let go of your marriage. Do you want to think about making a go of it?' But you *must not* push this on them (do not say: 'I don't think your marriage is over'). *Let them talk*, air their thoughts, let *them* say they want to work on it. If *you* say it, they (or one of them) will turn on you and say: '*No*; I'm determined to divorce' (personal communication with the author).

And yet, it is not just any decision that we want them to take. We are not equally happy to see a couple decide to divorce (especially where adultery is not a major factor) or remarry as we are to see them determine to seek reconciliation. One way in which we can enable a couple to take a decision in line with Christ's teaching is to help them to see the positive in their relationship. John Akers asks: 'Why did you get married?' He is not so interested in the external factors which brought them together – same school, same interests – as: 'What was the psychological fit?'

So the key is to ask good questions: 'What did you see in each other?', 'What are the good things you would be sorry to lose if this marriage broke up?', 'Is there anything you can still admire in each other?' As you listen to their answers to these questions as well as those which explore what has brought the marriage near to, or right to, breakdown, feed back to them the positive which 'I think I hear in what you say', while not ignoring or belittling the negative. This may be precisely what they need to help them decide to work on their marriage with fresh hope and determination.

g) Continuing

I have tried to emphasise that the pastoral care of people with severe marital problems cannot be accomplished quickly. Christian friends must be prepared to give a lot of time, whatever the individual's or couple's decision. On the one hand, this is so if they decide to act in the way that you had been, overtly or half secretly, hoping. If the couple decide that they want to work at reconciliation, and even move back together again after separation or divorce, they will need not only much prayer but also close friends who will ask out of genuine concern rather than curiosity – 'How's it working out?', 'How are you feeling now?', 'Are there more good days than bad days, or the other way round?' It will very likely be necessary for the couple to sit down and talk with a third party, friend or professional, several times in those early days and months.

On the other hand, continuing care is also necessary if one or both of the couple decide not to act in the way that you had been hoping; for example, if they decide to separate or to go ahead with a divorce. They may need conciliation help, to sort out the many financial and practical arrangements without bitterness. They will need emotional support. This may come from different people in different ways:

> Mary [a childhood friend] was always available when I needed her. I went over the same things a million times or more, at all times of the day and night, for about 18 months . . . She let me ramble on, weep and moan . . . My immediate neighbour . . . used to pop round, usually when I was alone in the evenings, for a cuppa and chat . . . Jane . . . was instrumental in my climb back to God together with Janet [another divorcee]. In the space of an hour they turned my inner despair and desperation to hope.

Despite the fact that they have gone against your counsel, you may, if you have established a good relationship, still play a key role in bringing pastoral care and support. Where, however, they have clearly gone against your (even gently expressed) hopes, this may not always be possible. Others may be God's provision of help for this next stage, and in some situations you may be instrumental in encouraging others to give this support and love, though of course the more naturally this can happen, the better.

So far we have been thinking in this chapter of the individual Christian: for the most part the 'ordinary' Christian friend or family member rather than the professional counsellor or even the clergyman. St Paul's view of the Church is that all 'the members [should] have the same care for one another' (1 Cor. 12:25 RSV). Of course this is very demanding, of course it is often emotionally draining; of course we must listen much more than we speak (Prov. 18:13; Jas. 1:19); of course we must know when we are out of our depth and should suggest bringing in professional help; of course we will need to learn from any listening or counselling courses our church may run. Nevertheless, this is a ministry that none of us can shirk. We all have friends who are going through marital difficulties, separation or divorce. If we have any sensitivity and compassion, we are bound to get involved.

## 2. The church

But of course the individual friend is not the only means through which care can be given. We turn now to the pastoral help and pastoral provisions offered by the local church as a whole.

a) Pastors
In the United States, where it is quite common for churches to have a large staff, there is often a staff member who is particularly responsible for the pastoral care of families and/or singles (both never married and previously married). Some larger British churches also have a member of staff, lay or ordained, who has as the whole, or part, of his job description a specifically pastoral ministry. In one UK church on the staff of which I served, a staff member had the rather grandiose title of Director of Pastoring; in our current, much smaller, church, the curate's job description is split between Training and Pastoral Ministry. In any case, of course, all clergy find themselves increasingly involved in marital counselling. As early as 1978 a Church of England Report recommended: 'Training for counselling in marriage and family life should be regarded as an essential part of the courses offered in theological colleges and diocesan training schemes' (*Marriage and the Church's Task* p.70).

But increasingly churches are also instituting 'lay pastors', men and women who are members of the congregation, have clear pastoral gifts (cf Eph. 4:11) and devote some of their time to parish-based pastoral ministry. It can be extremely helpful if one or more of these is officially designated as being Pastor to the Family or is recognised as having special skills in marital counselling. It is now very common for lay couples to be running a church's marriage preparation classes. Lay couples should also be used in helping to sustain, and repair, marriages that have run into difficulties.

Such lay pastors need to be officially (certainly by the local church, where appropriate by the bishop) designated, commissioned and trained (both before and after commissioning). Such official status will make it easier for some couples to turn to them and to seek help from them. It will also make it easier for the pastors themselves to take the initiative where they, or other leaders in the church, sense there may be marital problems.

b) A service of forgiveness

I cannot stress enough that one of the greatest needs of the divorcee is to deal with his or her guilt. He often finds it very hard to forgive himself or to feel forgiven by God. Indeed, Christian commitment frequently heightens his sense of guilt. It is also true that further feelings of guilt can be triggered off at any time; we should not imagine, when a person expresses delight in the knowledge of God's forgiveness, that the same feelings of guilt will not return. Very likely they will. When, for example, we talk about Christ's teaching on the permanence of marriage and the wrong of remarriage, it is very likely that the divorcee – even, perhaps especially, one who has remained single – will find feelings of guilt returning; he or she will not easily be convinced that Christ forbids remarriage because he is still married in God's eyes rather than because any sin involved in his divorce cannot be forgiven.

In these circumstances, it will be necessary over and over again to reassure many divorcees of God's forgiveness. Once again, the sharing of some key passage of Scripture can be very helpful: 'If you, O LORD, kept a record of sins, O Lord, who could stand? But with you there is forgiveness; therefore you are feared' (Ps. 130:3f). 'Very rarely will anyone die for a righteous man, though for a good man someone might possibly dare to die. But God demonstrates his own love for us in this: While we were still sinners, Christ died for us' (Rom. 5:7f).

Scripture alone, prayed over, looked at together, discussed (encouraging the person feeling guilty to say what it says to him) and prayed over again, can often bring all the help that is needed. But in addition a specific service of forgiveness – often a Communion service – can be of enormous help.

Sometimes this can be carefully arranged in advance. A woman described to me as 'a new beginning' a service with about 15 invited friends. Each friend read a relevant passage from the Bible or said a special prayer. 'Chris [the Vicar] prayed that now I would be able to put the past behind me and that I should feel accepted without any more fear . . . It was the most uplifting experience I have ever had in my entire life.'

But it does not need to be so formal. One day I was praying in church and a woman came in with the intention of praying by herself. Seeing me, she decided on impulse to approach me and poured out her feelings of guilt about her divorce. I asked the verger to produce some wine and sent someone else off to the local store for bread while I left her for a few minutes to review her marriage and confess everything quietly to the Lord. Then we had a simple and informal Communion Service.

It was a very important moment for her, not only in laying her guilt to rest (though not for ever; it returned, though less strongly) but in deepening her commitment to Christ. The experience of separation or divorce often makes people more open to sensitive witness about Christ. This should not be over-looked in our caring. While some – particularly those divorcers who leave their partner for another man/woman – leave behind their Christian faith altogether, many more find faith for the first time, especially if they are met with compassionate friendship from Christians who gently, and over a period of time, point them to the love and forgiveness of Christ.

c) Support groups

We have already referred, in the last chapter, to support groups for the married: groups set up for those in, say, the first five years of married life to discuss issues and problems that they are encountering in their marriages; groups for couples with young or with teenage children to discuss parenting and its effects on marriage; groups for older couples to discuss the changing pattern of life when children leave home or after retirement, again giving due weight to the effects of these changes on their marriage. Any discussion group in which marriage can be discussed in an open, confidential and constructive manner will serve to strengthen the marriages within the congregation.

Support groups can also be helpful for the single. So often sin-gles groups are purely social, or they are viewed, by those within and outside them, largely as dating agencies. In many churches they degenerate into meeting-places for those who find it hard to relate socially, and people without such problems – especially women – often steer well clear of these groups. Often it is more helpful if singles and marrieds can be mixed together in church groups, for example within home study groups or in ministry teams. But it can also be valuable, perhaps for a limited time, for single people to come together and discuss the issues and struggles raised by their own experience of singleness. For example, a clergyman about to preach a sermon, or a series of sermons, on the single life might gather together a group of single people (of all ages) to talk through their experiences and make his preaching more relevant. Apart from the benefit to him, the group would almost certainly be very helpful for those who were part of it.

Support groups can also be particularly helpful for the separated and divorced. Sadly, many Christian divorcees still fear the reaction of other church members; often they imagine that they are almost the only person in the church who has been divorced. It is therefore an enormous relief to be able to talk freely with others who have been through the same experience and who will understand, in a group where there is no fear of being judged.

In preparation for this book and for the series of sermons mentioned in the last chapter, I gathered together a group of about a dozen men and women who have been divorced. We met on five evenings and were supposed to meet for two hours, though we frequently (and with everyone's agreement) overran. Each evening was devoted to a different theme connected with divorce or remarriage, and before each evening the group members were asked to hand in a written reflection on their own experience answering a number of questions which I had put. In my many years of running church training programmes I have never known participants be so conscientious about their 'homework'. Then, in the evening spent together, we discussed various related questions. Any contribution was accepted, and any reaction to the biblical material. We were seeking to understand each other and Christ; not to sit in judgment on one another. It will not come as a surprise that trust and love grew (and the supply of Kleenex diminished) as the group continued to meet, and at the end the group members vowed they must all meet again and had a celebration dinner with conversation going on until 2 a.m.

Though it was at times a disturbing experience for everyone in the group, it was overwhelmingly positive for almost all. Many grew to understand themselves better. One man appended a letter to his first homework:

Writing about my marriage and its break-up was going to be a doddle, or so I thought until I got started. Probably because I went immediately into a very happy marriage with Jennifer . . . I had never spent much time analysing the past problems before now. What I have uncovered has genuinely surprised me. If anyone had asked me a month ago to apportion blame for the break-up of my first marriage, I would almost certainly have said that Cathy's behaviour was 75% of the problem. Now I think, perhaps, it should be the other way round or, at best, 50/50.

Others came to understand their partner's position for the first time. Commenting on the group evenings as a whole, one woman said that she had been initially disconcerted to discover that 'decisions and actions taken by my ex-husband were precisely those taken by some group members . . . It was helpful to see it from the other standpoint.'

Most encouraging of all was to see the healing that came to some. One man, quite recently separated/divorced for the second time, wrote:

For so many years now, my heart has been rock hard towards women and especially couples who look happy – arm in arm, holding hands, calling each other darling – I haven't been able to stand it. Not upset – but angry, so angry and bitter. I was so twisted – but could/would not give all this anger up to God to take it away. I needed to hold on to some of it as protection, as I saw it, so as not to weaken. Nobody was going to hurt me any more . . . By June [8 months after his separation] it had all got too much to bear and I told God: 'You've got to help me. I can't carry this weight around any more. *Please help me.*'

He found his attitude changed; he was able to attend a friend's wedding.

I was already feeling my burden was lighter when I opened your letter . . . inviting me to join this group. I saw this immediately as another step forward, to *maybe* bring myself to talk to someone and a recognition that I wasn't alone in my troubles . . . I didn't intend to write all this down when

I started [this homework] and it has been very painful to reveal. But I could not begin to love other members of the Church Family until I made the first steps to unload this burden and soften my heart.

Of the group evenings as a whole he wrote:

It has certainly been helpful to me to put down on paper things that have eaten away at me for years. To start unloading the hurt and anger – why didn't I think of it before! Also, I think I shall try to trace my first wife and write to apologise to her, with God's help and guidance in this.

It was probably beneficial for the group that they knew they were helping me, in my book and in my sermons. They mostly came to the group feeling that they would give, rather than receive, help. In God's goodness, I received much help and they also helped each other. But it would not be necessary, of course, to need help for a sermon series in order to form such a group. Gary Chapman's book *Now That You Are Single Again* is a very helpful collection of Bible study/discussion material with twelve sessions which can be used in a support group for the separated and divorced.

In fact, in our own church one couple from our discussion group have taken the initiative themselves. Realising how valuable our discussions had proved for almost all members, they proposed setting up a support group for others who are separated or divorced in Crowborough, both Christian and not yet Christian. After some months of prayer and planning – including a very helpful visit to a London church with a similar group – the support group has recently been launched.

d) Conferences
There are of course regional and national conferences specifically designed for single parents or for the divorced. In Britain, Lee Abbey, for example, runs an annual holiday/conference for single parents and their children. But not everyone can spare the time or money to get away to such conferences, even when children are adequately catered for.

It is therefore better still if a church can lay on its own 'in house' conference, either just for its own divorced members (if the church is comparatively large) or including divorcees from other nearby churches as well. One such conference (the Americans tend to call them seminars) is *Fresh Start*, used in churches all over the United States. The normal pattern is to meet in a church hall on Thursday and Friday evenings and all day Saturday. There are plenary sessions, on: 'The Stages of Divorce and Recovery', 'Life as a Single', 'Biblical Insights for the Divorced' and 'Working through Bitterness, Learning to Forgive'. There is also discussion in small groups (with more experienced leaders guiding these) and electives on a variety of subjects such as 'Communication and Conflict', 'Children of Divorce', 'Single Sexuality' and 'What does it Mean to be a Christian?' *Fresh Start* has proved so successful that it has now spawned a further conference, *Second Wind*, for those who have attended a *Fresh Start* weekend. Again, there are plenary sessions on such subjects as: 'Self-esteem and Goal-setting' and 'Fulfilled Singleness' and electives on, for example, 'Dysfunctional Families' and 'Remarriage'.

In the United States, a team from Fresh Start Seminars (651 North Wayne Avenue, Wayne, PA 19087) comes to lead these conferences at the invitation of the host church, but there is no reason at all why a church in Britain or any other country should not lay on a similar conference with its own speakers. It would be helpful if several (not necessarily all) of the speakers and group leaders were themselves divorced.

These conferences are of course explicitly Christian in outlook, but they are not by any means only beneficial for those who are already Christians. Much of the discussion will be just as relevant to those who are not as yet Christians, and as one elective already mentioned ('What does it Mean to be a Christian?') shows, the conference may very well lead participants to ask serious questions about the Christian faith. The experience of divorce often leads to all old assumptions and beliefs being questioned. This gives an exceptional opportunity to the Church to explain the gospel gently, clearly and sensitively.

e) Church Family life

A lot of healing and care can take place in the course of normal church life. While it can certainly be helpful to take part in specialist groups or conferences for a time, it is normally best if such groups run for a limited period only – perhaps with periodic (monthly or quarterly) reunions – and members are then integrated into mixed groups within the life of the church. Most divorcees do not want to be treated as different or to be seen as 'abnormal'. Often they have a decided ambivalence in their feelings about themselves. On the one hand, they feel a 'failure', a man or woman who has not been able to sustain the most basic and most important relationship in life; on the other hand, they strongly resent any comment or behaviour that seems to suggest they have failed or are in any significant way different. One example: they are often very conscious of the difficulties of bringing up children with one parent – or only one of their 'real' Mum and Dad – but are hurt and angry to hear their children described as coming from a 'broken home'. All this is part of the universal need of acceptance, and the Church, in its normal 'family life', can and must provide complete acceptance – an acceptance which treats the divorcee as a normal human being ('normal' in the Christian understanding includes problems, difficulties and forgiven sin) and which can itself be immensely healing.

It is important for Christians to realise some of the problems with which the 'single again' (especially after divorce) grapple. Many divorcees find that their circle of friends is drastically reduced. This is partly because some friends side with their partner and will now have nothing more to do with them. It is partly because many are embarrassed and do not know what to say; this is often true amongst those who are not Christians, but Christians have the added disadvantage that they may feel the divorce was unjustified and they do not want to give the impression that they approve. It is partly too because the husbands or wives of friends can become suspicious and protective of their partner; suddenly a single, and perhaps young and attractive, member of the opposite sex has become available within our circle of friends.

A further reason is that people are so used, once married themselves, to thinking in terms of couples. Dinner parties are arranged for 'other couples'; single people, it is felt, would somehow seem out of place. Theatre tickets are bought in multiples of two.

> When we were two
> we went about together –
> parties,
> dinner at friends,
> coffee with neighbours.
> Now that I'm one
> I wonder:
> Are the parties still happening?
> The dinners, have they stopped? . . .
> We have interests and talents
> and enjoy laughing among friends
> just as we used to –
> except, not as a couple anymore.
> This is a coupled society:
> two, four, six, eight.
> It's hard to be three, five, or seven. (Mattison p.33)

This narrowing of horizons and feeling of being unwanted, is not only imposed from outside, through the thoughtlessness and insensitivity of others. It also wells up from within. 'One of the hardest things about being divorced is going to all events . . . on one's own. Even now – 15 years later – I find it hard to turn up at any meeting or party on my own and usually make some excuse to cadge a lift from friends so that I can arrive in company' (a woman). 'I invariably stayed up well into the night watching TV . . . When most of your friends are married, you do not feel like going to parties or gatherings on your own' (a man).

This feeling of losing friends, perhaps of having no one to talk in depth to, is inevitably contrasted painfully with the best time of sharing with one's marriage partner, especially if communication continued to be good right up to the time of the separation. One divorced woman writes: 'I just have a great need to share with another person, a man. I had 28 years to get used to sharing . . . Then, suddenly, nothing. Even now after almost 10 years, there is still a great part of me very empty and sad. I am very lucky and blessed because I have a loving family and loving friends . . . None of these can take the place of a husband.' This highlights the need not only for friendship, but for friends specifically of the opposite sex. It seems – and is – a retrograde step to have only friends of the same sex again. Yet finding suitable friends is not at all easy, especially if the divorcee is to maintain Christian standards of morality. The same woman writes: 'I know from experience that it is as good as impossible to have a "friendship" with a man, Christian or otherwise. Bed is the ultimate aim, not mine.'

All this is well summed up in the last line of Sarah Anders' poem entitled *1 [i.e. One] People*: 'One people in a two-people world, needing only to be accepted as they are to be complete' (quoted in Hensley p.26).

It is precisely this acceptance, without ulterior motive, that the Church can offer. It is within the Church that human beings can experience that 'there is neither Jew nor Greek, slave nor free, male nor female, [married nor single nor divorcee], for you are all one in Christ Jesus' (Gal. 3:28). It is customary in Britain for Christians to knock the Church and say how dreadfully we fail in every area, particularly in caring for the divorced. Of course there are examples of failure to care, but in fact many divorcees have found that the Church is the only place where they are genuinely accepted and where friendships can be made, including with the opposite sex, without ulterior motives. What is more, of course, the Church is able to offer not only a network of genuinely caring individuals but a deepening relationship with God. Chapman is right to say: 'Of all the social institutions of our nation, no organisation is better equipped to care for the needs of the lonely than the Church. The Church offers not only a social support system, but a spiritual support system as well' (*Hope* p.77).

It is significant that the *Fresh Start* seminar, which is hosted by churches but often includes many non-Christians, deliberately points divorcees in the direction of the Church to find the support they need. One of the sessions begins with the fundamental point that we have a 'basic human need to be valued'. This is still more acute in the divorcee because there is nothing more devastating than to hear the person whom you have loved and relied on most in the world saying: 'I no longer love you or need you.' So we need relationships, companionship (cf Gen. 2:18): not (necessarily) marriage, but friendship. Instead of looking for romances, divorcees need to look for friends; not just one special friend, but a network of friends. 'You need love, compassion, support, helpfulness – with no possibility that anyone will take advantage of you', people who love you without wanting anything in response. 'One good place to meet people who really care is the Church' (*Fresh Start*, tape by Tom Jones).

The Church is not the only place to find this care and acceptance. One woman wrote to me of her involvement in a Choral Society and in other musical activities 'where singleness is not a disadvantage'. But the quality of genuine and unselfish love should be – and often, in experience, is – at its highest within the Church. Many have become Christians because of the love they have met within the circle of those who love Christ.

Much of this love is shown simply by the full inclusion – as 'normal' members – of divorcees in the ordinary life of the Church. The separated and divorced often long to be treated as normal human beings; and therefore to be accepted completely in a house group or in the social life of the Church can be enormously healing in itself. Of course there will be fears that 'they've only asked me on this walk because they are sorry for me' or 'he's asked me for this dance at the Church Harvest Festivities because he's got designs on me', but gradually these fears will be eroded as it becomes (or should become) increasingly obvious that, within the Church, people are accepted as they are and valued for their friendship and contribution to Church Family life.

Paula Clifford particularly stresses the need of the Church to see divorcees not merely as receivers (of care) but givers (of Christian service). This too is to treat them as normal members of the Church Family. A common feeling among the divorced is of 'inadequacy as a person' leading to 'a total loss of self-confidence . . . One of the most useful acts of friendship, therefore, can be helping to rebuild a person's self-confidence' (p.11), and this is often done by involving the divorced in service. This is only to follow the example of Christ who, in John 4:28f, 39–42, used a woman who had been divorced five times (and remarried four times) (p.13).

It may be particularly helpful for the divorcee to use his or her home in the service of others, partly because it may be almost the only resource a divorcee feels (s)he has to offer and partly because the home may have become a source of pain and, through being used to serve others, can become a joy again (Clifford p.77). It is also important to realise that divorcees may be able to offer help 'at unusual times when other help is hard to find', for example on a Saturday when the children are with the other partner and the divorcee may be at a loose end, or hospital visiting around Christmas time (ibid. p.107).

Many of these acts of service can be engaged in from comparatively early days after separation or divorce. But once the divorcee has, at least to some considerable extent, 'worked through' his pain as a Christian, he can be invaluable also in helping others. Hosier expands on this in a chapter entitled: 'Loneliness: Becoming Wounded Healers'. Jesus is *the* wounded healer' (p.141). Part of his power to heal comes from the fact that he himself is 'wounded' and therefore understands. There is a sense in which the more wounded we are – whether by our singleness (perhaps never having married) or by our divorce – the more we can bring healing to others, provided that we use our woundedness to understand ourselves and to reach out to others who are suffering (pp.138ff).

A by-product of getting involved in service is that it often enables us to make natural and unpressured friendships with others. Tom Jones asks a question to gauge emotional health after divorce: 'Can you be in a room full of the opposite sex and not be looking out for possible partners *or* be fearful of the opposite sex?' It is important to be in social situations in which the opposite sex *as* opposite sex is not important. As a way of doing this, Jones recommends joining a choir or getting involved in voluntary service (*Fresh Start* tape).

But of course a divorced person does have needs that other Christians can, and should, meet, as well as resources and love to give. Some women, for example, may have relied entirely on their husbands for decorating, carpentry and electrical work around the house; some men may not have the first idea how to cook. Partners of either sex may have left all the financial arrangements in the hands of the other. It can, therefore, be an enormous boon to have someone offering to give an afternoon for DIY jobs around the house, or to produce a casserole or pie that will last for two or three meals, or to offer financial advice – providing, of course, that there is no possibility that these offers of help could be misunderstood.

Children can be a special burden for the divorced – and not only for them, but for those also whose marriages have gone badly wrong. One woman wrote of how helpful it would have been, in the last period before her separation, if someone had offered to look after the children 'to give me some quiet time to think things through finally and make unhurried judgments on [our] current situation'. Another wrote of 'some friends who took the three of us [herself and her two children after the separation] camping in Germany with them – that was a wonderful break'. Baby-sitting, taking the children away for a weekend, doing things as families (two-parent and single-parent families) together can be enormously helpful to the divorced.

But not all divorced people have children. In fact for some their divorce has precisely robbed them of the possibility of having children, particularly if they accept Christ's teaching that they are still married, in God's eyes, to their partner and therefore remarriage is not an option for them. Margaret Evening, who was herself a single missionary in Zaire, writes: 'We all need children!' Third World countries have a valuable emphasis in which the family is seen as much wider than parents and children: 'Everyone in the family [including the single] has a responsibility and share in the upbringing of the children' (pp.155f).

Evening writes for the never married, but what she says is equally applicable to the divorcee without children. Amongst their relatives, it can be a tremendous boost for a divorced person to be known as 'your special uncle' or 'our favourite cousin'. And exactly the same is true in the Church Family. Our eldest daughter used to spend a morning a week with a single woman in the congregation. This was a considerable joy to the woman, as well as fun for our daughter and a great help to us as a family.

Separated and divorced people are striving to come to terms with enormous hurts and often a profound questioning of their own identity and worth. Sometimes a single event will help healing forward. One divorced woman, for instance, recently asked for prayer in one of our normal Communion services. There was nothing unusual in that; other church members will, at the same service, have asked for prayer for a bad back or for finding a job. Two days later the staff member who had prayed for her met her in the town and invited her back for tea. They talked, prayed a little more and God met with her powerfully. A few days later she came to a mid-week Communion service, beaming: 'I'm a new person.'

But, much more often, progress will be gradual. I have tried to stress in this section that much of the deepest, and most long-lasting, healing comes simply by being accepted, cared for, and put to service within the ordinary life of a Church Family.

f) Discipline

Church discipline is a vexed and very difficult subject. On the one hand, most Christians do feel that for the Church never to exercise discipline is a mistake. There were clearly cases in the New Testament Church when disciplinary measures, sometimes of a fairly severe nature, were taken. Discipline has also been regularly practised in most churches right up to our own century. And it seems wrong for the Bishop of Durham, and the Bishop of Newark, New Jersey, having subscribed publicly to the traditional formularies of the Church, to be allowed to call into question the historical nature of the Virgin Birth or the Resurrection, or to ordain an openly practising homosexual, without any obvious disciplinary action being taken. On the other hand, discipline is out of fashion in the Church as in society. In the Church, even where sin is clearly involved, 'the accent is on forgiveness and acceptance rather than correction' (Phypers p.142). And especially when it is a question of disciplining not some distant bishop, but a member of *our* church, whom *I* know, we all shrink back. 'Discipline has virtually disappeared in many parts of the modern Church' (Heth and Wenham p.44).

Some of this is laudable: any kind of pleasure in discipline or any gloating over another person's being exposed as sinful is abhorrent. Nevertheless, the abuse of discipline should not put us off its proper use. St Paul was deeply sorry that he had to bring disciplinary action sometimes, but he did not shirk it. Indeed, he saw it as part of his care for the churches (hence the

inclusion of this subject in a chapter on Caring): 'Everything
we do, dear friends, is for your strengthening. For I am afraid
that when I come I may not find you as I want you to be,
and you may not find me as you want me to be. I fear that
there may be quarrelling, jealousy, outbursts of anger, factions,
slander, gossip, arrogance and disorder. I am afraid that when
I come again my God will humble me before you, and I will
be grieved over many who have sinned earlier and have not
repented of the impurity, sexual sin and debauchery in which
they have indulged . . . Every matter must be established by
the testimony of two or three witnesses. I already gave you a
warning . . . I now repeat it . . .: On my return I will not spare
those who sinned' (2 Cor. 12:19–13:2).

We today, therefore, cannot shrink from discipline in the
Church where there has been overt sin in any area, and specifically (in the context of this book) in sinful instances of divorce
and remarriage. The Church must act; it must re-establish a
practice of discipline, if it is to remain true to Christ. We will
look in turn at motives, at the process and at the forms of Church
discipline.

*i) Motives*
There is always the danger of taking the right action for the
wrong reasons. In these days, the church leaders, who have to
take the final decision about discipline, rarely do so out of sheer
vindictiveness. This may have been the reason why a church
member brought another's sin to the attention of the leadership
– out of a desire to see an enemy publicly put down – but the
leaders themselves seldom have such motives. They could, however, be acting simply to feel better themselves, because while
they do nothing about blatant sin they feel guilty and even somewhat implicated in the sin. 'At least we are doing something.'

These feelings are wholly understandable, but are of course
utterly inadequate as a reason for exercising church discipline.
The New Testament, by contrast, puts several motives for discipline before us.

• To show the sinner his sin
The famous passage where Jesus explains the process by which
Church discipline should be carried out starts with the words: 'If

your brother sins against you, go and show him his fault' (Matt. 18:15). It is inevitable that if a Christian sins and the local church does nothing, it will be assumed – by the man himself first, and then by others who know of the situation – that the church does not consider that anything seriously wrong is being done.

In a church that I know quite well in Carlisle, a church member left his wife (another church member) for another woman. The man and his new girlfriend (later, his wife after his divorce) became more regular at the church (where his [first] wife was still worshipping) and joined a home study group. The new couple was completely accepted by the church, no disciplinary action was taken and indeed the couple became greeters to people as they arrived for worship. The scandal that the deserted wife felt is exactly mirrored in St Paul's comments to a church which did nothing to discipline a man in an incestuous relationship: 'It is actually reported that there is sexual immorality among you, and of a kind that does not occur even among pagans: A man has his father's wife. And you are proud! Shouldn't you rather have been filled with grief and have put out of your fellowship the man who did this?' (1 Cor. 5:1f).

Recently, a woman in a neighbouring parish left her husband. He was and is an exceptionally difficult man and the marriage cannot have been at all easy. Nevertheless, there had been no sexual infidelity involved and no biblically justified reason for the separation. The woman moved away, living on her own, but continued to return to the locality as she was an interior designer, and therefore returned sometimes to the same church. The minister immediately called his elders and discussed what action should be taken. To do nothing, he believed, would encourage her to feel that she had done nothing wrong, whereas it is incumbent on a church to show a sinner his or her sin (even while recognising that there may have been provocation). This is an essential motive for discipline and sufficient in itself for taking action.

• To bring the sinner back to obedience to Christ
Nevertheless, that in itself is not enough. The Church's desire – and its reason for exercising discipline – is not merely to reveal to the Christian that he has done wrong but to help him repent

and turn back in obedience to Christ. The aim is not that he should feel condemned and be an irredeemable outcast, but that he should feel shame and so return to the family of God: 'If anyone does not obey our instruction in this letter, take special note of him. Do not associate with him, in order that he may feel ashamed. Yet do not regard him as an enemy, but warn him as a brother' (2 Thess. 3:14f).

Indeed Paul warns the Corinthians against prolonging discipline after the sinner – in this case someone who hurt Paul deeply – has shown signs of genuine 'sorrow' and has honestly repented: 'The punishment inflicted on him by the majority is sufficient for him. Now instead, you ought to forgive and comfort him, so that he will not be overwhelmed by excessive sorrow. I urge you, therefore, to reaffirm your love for him . . . If you forgive anyone, I also forgive him. And what I have forgiven – if there was anything to forgive – I have forgiven in the sight of Christ for your sake, in order that Satan might not outwit us. For we are not unaware of his schemes' (2 Cor. 2:6–11). Discipline prolonged after the sinner has repented and returned to Christian obedience merely plays into the devil's hands.

Even the somewhat chilling judgment in the case of the incestuous relationship has ultimate restoration in mind: 'When you are assembled in the name of our Lord Jesus and I am with you in spirit, and the power of our Lord Jesus is present, hand this man over to Satan [cf 1 Tim. 1:20], so that the flesh [literally] may be destroyed and his spirit saved on the day of the Lord' (1 Cor. 5:4f). Whether this means that the immediate result of discipline will be his physical death – the destruction of his body (so NEB, GNB) – or the subjugation of his evil desires – the destruction of his sinful nature (so NIV text) – the ultimate aim is clear: that his 'spirit' should be 'saved'. Here too, then, it is not a case simply of desiring the punishment of evil. This thought will not be absent since the entire Bible is convinced that evil should not go unchecked and must be punished. But the main aim of Church discipline is renewed fellowship with, and obedience to, Christ and, where possible, renewed fellowship with other Christians.

So, in my last church, an engaged couple, who were regular worshippers, were living together. I excluded them from Communion (and immediately told the bishop I had done so, as

Anglicans are obliged to do) not because this is always and the only right means of disciplining but because it seemed inappropriate for them to receive the bread and wine when they were not repentant and because, in a church that was eucharistic in emphasis, this exclusion from Communion would be something they found painful. I put to them two options for action: one (which I said was really the right course) was to live apart again until their wedding day; the other (if they found that too hard) was to arrange a civil wedding as soon as possible, after which we would still have a great celebratory service in church on the already agreed date. They would be married by then but it would be a celebration of their marriage. They knew already that in living together they were sinning, chose the latter course and had a civil wedding out of obedience to Christ. My wife and I went as witnesses. It was then of course right to remove immediately the discipline of exclusion from Communion.

So the aim of Church discipline is 'restoration: to bring a fallen member back to the full status of an active participant in the fellowship' (*Fresh Start* p.49). Indeed, discipline is normally a process in which various steps are progressively taken before disciplinary measures are imposed. It is important to remember that at every step, even when the sinner is quite unresponsive or recalcitrant, the aims remain renewed obedience to Christ and full reincorporation within the Christian fellowship. Commenting on Matthew 18:16f, Phypers says: 'only if the witnesses agree together, and the offending brother rejects their appeal for repentance and reconciliation, should his church be told. Even then suspension, and exclusion from membership, is not the aim, but forgiveness and restoration' (p.145).

But what does this mean in practice? It is comparatively easy to see what it means to come 'back to obedience to Christ' when two people are living together before marriage, but what does it mean for the man who has separated from his wife because life with her became unbearable (but where there was no adultery on her part) and whose divorce has long since come through? What does it mean for the single woman who knew she should not marry a divorced man but went through with it anyway?

First, it must mean *repentance*. The divorcee normally wants to justify himself. Even if he was the one who actually separated, the break-up was mainly his wife's fault. Repentance does not mean swinging to the other extreme and claiming that all the guilt is his and she had no part to play in the marriage problems, but it does mean acknowledging that he contributed major faults to the marriage and (probably) that if he had not contributed his significant part to the difficulties, they would still be together now. Compare the man, quoted earlier in this chapter, who as a result of a church support group for the divorced wrote: 'If anyone had asked me a month ago to apportion blame for the break-up of my first marriage, I would almost certainly have said that Cathy's behaviour was 75% of the problem. Now I think, perhaps, it should be the other way round or, at best, 50/50.'

This repentance must also include (assuming that the divorce was not for repeated adultery or gross physical abuse) a recognition that it was wrong to divorce. It is always hard to acknowledge that we have done the wrong thing, especially in a very major decision, and more especially still if the overall result has been relief from tension and pain, new openings in life and perhaps a new and happy marriage. Nevertheless *metanoia* (repentance) means a change of mind: coming to see things God's way. This may take some time but the one who has initiated divorce on unbiblical grounds has not truly repented until he has come to admit – at least with his mind, if not with his emotions – that he was wrong to divorce his partner.

Second, a return to obedience to Christ must mean *reconciliation*. If the divorce should never have taken place, then it must be right to undo that wrong and to seek to restore the marriage, even after legal divorce. Of course full reconciliation may prove impossible. The other partner may refuse any thought of it: she (or he) may have remarried. But wherever possible there must be genuine and sustained attempts at reconciliation, since this is so clearly the will of Christ (see chapter 11). Even where full reconciliation is impossible, the Christian must seek that measure of reconciliation which can be achieved: a frank admission to his ex-partner of his own past failures, a genuine desire and request to be forgiven, an openhearted readiness to forgive any past hurts he himself has suffered.

But what if he has already remarried? Or what if a single person has already married a divorcee? What does a return to

Christian obedience mean in these cases? It must begin with an acknowledgment that the marriage was a mistake, not in line with the teaching of Christ. This does not mean twisting our minds into saying something which is manifestly untrue: that we only feel regret at this remarriage. On the contrary, we can still say that we find it hard to feel sorry about this marriage. We can still praise God for all the good he has given us in this marriage. We can still rejoice at the wonderful gift of children born in this marriage. We can still acknowledge that we have grown spiritually, and even become Christians, as a result of this marriage. Nevertheless, we will have to admit – again with our mind, if not with our emotions – that we were mistaken, and disobedient (perhaps unwittingly) to Christ, in entering into this marriage. Unless we can admit that, we are still kicking against Christ's teaching.

But should we then dissolve the second marriage and return to our first partner? Almost all writers say no. Heth and Wenham, put this clearly ('We believe that . . . your present marriage is now God's will for you') and give three reasons (pp.200f). Probably the most important is that to leave the new marriage would only be to compound evils: 'To . . . seek to return to your former partner . . . will surely bring great grief to your second partner' (p.201). In other words, it was certainly wrong to enter into this second marriage, but having entered into it, and having promised your new partner perpetual faithfulness, it would be a worse wrong to renege on your vows and repudiate this relationship which you have solemnly entered into.

A second reason is that every action of ours – particularly the act of marrying, which affects us and others so profoundly – has repercussions, and brings with it obligations, that we cannot extricate ourselves from, however mistaken we know the original act was. 'All Christians, from the apostle Peter onwards, recognise that their past sins have inevitable consequences which we cannot alter' (p.201). Yes, it was a sin, it was disobedience to Christ, to enter into this new marriage. That sin, however, like any other can be entirely forgiven. Indeed, it is not as if it were a heinous sin, particularly if (as is often the case) the couple were largely unaware of the teaching of Christ at the time of their remarriage. It was a covenant that was entered into, a binding covenant. The covenant itself should not have been made in the first place, but now that it has been made, it remains binding, just as a Christian would be bound to honour any agreement he solemnly entered into (even if not legally binding), even though he subsequently recognised that he should not have entered into it in the first place (for the necessity of abiding by even rash vows, see Num. 30, especially vv.6f; Eccles. 5:4–7).

There is of course a very clear analogy from within the marriage realm itself. Christians are forbidden to marry those who are not committed to Christ (1 Cor. 7:39; 2 Cor. 6:14–7:1), yet once they have entered into this relationship, they are to honour it; even the strong language used of incompatibility between a Christian and a non-Christian (righteousness and wickedness; light and darkness; Christ and Belial; believer and unbeliever; temple of God and idols: 2 Cor. 6:14–16) does not justify a Christian's initiating of divorce (1 Cor. 7:12–16). The initial marriage was wrong (if the Christian was already a believer at the time of the wedding) but the marriage is not to be repudiated now, even though the Christian should be prepared to admit he was at fault in marrying.

A third reason is taken from the Old Testament. Deuteronomy 24:1–4 forbids a return to the first partner after a second marriage has been entered into. We saw in chapter 4 that this is a difficult passage but it clearly teaches that the woman has been 'defiled' (4) in the eyes of her first husband and probably that this 'defilement' in his eyes comes from her second marriage (even though it was he who initiated the divorce). If this interpretation is correct, then the Old Testament prohibits a return to the original marriage partner even if the wife is repentant for whatever (her immodest or indecent behaviour, according to Deuteronomy 24:1) caused the original divorce.

These three reasons, taken together, show that repentance and a renewed obedience to Christ do not mean that the remarried divorcee, or the person who has married a divorcee, should leave his second marriage, but rather that he should stay within it and seek to enrich it, recognising that this is now – now that he has entered into a new marriage covenant, however mistakenly or even wilfully – God's will for him.

But how should the couple regard themselves when one or both are divorced? Are they, in God's eyes, married or not? The New Testament gives no definitive answer to this. It does indeed say that to enter into a second marriage after divorce is adultery, but it says nothing about the need to dissolve second marriages – a question which must have arisen, given the ease of divorce in both Jewish and Roman society and the assumption that a divorced person would remarry.

The overwhelming majority of commentators conclude that the couple are indeed married. It is interesting to see the Mishnah addressing this issue. The specific question discussed is: What is the status of children where a divorce is invalid? 'Three kinds of bills of divorce are invalid, yet if she [the invalidly divorced woman] married again, the offspring is legitimate. [The Mishnah then mentions the three situations which invalidate a divorce and concludes:] Lo, these three bills of divorce are invalid, yet if she married again, the offspring is legitimate' (*m. Git.* 9.4). Here, then, despite an illegitimate divorce, a second marriage is recognised.

The Church of England Report *Marriage, Divorce and the Church* addresses the same issue and notes that Anglican practice has been to refuse Communion for a period to those involved in remarriage. Clearly the Church disapproves because discipline is exercised but equally clearly the couple are not regarded as 'living in sin' because exclusion from Communion is only for a period and particularly because the couple are not asked to separate before returning to Communion (p.65).

Murray also asks about the status of a remarriage which Christ has forbidden:

The second marriage is undoubtedly adulterous and, there- fore, illegitimate. But we are not prepared to say that it is invalid . . . Though illegitimate, it is a real marriage and should be regarded as such . . . The parties have illegiti- mately pledged troth to one another and consummated that pledge in the conjugal act. That troth was wrong but it still binds them to observance of what was contracted and consummated by it (pp.111f).

In other words, they should not have married, but they are married.

This of course does not dissolve their first marriage; only death can do that. It therefore means that they are in a similar position to those who practise polygamy. Of course their living conditions are entirely different because they are not living with two husbands (or wives) at the same time. Nevertheless, they have contracted a second (valid, though illegitimate) marriage while their first marriage still continues (since legal divorce is unable to end it). It is therefore instructive to see what Christians have written about polygamy.

The Reformer Peter Martyr (1500–62) wrote about Old Testament polygamous marriages:

Undoubtedly marriages they were . . . If an infidel were in our day converted to Christ, having two wives, could such polygamy be endured under the Christian dispensation? Certainly, for the time. For they contracted with each other in good faith . . . That law . . . which Christ gave [lifelong monogamy] ought to hold for the future, but what has been done, and done with good faith, probably in ignorance, cannot be rescinded (quoted in Powers p.353).

B. Kisembo, L. Magesa and A. Shorter discuss contemporary polygamy in their book *African Christian Marriage*. Some of their conclusions are that: polygamy 'is also a permanent, lifelong relationship, as indissoluble as monogamous marriage'; 'baptised Christians should not be allowed by the Church to contract polygamous marriages'; 'Christians who have lapsed [presumably after baptism] into polygamy . . . under social or economic pressure or the burden of childlessness should be treated with equal consideration and sympathy, and even re-admitted to Communion' after repentance but 'the indiscriminate baptism or re-admission to Communion of all polygamists is definitely not recommended'. The authors state that their proposals are in line with 'the recent recommendations of the Anglican Consultative Council [in July 1973]' (quoted in Powers pp.354f).

For many it will be uncomfortable, even distasteful, to think of a remarriage as analogous to polygamy, especially if the second marriage has been an obvious source of blessing to the couple themselves, their families and their friends around them. But their only alternative, given Christ's teaching, is to treat a second marriage as a forbidden liaison which should be abandoned as quickly as possible. We believe, however, with the majority of commentators that the remarriage should indeed be seen by the Church, as well as by the couple, as a marriage – valid though illegitimate. Since the first marriage is, according to Christ, not at an end, the analogies with polygamy are inescapable. Taking our cue from the discussion above of polygamy, we must regard a second marriage as not to be dissolved – in fact, as indissoluble (Kisembo *et al.* say: 'as indissoluble as monogamous marriage'). The couple will not be encouraged to break up their new marriage but obedience to Christ will entail an acknowledgment that they were mistaken to remarry in the first place. Where there is an adamant refusal to acknowledge this, some discipline should be exercised.

• To protect the Church against similar acts
We have seen that it is important, in Church discipline, to have true motives. Vindictiveness is an entirely unworthy motive. Biblical motives are to show the sinner his sin and to bring the sinner back to obedience to Christ. A third scriptural motive is to protect the Church against a gradual acceptance of sin in its midst. Paul concludes the discussion of the necessity to discipline the incestuous man: 'Your boasting is not good. Don't you know that a little yeast works through the whole batch of dough? Get rid of the old yeast that you may be a new batch without yeast' (1 Cor. 5:6f). A slightly different, but related, reason – the idea of guilt by association – comes in John's second letter: 'If anyone comes to you and does not bring this teaching, do not take him into your house or welcome him. Anyone who welcomes him shares in his wicked work' (2 John 10f).

Christian moral teaching burst upon a world that was largely inimical to it, especially in the marital sphere. It was partly by clear and compassionate discipline that this moral teaching became accepted and established. 'Besides the transforming power of the Holy Spirit and solid, constant instruction in Christian living, the early Church also established Christian standards of sexual and marital behaviour among its converts by fearless discipline of those who failed' (Phypers p.141).

The sad fact is that these moral standards have now been largely whittled away within the Church by an equivocation, and even cowardice, in standing up against prevailing standards and giving straightforward Christian moral teaching, and perhaps even more by a shying away from any exercise of discipline. The result is that fewer and fewer Christians take the Bible's moral teaching, especially as regards marriage and sex, with any degree of seriousness. 'Where there is no discipline in the Church, moral and doctrinal anarchy reigns' (Baughen pp.61f).

Church leaders often imagine that there is no point in exercising discipline where there is little or no hope of repentance and restoration. If, for example, a church member leaves her husband for another man and leaves the church at the same time, is there any point in discussing among the leadership, and then with the church, what kind of relations Christians should have with the new couple? Certainly there is. If the church leaders seem to be pretending that nothing has happened because they never mention it, those within – and those outside – the church will imagine that such desertion is accepted, or at least tolerated, by Christians. Appropriate discipline – which will almost certainly mean partial, or complete, breaking off relations with the couple, and which will prove quite as painful for the Church Family as for them – gives the essential message to both Church and World that Christians stand for lifelong marriage and that marital desertion is taken very seriously indeed.

*ii) The process*
Church discipline is not to be imposed suddenly, so that one minute the Christian is quite unaware that anyone disapproves or that he has been detected, and the next minute the full weight of Church discipline has descended. On the contrary, there is to be a gradual process before any discipline is imposed: 'Warn a divisive person once, and then warn him a second

time. [Only] after that, have nothing to do with him' (Titus 3:10).

It is Jesus, in Matthew 18, who spells out this process most fully:

> (15) If your brother sins [the best manuscripts do not add: against you], go and show him his fault, just between the two of you. If he listens to you, you have won your brother over. (16) But if he will not listen, take one or two others along, so that 'every matter may be established by the testimony of two or three witnesses'. (17) If he refuses to listen to them, tell it to the church; and if he refuses to listen even to the church, treat him as you would a pagan or a tax collector. (18) I tell you the truth, whatever you bind on earth will be bound in heaven, and whatever you loose on earth will be loosed in heaven.

It is, of course, not necessary to follow this exact process in every particular on each occasion. For example, if a man who has left his wife for no reason that can be justified from Scripture and has scorned a private reproof (15), immediately leaves the area but starts writing letters and making phone calls that spread lies about what has been said to him, the second stage (16) may be impossible and the whole church may need to be told at once (17). Again, it will not always be right, in every circumstance where the initial stages of reproof and correction have been spurned, to make excommunication the form of discipline (17). But there are two important principles to be drawn from this passage:

• Keep it as private as possible for as long as possible

Jesus says that at first only one individual (other than the one who has sinned) is to be involved. The discussion is to be 'just between the two of you' (15). If that fails, only one or two others are to come along (16, cf 2 Cor. 13:1; 1 Tim. 5:19). The hope is of course that at either of these early stages 'he will listen to you' (15) and then there will be no need for anyone else to know. Once there has been repentance and a return to Christian obedience, the matter can be considered closed.

This is tremendously important. Far too often, where there has been an illegitimate divorce or a remarriage, the church does nothing for a long time. Then, after having given the impression that it really does not mind too much because nothing much has been said and certainly nothing done, suddenly it comes down with a heavy hand and excludes from certain public privileges of church membership.

If, however, we are to follow Christ's teaching, discipline must begin with an entirely private conversation – or, at most, a conversation in which only one or two others are present (this may be necessary right at the outset to prevent subsequent misrepresentation). This should be done as soon as anyone knows, for example, that a man is considering separation from his wife or a woman is thinking of marrying a divorcee. It will not necessarily take the form of 'warning' (Titus 3:10) straight away. We will want to listen much before we speak. But if it is clear that there is some 'fault' (Matt. 18:15), it needs to be pointed out.

It is essential too to realise that discipline can be initiated by anyone in the church. Jesus' instruction in 15 is not at all just to the leadership. This does not mean that any Tom, Dick or Harry can start excommunicating left, right and centre. But it does mean that when an 'ordinary' Christian becomes aware of another Christian's fault – for example, that she is leaving her husband or going out with a divorcee – he cannot wait for the leadership to take action, nor should he immediately go and talk to the minister. The principle that Jesus enunciates in 15f is that all Christians must be involved in correcting each other and that, initially at least, the sin and the gentle but firm correction should be kept as private as possible.

• The whole church must ultimately be involved
First there is to be an utterly private conversation. Then one or two others are to be involved. But if that too fails, further action must be taken: 'If he refuses to listen to them, tell it to the church; and if he refuses to listen even to the church, treat him as you would a pagan or a tax collector' (17).

It is important to realise that two stages are involved here. The first is that the church should be told. Still no positive disciplinary action has been taken. The hope is that the sinning person will be so ashamed, and will have so many of the church membership talk with compassion but firmness to him, that he will at this stage repent.

If, however, he refuses to repent even now, then the church is to take corporate action. Of course the church membership cannot *en masse* decide what disciplinary action should be taken. That is a job for the church leadership. It should rarely be a decision taken by just one – the minister or rector – but by a 'small group of caring folk . . . who can talk and pray together in pastoral situations, to seek and discern the mind of Christ. When a group makes a decision, . . . rather than an individual, responsibility is shared and the decision is unlikely to reflect personal views and prejudices' (Phypers p.125).

But once the decision has been taken, it needs to be explained to the church (at least if the discipline has any significant public dimension) and acted on by the church. 'If the situation continues to deteriorate [after the more private beginnings: 15f], then the church leadership must take action. This will demand time and effort if they are to properly understand, negotiate and exercise authority . . . If the problem comes before the entire congregation, there is a need for each member to clearly understand and consistently follow through on the decision of the fellowship' (*Fresh Start*, p.49).

This is particularly true if there is any question of excommunication, by which I mean not exclusion from Communion but the normal New Testament practice of shunning the company of a sinner as a form of discipline (17, cf 1 Cor. 5:9–13; 2 Thess. 3:6, 14; Titus 3:10; 2 John 10f). This was probably the 'punishment . . . by the majority' of 2 Corinthians 2:6. It is then essential that the whole church understands, accepts and carries out the discipline that the leadership is imposing.

In a church which I know well, the curate left his wife and children, and ran off with the (female) youth worker. The leadership decided, after much prayer and discussion, that the couple should be excommunicated (as in Matt. 18:17). It was very important that the church membership, whether or not they agreed with the leaders' decision, acted upon it. Any disunity, any breaking of the silence from the church, would have under-mined the entire disciplinary action.

And it is not only the original church which must not under-mine the discipline. It is essential that the new church, to which a couple may well have gone, should also uphold the discipline. Fee is right, commenting on 1 Corinthians 5:1–5, to say: 'The great problem with such discipline in most Christian communities in the Western world is that one can simply go down the street to another church. Not only does that say something about the fragmented condition of the church at large, but it also says something about those who would quickly welcome one who is under discipline in another community.'

Of course it is up to the disciplining church to inform the new church to which the couple have gone. But this is not always possible, for example, because the new church may not be known. This places a responsibility on churches to find out more about the background of new arrivals. Of course this is not to advocate an inquisition where the message is: you are not accepted unless you can prove that your past is lily white. However, it is not genuinely caring to accept people with no questions asked, and at the very least we should follow up, with the past church, any hint that an individual or couple may have 'left under a cloud'. 'When divorced and remarried people come as Christians, seeking to join a particular congregation, more caution may be required. Have they left an estranged partner in another congregation angry and hurt at their action? . . . Are they conscious of their sin and sorry for it? Did they remarry against the advice of fellow Christians, and are they obdurate in justifying themselves?' (Phypers p.125). If there is any doubt on these issues, then they should be further discussed and investigated in a pastorally responsible manner. The sad fact is that in the case mentioned above, a nearby church and the Diocese as a whole accepted the curate and his new girlfriend (later wife) without any disciplinary action being taken.

Discipline imposed by the church as a whole must of course be removed by the church as a whole where there has been genuine repentance. It is to make precisely this point that Paul wrote 2 Corinthians 2:5–11. Someone had hurt him personally and, through him, offended the whole body of Christians (5).

Discipline had been imposed by the Christians together (6). Now the man in question has proved to be genuinely sorry (cf 7) and Paul has forgiven him (10). But this is not enough. He must be forgiven and comforted by the whole body of Christians (7f, 10f). Just as everyone had to be involved in shunning him when he was unrepentant, now everyone must be involved in receiving him back with love.

*iii) The forms*

What form should discipline take? In particular what kind of discipline should there be, and how long should it last, when there has been a remarriage and the divorced partner is still living?

Opinions on this have varied down the years and in different places. In the canons of Basil of Caesarea (Bishop: 370–9) it is stated: 'He that divorces his wife, and marries another, is an adulterer; and according to the canons of the Fathers, he shall be a mourner one year [outside the door of the church during the service], a hearer two years [in the vestibule], a prostrator three years [among the catechumens], a co-stander one year [among the full congregation but not receiving Communion] if they repent with tears' (Canon 77). Augustine shows that debarring from Communion was also practised in the Western Church, though it is not clear how long a period was involved (Heth and Wenham p.42). It is interesting to note that no mention is made by Basil of the need to dissolve the second marriage, and that the discipline imposed was less severe than that for straight adultery: seven years of penance as against fifteen (Canon 58).

In the twentieth century, it has been normal Church of England practice until comparatively recently to debar someone who had remarried from Communion for one year. The 1957 Resolutions of the Convocation of Canterbury also declared that if a remarried person wanted to be baptised or confirmed or receive Holy Communion, the matter should be referred by the incumbent to the bishop. Within the Roman Catholic Church, a divorcee who remarries may never receive Communion.

It is understandable that churches should want to standardise practice and lay down formulae for Church discipline. Wide discrepancies of practice from one church to another are very unfortunate. But it seems quite clear from the New Testament that it is quite impossible to stipulate in advance how long church discipline should be enforced. We have already stressed that the whole purpose of discipline is to lead the sinner to repentance. Once he has repented, therefore, the discipline should be removed as soon as possible. This is the whole purpose of Paul's teaching in 2 Corinthians 2:5–11. It seems extraordinary that Basil should insist on seven years of penance when the people concerned 'repent with tears' (Canon 77). In practice, this will indeed mean that for some people church discipline will last their entire lifetime (though in reality these will probably long since have left the church); in other cases, it will last only a few days. Immediately it is clear that the repentance is heartfelt the discipline can be lifted.

But still the question comes: what form should church discipline take in the case of remarriage? This too cannot be answered with a set formula. While obviously there must be some consistency (or a church will lay itself open to the charge of injustice), it must be acknowledged that some people are quite unaware that they have sinned while others know precisely what they are doing. The Old Testament distinguishes between the person who sins unwittingly and the one who sins 'with a high hand' or defiantly, the penalty being much severer in the latter case (cf Num. 15:22–31). This distinction is upheld by Jesus. At the end of a parable about being ready for the Second Coming by continuing to act as a servant who does the master's will, Jesus adds: 'That servant who knows his master's will and does not get ready or does not do what his master wants will be beaten with many blows. But the one who does not know and does things deserving punishment will be beaten with few blows. From everyone who has been given much, much will be demanded; and from the one who has been entrusted with much, much more will be asked' (Luke 12:47f, cf Acts 17:30; Jas. 4:17).

There are any number of different attitudes which people may have held at the time of their remarriage and may hold now:

● 'It never crossed my mind that remarriage might be wrong'

- 'I was genuinely and thoughtfully convinced that it was right to remarry'
- 'I refused to look at the issue from a Christian point of view because I feared what I might find'
- 'I knew what Christ says on the subject but I went ahead anyway because I couldn't bear to remain without X [my present wife]'
- 'I had real hesitations but suppressed them and convinced myself that I was doing the right thing. Other people supported me in this'

It is immediately obvious that all these situations are different and that while some form of church discipline is appropriate in every case where Christ's will is now known and is being resisted – in other words, where there is a determined refusal to recognise that the remarriage was a mistake – it will vary greatly from situation to situation. For example, it would almost certainly be right to relieve a Christian of all church office and perhaps debar him from Communion if he knows full well that Christ forbids remarriage and yet he goes ahead. In the case, however, of someone who remarried at a time when he had no idea that Christ forbade it and now resists admitting that his own marriage, which has brought him such happiness, should not have been entered into, the only action might be to decide that some areas of Christian ministry – for example, teenage youth work and leading marriage preparation classes – should not be open to him.

Kasper is one of many who argue that we should also take into account the situation in which the contemporary Christian finds himself and especially normal attitudes in society towards divorce and remarriage (p.66). This is indeed important for a pastoral and compassionate understanding of why a Christian has thought and acted in a way contrary to Christ's teaching; it is necessary for determining how inadvertent or wilful a Christian's disobedience has been; it may also, from a pragmatic point of view, be essential if the whole church is to 'own' the discipline which the leadership decides on, but it leads all too easily to the Church's simply following a few steps behind society's drift away from Christian standards.

And that does not accord with New Testament practice. We have seen in previous chapters that in Jewish society it was comparatively easy for a man to divorce his wife, and in Graeco-Roman society it was practically as easy, with the added fact that the wife, provided she had or could find alternative sources of maintenance, could divorce her husband. Yet the New Testament took a tough line on remarriage, and the early Church used discipline to instil moral standards that were consciously different from the world's. As one example, in 293 Diocletian passed a law that allowed women to dissolve their marriages simply by writing a bill of divorce, without even giving it to their husband or telling their husband about it. Heth and Wenham (p.43) believe it was to 'counteract the civil legislation' that the Council of Elvira (AD 306) enacted that women who desert their husbands without reason and remarry should never again receive Communion even on their death bed, and that women who divorce for adultery and remarry should not receive Communion until their first husband's death (Canons 8 and 9).

So, the severity of discipline must be determined primarily by the extent of wilful disobedience to Christ's command, and discipline must be lifted where there is repentance. Repentance will not mean breaking up a remarriage that has already been entered into, but it will mean recognising that this second marriage – however much it is, rightly, a cause of praise to God – should not have been embarked upon, and attempting to be reconciled – to ask, to receive and to give forgiveness – with one's first partner.

I have spent a large part of this chapter on the question of church discipline because it is a thorny, and much neglected, subject, and I have deliberately concentrated on the hardest question of all: what discipline is appropriate in the case of remarriage? I want to stress again that this has very deliberately been included in a chapter on Caring. To avoid discipline in cases of divorce and remarriage is not to care for the emotional or spiritual welfare of the individuals involved or – quite as important – the church as a whole. To exercise church discipline, after much heart-searching (though not after much delay), is to act with the aim of restoring those who have gone astray from Christ (Gal. 6:1) and protecting the church as a whole from moral decay.

## 3.   The legal profession

In the final section of this chapter, we look more briefly at what
the legal profession can do to care for those whose marriage is
in difficulties and who are beginning to head towards divorce.

a) The solicitor
Solicitors are encouraged by law, in cases where clients come
seeking a divorce, to discuss the possibility of reconciliation.
The 1969 divorce legislation requires the solicitor to certify
whether he has discussed reconciliation. In practice, this has
become a formality which is often omitted altogether. A Bristol
University research study of recently divorced people in the
South West (published in 1982) found that 34% of respondents
(as opposed to petitioners) did not regard their marriage as
irretrievably broken down. A further 5% would have preferred
to continue their marriage for the sake of the children. And
20% of petitioners reported that their solicitor had not checked,
even for form's sake, to see whether there was any prospect of
reconciliation (Parkinson p.3).
    The reality in most cases is that 'once solicitors get involved,
it is even more difficult to attain a reconciliation' (one divorcee, writing from his own experience). Another writes how
easy it is for 'the legal situation to degenerate into a bitter
war'. This is partly because lawyers are trained to take up an
adversarial position: they are out to get the greatest advantage
for their client, without taking too much account of the damage
caused. 'A divorce lawyer has got to be a fighter, to fight
his client's corner hard' (a divorce lawyer on: *Say It With
Lawyers*, BBC2, 13 June, 1991).
    It is also often a result, at least in Britain, of the Legal
Aid system. Phypers makes this point and also sketches the development of a typical scenario: A woman goes to her solicitor not
because she really wants a divorce but because she wants him to
write a letter to her husband which will give him a shock. But the
solicitor is not a marriage guidance counsellor, and has not
the skill, and especially the time, to listen pastorally to what she
says. She will need Legal Aid, and the initial grant of aid is only
for three hours of a solicitor's work (after that the solicitor will

have to justify the extra expense to the Legal Aid Department).
So he gets her to fill out the forms at the initial interview. 'The
juggernaut has started to roll . . . No one has asked her to pause
and think. No one . . . has pointed out the alternatives . . . No
one at all has suggested reconciliation, offering . . . help in
settling their quarrels and living more peaceably together.' The
husband receives the letter and is devastated. He sees a solicitor
who advises him to allow the divorce to proceed and says that
he will work at getting the best deal possible. If the husband
insists on fighting the petition, the husband and wife will meet
before a judge. 'If the reconciliation cannot be achieved there –
and the setting is hardly conducive – he will again be urged [by
his solicitor] to allow the divorce to proceed . . . Divorce suits
engender bitterness and bring out the worst in people, so even
if the marriage had not broken down, . . . the legal process will
almost certainly finish it off' (Phypers pp.132f).

The Christian solicitor must, by his practice, help his client
to break free from this destructive cycle, wherever possible. As
a Christian, his overriding desire must be to save the marriage.
And this desire will of course be shared by many conscientious
solicitors who are not committed Christians.

In the first place, this will mean a great deal of *listening*:
listening not just for the facts which will be needed in any divorce
petition, but listening especially for any sign of ambivalence
on the part of the client; it will frequently be there. 'A lot
of people say their marriage has finished when they're really
asking if it could continue. Several divorced people [whom
the author interviewed] expressed regret that they had gone
ahead with divorce proceedings without really considering the
alternatives' (Green p.40). A divorcee wrote to me: 'I decided
that I would seek a divorce, believing that at some time he [my
husband] would try to stop it and see that he really loved me.'
She did not want the divorce, but once the solicitors became
involved it proved unstoppable.

By contrast, a woman was urged by friends to seek a divorce
from her husband who had left her for another woman. The
solicitor was wise enough to see that she was still very much
in love with her husband and helped her to realise that she did
not really want a divorce. This situation is not uncommon. The

client, at the time of seeing the solicitor, may be unaware of his own ambivalence. The solicitor should be listening out for possible signs of it and will then need considerable sensitivity and skill in steering the client away from divorce proceedings which he does not really – or wholly – want.

Even if the solicitor does not sense any ambivalence, it is important for him to give his client *time to reconsider*. The appointment may well have been made in haste, after a major row or the discovery of an affair; at the moment, the client is extremely angry, but things may look quite different in a few days' time. If the solicitor immediately starts writing letters or sets proceedings in motion, it may well be that the client will become trapped in a legal process which he entered into over-hurriedly but now feels powerless to stop. Some solicitors will advise their clients to wait until the dust has settled a bit and things have become clearer. Green reports one solicitor whose regular practice is to spend about an hour with each client, finding out all the relevant facts about the marriage. He then puts the different options for the future. If the client wants a divorce, he takes down all the necessary information, explains the procedure and then says: 'Think about it and phone me if you want to go ahead' (p.65).

This *discussion of alternatives* is tremendously important. The client will often be thinking of divorce. It is important for the solicitor also to talk about judicial separation, less formal separation and, most importantly, various ways of moving towards reconciliation. It is also important that the solicitor should make his client aware of the various likely outcomes – emotional as well as material – in each case. He cannot, especially if he is a Christian, avoid this by claiming that he is just not equipped for this sort of work. In practice, it may be his whole approach that either finally breaks or begins to remake the marriage. One solicitor reports: 'We get a lot of people phoning up . . . screaming blue murder, but when I actually sit them down and we talk about the implications of divorce, it seems to fizzle out. In about half the cases, that's the last I ever hear' (quoted in Green pp.58f). 'Divorce is often seen by the petitioner as the solution to an unhappy marriage, without possible alternatives being sufficiently clarified and explored and without sufficient understanding of the reality of divorce' (Parkinson p.5).

All this of course takes much more time than if the solicitor simply acts on the client's request to begin divorce proceedings. It may mean a loss of income. It may mean taking some training in basic marital counselling. But it is well worth it if it results in a marriage being saved rather than destroyed, and a family kept together rather than wrenched apart.

b) The courts
The stated intention of the divorce legislation in Britain is that the courts should support marriages in difficulty and aid reconciliation. In practice, however, the divorce courts are so overwhelmed by the sheer volume of work that they do almost nothing to help reconciliation and only concern themselves with practical arrangements, especially about finance and custody of, and access to, any children.

The Children Act 1989 (which came into force in October 1991) seeks to remove many of these decisions about children from the courts and encourages parents to make their own arrangements. It is too early to say what effect the new legislation will have but the Act itself clearly envisages a continuing need for court orders about 'residence' (the replacement term for 'custody') and 'contact' (the replacement for 'access').

In fact, far from helping reconciliation, court proceedings normally make it even less likely. This is, again, because of the very nature of the courts: they are seen to be, and experienced as, adversarial rather than conciliatory. Meg Scott writes of her experience of the divorce courts: of the clerk who 'seemed . . . to be filled with vengeance and bitterness towards the male in every divorce case he had ever dealt with: "They [the husbands] think they're so clever . . . but we soon cut them down to size"', and of 'the acrimony which seems inevitably to surround such litigation' (pp.47, 54).

Therefore it is essential that there are statutory Reconciliation and Conciliation Services and that it should be a requirement, in all normal situations, for these Services to be used before a court grants a divorce petition. Encouragement for parents to sort out post-divorce arrangements is simply not enough.

It is important to make a distinction between reconciliation and conciliation. The Finer Report on One-Parent Families (1974) defined the distinction in this way: 'Reconciliation . . . is the act of reuniting persons who are estranged; whilst conciliation . . . is the process of engendering common sense, reasonableness and agreement in dealing with the consequences of estrangement' (quoted in Order of Christian Unity p.3).

Reconciliation must be the main aim because it keeps marriages, and families, united. It can be the overt aim when both partners have at least some conscious desire to mend the marriage. But where at least one partner is – or believes he is – not at all open to reconciliation, conciliation deals with the practical aspects of divorce with the minimum of acrimony – and can do much more.

> It is the openendedness of the outcome [separation, divorce or reconciliation] which can make conciliation acceptable both to the partner wishing to end the marriage and to the partner wishing to preserve it. This is of crucial importance. Many petitioners . . . refuse to see a Marriage Guidance Counsellor because they believe . . . that the Marriage Guidance Counsellor is committed to saving the marriage. A counsellor who is perceived to have a vested interest in marriage may be ruled out as a conciliator, or be unable to conciliate effectively. If the offer of counselling is refused by one partner, the opportunities for reconciliation and conciliation are greatly diminished (Parkinson p.7).

But once a conciliator has been accepted, it may in fact be possible to move towards reconciliation. Parkinson is co-ordinator of the Bristol Courts Family Conciliation Service. She reports that in 1981 one in six cases 'moved from conciliation to reconciliation (16.5%), including four couples who reconciled after a divorce decree. These reconciliations, which may be unpredictable at the outset of conciliation . . . resulted from the couple's increased ability to listen to each other and to correct . . . false perceptions of each other.' This is all the more striking as 'one of the criteria for referral to the Bristol Courts Family Conciliation Service is that one or both partners believe that the marriage has broken down irretrievably; separation is imminent or has taken place' (p.7).

The Order of Christian Unity Report believes that separation, rather than divorce, is the more crucial moment: 'Of the two events, it is separation which is often more important for the welfare of the children and often presents the more acute financial problems; and it is separation which presents the best opportunities for reconciliation and conciliation' (p.12). The report therefore urges the formation of a National Reconciliation and Conciliation Service, to be attached closely to the Magistrates (rather than the Divorce) courts. 'Petitions for divorce should not normally be filed until the parties have first tried the remedies in the Magistrates courts, and there has been a ' "cooling-off" period, which we believe should be 12 months' (p.21 ) .

It is interesting to see that some of these ideas have been incorporated into the 1990 Law Commission's proposals on divorce law reform. In particular, the Commission suggests that there should be a twelve-month period between a formal submission of marital breakdown and an application for divorce. This is to allow time for conciliation or reconciliation. G. B. Bentley, the secretary to the Church of England's Report on divorce law *Putting Asunder* (1966), wrote to the *Church Times* welcoming the Law Commission's proposals: 'During the year that must elapse between the initial declaration of breakdown and application for divorce, the parties will have to face the meaning of divorce in terms of problems of finance, problems about children, and so on; and the hope is that in some cases at least the application will never be made' (*Church Times*, 30 November, 1990).

Of course the statutory Reconciliation and Conciliation Service would cost a lot of money. But when one considers that in the 1980s the cost of marriage breakdown was reckoned at one thousand million pounds per annum (Order of Christian Unity, p.9), any attempt to salvage marriages must be worth it on financial grounds alone. Add to this the much more important saving of marriages and protection of children, and further statutory help for marriages in trouble becomes essential. Moreover, this approach is not untried. New Zealand and about a third of the States in the USA insist on mediation before a petition for divorce can come before the courts.

This chapter has been about caring. A description of the Lord's servant – a description, in the first place, applied to Jesus – is also very apt for the Christian – whether 'ordinary' church member, church leader or lawyer – who is seeking to care for those in marriage difficulties:

(1) The Spirit of the Sovereign LORD is on me because the LORD has anointed me to preach good news to the poor. He has sent me to bind up the broken-hearted, to proclaim freedom for the captives and release from darkness for the prisoners, (2) to proclaim the year of the LORD's favour and the day of vengeance of our God, to comfort all who mourn, (3) and provide for those who grieve in Zion – to bestow on them a crown of beauty instead of ashes, the oil of gladness instead of mourning, and a garment of praise instead of a spirit of despair. They will be called oaks of righteousness, a planting of the LORD for the display of his splendour (Isa. 61, cf Luke 4:17–21).

We must never forget the great *pain* of those going through very serious marriage difficulties or divorce. They are broken-hearted (1), mourning (2, 3), despairing (3). They are often prisoners (1), trapped in feelings of bitterness and guilt. And it is an extraordinary and moving privilege to be anointed by the Spirit of the Lord (1) – because it will not be possible if left to our own resources – to 'bind up the broken-hearted' (1), to bring comfort (2) and to be a catalyst for the extraordinary transformation which turns ashes into beauty, mourning into gladness and despair into praise (3).

Some of this chapter may have seemed hard, difficult to see as an aspect of genuine 'caring'. This is because we too often have a man-centred view of happiness which leaves God's righteousness (3) out of the picture and which finds it impossible to conceive that the 'Lord's favour' towards the broken-hearted may have to go hand in hand with the 'vengeance of our God' against sin (2). Bromiley has summed this up well. Writing in the context of divorce and remarriage, he says: 'Happiness . . .

is a gift from God, and it cannot be attained, nor human life
be fulfilled, where there is a conflict with God's stated will or
a defiant refusal to see that true happiness and fulfilment lie in
a primary commitment to God's kingdom and righteousness'
(p.41). The only real care is one that helps another person, or
couple, look to God and obey God.

# 11

# Reconciling

There are many ways in which Christians can care for those in marriage difficulties, for the separated and the divorced. But there is absolutely no doubt that the greatest service which Christians can render – and therefore the goal they should always be aiming towards – is to help bring about the reconciliation of the husband and wife.

Reconciliation is, in fact, *the most important ministry and responsibility of the Church*. In putting this work at the centre of its life, a Church is only imitating God; reconciliation is God's main ministry. The New Testament picture of human beings is that we are naturally 'separate from Christ . . . without hope and without God in the world' (Eph. 2:12; there written specifically of Gentiles, but the Jews are clearly in a very similar position: Rom. 2:17–3:20). Moreover, we and our basic way of thinking are 'hostile to God' (Rom. 8:7). This leaves us in a desperate situation, partly destroyed already and partly bound for destruction. But God's great desire, and his greatest work, is to reconcile us to himself, and he has done this reconciling work in the death of Christ: 'Once you were alienated from God and were enemies in your minds because of your evil behaviour. But now he has reconciled you by Christ's physical body through death to present you holy in his sight, without blemish and free from accusation' (Col. 1:21f). 'When we were God's enemies, we were reconciled to him through the death of his Son' (Rom. 5:10). 'God . . . reconciled us to himself through Christ . . .: God was reconciling the world to himself in Christ, not counting men's sins against them' (2 Cor. 5:18f). So, the estrangement is brought to an end, and the intimate relationship between God and man can be resumed.

But there is more than that. Hostility exists not only between man and God but between man and man. God's further desire, and further work, is to break down this second kind of hostility and to reconcile man with man: again he has done this work through Christ and his death. The great example in the New Testament of this hostility between humans is the suspicion and alienation that divides Jew and Gentile. In a famous passage, Paul speaks of how Christ died to break down the hostility and reconcile the two groups:

> For he [Christ] himself is our peace, who has made the two [Jew and Gentile] one and has destroyed the barrier, the dividing wall of hostility, by abolishing in his flesh the law with its commandments and regulations. His purpose was to create in himself one new man out of the two, thus making peace, and in this one body to reconcile both of them to God through the cross, by which he put to death their hostility (Eph. 2:14-16).

It is true that the work of reconciliation is primarily God's/ Christ's. Without his work there could be no reconciliation between God and man, and the likelihood of reconciliation between any warring human individuals or groups would be very seriously reduced. Nevertheless, he enlists Christians to further his reconciling work. We are to engage in 'the ministry of reconciliation' and to go out with 'the message of reconciliation': 'God . . . reconciled us to himself through Christ and gave us the ministry of reconciliation: that God was reconciling the world to himself in Christ, not counting men's sins against them. And he has committed to us the message of reconciliation' (2 Cor. 5:18f).

In 2 Corinthians 5, our ministry is to urge humans to 'be reconciled to God' (20). But it is also our responsibility to foster reconciliation between man and man. Philippians 4:2f is a famous example: 'I plead with Euodia and I plead with Syntyche to agree with each other in the Lord. Yes, and I ask you, loyal yoke-fellow, help these women who have contended at my side in the cause of the gospel.'

Since the most important human relationship is between man and wife, here too God's great desire is for reconciliation if at all possible (1 Cor. 7:11). He will certainly be working to bring it about (cf Hos. 3), and clearly Christians must do all they can to instigate, aid and support marital reconciliation. At every marriage service in the US Episcopal Church, the Celebrant asks the couple's family and friends: 'Will all of you witnessing these promises do all in your power to uphold these two persons in their marriage?', and they promise: 'We will.' The Episcopal Church also has a canon entitled: 'Of Regulations respecting Holy Matrimony: Concerning Preservation of Marriage, Dissolution of Marriage and Re-marriage'. Its first words are: 'When marital unity is imperilled by dissension, it shall be the duty of either or both parties, before contemplating legal action, to lay the matter before a Minister of this Church; and it shall be the duty of such Minister to labor that the parties be reconciled' (1985 Canons I.19.1). Once again, we must add that this is the responsibility not just, or even principally, of the minister, but of all Christians, especially those closest to the couple themselves.

Commenting on the exception to Christ's prohibition of all divorce (in Matt. 5:32), Stott says:

This reluctant permission . . . must always be read both in its immediate context [Christ's emphatic endorsement of the permanence of marriage in God's purpose] and also in the wider context of the Sermon on the Mount and of the whole Bible which proclaim a gospel of reconciliation. Is it not of great significance that the Divine Lover was willing to woo back even his adulterous wife, Israel (cf Jer. 2:1[ff]; 3:1[ff]; 4:1[ff]; Hos. 2:1–23)? . . . [Jesus'] whole emphasis . . . was . . . on God's original institution of marriage as an exclusive and permanent relationship, on God's 'yoking' of two people into a union which man must not break and (one might add) on his call to his followers to love and forgive one another, and to be peacemakers in every situation of strife and discord. Chrysostom justly linked this passage with the beatitudes . . . 'For he that is meek, and a peacemaker, and poor in spirit, and merciful, how shall he cast out his wife? He that is used to reconcile others, how shall he be at variance with her that is his own?' . . . Speaking personally as a Christian pastor,

> whenever someone asks to speak with me about divorce, I
> have now for some years steadfastly refused to do so ...
> until I have first spoken with him (or her) about two other
> subjects, namely marriage and reconciliation. Sometimes a
> discussion on these topics makes a discussion of the other
> unnecessary (Stott on Matt.5:32).

Reconciliation is also *the most important responsibility of the
estranged themselves*. It is not only a vital ministry of other Christians to help those who are estranged. It is the principal duty of
the estranged themselves to seek reconciliation with each other.
This is true wherever there has been a breakdown of relationship:
'If you are offering your gift at the altar and there remember that
your brother has something against you, leave your gift there in
front of the altar. First go and be reconciled to your brother;
then come and offer your gift' (Matt. 5:23f).

If this is what God asks of us in ordinary (less important)
relationships, how much more must we seek reconciliation in the
most important human relationship of all: marriage? As we saw
in chapter 4, God has shown us the way. He has been appallingly
let down by his wife who has been repeatedly unfaithful. Yet it is
he, the one who has been sinned against, who takes the initiative.
He does not even wait for her repentance before beginning to
woo her back: "She decked herself with rings and jewellery and
went after her lovers, but me she forgot," declares the LORD.
"Therefore I am now going to allure her; I will lead her into the
desert and speak tenderly to her" (Hos. 2:13f). He quickly turns
from his (quite legitimate) anger and "with deep compassion
I will bring you back ... Now I have sworn not to be angry
with you, never to rebuke you again. Though the mountains
be shaken and the hills be removed, yet my unfailing love for
you will not be shaken nor my covenant of peace be removed,"
says the LORD, who has compassion on you' (Isa. 54:7–10). He
renews his 'everlasting [marriage] covenant' with her before she
has shown shame at her actions (Ezek. 16:60–63).

What God does himself, he asks his servants to imitate.
Hosea is married to a woman who is adulterous (1:2), and his
instructions are: 'The LORD said to me, "Go, show your love to
your wife again [the Hebrew word can mean 'woman' or 'wife',

but the whole symbolism is entirely lost if Hosea is told to love another woman and not his original wife], though she is loved by another and is an adulteress. Love her as the LORD loves the Israelites, though they turn to other gods"' (3:1).

It might be argued that Hosea is a special case, but this instruction is continued in the New Testament. Even if there has been a divorce, the goal of the estranged Christian should still be reconciliation if at all possible: 'To the married I give this command (not I, but the Lord): A wife must not separate from her husband. But if she does, she must remain unmarried or else be reconciled to her husband' (1 Cor. 7:10f). We have seen in chapter 6 that the only possible explanation of Paul's exception ('but if she does') is that he is echoing Christ's exception (there is to be no divorce 'except for marital unfaithfulness': Matt. 5:32; 19:9). Even where there has been a divorce for adultery, reconciliation should still be the hope, and goal, of the Christian. Hermas, one of the earliest post-New Testament writers (date uncertain; somewhere between the end of the first century and 150), endorses this. He is discussing what should happen when a woman has been divorced for adultery: ' "If then," I said, "sir, after the wife is sent away the woman repents, and she wishes to return to her own husband, she will be taken back, won't she?" "Indeed," he [the heavenly guardian] said, "if her husband will not take her back he sins and brings upon himself a great sin" ' (*Mandate* 4.1.7f). So, even where there has been adultery, and even where a divorce has been entirely justified, reconciliation must remain the ultimate goal.

But 1 Corinthians 7:11 recognises that a reunion of husband and wife may not be possible. The other partner may be unwilling to contemplate living together again; he or she may have remarried; and indeed the Christian considering what action to take may be so deeply hurt, and have such a profound sense of betrayal, that any attempt to start the marriage again, even on a totally different footing (cf Hos. 2:16–20; 3:2f), is out of the question, at least for the foreseeable future.

Yet even then the Christian's goal should be at least some measure of reconciliation, if not immediately then at some stage; at least an attempt to diminish the bitterness and lay to rest some hurts, by confessing his own part in the failure of the marriage and by asking, and offering, forgiveness.

Of course this calling – whether it is to work towards full reunion or towards mutual forgiveness – is hard. We would often much rather have nothing to do with our partner ever again. But reconciliation is a primary duty of all estranged Christians; it is what God asks of us. 'If the readiness for reconciliation makes a stern demand, this, after all, is what being a disciple is all about. Christian conduct exacts a price from us, as God's atoning work exacted a price from him. Grace practised as well as grace received is not cheap' (Bromiley p.69). Chapman says much the same, addressing directly the separated Christian:

> The choice to . . . pursue reconciliation is a step of faith. But . . . it is faith based on the counsel of God . . . It is a choice against continued separation . . . It is a choice to reaffirm your marital vows and actively seek to rediscover . . . [what] God had in mind when he instituted marriage. It is not a choice to go back to the kind of relationship you had when you separated, but to work towards establishing something far more meaningful . . . The choice for reconciliation is not popular in our day. A thousand voices will seek to allure you to the supposed happiness of divorce and remarriage. Others will call you to join them in sex without commitment. You stand at the crossroads. The decision is yours (*Hope* pp.88f).

## Acceptance

What does this mean in practice? One way to begin an answer is to face the question: should Christians 'accept' a divorce? If my wife has left me, and later legally divorced me, at what stage – if ever – do I accept this? Does openness to reconciliation mean that I never fully accept it? Or is it, after a certain point, both unrealistic to continue holding out for reconciliation, and unhealthy?

## 1. Not accepting too quickly

Mike's story is typical (and true). For many months his wife threatened to walk out on him, and he did everything he could to keep the marriage from falling apart, even making an effort to 'become a Christian' when his wife had clearly come into Christian faith. But he could not stop her, and she eventually left. When I visited him, he said: 'I'm deliberately trying to make myself bitter. It's my only defence.' And, sadly, his tactics worked. He nurtured the anger and bitterness which were welling up anyway, and deliberately and systematically killed off his affection for his wife. Many people do the same; they want to do as the song says: 'I'm going to wash that man right out of my hair.'

Very frequently friends and relatives urge this reaction. They see – and are often taken aback by – the strength of the emotion: anger, pain, love, guilt, bitterness and yearning all jostling together. They rarely believe that there is any hope of reconciliation. They may well be angry – often angrier than the deserted partner – with the one who has gone away. And so their advice is: 'Forget him', 'Try and get rid of any thought of him', 'Look for someone nice you could have a good evening out with.' In their confusion, those who have just experienced separation often accept this well-intentioned advice. Some of course still cling to hopes of mending the marriage, but others give way to bitterness, a fevered search for a new relationship, or despair. Yet to accept the new *status quo* too readily, and especially to harden one's heart deliberately against one's partner, may well make one miss opportunities, which would have come otherwise, for reconciliation.

## 2. Accepting

Yet Christians must not live in a world of unreality: continuing to hope when it is obvious that reconciliation is out of the question, at least for any foreseeable future. Moreover, we are not committed, as Christians, to using every means to block a divorce because it is morally unacceptable to us. It was to make precisely this point that St Paul wrote 1 Corinthians 7:15, 'But if the unbeliever leaves, let him do so. A believing man or

428                    DIVORCE AND REMARRIAGE

woman is not enslaved [literally] in such circumstances; God
has called us to live in peace.' Some Christians in Corinth
might be thinking that if Jesus forbade divorce (10f), then even
if a non-Christian partner wants to leave, the Christian partner
should do everything in her (or his) power to stop him doing so;
her vows 'enslave' her to fight any possibility of divorce even if it
causes great bitterness and anger (the opposite of 'peace'). Paul's
advice was, on the contrary, to accept the divorce. The principle,
while discussed specifically in the context of a marriage between
Christian and unbeliever, will hold good where any partner is
absolutely determined to divorce: the other partner is not to
initiate the divorce (12f) but equally need not feel 'enslaved'
in such a way that he must resist the divorce at every point.
He can with a good conscience, and indeed should, accept it
in the sense of: letting it go ahead.

A man came to see me recently worried about what he should
do. His wife had left him; he did not want a divorce but she
did and was putting pressure on him to agree. She could have
a divorce almost immediately if he consented but it would take
several years longer if he withheld his consent. He felt that
only further bitterness would result if he did not agree, yet as
a Christian he believed that divorce was wrong. In the end –
rightly, I think – he gave his consent.

Sometimes it may be helpful thoughtfully to set aside 'a
particular period in which you will pray for and be open to the
prospect of reconciliation' (Crispin p.184). During that time –
perhaps six or nine months – you will not do anything (such as,
moving house to another town) or say anything, particularly to
family or mutual friends, which will make reconciliation more
difficult. You will resist advice to 'cut yourself off' from your
partner; you will seek God's help against those emotions which
harden you towards your partner. More positively, you will see if
there are ways in which you can keep in touch with your partner
and keep lines of communication open (as much as he will allow
and your emotions can stand).

In some cases – where your partner says that he is open to
reconciliation but seems to do nothing about it – it may even
be helpful to tell your partner what your timetable is. *Fresh Start*
quotes with approval a woman who said: 'You keep saying you

want us to get back together again. I believe you. I think you should find some way to leave June [the other woman] – not necessarily to come back to me – in the next 3 months' (*The Separation and Reconciliation Struggle – Fresh Start* tape by Bob Burns).

The reason for setting such a timetable, whether for oneself only (this would be more normal) or for one's partner also (when a professed desire for reconciliation does not seem to be put into practice), is that it is emotionally and practically impossible to be *actively* seeking reconciliation for ever. There comes a point where one has to accept that, at least for the foreseeable future, there is not going to be a reunion. One can continue a *passive* openness to reconciliation – if a significant move comes from one's partner, or God seems to be prompting a resumption of an active search for reconciliation – and at the same time begin to build a new life with the assumption that one's partner will not be there.

Some people are never able to get to this stage. They never 'accept' the separation/divorce – not, at least, for a long time. A remarkable number seek to be 'closet divorcees', for as long as possible hiding from friends and family the fact that their partner has left them. Others 'are held up from growth because deep down they *know* their wife is going to come back and make it all right. She will realise she has made a fearful mistake. So you wait and do nothing' (*Re-entry into the Single Life – Fresh Start* tape by Tom Jones).

In these cases, adjustment takes far longer. The Christian is called to tread a difficult middle course: neither denying that the separation has definitely taken place (at least after a legitimate period of hope and active seeking of reconciliation) nor becoming embittered and so closing off any possibility of reunion. He is to be honest enough with himself to accept what he cannot change, and yet constantly (if after a time, passively) to be open to any, perhaps sudden, opening for reconciliation (or for working towards it).

## 3.  Not accepting

It is in this last sense that the Christian never accepts separation or even divorce. He never accepts that the break-up of the relationship is the last word; he always remains open to reconciliation.

I added the phrase at the end of the last paragraph – 'or for working towards it' – because this does not mean that the Christian will accept reconciliation on any terms. A man leaves his wife for another woman; after six months the new relationship breaks up. The man then returns to his wife and wants instantly to move in and resume the marriage as if nothing has happened. The woman is quite right not to accept this. A marriage that has broken down cannot simply be resumed on the old terms. There will be much to talk about; it may not be appropriate to move back together again immediately.

Nevertheless, the Christian's great desire is for reconciliation and he (or she) is always ready to work towards it. Indeed, even after his desire for reconciliation has become passive rather than active, he will always be ready to change back to a more active mode, if the time and opportunity seems right. It may be that he will have to make the first move.

This also applies to Christian friends of the couple. They may counsel a greater acceptance of what has happened – if their divorced friend is clearly refusing to face up to reality – but they will never counsel closing oneself against genuine attempts at reconciliation. Moreover, there may well come a time when it is right for a Christian friend, tactfully and after much prayer, to take the initiative in suggesting reconciliation (see below).

It is certainly true that of the two options in 1 Corinthians 7:11 – remaining single or being reconciled – all Christians (the couple themselves and their friends) will always feel that reconciliation is better, not because of any downgrading of the single life but because God's desire is that broken human relationships should be mended.

# When the Marriage is in Danger

The search for reconciliation is, of course, very different when the marriage is still just holding together from when there has already been a seemingly final separation or divorce. In this section, we think of marriages which are still intact but are in trouble, or indeed in serious danger of breaking up. Many suggestions on how Christians can help in these situations have been covered in the previous chapter, but some further points need to be made which relate specifically to the question of reconciliation.

## 1. *Talking*

It is impossible to overstress the importance of a couple in marriage difficulties talking together about their problems and feelings; and this is almost always best done in the presence of a third party, not necessarily a professional counsellor.

Time and time again one of the fundamental causes of marriage failure is a breakdown of communication. Chapman reports a study of 'Why did your marriage fail?' in which '86% said that the main problem was deficient communication' (*Now That*, p.48). Couples have reached a situation where they do not communicate at all or can only communicate destructively, with one accusation capping another. Edward Albee's *Who's Afraid of Virginia Woolf?* is a chilling example of this and shows how every ability – in this case, above average intelligence – can be hijacked into causing pain, mental or physical, to one's partner.

One man wrote to me: 'The root cause [of what had 'become a love/hate relationship'] was of course that we had never really been able to communicate with one another about our deepest feelings.' A woman wrote:

> Instead of ignoring, forgiving or forgetting the minor irritations, each seemed only to be able to turn them into horrific rows, accusing the other of all kinds of things. Real communication was difficult, and I was very frustrated time and again to hear the same answer to my request to talk things out. It was always 'not now' for all sorts of reasons, then 'What

is there to talk about? – Problems, what problems? I haven't got any problems. If you have, sort them out yourself!' I felt then, and know for certain now, that if we could have talked openly and honestly, each seeking a satisfactory solution . . . most of the later aggravation would have been avoided.

Once communication has broken down, or become destructive, it is almost always best to seek another couple or individual with whom to talk. Talking just between the marriage partners can easily degenerate again into accusations and scoring points. And it is often preferable to talk with another couple rather than an individual. Both partners then feel supported – the husband will often feel that another man will be able to see things from his point of view, and it is the same with the wife – and both members of the 'third party' couple can listen, and add to, or modify, each other's response, where appropriate.

Some couples who have been unable to communicate their feelings at all will, for the first time, be able to express their anger or resentment or ambivalence. They may at last feel they can speak and 'be heard'. Others will be able to be much less destructive when in the presence of a third party and realise perhaps much more clearly than before   maybe with the help of 'reflections' from those who have listened – that there are within them both positive and negative feelings, both love and anger. If anger can be expressed and yet not allowed to run riot, if it can be acknowledged (in some cases for the first time) and yet not permitted to dominate, it can be partly dissipated by the very act of speaking about it, and sometimes this is the first significant step towards both parties asking forgiveness and towards genuine reconciliation.

It is normally far better for Christian friends or a counsellor to see both marriage partners together. Otherwise, there is a grave danger of only discovering part of the story and taking sides with the person who has spoken to you. It is often the case, however, that one partner will approach you first and the other partner may be reluctant. It is good if the more reluctant partner can be helped to see that he will have something to gain from joining his partner in meeting with a third party (e.g. 'You have a point of view and legitimate needs too!').

Freeman suggests that a counsellor might offer a 'time-limited service', for instance: three interviews only, so as to encourage a partner to attend who might be unprepared to do so if the commitment seemed open-ended (p.195).

But there can be wisdom in also seeing marriage partners individually. Freeman's practice is always to say 'at the outset that I reserve the right to see them separately and confidentially' and she normally does so if the initial interviews reveal that the couple are deadlocked and the marriage is moving in the direction of divorce.

The outlook is much less encouraging if one partner refuses altogether to talk, but even then it can be constructive for the marriage (as well as supportive for the individual) for the other partner to talk to a third party. One woman wrote of a time when her marriage was in deep trouble: 'I had one friend who became very close, she tried to be objective for me and allowed me the privilege of talking in depth – this is one of the most useful things that can happen: having the opportunity to sort out your own thoughts and feelings. My family were very supportive and at the same time managed to keep out of the arguments and remained just a listening ear.' This again can be an enormously important ministry to a friend – just allowing him or her to talk – provided you seek to 'be objective for me' and provided your overriding aim is unobtrusively to support, and sustain, the marriage.

## 2.  Divorce

No Christian friend or counsellor should support the idea of a divorce. Our conviction is that God has joined this couple together, that they are in God's eyes one flesh and that they should not be put asunder. We are certainly not going to go against Christ's instructions and help to separate what God has joined.

Of course there are occasional exceptions – a battered wife may need to be encouraged to leave her husband – but we will not normally advocate, or support, divorce even in the case of adultery. Christ permitted divorce for adultery; he did not command it. And in most cases it will be far better if the couple can work through this very substantial blow to their marriage, forgive one another and learn gradually to trust one another again.

> The covenant relationship envisaged in marriage (the 'one flesh' union) is far deeper than other covenants . . . [it] is not an ordinary human contract which, if one party to it renegues, may be renounced by the other. It is more like God's covenant with his people. In this analogy (which Scripture develops) only fundamental sexual unfaithfulness breaks the covenant. And even this does not lead automatically or necessarily to divorce; it may rather be an occasion for reconciliation and forgiveness (Stott p.274) cf Ezek. 16:59f.

Schweizer makes the same point and acknowledges that often the 'innocent party' has contributed to the adultery by his behaviour or attitudes within the marriage. He counsels against jumping on adultery too quickly as a reason for divorce and adds: 'The very infidelity of the parties can, for example, bring about a crisis in which both may once more communicate with one another and thus find the way back together.' If the 'offended partner' leaped to the idea of divorce, he 'would then be missing the chance, given him by God, of recognising the failure on his part that has driven his partner to infidelity, and miss the chance of doing something about it' (on Matt. 5:32).

The fact is that, sadly, an enormous number of marriages do have to weather an extramarital affair, and many of them survive. In Britain, according to Anne Kelleher, 6 out of 10 wives and 7 out of 10 husbands are unfaithful to their partners (*Byline*, BBC1 programme, 10 July, 1989). For the USA, Richmond says that in a ten-year marriage 45% of women and 55% of men have extramarital affairs. He adds: 'One affair does not indicate a pattern, and in our society, which is pleasure-orientated without self-control, it would be unrealistic to think that divorce is always the best course of action' (p.122).

Moreover, Christians need to be as honest as possible with themselves. When they are seeking a divorce and there has been adultery, is it really the adultery that has made the marriage intolerable for them? Jesus says that only adultery provides a just cause for divorce. If, then, a husband could actually have coped with his wife's adultery and really wants to separate from her because of constant tensions in the home, her affair cannot be seen as justification for his divorce.

In my counselling experience, I have quite frequently come across precisely this situation. For example, an engaged couple came to see me: she had never married, he was a divorcee. When I asked him why he had left his wife after 12 years, he replied: 'There was nothing in it for me.' His fiancée said that she had initial hesitations about going out with a divorcee but said to God: 'If this is wrong, you are going to have to get me out of it. I haven't the strength.' She said that in her view the relationship was obviously right because 'I've been so much happier . . . I've been in wrong relationships before and God has . . . always put up roadblocks.' Later on in our conversation, I discovered that there had been adultery on his first wife's part, and they began to shift their argument for their marriage in this direction, but it was obvious what their real reasons were: there was 'nothing in' the first marriage for him; she felt 'much happier' with him; and both concluded that the new marriage must be God's will.

It is often argued in favour of a laxer approach in the Church[1] to divorce that when English and American law allowed only adultery as sufficient grounds for divorce, individuals or couples manufactured affairs, and arranged for witnesses, in order to get out of an unwanted marriage. This of course is no argument against Jesus' teaching at all, since divorce would clearly not be permissible in these cases. Adultery is not the reason for divorce in these instances; it is merely the artificial means of complying with the law. The real reason lies elsewhere – perhaps in the fact that one partner has lost all love and respect for the other – and this does not constitute sufficient grounds, according to Jesus, for his followers to contemplate divorce.

Obviously those experiencing severe marriage difficulties will find counsellors and friends outside Christian circles who will encourage them to divorce, but amongst their Christian friends

---

[1] The difficult question of what the divorce laws of the State should permit lies outside the scope of this book. Some allowance should certainly be made for 'the hardness of men's hearts' as in the Mosaic legislation (Mark 10:5//Matt. 19:8),but since the preservation of marriage is so important for the well-being of society as well as for the upholding of God's will, individuals or couples should be required to show weighty reasons for breaking solemn vows that they have entered into and should normally be required to have a 'cooling-off' period during which the help of a Reconciliation and Conciliation Service would be mandatory.

(except in rare circumstances) they should find no one who suggests this. One woman who did eventually divorce (with very good reason) nevertheless, as she looked back on her past marriage difficulties, said it was very helpful that 'Nobody urged me to leave. They would give me Bible passages to help me find strength and comfort to carry on.' It is worth noting both parts of her friends' advice: they did not only advise her not to separate, but gave her positive help from Scripture which strengthened her to carry on.

When someone becomes desperate about his (or her) marriage and has really – even if he has not admitted it to himself – decided to leave the marriage, he longs to hear anyone with whom he discusses it agree with him. In particular, it matters to him enormously that his family and friends should agree with his course of action. If anything, this is still more pronounced in the Christian who knows what Scripture says about divorce and is almost certainly deeply troubled in his own conscience. Any disagreement from friends can result in anger – 'they don't (or: haven't even really tried to) understand' – and any agreement leads to an enormous sense of relief. One example:

> I discussed the biblical attitude with Dave [a close Christian friend] and found to my dismay that he was very black and white in his interpretation . . . I found it only added to the pressure I was under to be told that I should make every effort to keep my marriage intact. I felt guilty enough about wanting a divorce – I didn't need to be told that I was going against God's law. Unless you have been in the situation of an unhappy marriage, it is impossible to comprehend the depths of despair reached when living in those circumstances.

But in the end Dave changed his mind because of her insistence: 'I can remember talking to Dave and telling him that I couldn't stand this sort of life any longer . . . He did his best to dissuade me, but finally after many such discussions even he agreed that if I really felt divorce was the answer, then the time seemed to have come. I vividly remember the relief I felt when he actually said that. Suddenly I wasn't battling completely on my own.'

It is probably true in this case that Dave's acquiescence was the catalyst which finally allowed his friend to divorce. This puts an enormous responsibility on us as Christian friends and counsellors. But despite the fact that we know what our friends are longing to hear us say, our first allegiance is to Christ and we must be very certain that our words do not contribute to putting asunder the two whom God has joined together as one flesh.

## 3. Trial separation

Because Christians are aware of Christ's teaching on divorce, they often opt for a 'trial separation', a time of living apart to 'take stock' and see where the marriage is going and whether it can be saved. Crispin's comments on this seem quite harsh but are, in many cases, only realistic: 'The decision to separate [the decision; before the *actual* separation] will almost inevitably be followed by pangs of guilt . . . There may be enormous guilt over the prospect of the effect on the children . . . Yet, on the other hand, one may feel that to stay would be intolerable. A "temporary" separation may be arranged as a sop to the conscience' (p.123). In other words, the person is almost entirely convinced that he will leave the marriage permanently but decides for now on a temporary separation only because that is all his conscience can live with. Later he will be able to say: 'I did try, but it obviously wasn't going to work.'

Christian friends also frequently suggest a trial separation. This is partly because they can see that the marriage is not working but cannot bring themselves to suggest a permanent separation, and partly because they hope that absence will make the heart grow fonder and that, when apart from each other, the partners will recognise many of the good points in each other.

In fact, Christians should not normally support the idea of a trial or temporary separation. Crispin rightly points out that, because for us in the contemporary West marriage break-up almost always comes in two stages: separation and divorce, we tend to imagine that the New Testament teaching relates to the second stage and has nothing to say about separation. In fact, the New Testament recognises no such distinction (pp.10–18). It frequently uses the normal word for to 'separate' (*chōrizō*) to mean 'divorce' (Mark 10:9//Matt. 19:6), and we have seen how *chōrizō* is used in parallel with *aphiēmi* (send away, divorce) throughout 1 Corinthians 7:10–16. Of course some factors – for example, illness, war, imprisonment or (for short periods) business – may force an undesired separation on marriage partners but

> a spouse may not voluntarily separate himself or herself from the other spouse and thus wilfully refuse to perform the debts [= duties] incident to the marriage relation. And neither may the spouses by mutual consent agree thus to separate from one another . . . The spouses are under obligation to live together in the discharge of all mutual debts unless, for some reason of divine providence beyond their control, they are compelled to be separated from one another (Murray p.105).

Does this mean that a 'trial separation' will always be wrong? I think we must answer 'yes' because the very word 'trial' implies that no decision has yet been taken as to whether the separation will be permanent. But a *temporary* separation may be occasionally advisable, but only if both parties realise that it is only temporary, that it will soon be reversed and in fact that it adds a further unfortunate feature to the marriage but only with a view to making the marriage better. Only under these very limited conditions could a Christian embark on, or advise, a temporary separation (cf what St Paul says about a mutually agreed temporary abstinence from sex: 1 Cor. 7:3–6).

## 4.  Hope

It is not enough for the Christian friend or counsellor to be negative: 'Don't allow yourself even to think about a divorce or a separation.' It is not enough to be neutral: 'Let me help you to talk together and you work out your own decision. Whichever way you decide is fine, so long as you are able to come to a decision' (cf Freeman's remarks, quoted in the last chapter, about the unfortunate effects of supposed neutrality: Freeman p.194). It is not enough to be an upholder of the *status quo*: 'Just hang in there. Maybe you'll be able to stick it out and pull through.'

The Christian's aim is reconciliation: the rediscovering, or constructing, of a healthy foundation for marriage on which the couple can build. This is in part salvaging the good that is already there, and in part discovering new and better ways with which to build the marriage. In all this, it is essential that the Christian friend is realistic certainly but also, and self-evidently, hopeful. This hope stems partly from what is good within the marriage and the partners' attitudes (however slight this may be) and mainly from the conviction that God wants this marriage to be rebuilt and will give the resources to do so. 'Wherever God is in control, there is hope; not necessarily the hope of an instant cure, but the promise of support and change' (Clifford p.34).

Because divorce is so prevalent today, it is easy to lapse quickly into pessimism: 'Here we go again. Yet another marriage breaking up', 'I suppose it had to happen sooner or later.' As Christians, men and women who believe in God, we should be those who clearly stand up against that trend. Joyce Huggett writes in the preface to her book *Marriage on the Mend*: 'I write this breathing a prayer that in some way this book may pierce the pessimism with which the marriage relationship seems to be surrounded today and raise the level of hope in the hearts of those whose marriages are under pressure' (p.11). Later on she adds: 'Some of the richest marriages are those that have worked their way through disasters that would have shattered others, but because they refused to give up and worked towards a solution in partnership with God, they reached a maturity and a joy they had never imagined possible' (p.87).

Phypers makes the same point in a different way. We have become aware that more and more are 'coming to marriage with such deep wounds and hurts from their childhood that they are unable to relate to each other with the depth which is necessary'. This might cause us to despair, except that the Christian Church is also rediscovering the healing ministry: 'Through a living relationship with Christ himself, and the healing power of the Holy Spirit, we can be delivered from the wounds that bind us' (p.63). 'The whole idea of education, spiritual conversion and Christian growth stands in opposition to the idea of determinism . . . that our . . . life is determined [inexorably] by patterns established in childhood' (Chapman: *Hope* p.35).

Chapman, to whose excellent book I owe many of the thoughts in this chapter, deliberately gives it the title: *Hope for the Separated*. 'The greatest thing a counsellor brings . . . is hope. A listening ear, a caring heart, communication skills, biblical teachings – all are necessary to successful counselling, but without hope all will fail' (p.68). Chapman says to those whom he counsels: 'Your attitude is important. Don't say: "I might fail", but rather: "I must succeed"' (p.98). Even if he is talking to only one partner and the other shows no sign of wanting to talk, he says: '[You may be thinking:] "It sounds good, but it won't work. We've tried before. Besides, I don't think my spouse will even try again." Perhaps you are right, but do not assume that the hostile attitude of your spouse will remain forever . . . Two weeks or two months from now . . . your mate may be willing to talk' (p.12).

Of course we must not give false hope to people, where it is abundantly clear to us that there is not, and will not be, any possibility of reunion. But we, and the marriage partner(s) with whom we are talking, must not give up hope too soon. God wants to save this marriage, God is at work, God may provide an opportunity for reconciliation; and we will be much more able to seize that opportunity constructively if we have learned to be both realistic about the difficulties and hopeful. Almost the last words in Bromiley's book are: A truly Christian marriage 'is a possibility, not for a few specially gifted people, but for sinners who in and of themselves really have no such possibility' (p.81).

Within this atmosphere of realistic (not naïve) and God-centred hope, we are wanting to help the couple – who are always the ones who have to make the decisions – to forgive each other and to build a new and better relationship. To do so, our input needs to centre on the positive: the positive that there was, and still is, in the marriage, and the positive action that the partners can take. Insofar as there is, and must be, some evaluation of the negative elements in the marriage, each partner should be encouraged to think more about his (or her) own negative contributions rather than his partner's.

You might ask: 'What are the good things in your relationship (if any) which you want to hold on to?' This helps them to think positively about each other and about the marriage. Hosier tells the story of a woman called Mitzi who had already been separated from her husband for four months and had begun divorce proceedings. Fairly early in the conversation, Hosier asked: 'What do you want out of life, Mitzi?' 'Happiness.' 'And you think on the other side of divorce you will find that?' 'I'm not sure.' Hosier thought that reply was hopeful as 'it told me that Mitzi wasn't sure she was making the right decision'. Later, 'I suggested to Mitzi that . . . she write out the qualities she first admired in her husband, adding to it other qualities that had emerged through the years of their married life – that she write down the good things they had going for them' (pp. 45, 49).

Turning to what has caused tensions and great strains within the marriage, it may be helpful to ask: 'What are the difficulties you – not your partner – have contributed to the relationship?' And again: 'What are the ways in which you – not your partner – need to change?' This was of course exactly the way Jesus told us to tackle relationship difficulties (Matt. 7:3–5). It can often be helpful if the partners are encouraged to take time, think and pray about their responses, write them down and then share and discuss them at a meeting in the presence of a Christian friend or counsellor. It can make a very useful 'assignment' between sessions with a trusted friend or couple.

Other questions that can be helpful, either in a session of open talking as a couple or as an assignment (to be discussed together later) are: 'What are the practical steps you can take this week to bring about a change needed in you?', 'How would you like to feel about your partner?', 'How do you think that God feels about your partner?', 'Is it possible to forgive someone when they refuse to acknowledge that they've done wrong?', 'Where are you in the struggle to forgive yourself?' (cf *Fresh Start* p.112).

In all this, there is the determination to remain realistic – not underestimating the extent of the pain or the difficulties or the number of occasions in which the couple have tried to work things out before and failed – but also hopeful, a hope that springs principally from a profound faith in God and a conviction about his purposes for marriage.

## When there has been a Separation or Divorce

Chapman, in his book *Hope for the Separated,* makes a strong distinction between those who are separated (where he still sees much ground for hope that they may be reconciled) and those who are legally divorced. Of course it is more difficult to work towards reconciliation after divorce, especially if there has been bitter wrangling over the arrangements for custody, access and finance. The sad fact is that often 'the court system generates and perpetuates division between the parents' (Richard Tur in *Say it with Lawyers,* BBC2, 13 June, 1991), making reconciliation all but impossible.

But we have already seen that the New Testament makes no real distinction between separation and divorce. And in practice, it is possible to achieve reconciliation after divorce; there are many examples. In our own congregation, there is already one such couple and another who, we hope, are working towards reconciliation after several years of divorce. What, then, can the Christian friend, family member or counsellor do to aid reconciliation, whether the couple are separated or divorced?

### 1.  Not enlarging the rift

There is obviously a rift already; it is already a large rift. Otherwise the couple would not be separated. If the couple is divorced, the rift is likely to be larger. But if reconciliation is the ultimate goal – or, at least, in the case where only one partner is prepared to work at the marriage, an openness to reconciliation – then no one will want to make the rift larger still. Sadly, this is precisely what many well-meaning friends do.

a) Friends and family
'Friends often side with one spouse or the other, frequently without much understanding of the real issues that led to the marital breakdown' (Hurding p.123). This is precisely what we must studiously avoid.

We must be careful not to 'do down' the other party. Friends often think this will help: 'I never liked him anyway', 'I couldn't understand why you married her. I always thought she couldn't be trusted.' Friends are often taken aback by what a negative reaction such comments receive. Quite frequently the separated person leaps to his partner's defence; he still retains many vestiges of affection and does not want to be told that anyone could have seen the marriage was a disaster from the beginning. But even where such comments would be warmly greeted and agreed with, they are to be avoided, as they only make the rift wider.

It is also not helpful for friends to keep supplying information about the other partner's movements, and especially his movements and activities with his new girlfriend, even if the wife asks and seems hungry for these details. A divorcee wrote about the time after she and her husband had separated: 'Definitely unhelpful: friends tended to repeat gossip about, and sightings of, James and Tracey. I had a morbid curiosity and had to know, even though it caused pain.'

Rather, in talking about a friend's separated partner, we need to be gently positive about him, neither damning him for his outrageous behaviour nor of course praising him to the skies, but speaking of him with courtesy and respect. Another divorcee, having said: 'It was definitely unhelpful when people chose to blame your partner for you', wrote about what she had found helpful: 'My sister came to the house and helped me pack and made me laugh, and she remained kind and nice to my former husband. My family looked after my children for a week during the move and that helped relieve pressure . . . My ex-mother-in-law was kind and never apportioned blame. My solicitor was very good; he listened to me and did not try to enlarge his fee by a vindictive approach.'

This positive attitude towards the other partner is often most difficult for the family. Parents and grandparents see their (grand)child's hurt, normally hear only his side of the story and almost inevitably sympathise mainly, or exclusively, with him. If, however, they can keep up relations with their (grand)son-in-law (or daughter-in-law), or at least continue to speak positively and respectfully about him, the likelihood of the marriage being restored and of their own son's (or daughter's) happiness is very greatly increased.

Of course the greatest enlargement of the rift often comes

when a new relationship begins for one partner or both. When a man sees, or hears of, his wife going out with another man and perhaps expressing affection in public, this is deeply hurtful and he may deliberately increase the emotional rift – and perhaps the physical rift: breaking off all contact – in order to deaden the pain. Therefore any encouragement to start looking around for another companion, and to think about a new relationship – which is so frequently recommended by friends and family – makes reconciliation a great deal more difficult, as well as being against the express teaching of Christ.

b) The separated or divorced Christian

It is not merely friends who need to ensure that they do not enlarge the rift, it is the separated Christian too. Right from the earliest days of separation, arrangements will need to be made over money and the care of the children. Paradoxically, many couples find that they are able to communicate better at this point than for months past.

It is essential that these arrangements are conducted in an atmosphere that is as little adversarial as possible. This may be possible simply between the couple themselves, but will often be better accomplished by making use of a Conciliation Service of which there are now (1991) 66 in Britain. Of course lawyers will have to become involved, especially if it comes to a divorce, and even at the separation stage it may be helpful to check with a lawyer the implications of any arrangement. However, it should be remembered that the involvement of lawyers normally makes the relationship more adversarial and increases the rift and, sadly, the more that lawyers suggest approaches and courses of action, the more embittered the relationship between husband and wife is likely to become. In one case of divorce both husband and wife went off with another partner. The relationship was then, and is still now, relatively cordial and this is put down to 'the determination by all four parties involved . . . to tell the solicitors how we wanted the matter to be sorted out and not to allow the legal situation to degenerate into a bitter war'.

Above all, arrangements over the children need to be discussed, and carried through, with as little rancour as possible.

The custodial parent – whether custodial in practice and ideally by agreement, or in law after a court order – needs to be as generous as possible in offering access to the children, seeking to avoid showing any signs of resentment at this contact, and not restricting access to the precise letter of a personal, or legal, agreement. Crispin quotes with approval the saying that access is a right not of the parent but of the child (p.266). 'The children of divorced parents need both a mother and a father. Don't deny them this right because of your anger, hostility, guilt or vengeance' (*Fresh Start*, p.92).

But it is not only for the children that a Christian parent will be generous over access. If she (or he) is wanting to remain open to reconciliation – however hard or remote that may seem – she enhances the likelihood of this immeasurably by her generosity over sharing the children. My experience has been that reconciliation is much more frequently achieved, even after divorce, where the non-custodial parent has been able to see the children frequently and easily.

The non-custodial parent, for his (or her) part, must keep visiting the children. Painful as these visits may be because they involve continuing contact with his wife and because he may feel unwanted by the children ('Fathers tend to visit younger children regularly. They tend to visit older children less frequently, especially those who are resentful' (Freeman p.203)), he needs to see as much of his children as he possibly can. If possible, he should continue to live in the same town, near them. Yet he must also be careful not to spoil them, and in particular not to shower them with gifts which he knows his wife will not be able to afford; this only causes resentment. One woman's experience is typical: she writes that the hardest part of divorce 'was when Laura [her daughter] went on her fortnightly visits to stay with her father. I hated it when she went and yet I was desperate not to let her see my anguish as I didn't want her to feel guilty about wanting to visit her father. On her return she nearly always came back with new clothing or a doll, which again I found difficult to deal with.'

And both parents – custodial and non-custodial – must encourage their children to love and respect the other. Those wives (for example) who poison their children's minds against their father normally find that this policy backfires on them. It may work while the children are young, but later in life the children often want to re-establish contact with their father and then frequently blame their mother for keeping him out of their lives. It is, of course, deeply detrimental to any reconciliation if a father (or mother) knows that he is being systematically vilified, and in contrast reconciliation becomes much more possible if the children clearly show that his wife has been encouraging respect for him in the children.

Children are the greatest catalyst for reconciliation. They normally desire it, and hope for it, more than any other human being involved, and where the partners are generous over access to the children and over talking to the children positively about the other parent, there a real hope for reunion can blossom.

## 2.  *Taking the initiative*

If a reconciliation is to come about, or even be tried for, someone will have to make the first move. It may be that one of the couple can do this. Most partners, in the months that follow separation, consider at some time or another suggesting 'a try at getting together again'. But most never translate this thought into action. Sometimes this is because of a deep sense of *being wronged*. I feel that I am much more sinned against than sinning, that I have been much more hurt than the hurt I have given; therefore, if anyone is to make the first move, it should be my partner.

This may be the case, but Jesus laid down that it is our responsibility to make the first move whether we have sinned (Matt. 5:23f) or been sinned against (Matt. 18:15). The fact is that within our marriage we are almost certainly both a sinner and sinned against. So, despite a probably very legitimate sense of having been wronged, we are if at all possible to take the initiative. 'You may not be able to effect reconciliation, but you must seek it' (Chapman, *Hope*, p.54).

More often still a partner is held back from suggesting a move towards reconciliation because of *fear of being rebuffed*. He has been hurt so many times already by his partner; he has been put down again and again; he does not want to put himself in a position in which he will be rejected all over again. This is very understandable, but perhaps the possibility of reconciliation is worth the risk of rebuff. One woman's experience is not untypical. It was she who had left and she put up a brave front that she was coping well. She was also having an affair. Yet inwardly things were very different: 'I missed Frank [her husband] dreadfully during the months we were separated and I quickly realised that I still loved him deeply. I did not confide in Frank as to how I felt because I thought that he would resent the way I had treated him . . . I regret not having told him much earlier.' This couple divorced but are now back together again and legally remarried.

The fact is that most couples have very ambivalent feelings after separation. There is almost always some measure of relief but, even for the partner who walked out and even if this was to go to another relationship, there is often a great mixture of guilt and doubt. One woman had been considering divorce for many years and had in fact left her husband for a time. Finally *he* left her. 'I felt really happy for the first time for years', yet three months later 'suddenly and without warning I began to suffer severe depression and felt weighed down by the responsibilities which weighed upon me . . . I had looked forward to being independent and was confident that I could cope' but now 'the future stretched out in front of me like an endless ocean – an endless period of time for which I was totally responsible'. She found she missed sex as well: 'Although it wasn't marvellous, 21 years is a long time to establish habits that abruptly ceased.'

Most people find that being on their own again is much harder than they expected; it is then that they can begin to hanker after the life they knew, despite all its difficulties, and wonder whether the marriage could start again, on a better footing. Another person's experience: 'In a practical way . . . I managed fairly well . . . Emotionally I found [it] very hard. The loneliness was very hard to bear . . . I was very up and down. I would feel chuffed because I was coping so well and then wake up one morning and be back to square one. This went on for more than a year . . . I have smashing children . . . but there is a different kind of emptiness, a kind of deep void, which at times is almost physically painful'. That was written by someone who was left by her husband. Here is the experience of someone who did the leaving: It was wonderful that 'the endless arguments came to an end' but 'it was far more tiring than I had anticipated looking after the children. It is surprising how much easier it is when there are two of you . . . I was extremely lonely, because I had no one to share things with.'

It is not surprising, then, that a Bristol University research project revealed that 51% of men and 41% of women regret having divorced. Of course the majority of these are partners who have been left, rather than those who have done the leaving. But even after remarriage 37% of men and 21% of women wish they were still married to their former partner (quoted in Polly Toynbee: 'The Worm Turned Syndrome' – *Observer*.

'Many people vacillate in their attitude to a former spouse. One day they may be angry . . . The next day there may be a feeling of resignation about [their] marriage [i.e. it is over] . . . The next day something may happen which triggers a memory of happy times together. Abruptly the resignation has given way to nostalgia and a real sense of loss. Hopes of reconciliation may be kindled, dashed and then revived' (Crispin pp.230f).

Mattison captures this vacillation well:

> Since we had planned so carefully
> and thought so rationally,
> cautiously making our decision,
> I thought I would not feel much pain.
> But there was something about the sunset
> and the tiles in the street
> and the fragrance of honeysuckle
> that hurled me backwards,
> to times before all that rationality,
> to moments when planning to be apart
> had never entered our minds.
> It is inevitable.
> I will at times feel great pain,
> because I am not only a mind and a plan
> but a heart and a memory as well (p.47).

This may remain only a painful, wistful thought ('If only . . .'), as it did with Mattison. Or it can lead, as it did with one woman quoted above, to taking the initiative and seeing if there is any possibility in trying for reconciliation. The suggestion needs to be put very tentatively, and it will much better be done in person rather than by letter or over the telephone. It is often best not to request an answer immediately, but to ask for one's partner to 'think about it and let me know', agonising though the wait may be. Of course reconciliation will not be possible in every case, nor probably in the majority, but Chapman's experience is echoed by several: 'I have never met an individual who sincerely, consistently and lovingly tried to find reconciliation after separation and regretted the effort. I have met scores of individuals who have succeeded and today are happily restored to their mates' (p.98).

Yet, because of the reasons mentioned above, it can be difficult for either partner to take the initiative in reconciliation, and it may therefore be up to their friends, with great sensitivity and gentleness, to suggest it (cf Green p.59). One man said how much he wished someone had suggested reconciliation to him; instead his friends tended to criticise his wife: 'I needed someone to sit me down and discuss the situation. At this stage it is often difficult to see the wood for the trees, particularly when you are as stubborn as I am.' Another man: 'I needed an impartial ear and mouth to listen and speak when necessary and not be afraid to tell me if I was wrong' (though certainly this needs to be done with great gentleness). At the time of writing, I am about to approach both partners in a situation where they were divorced many years ago but where the four children have kept them in close contact, and suggest a possible move towards reconciliation.

Friends normally need to make any move sooner rather than later. This should not be done immediately. The initial reaction to separation is often relief, and perhaps also (or instead) a great deal of bitterness and anger. At that time friends simply need to show support and not suggest any coming together again: 'Initially I had no wish for reconciliation; then a couple of months or so later I would have liked an opportunity to discuss, as I felt we had had a sound partnership.'

But after an initial few months have elapsed, the earlier that friends can tactfully bring up the subject of reconciliation, the better. The Royal Commission on Marriage and Divorce (1951–5, the 'Morton Commission') gave as some of the prerequisites for successful reconciliation: an early start, a positive attitude on one side at least and complete assurance of confidentiality about anything disclosed to a counsellor. If a friend is to take the initiative in discussing possible reconciliation, it will need considerable courage. He too may perhaps be rebuffed. He must be careful not to raise his friend's hopes too high. But it is so much better to try five times and have some measure of success twice, than never to be courageous enough to try at all, and so see no measure of healing or reconciliation in a broken marriage.

Often of course what causes the separation to take place is an affair. The husband leaves his wife for another woman; or he discovers that his wife is having an affair, cannot stand it and leaves her (or demands that she leaves). But 'affairs usually come to an end. When they do, you sometimes get a window to launch a reconciliation' (Richmond p.161). It was when the Prodigal Son's 'wild living' had come to an end, that he was open to reconciliation with his father (Luke 15:13–20). When this happens, it would normally be a mistake for friends to act immediately, suggesting reconciliation with the separated partner as soon as they hear the news, but again it is a mistake to delay too long. This 'window of opportunity' may not last; your friend may start another temporary relationship quite quickly.

Of course any suggestion about reconciliation must come from the basis of a genuine and continuing friendship. Someone who does not really know the people concerned will not be able to say anything effective. Similarly, if a friendship was cut off abruptly and without explanation when the man began an affair, it will be impossible to say anything helpful to him when the affair comes to an end. Those who have experienced the pain of separation will only listen to a friend who has stood by them throughout these dark days. A clergyman does have a certain *entrée* and (it is hoped) respect because of his leadership position, but it will often be better for him to suggest that a close friend raises the subject of reconciliation rather than doing so himself.

And in any case, the subject will need to be raised with great care. Far from there being any attempt to push either partner into action, the suggestion should be made very tentatively: 'Has it ever crossed your mind that you might . . . ?', 'Do you think there could be any mileage in the two of you meeting with another person, me or someone else . . . ?' A similarly tentative approach will need to be made if it is one of the partners who is taking the initiative: 'I've been thinking a lot about our marriage. I've seen much more clearly the ways in which I contributed to where we are now. I've just been wondering whether you'd be prepared to talk about it some more, perhaps with someone else there. I feel we could talk more constructively now . . .'.

Anyone who takes his courage in both hands and suggests reconciliation must be ready for a rebuff, even for anger. Moses was manhandled when he tried to bring together people who had quarrelled (Acts 7:26–29). We must be prepared to back off, at least for a time. But it will have been very well worth that risk if the other person responds positively; and even where that is not the case, there will be a sense of having done God's will, providing the suggestion was made with sensitivity and with much prayer.

## 3. *Starting a new relationship*

If reconciliation is going to be possible, it is very important that both partners realise it will not be a restoration of the old relationship. The partner who has left for another man and who is now wanting to return to her husband cannot expect simply to 'take up the threads again' as if nothing has happened and there is nothing to be resolved. The partner who was left and still hankers after his wife must not say: 'Come home and I won't ask any questions. I'll let you do exactly as you like.' That resolves nothing. It does not inspire any respect and, even if accepted, will almost certainly break down sooner rather than later.

So it is essential that new patterns of relationship are fully discussed and agreed upon before the partners move back together. One woman lived under the same roof as her husband for many months without any communication at all and with letters coming to each from the other's lawyers. But 'immediately I left home [after the divorce came through], I realised I'd made a mistake. I made every effort during these visits [her husband's to the children] to show my feeling for John.' Eventually they met to discuss the future. They had already, by this time, both decided to get back together 'but I needed reassurance that our relationship would not continue as it had been when we had been married'. These initial discussions may be best conducted with a third party present.

All this may take time. It may be necessary to start seeing each other, perhaps also having sexual relations again, before moving back under the same roof. Trust will need to be restored and sometimes this is best begun while living apart. But often it will soon be possible to start living together again. The important thing is to work out a genuinely new foundation to the marriage, based on forgiveness and on new agreed patterns of marital behaviour and relationship.

## 4. *Acknowledging faults and forgiving*

One of the most common reactions to separation, or divorce, is a deep feeling of guilt. The partner who has been abandoned is often just as plagued by guilt as the partner who has left, sometimes more so. And often individuals blame themselves for events which have little or nothing to do with them in any direct way. Children frequently blame themselves for their parents' splitting up. Some bad news comes to one of the partners who instantly thinks that it must be punishment from God. One typical example: 'On the day that George left, he was obviously angry and upset, a fact proved when he pulled straight out into the main road and hit a pedestrian . . . The pedestrian was taken to hospital with a broken arm and eventually George and Johnno [one of their children, who was going to live with his father] left again. *It was all my fault, I reasoned*' (my emphasis).

Yet, paradoxically, there is also a great reluctance to acknowledge any guilt. Both partners are quite clear that it was mainly the other's fault, that it was he (or she) who made the marriage a failure, while they perpetually tried to keep it going. Chapman has a section entitled: 'Don't proclaim your own righteousness . . . It is so easy to look back and announce all your righteous acts in the marriage while overlooking your weaknesses. "I was faithful to you. I cooked your meals, washed your shirts, cared for your children, and where did it get me? You cannot say that I did not try" ' (*Hope* p.64).

The fact is that in every separation or divorce there are deep hurts. Each of the partners has been hurt very badly, and each has hurt the other. Reconciliation can only begin with an acknowledgment that I have hurt my partner too, and hurt him deeply; that I am in the wrong too. ' " 'Return, faithless Israel', declares the LORD. 'I will frown on you no longer, for I am merciful,' declares the LORD, 'I will not be angry for ever. Only acknowledge your guilt . . . for I am your husband " ' (Jer. 3:12–14).

Failure to acknowledge this will make reconciliation impossible. I am in correspondence at the moment with a couple who separated and were both desperately unhappy. In the end, mainly because of the children, they moved back together again. But neither of them are prepared to admit that he/she has contributed in any major way to the marriage problems; it is all the other's fault. The result is that living together continues to be searingly painful for them both. This is exactly what Scripture leads us to expect in any broken relationship:

> Blessed is he whose transgressions are forgiven, whose sins are covered . . . When I kept silent, my bones wasted away through my groaning all day long. For day and night your hand was heavy upon me; my strength was sapped as in the heat of summer. Then I acknowledged my sin to you and did not cover up my iniquity. I said, 'I will confess my transgressions to the LORD' – and you forgave the guilt of my sin (Ps. 32:1–5).

It is also very important, if any progress is to be made towards reconciliation, that we should be more interested in acknowledging our own faults than in hearing our partner acknowledge his. If we begin communicating with our partner again thinking that reconciliation will perhaps be achieved when our partner sees that it was principally he who was at fault, we shall get nowhere. And we must be particularly wary of meeting together with any third party in the hope or confidence that (s)he will bear us out and show our partner to be the one who is mainly responsible for the problems. If so, we will probably be bitterly disappointed by the third party's response; and even if he does back our assessment up – or we believe he does – we may win the argument and lose any prospects of reconciliation.

Nor can we shrug off any idea of guilt and pretend it is not present on either side. Atkinson admits that 'no fault' divorce may have advantages [as well as several disadvantages] from a legal point of view, but it is not helpful in coming to terms with divorce, nor in moving towards reconciliation; nor is it true to the biblical picture:

> Covenants do not just 'break down', they are broken; divorce expresses sin as well as tragedy . . . From a biblical moral perspective, we cannot dissolve the category of 'matrimonial offence' . . . into the less personally focused concept of 'irretrievable breakdown' . . . 'Marriage breakdown' transfers all question of blame from the partners to the marriage itself . . . A denial of personal responsibility is ultimately a denial of an important part of what it means to be human (pp.151f).

So how can we begin, especially when we are naturally reluctant to acknowledge our own faults? Chapman suggests a 'learning exercise' which he says 'may be one of the most difficult and yet most healing things you will ever do'. He begins by drawing our attention to Matthew 7:3–5. Then he adds: 'In a quiet setting with time to reflect, say to God: "Lord, where have I failed my ex-spouse? You and I know that person has failed me, but right now I want to concentrate on my failures." List . . . whatever comes to mind. Be as specific as you can. Include failures when you were living together and failures since you have been separated' (*Now That*, p.35).

This is an exercise to do on our own; and very often acknowledging our faults brings us to God. Many who are Christians have been brought much closer to God as they have seen the depth of their sin and therefore the enormous generosity of God's forgiveness (cf Luke 7:37–47). Others who have not been Christians before find that the great unforeseen blessing of what seemed like unmitigated darkness is that they have found God. Returning to God like the Prodigal Son proves to be a gain that can stand comparison with all the losses of divorce.

And Christ not only brings forgiveness but the power to change. 'Failures come in two basic areas: first we fail in meeting the needs of our partners, and second we fail by doing and saying things that actually are designed to hurt them.' Romans 7:15 often aptly describes marriages. 'Our only hope for change, Paul says, is to allow Jesus Christ our Lord to control our lives [Rom. 7:24–8:14]. He alone can give us the power to do what we know is right' (Chapman, *Hope*, p.55).

But this acknowledgement of failure cannot remain purely between ourselves and God, or even between ourselves and a close friend. If we are to move towards reconciliation, we must be prepared to admit our faults frankly to our partner. This will not normally mean reading out a great list of failures (which may well be helpful in coming to terms with our guilt privately and receiving forgiveness from God) but rather acknowledging the main ways in which we have failed our partner and asking his (or her) forgiveness. In the context of prayer for healing, James says: 'Confess your sins to each other and pray for each other so that you may be healed. The prayer of a righteous man is powerful and effective' (Jas. 5:16). In a past generation, this Scripture might have been considered irrelevant because it would have been assumed that James had only physical healing in mind. Today it is afresh being realised – as it seems to have been in the first-century Church – that emotional and spiritual hurt cannot so easily be separated from physical pain, and can also be healed not just by prayer alone but by confession to each other as well.

The open admission of failure by both partners is, then, the only firm base on which reconciliation, and a new relationship, can be built. It will not be based on anything solid if, as is the case with an electrician friend of ours at the moment, one partner moves back only because he has nowhere else to go. Nor if, as with another friend of ours, the move back comes merely for financial reasons. Nor out of a general sense of guilt – because divorce is not God's will – but without any real facing up to, and acknowledgment, of personal failures. The only solid foundation will be an admission of my own sins, the hurts that I have caused my partner.

But hand in hand with this, and equally important though

also equally difficult, must be a willingness to forgive. If one, or both, of the parties is willing to acknowledge their own faults, but one, or both, of the parties is unwilling to forgive, reconciliation will again prove impossible. Of course we may well not feel like forgiving; our hurts may be so deep. But ultimately our feelings are not where the battle will be fought: 'True forgiveness involves not warm feelings but the will . . . The question to ask yourself is not: "can I forgive?' but "will I forgive?"' (Huggett p.132).

And that question can only be answered in one way by the Christian. 'Forgiveness is in no way an option; it is an obligation to God . . . Forgiveness is the door that opens up the possibility of reconciliation' (Richmond p.175). It may help forgiveness to understand our partner's circumstances, the pressures that he is under. Many have found it helpful to realise that their partner has no idea just how much pain he has caused and have used the prayer: 'Father, forgive them, for they know not what they do' (Luke 23:34 (RSV), cf Acts 7:60).[1] But even this is not enough. C. S. Lewis points out that to seek to understand someone and therefore excuse his wrong 'is not Christian charity; it is only fair-mindedness. To be a Christian is to forgive the inexcusable because God has forgiven the inexcusable in you' (quoted in R. F. Wilson: 'Don't pay the price of counterfeit forgiveness', *Moody Magazine*).

And once our partner has confessed his own failings, and we have promised forgiveness, we must try never again to remind him of how he has failed in the past. In this, we must imitate God who forgives freely and does not continually throw our past sins in our teeth. 'Your well-being is not determined by the past but by what you do with the future. What is important is how you treat each other today, not how you treated each other last month' (Chapman: *Hope* p.67, cf Phil. 3:13f).

There can of course be no reconciliation until both partners are able to acknowledge their faults and to forgive, but the

---

[1] 'I invited her [a friend] to picture our Lord hanging on the Cross, and to imagine herself standing at the foot of that Cross with her husband . . . [Then] look from Jesus to your husband and when you are ready, pray the prayer Jesus prayed: "Father, forgive him, he didn't know what he was doing . . . He didn't realise how much he was hurting me"' (Huggett p.132).

partners may be out of sync. One may be willing to confess – and may indeed do so, to his partner – before the other is willing to reciprocate. It can be extremely painful to acknowledge one's faults to one's partner, and perhaps receive a forgiveness which seems patronising or half-hearted, and then to hear no corresponding admission of guilt from the other person. But this may come later: 'You must stand ready to forgive and receive . . . You must be willing to wait, pray, and love, even if at a distance.' God allows your partner to resist him and to turn away from reconciliation. You must allow your partner the same liberty, hoping that it will just be for a time (Chapman: *Hope* pp.56f).

It may be necessary for family and friends to help each marriage partner to see and identify his own wrong and to forgive the other. But this must be done with the utmost tact and gentleness. It is absolutely essential that the individual himself (or herself) takes the decision to acknowledge his failings and to forgive. Friends can act as catalysts for this decision – for instance by gently suggesting an exercise in which the individual privately writes an account of his own part in the marriage – but they must beware of forcing another person into a half-hearted acknowledgment of failure, or of pushing him before he is ready to see his own faults or to forgive.

Where friends can often be extremely helpful is in arranging for the couple to meet and talk. Many marriage partners do recognise in time that they contributed many faults to their marriage; if they heard their partner honestly and humbly admitting the same, they would be prepared to forgive. But it costs a lot in pride to be the first one to make the move, especially if (as mentioned above) there is a fear of rebuff. Friends – especially those who have remained friends of both partners – can talk to both individually and bring them together.

## 5. *Working out the practicalities*

Couples do get to the point of acknowledging their faults to each other and of seeking genuinely to forgive. But where do they go from there? It cannot be left at the general level: 'We want to start out again, to rebuild our marriage'. It must be worked out in practical details.

I talked recently with a man who had had a very detailed contract at work. His employers had insisted on its being carried out to the last letter and had constantly thrown it in his teeth, so that the contract had become a millstone round his neck. About the same time his wife left him, but after a time, largely because she could find no decent alternative accommodation, she moved back in. Nothing was properly discussed; nothing was resolved. The old rows continued. I urged the man to work out, in detail and in the presence of a third party, what each would expect of the other and how in practice they would seek to resolve their differences and rebuild their marriage. But his experience with his employer's contract had been so awful that he could not face sitting down and drawing up an agreed way forward.

His reaction was wholly understandable but mistaken; the marriage simply continued to deteriorate. Instead, it is vital for a couple to work out together how they are going to live, and this must be done from a position of mutual respect. Even though one partner may desire reconciliation more than the other, he must never say, whether in so many words or in effect: 'You can come back any time, under any conditions you like – no questions asked.' This will merely evoke disdain and will not prove any kind of foundation for a lasting relationship.

The partners will need to discuss as equals. As they do so, it will often be helpful to work together on specific and concrete goals. Richmond suggests that each partner separately makes a list of ten goals for the marriage. These should take the form 'That we should . . .', not 'That you should . . .'. They should then be shared with the other partner in the presence of a counsellor. The couple should then go away and combine their two lists into one set of ten priorities. This in itself will unify their vision for their marriage and help them to work together (pp.180–2).

Normally it will be best to work out the practical details in the presence of a third party: a Christian couple or friend whose wisdom both partners respect or a clergyman or professional counsellor. One role of this third party can often be to set the couple an assignment which they can agree upon and which can be talked about and evaluated next time they all meet together. One such assignment might be: make a list of specific ways

you could express your love to your partner. Choose one of
this list in particular and ask God to show you ways in which
you could particularly work on that and express your love to
your partner in that area (cf Chapman, *Hope*, p.69). At the
next meeting with the third party, you would share what you
had written and what success you had had in putting your
best intentions into practice. In this way, despite continuing
difficulties, progress can be seen to be made.

## 6.  *Being patient*

Yet progress will be variable; reconciliation is rarely one smooth,
continuous success story. It will frequently be a case of two steps
forward, one step back. And sometimes it will seem more like
one step forward and two steps back. The marriage did not get
into trouble overnight, and it will not be the work of one day to
put it on a sure footing again. Trust will need to be rebuilt, and it
will be important for each partner to give the other the benefit of
the doubt. The temptation will always be there to be suspicious,
not to trust the other's word, to read deliberate hurtfulness into
the other's words or actions. These temptations must be resisted
if genuine progress is to be made.

It may be, as a couple move towards reconciliation, that one
partner seems to be saying quite contradictory things from day
to day. It is unlikely that this is because he is lying. Rather, he is
expressing the confusion, the conflicting thoughts and emotions,
within himself: one moment wanting to get back together, the
next remembering all the hurt and not even wanting to consider
reunion, the next attracted by another woman. This again calls
for great patience in the other partner. Tertullian wrote:

> On a disjunction of wedlock – for that cause, I mean, which
> makes it lawful, whether for husband or wife, to persist in
> the perpetual observance of widowhood [i.e. in the case of
> divorce for adultery; note that there is to be no remarriage]
> – [Patience] waits for, she yearns for, she persuades by her
> entreaties, repentance in all who are one day to enter sal-
> vation. How great a blessing she confers on each! The one
> [the partner who has not committed adultery] she prevents

from becoming an adulterer [by remarriage]; the other [the adulterer] she amends (*De Patientia*, 12).

It is not only our partner with whom we will have to be patient; it is with ourselves also. Old bitternesses, which we thought we had discarded, will resurface. When our partner shares his feelings honestly, we will find it hard not to leap to our own defence and get back into a cycle of accusations. We will have to ask for God's forgiveness and for fresh power again and again. But gradually we will see progress, especially if we measure it not from day to day, or even week to week, but from month to month.

All this will mean that it will not necessarily be right to move back together again immediately. I recently met a clergy couple in which the husband had been repeatedly unfaithful. The couple were seeking reconciliation but the wife did not feel able to move back permanently until a real measure of trust had been built up. Meanwhile, they were continuing to see each other regularly for visits and weekends, and hoping that full reunion would soon be possible.

It will also mean that it may be unwise to tell the children too early that reconciliation may be possible. Most children long for their parents to reunite, even years after a divorce has gone through and often even after there has been a remarriage. They are likely, therefore, to be overjoyed at the prospect of 'Dad moving back with us' and may put enormous, and unwanted, pressure on their parents to speed the process up. Their disappointment is correspondingly enormous if reunion does not work out. One family with whom I am in correspondence was deeply fractured because the teenage daughter was told too early – when discussions between her parents had scarcely begun – and was very angry with her Dad (with whom she was living) when things did not work out.

A friend or counsellor will normally have helped a couple to get back together. It is vital for the reunited partners to keep seeing this same person, or couple, after they have moved back together. There is a great temptation for friends, in their joy, to think: 'It's all now solved.' But normally there will be continuing problems and a long period of adjustment until the marriage is on a really sound footing. To 'fail again' would be devastating. It is therefore very important to keep meeting to talk, probably in the presence of the same third party. Genuine progress will be seen as these meetings can have longer and longer intervals between them.

## Conclusion

It is perfectly apparent, from all that has been said in this chapter, that reconciliations rarely come easily. Normally they need an enormous investment of time and effort, of prayer and emotional energy, not only from the couple themselves but from their friends and from the Christian Church. Can all this expenditure of time and energy be justified?

Surely the answer must be: yes. First and foremost *because it is God's will*. God has said unequivocally: 'I hate divorce' (Mal. 2:16). This does not at all mean that he hates divorcees, so that they are permanently under his displeasure; but it does mean that he hates divorce itself and will put all his resources at the disposal of those who are seeking to avoid a separation/divorce. Moreover, it is not merely true that he hates the break-up of families. It is his delight to see families reunited. Indeed, he sends his servants precisely to bring about family reconciliation (cf Mal. 4:5f). We can therefore be certain that we are at the centre of God's will as we seek reconciliation with our partner or seek to help a couple be reconciled.

Then also all the necessary effort is well justified *because of the hurt involved* in separation/divorce. Hurt is there for everyone connected with the marriage, and in the first instance *for the couple* themselves. That hurt is, literally, incalculable. Many who separate think they have calculated how much pain there will be for themselves and their partner, and are completely taken aback when the suffering proves to be so much greater. Bellah states what his research reveals as the normal and accepted attitude towards marriage in America today, underlying most people's behaviour if not openly acknowledged: 'A relationship should give each partner what he or she needs while it lasts, and if the relationship ends, at least both partners will have received a reasonable return on their investment' (p.108). It is extraordinary that such a coolly calculating attitude to marriage and marriage breakdown should persist, when almost all experience shrieks that it is not so. One example must suffice:

> I couldn't concentrate on anything for very long and was ultrasensitive to criticism . . . Because of my increasing depression, I became isolated and withdrawn. I found it difficult to be part of all the usual activities that I had previously enjoyed . . . None of these aftereffects were things I had ever considered when thinking about a break-up . . . I had foolishly imagined that life would be much the same as before, with the difference that Chris wouldn't be there and thus harmony would be restored.

The hurt normally goes on, also, for much longer than the couple anticipated. The group of divorcees who met and discussed their experiences to give me further help with this book found that thinking again about their marriages was a very helpful experience but painful. Two people whom I invited felt unable to accept. In both cases they had been remarried, happily, for many years. One wrote:

> Colin's [his son's] wedding [recently] was a very emotional time for me . . . Their wedding brought back so many memories. When I came to see you at the Vicarage you said: 'Divorce doesn't go away; it's always there' and it is true. The hurt, although dulled, can be reawakened at any time . . . I know I would probably benefit from joining other Christians but I also know that it would be too painful for me. It is not something that is over that I could discuss with others.

Any effort at reconciliation is also very worthwhile *because of the hurt for those who are close to a separated couple*: their parents and grandparents, brothers and sisters, friends and especially their children. So often the partners are asked: 'How are the children doing?' and often the reply is: 'Remarkably well, considering.' Some children of course do cope well, but we should always reckon with the fact that the parents want desperately to believe that their children are not adversely affected by their separation and so tend to play down – at least to others, they may feel worried and guilty themselves – any signs of disturbance. Moreover, one of the principal conclusions of Wallerstein's long-term study of the effect of divorce on children is that: 'One cannot predict long-term effects of divorce on children from how they react at the outset.' It is true that some who react badly initially may adjust well later on, but also 'some of the least troubled, seemingly content and calmest children [initially] were in poor shape ten and fifteen years later' (p.44).

Once again every attempt at reconciliation is justified *because of the hurt caused to society* by separation/divorce. It has been said again and again that the family is the basic building block of society. Every permanent separation undermines society, and every reconciliation makes our society stronger.

As I have continued this research, I have been struck by the number of those who are not only remarried but happily remarried who nevertheless still feel wistful about their first marriage: 'If only we'd had more help . . .'. It is worth an enormous sacrifice of time and effort to give that help. Green's conclusion from her own research is: 'In spite of the fears and forebodings, in spite of a double portion of failure and rejection [for those for whom reunion proved impossible], I met no one who regretted making a second attempt at their marriage. If nothing else, they felt they had not given up without an effort' (p.63). That in itself is worthwhile. And how much more rewarding when a couple get back together again and, because of the help of God, their own efforts and the encouragement of their friends, build a new and stable marriage.

# 12

# Bearing Witness

The Church is not to be moulded and remade by the world in its own image. This is precisely St Paul's point at the famous start of a new section in the Epistle to the Romans: 'Therefore, I urge you, brothers, in view of God's mercy, to offer your bodies as living sacrifices, holy and pleasing to God – this is your spiritual act of worship. Do not conform any longer to the pattern of this world, but be transformed by the renewing of your mind. Then you will be able to test and approve what God's will is – his good, pleasing and perfect will' (Rom. 12:1f). Yet sadly the Church has in fact 'conformed' to the world in this century, in the sexual and marital sphere; or more precisely, limped along behind the world. If liberal secular thought has accepted pre-marital sex and even advocated it, many in the Church – both among its leaders and among its ordinary members – have at least become resigned to it, and perhaps been prepared to argue for it, a decade or so later. If secular thinkers have long since abandoned any opposition to remarriage, the Church also has forgotten why it ever opposed it (and officially within some Churches, for example the Church of England, continues to oppose it) and Christians tend to offer congratulations, like anyone else, and genuinely to rejoice, when a divorcee announces his engagement.

But instead, the Church's calling is to mould and remake the world, to help the world listen to the teaching of Christ, to encourage the world to obey Christ. The striking fact is that the Church has achieved this before now, precisely in the area of sexual and marital morals. The Church of the first centuries brought about a sexual and marital revolution within the society of its day. To admire that courage, to marvel at that achievement, to aspire to emulate that influence is not to justify everything that was taught in the early Church – of course it had its extremes, both in teaching and in practice – but it is to point out the extraordinary power of Christian ideas and moral standards, and the transformation of society they can bring about. If it can be argued that these were new ideas bursting on the Graeco-Roman world and that Christian teaching could not have the same effect on societies that have been exposed to the New Testament already, we must answer that our own society is almost entirely ignorant of Christian teaching about marriage and singleness, and that if it were forcefully and persuasively presented, it would explode like a bombshell on Western society today and could have the same transforming effect. Already we see this to be the case in many individual lives, the lives of people who have been brought up with teaching on marriage and sex that has almost nothing in common with Christianity and have lived according to this non-Christian teaching.

So the Church is to bear witness to God's standards, to Christ's teaching. It is not a comfortable calling. Jeremiah, in the Old Testament, was taken aback by the ferocity of the antagonism to him and complained bitterly to God, though in fact God had warned him what would happen (e.g. Jer. 15:10–18; 1:17–19, cf 15:19–21). Christ also warned his followers:

> If the world hates you, keep in mind that it hated me first. If you belonged to the world, it would love you as its own. As it is, you do not belong to the world, but I have chosen you out of the world. That is why the world hates you. Remember the words I spoke to you: 'No servant is greater than his master.' If they persecuted me, they will persecute you also. If they obeyed my teaching, they will obey yours also. They will treat you this way because of my name, for they do not know the One who sent me (John 15:18–21).

So we can expect opposition, but we can also expect God's help. God is also concerned with the transformation of society, with people thinking and living righteously (Matt. 6:10), so that we can expect to meet with (perhaps hard-won) success as well.

But whether we succeed or not in changing our society – and of course our record will be mixed – our prime responsibility is faithfulness to God. It is extraordinary how, even from within the churches, pragmatic arguments are used to deflect us from this faithfulness. I remember in the United States being part of a clergy discussion on baptism policy. I was arguing for a somewhat more thoughtful policy than indiscriminate baptism for all who asked. No one put forward any biblical or theological argument against this; the only counter-argument was: 'We could never change. We would lose a few key families and the giving would go down.' Sadly, precisely the same argument is used against any stand over divorce and remarriage, in Britain just as much as the United States.

A more attractive argument, which I have also heard often on both sides of the Atlantic, is that any refusal of remarriage, or teaching against it, would make it harder to evangelise; divorcees, who are a growing percentage of the population, would simply stay away. This is an unfortunate way of speaking; it presents Christ's teaching in purely negative terms ('refusal of remarriage', 'teaching against remarriage') and we have of course to labour hard (see chapter 9) so that the teaching of Christ is not perceived as negative (which it is not) but as positive: that God joins a man and his wife together for life, that they become inextricably one flesh, that God gives them the resources to maintain even a very difficult marriage. But Christ's teaching has always been thought hard; it has always lost him adherents (John 6:60, 66). This cannot be a reason for toning down, or keeping silent about, Christ's teaching about marriage (cf 1 Cor. 1:18–25).

Faithfulness to God in this area is also pilloried, by some Christians, as being against the spirit of the age. It is 'fundamentalist', 'outmoded', 'unaware of how society has changed', 'turning its back on the insights of contemporary psychology'. Of course it is true that Christ's teaching can be presented in an obscurantist and utterly unpersuasive way. But since when was it the Church's calling to cut its moral cloth so that it fitted the desires and attitudes of the age? There is much in Scripture which says precisely the opposite (e.g. Eph. 4:14f; 2 Tim. 4:1–4).

But perhaps the single factor, more than any other, which keeps ministers quiet is that 'my church will not agree'. It is bad enough having members of the wider community speaking behind one's back about one's 'harshness' and 'insensitivity'; it is worse when members of one's own Church Family are saying the same. I can sympathise very much with that feeling; in both the churches of which I have been Senior Pastor there have been some in the church who have been opposed, and outspoken in their opposition, to what I have sought to show is the New Testament's teaching on singleness, marriage, divorce and remarriage. Yet it has also been my experience that, where the teaching stems from an exposition of Scripture and is consistently carried through in church practice, one is met with much more respect and, for the most part, agreement than opposition. But even if that were not the case – as it was not for Jeremiah – still it would be right to remain faithful to God and to bear witness to the teaching of Christ.

But how can a church bear witness? By example and teaching. Both are necessary. Teaching without example is hollow. If a church teaches about the lifelong nature of marriage, but its members are divorcing in large numbers and its leadership is doing nothing to help marriages in difficulty nor to discipline those who separate contrary to the will of Christ, then that church will have no impact on the attitudes to marriage of the society around it. And example without teaching is ineffective. If a church has a membership whose marriages are largely stable and yet never speaks of Christ's command to man and wife not to separate nor his power to sustain even difficult marriages, society will simply imagine that these Christians happen to have good marriages but will remain unaware that Christ's teaching is radically different from their own presuppositions. Teaching and example must therefore be kept together in every church's witness.

And to whom should a church bear witness? Both to its own members and to the outside world. As we have said earlier, many are coming into our churches, or have always been in our churches, who have accepted late twentieth-century Western attitudes to singleness and marriage without any questioning. They need to be helped radically to overhaul their own thinking and practice, and to bring it into line with the teaching of Christ. But our ambition should be greater than that. We also want to

468 DIVORCE AND REMARRIAGE

influence, and commend Christ's teaching to, the wider world. It is one of the limitations of this book that it is addressed to a Christian audience; my prayer is that others will write books on these subjects for the secular market, to persuade the world of the rightness of Christ's teaching. Similarly, a church should not be content to teach its own members a Christian view of marriage, divorce and remarriage. Through its Sunday schools, its marriage preparation and simply as Christians rub shoulders with non-Christians, it should be seeking to win over society to obedience to Christ, in thought first and then in action.

But what exactly are we wanting to say and live out? What are we bearing witness to?

## 1. *To the happiness of the single life*

The New Testament, as we have seen, has a very high view of the single life. One of the many ways in which it describes singleness is *makarios* (1 Cor. 7:40) which means either blessed or happy 'usually in the sense: privileged recipient of divine favour' (Arndt and Gingrich). This is a truth which contemporary Christians are remarkably slow to assert. The assumption is so widespread within the Church that singleness is a worse and more unhappy state to be in (cf 1 Cor. 7:38, 40), so that single people themselves have been deeply influenced by this attitude, have often accepted it entirely and missed the opportunities and richness that the single life can bring. How refreshing, by contrast, to receive this letter from a woman recently: 'I am 30 this March and firmly entrenched on the shelf, but the wonderful thing is that it's quite nice up here and not at all the miserable place that I was led to believe. It's lovely to have the freedom to do this [Social Work] course in Cardiff, and I am going to Malaysia in the summer, before I get started. This, as you may remember, has been a very long-standing ambition.'

The fact is that often the role models in our churches are single. We admire them, speak very highly of them, yet do not seem to have noticed the connection between their singleness and the qualities and dedicated service which we admire. Yet these qualities are precisely what the New Testament leads us to expect in the single man or woman of God. Therefore, in both our public Christian teaching and in our private conversation, we need to point out these connections which, once we have thought about them, are often very plainly present.

St Paul speaks about a strong connection between singleness and closeness to Christ – at least for those who make wise use of the advantages of singleness (1 Cor. 7:32–35). This is precisely what I see in practice. If I think of those in my own congregation whose lives are most conspicuously holy, and who give a great deal of their time to prayer, my mind goes immediately to two single women. If I were to ask the congregation whom they admired most as Christians, I am convinced that these two women would come at, or near, the top of the list. This is precisely what 1 Corinthians leads us to expect, and we must draw people's attention to the connection between their closeness to the Lord and their singleness.

Jesus for his part speaks of a connection between singleness and service for God (Matt. 19:12, cf 1 Tim. 5:3–15). Again I see exactly this in practice. I think of two young men who have led our large teenage group. Of course they may get married; one of them indeed has married recently and moved away. But undoubtedly they have been able to put far more time and energy into this vital work of leading young people to Christian faith and building them up precisely because they have been single. Or again I think of an older woman who has devoted herself unstintingly to making happy the life of some aged friends as well as relatives and caring for them, in her own home, until their death. What she has done would have been quite impossible if she were married. But again these connections, though real, are so often missed – even, sometimes, by the individuals themselves – and need to be pointed out.

Frequently Christians' reactions and attitudes are precisely the opposite. A church in our town has recently lost their minister after many years; he was single. When the name of the man to replace him was known, almost the only question I was ever asked, and I was asked it repeatedly, was: 'Is he married?' And always, when it was discovered that he is: 'Oh good! It's so much better that way.' I often think wryly that St Paul and Jesus himself would have been turned down by many churches.

But what blindness! Of course it is true that some avenues of ministry are more difficult for the single, but often their service is richer and more self-giving than the married person's. Margaret Evening tells of how one day she was reading *The Dean's Watch*, a novel by Elizabeth Goudge. In the story, a cripple gradually realises that a good job and marriage are not likely to be possible for her. Evening read: 'With no prospects of a career and marriage, it seemed that she was doomed to lifelong boredom. But then in a moment of awakening, it dawned upon her that *loving* could be a vocation in itself, a life work. It could be a career, like marriage, or nursing or going on stage . . . Quietly, she accepted the vocation and took a vow to love.' Reading this was for Evening, herself single, 'a sudden moment of clarity . . . I knew God was placing on me a vocation for life', and she began immediately to fulfil her vocation by inviting a lonely person round for the weekend (pp.200f).

It is often said that St Paul (and Jesus) were men and did not understand the needs of women. In particular, there is in most women a God-given and strong desire to have children. Evening certainly points out how single people can develop special relationships with the children of brothers and sisters, or of friends. But she also says that there is enormous richness in having spiritual children with whom single people, precisely because they do not have any physical children of their own, can often develop a particularly intimate and mutually satisfying relationship. Paul uses maternal language of his relationship with his children in the Lord: 'My dear children, for whom I am again in the pains of childbirth until Christ is formed in you' (Gal. 4:19). 'As apostles of Christ we could have been a burden to you, but we were gentle among you, like a [nursing] mother caring for her little children' (1 Thess. 2:7). And Evening quotes Max Thurian who says that the single Christian 'will find the fulfilment of the hundredfold promise made by Christ (Mark 10:29f and parallels [note the mention of children]). He [or she] experiences a spiritual fatherhood [/motherhood] of those who freely confide in him [/her]' (Evening pp.118f, quoting Thurian: *Marriage and Celibacy* p.108).

For the Church to bear witness, in its public teaching and everyday conversation and in the example of its contented single members, to the happiness and blessedness of the single life, can be an enormous encouragement and help to many. In the first place, it is an encouragement to the single themselves. Recently I visited a man in his seventies. He served for most of his life as a missionary in Japan; he is an exemplary man of God whom his whole church looks up to. Somehow the conversation came round to marriage and he said wistfully: 'I know there is no marriage in heaven but I am hoping there may be a woman with whom I will have a special relationship.' This saddened and angered me. I was angry because I felt that we, his fellow Christians, have stirred up this feeling in such a good, and otherwise contented, old man. We have so trumpeted the virtues of marriage and so denigrated singleness (often implicitly, by our attitudes and remarks) that he has imbibed a negative attitude towards his own singleness, even though it has quite manifestly led him closer to Christ and opened for him very fruitful service. How different was the attitude to singleness of the Church in the first centuries; then men and women were taught to be proud of a single life devoted to God. And what a service we could do to such people by discovering and again proclaiming the tremendously positive teaching in the New Testament about the single life.

This could, if anything, bring still greater encouragement to those who remain single after divorce. Not all divorcees by any means remarry. In particular, the older you are when you divorce, the less likely you are to remarry. In Wallerstein's study, half of the men over forty at the time of separation, and all of the women in the same age bracket, had not remarried ten years later. Wallerstein quotes a 1985 US Census Bureau survey which shows that 65% of all women who have divorced once (statistics are different for those divorcing a second time) remarried. Of these women almost half (48%) remarried in their twenties, but only 3% remarried in their fifties (pp.73, 80). So, a substantial minority of men, and a larger number of women, do not marry after divorce. And if they are to follow the teaching of Christ, they should not remarry, at least during the lifetime of their partner.

Yet the Church, far from supporting them in this (admittedly, for many, difficult) decision, frequently makes it harder for them. Divorcees often already feel that they are failures because of the breakdown of their marriage. Society then pities them for their singleness and perhaps (unwittingly) makes them feel a failure again because of their inability to form a second marriage. And the Church, because of its great emphasis on marriage and its almost total silence on the obedience of remaining single after divorce or the blessedness of the single life, merely reinforces this sense of inadequacy and failure. By contrast, if the Church were to show – both by clear teaching and equally clear example – that the single life can be one of great contentment in which it is possible to develop a special closeness to God and ways of service which are not always open to the married; if, in other words, the Church could affirm and honour, rather than merely pitying, the single divorcee, this would be a tremendous encouragement to those struggling to find a new identity.

Bearing witness to the happiness of the single life can also be an encouragement and help to the young. After a certain (increasingly young) age, everything conspires to pair young people off. There is *kudos* among one's peers in having a boyfriend or girlfriend, and boys and girls will frequently boast of their romantic and sexual involvement, exaggerating much of their experience in order to gain respect. Parents will often encourage their children to take a romantic interest in the opposite sex. Christian youth groups also, if only by their off-the-cuff comments and humour, positively encourage boyfriend-girlfriend relationships.

Some of this of course is perfectly healthy. It is part of maturing to learn to relate to the opposite sex. Yet a quite inordinate amount of time and energy is often devoted to thinking about, hankering after, seeking to win and going out with another teenager (or, nowadays, pre-teen). Some of this energy could fruitfully be channelled in other directions, especially in going deeper with Christ and serving him. Moreover, many teenagers who are – for whatever reason – unable to form an exclusive relationship with the opposite sex feel misfits, failures, abnormal. Something must be wrong with them.

Much of this energy would be redirected, and much of the agonised self-doubt allayed, if the Church, and especially leaders within Christian youth groups, were showing – by example and teaching – that it is very possible to be happy and single, and that there are great advantages in not being exclusively 'attached', whether this freedom lasts for a few more years only or for a lifetime. The boy or girl without a partner is not missing out on the most important thing in life, but is freer to develop what really is the most significant relationship: with Christ. Of course he must be gently encouraged to mix with, and form friends with, members of the opposite sex, but if he reaches his twenties or thirties without having had an exclusive boyfriend or girlfriend, this does not in any way make him an inadequate person. On the contrary, he should see it as an opportunity, given him by God, to make Christ the one he is devoted to and Christ the one he longs to please. Moreover, as he looks to the longer term, a lifelong single life is a very viable option which he can contemplate not only with equanimity but with the same kind of eager anticipation as a married person: he anticipates getting to know Christ more deeply (and more wholeheartedly than is possible for the married) just as the married person anticipates getting to know his partner more deeply.

I have known Christian youth groups where the whole ethos is one of pairing off; I have also known such groups where the emphasis is on natural befriending across the sexes without necessarily forming exclusive attachments and indeed where such exclusive relationships are, if anything, gently discouraged. I have known Christian groups for those in their twenties which are openly referred to, and thought of, as marriage bureaux, and others where the whole emphasis has been on growing as Christians. There is no doubt in my mind which group is more healthy (providing that our sexuality is openly acknowledged and, when appropriate, discussed) and is more true to the teaching of the New Testament.

And this points to the last reason for wanting to bear witness to the happiness of the single life: because it is the truth, according to the New Testament. It is a much neglected area of New Testament teaching, and a much neglected fact of Christian experience, but for those who are taught it and then 'accept' it (cf Matt. 19:11f), it becomes a very wonderful reality. By teaching this truth, and living it out, Christians will help many people to appreciate the 'gift' God has given them (Matt. 19:11; 1 Cor. 7:7) and to make the very most of it.

## 2. To the Christlikeness of forgiving and working through difficulties

Not so long ago we preached a series of sermons on forgiveness at our church. This series, together with that on marriage (see chapter 9), has undoubtedly had the most impact on the church in the last 18 months. We first preached five sermons on different aspects of God's forgiveness, before looking at a further six aspects of our need to forgive each other. This is the New Testament teaching: we are to forgive because God has forgiven us: 'Bear with each other and forgive whatever grievances you may have against one another. Forgive as the Lord forgave you' (Col. 3:13). 'Do not grieve the Holy Spirit of God, with whom you were sealed for the day of redemption. Get rid of all bitterness, rage and anger, brawling and slander, along with every form of malice. Be kind and compassionate to one another, forgiving each other, just as in Christ God forgave you' (Eph. 4:30–32).

It is Godlike to forgive. When we forgive, we are acting as God acts habitually towards us, and particularly as he acted in the death of Christ. Indeed, because God has forgiven us, it is our inescapable responsibility to forgive others who have hurt us (Matt. 18:21–35).

This duty to forgive extends of course to all who have wronged us. But it is especially necessary within a marriage; it may be significant that in Matthew's gospel the discussion of divorce comes immediately after Jesus' strongest teaching about the need to forgive (Matt. 18:21–19:12). But it is the very opposite of the action often urged by friends on those whose marriage partners are treating them unreasonably: 'Stick up for your rights', 'Get your own back', 'Give her a taste of her own medicine', 'Refuse to have sex with him', etc. This kind of response rarely has the effect of bringing the partner back to his responsibilities and normally turns the marriage still more sour. Margaret Havard, faced with a deeply hurtful coldness and hardness from her husband, was tempted to act in precisely this way, but saw that, at least for many months, 'the giving had to come from me . . . [I had to] get my priorities into perspective. What did I want most of all – my marriage or my feeling of self-righteousness?' (pp.53f).

But this response of giving and forgiving is not only the way (normally) to provide one's marriage with a chance of being saved and healed. It is specifically to act like Christ. Many teach, or imply, that if one marriage partner fails signally in his marital duty, the other is free not to carry out her responsibility; thus, if a husband does not sacrificially love his wife, she is under no obligation to submit to him (cf Eph. 5:22–33). But in fact Christlikeness consists precisely in receiving unjust treatment and not retaliating, in going on loving and serving even when one meets only with hostility.

Thus 1 Peter 3:1–7 describes how husbands and wives are to relate to one another: wives are to be submissive to their husbands, just as much if the husband is not a Christian (1) as if he is a man of God (5f); and husbands are to 'be considerate as you live with your wives' (literally: 'live together in accordance with [Christian] knowledge' (Arndt and Gingrich)) and 'treat them with respect'. These verses come in a longer section which speaks of the Christian duties of citizens towards the authorities (2:13–17), slaves towards their masters (2:18–25), and wives and husbands to each other (3:1–7, cf Eph. 5:21–6:9; Col. 3:18–4:1). In the longest of these sections, the question is specifically raised: what should a slave do whose master clearly defaults in his responsibility and treats him unjustly? The answer is that the Christian should continue to fulfil his side of the relationship even when the other party is manifestly failing in his duty (1 Pet. 2:18). Significantly, the second half of this section is devoted entirely to the example of Christ who himself was treated with gross injustice yet refused to retaliate and instead carried on doing God's will and sacrificed his life to bring healing – specifically healing to those who had 'gone astray' from him (2:21–25).

The implications are clear. First, the Christian wife or husband also (3:1–7), if (s)he is let down by her marriage partner, must go on loving him and working to maintain the marriage. His unjust and even harsh treatment gives her no grounds for shirking her own responsibilities within the marriage. Second – and this is especially clear when the whole context of 1 Peter is taken into account – the Christian is called upon to suffer as part of his obedience to Christ (cf 1:6f, 10f; 2:11f, 18–25; 3:9, 13–18; 4:1–6, 12–19; 5:1, 8–11). So often, perhaps particularly in the United States, men and women leave a marriage because they believe they have a right to be happy, and separation with a view to a new relationship is seen as their chance of happiness. Richmond quotes a woman who left her husband with, at that stage, no new partner in view, saying: 'I have another chance to be happy and I'm just not going to miss it.' The frequent attitude is: 'My happiness is more important than your happiness, or the children's happiness or anybody's happiness' (pp. 29, 117).

All too frequently this happiness proves quite illusory and in fact the separation merely brings different, and often deeper, unhappiness to all concerned, even to the one who has decided to separate. But in any case the Christian is *not* called to be happy. He is called to experience life in all its fullness (John 10:10) and to have inexpressible joy in the midst of suffering (1 Pet. 1:3–9), but this life and joy stem specifically from obedience to Christ. The pursuit of happiness for its own sake was never part of the Christian's calling.

All marriages bring some suffering; some marriages bring a terrible amount of suffering. But as Christians we are called to accept suffering for Christ's sake and with the help of Christ. That suffering involves not only stoically putting up with a very difficult marriage, but continually seeking to understand my partner, to forgive him and to act in sacrificial love towards him.

Yet there can be no complete forgiveness without repentance. We can offer our forgiveness, but it cannot be fully appropriated or do its healing work unless the other party is sorry for the hurt he has caused. And there can be no real progress in the marriage without both parties working together to build a new relationship.

Obviously both partners may not be willing to participate in this healing process. Yet the willing Christian partner, and the Church Family as a whole, should refuse to work towards anything less than the rebuilding of the marriage. Many partners try for a time and then give up all hope or effort. Many friends encourage reconciliation for a time and then give in to what they see as the inevitable. And indeed it may be true that some other route – separation, divorce or just retreating into one's own self-contained world – presents itself as easier and quicker. But only continued loving and forgiving, only continued suffering and seeking to work through the difficulties, is walking the way of Christ.

This may mean hanging on for a long time before we see any change. It may mean months or years of difficulty and almost constant pain. But it does not mean putting off the start, or the starting again, of praying and working for change. Yet whom are we trying to change? If our principal desire is to change our partner, it is probable that we will not get far towards reconciliation. I must pray that God will show me where I must change, I must put my energy into becoming myself a more considerate marriage partner, if our marriage is to stand any chance of being rebuilt.

It is to this Christlike work of forgiving and refusing to give up on a marriage that the Church must bear witness, and marriages that have been through these fires and come out securely on the other side should be much more spoken about in sermons, in books, in public testimony. The truth is that while many Christian marriages have got into very serious difficulties which have perhaps never been repaired (with God's help and our willing obedience they are not irreparable), many more have been through equally serious problems and emerged the stronger. Far from keeping these experiences to ourselves, we should humbly and honestly share them, as they will be a great encouragement and practical help to others, Christian and non-Christian, struggling with similar difficulties.

## 3.   To the lifelong nature of marriage

Not only do many marriages not hold together today, increasingly people are repudiating the whole idea of lifelong marriage. They do not expect marriages to last, either other people's or their own, and a growing number are not even too concerned (in advance; the experience itself is often quite different and much more painful) whether their marriage does last or not.

Bellah's research concludes that the normative approach to marriage in the USA today is what he calls 'the therapeutic

attitude'. We have already quoted his description of it: 'A relationship should give each partner what he or she needs while
it lasts, and if the relationship ends, at least both partners will
have received a reasonable return on their investment' (p.108).
So Jody Foster can say: 'I do think about [marriage] . . . I'm
sure I will [get married]. I'm sure I'll get divorced too. Why not?
You've got to do it once. Everyone seems to' (*Parade* magazine
11 December, 1983, quoted in Yates p.157). In the USA a 1990
survey of *Wedding and Home* readers revealed that nearly 40% of
engaged couples accepted that their marriage would not last.

The same attitude can be found even amongst those who
are content in their marriage. Bellah cites Ted Oster who has
been married more than ten years and intends to maintain
his marriage. Why? Because 'he has found the best possible
partner, the one who will bring him the most happiness. He
is unsure whether he has any obligation to his marriage, or
stays married only because he continues to prefer his wife to
available alternatives' (p.104).

Yet lifelong marriage is what (almost) every couple promises
at their marriage, and it is rightly what both Church and State
normally insist on. This is part of what marriage, as created by
God, is.

> Notwithstanding the custom in some American churches of
> allowing the couple to write their own vows, there can be no
> individually-drafted form of marriage contract, no special
> stipulations about what they will and will not agree to. One
> of the things meant by the claim that marriage is a divine insti-
> tution is that God . . . has made the terms what they are. And
> what they are, effectively, is not terms at all but unconditional
> self-offering (O'Donovan: *Marriage and the Family* p.96).

Marriage partners 'do not have the choice *what* [marriage is],
but they do have the choice *whether*, and they do have the choice
*whom*' (O'Donovan: *Marriage and Permanence*, p.5).

And it is not simply that the partners solemnly *vow* that their
marriage will last until death them do part. Their marriage will
in fact last that long. God is not mistaken; and what he sees, is
the truth about a situation. In his eyes lifelong marriage is not

just an ideal which some of us are not able to live up to. It is of the nature of marriage that it lasts for life, that only death can destroy it. 'God himself is also at work in the act of creating community in that he causes man and woman to become one flesh.' That is why 'the marriage contract is simply not subject to recall – even by consent of both partners – and that [unlike almost every other contract] it contains no conditions on the basis of which it could be terminated' (Thielicke p.175). There is in fact one condition, and that is explicitly stipulated: death.

Bearing witness to the lifelong nature of marriage must mean refusing remarriage in church. It is very important that we give the reason for this decision. We know it will be unpopular, especially when the people asking the question are an engaged couple, at least one of whom is divorced. And therefore we tend to deflect criticism from ourselves elsewhere: 'I'm so sorry. It's the policy of this diocese . . . My bishop won't allow it . . . We can't remarry in the Church of England.' These are not the main reasons at all. If we are to deflect criticism from ourselves, let us deflect it on to Christ. We should make it absolutely clear that it is because of what Christ taught about marriage that, in obedience to him, we are not able to perform the wedding ceremony or allow our church to be used for this purpose by another minister.

Nor should the message come across in a purely negative way: 'We don't remarry people who have been divorced . . . Christ didn't allow remarriage where there has been a divorce.' This answer is incomprehensible to most people and it is no wonder they believe that divorce is being treated as a sin which cannot be forgiven.

Imagine the following conversation which must frequently take place:

'St Anne's won't marry Elizabeth and Richard.'

'Why?'

'Because Richard's divorced.'

That is not the reason at all. Richard's divorce has nothing whatsoever to do with the decision not to celebrate a second marriage for him. The only true answer is:

'Because Richard's married.'

Only this answer is true to Christ's teaching. And it shows

immediately that it has nothing at all to do with some sin which apparently cannot be forgiven. Marriage is not a sin; but it is an indissoluble bond. It is because of this bond that it is unthinkable to support Richard in his plans for a second marriage.

This teaching of Christ's – that marriage is lifelong – will need to be explained again and again. One of the most common objections to the Church's practice is that it is unjust. One man expressed the accusation in this way:

> In our modern society pre-marital sex is rife. Non-Christians (in particular [but not exclusively]) will often have all sorts of sexual relationships, some of them quite long lasting; none of them may be legalised as marriage. Why should people who . . . have such relationships be permitted . . . to get married, whereas someone who . . . tried to be 'moral' and got married, but whose marriage broke up, [is] prohibited from marrying again? . . . It is almost as though promiscuity paid, if the utterly immoral can legally take a new sexual partner with the church's blessing . . . Whereas the once-divorced [person] is told: 'You must remain single for the rest of your life', because . . . you made a public commitment instead of just cohabiting.

There is a lot of force to this argument. At first sight it does seem unfair that marriage should not be a possibility for the person who 'tried to be moral' while no objection is raised to the marriage of the sexually promiscuous. It does seem as if divorce is being treated as a more heinous sin than promiscuity, and this seems even more unjust when the divorcee wanting to remarry is the one who was abandoned and who fought to keep the marriage going.

But to reason like this is to show a misunderstanding of the teaching of Christ. On the one hand, of course promiscuity does not pay. Promiscuity angers God and threatens to exclude those who practise it from the kingdom of God (Eph. 5:5f; 1 Cor. 6:9f). It scars and distorts lives. It is not because people are promiscuous that marriage is open to them, but because they have never married.

On the other hand, we need to stress again that it is not

because he is divorced that marriage is not an option for the divorcee (whether he deserted his partner or his partner deserted him, whether the divorce was morally justified or not) but because he is still married. Cohabitation is not marriage. In order to be married, a couple must, among other things, fulfil two criteria: they must promise that their relationship will be permanent and they must give their voluntary consent to be married now (not: to be married at some future date, which is engagement). Certainly the second criterion, and normally the first, is missing in cohabitees. They are not married (see chapter 1).

Those who are married, however, have entered into a lifelong union. They promised this solemnly at their marriage. And whether they realised it at the time or not, God joined them together as one flesh. This marriage lasts until death; legal divorce does not undo it. And it is for this reason rather than any other – it is because they are still married – that Christians are unable to support them in any second marriage.

So, as we explain the reasons for our lack of support for a second marriage, and specifically for refusing a church wedding, we need to say something like: 'Christ said that marriage is for life. That God joins a man and his wife together and only death can actually separate them. So people can't really get married again because they're married already.' That may be greeted with impatience or anger; it may, in some cases, make it harder to have further contact with that couple. But nothing less than this kind of explanation does justice to Christ's teaching and we are called to bear witness to his truth, whatever reception it and we are given.

And in fact more people than one imagines respect the position of a church that refuses remarriage. One man, not at the time a committed Christian, wrote to me: 'I felt disappointed that we couldn't have a church wedding because for me this was the real thing whereas my first marriage had been "bogus" in some way, but I knew somewhere deep down that the Church was right not to be willing to remarry us.' A woman wrote: 'I feel I wouldn't want to remarry in church. Despite what has happened, I still feel that my first marriage in church – when I *wasn't* a Christian – is sacred to me and I would not like a "repeat performance". I would feel uncomfortable.'

This last quotation of course assumes that a registry office wedding would not be so great a problem. There are however no biblical grounds for making any distinction between a wedding in a church and a wedding in a registry office. As we have seen, an Old Testament wedding might take place with a minimum of ceremony, of which nothing was very specifically religious (cf. Gen. 24:62–67). Therefore it is just as impossible for a Christian to encourage a divorcee to marry in a registry office as it is for him to suggest a wedding in church, and for precisely the same reason: the person concerned is still married.

If it is impossible for Christians to support plans for a re-marriage – whether by Church or State – after a divorce, then it cannot be right to offer a service of blessing after a civil wedding. Many clergy reach for this solution as it seems pas-torally constructive: it upholds the witness to (the original) marriage being lifelong and yet it offers God's blessing on a new beginning. But in fact it does no such thing. It denies the lifelong nature of marriage because it asks for God's blessing on a second marriage while the first partner is still alive, it winks at Christ's teaching that remarriage is adultery and it offers God's blessing on what Jesus has called a sin. The practice is widely perceived as at best awkward and at most hypocritical. Even non-Christians sometimes ask angrily: if you deny remarriage, how can you suggest a service of blessing?

The most recent example before me so clearly reveals the muddled thinking involved in services of blessing. A married man was severely crippled in a car accident ten years ago; his wife of thirty years' standing looked after him with help from a housekeeper. Then the wife, who had been having an affair for many years, left him for her lover, forcing him into a nursing home. She married the lover, and the vicar, knowing the full circumstances, agreed to a service of blessing. Speaking to the distressed daughter of the first marriage, he said that he would make sure the service 'should in no way be a "big do"'. He said that on the one hand he wanted to maintain Christian standards but on the other also to show God's forgiveness. How can it possibly be 'to maintain Christian standards' when offering God's blessing on an adulterous relationship with a callous disregard for the needs of the previous husband? How can it be a demonstration of 'God's forgiveness' when clearly there is no repentance for the original act and its continuing effects?

This may be a particularly clear example, but services of blessing are never appropriate where a remarriage cannot be justified. The Commission which produced the 1978 Church of England Report *Marriage and the Church's Task* was divided on the question of whether remarriage should be permitted in certain limited circumstances, but it was unanimous in condemning services of blessing: 'We are therefore of one mind in rejecting the suggestion of a public service of prayer and dedication. *We recommend that the present use of such services should be brought to an end*' (p.84. Their emphasis). The reason given is that, however much such a service is explained, the impression is given that this is a marriage service, especially where, in practice – the bride in white, the ringing of church bells, the use of the wedding march, etc. – or in wording, the service closely resembles the marriage service (as the 1985 Church of England Services of Prayer and Dedication after Civil Marriage do). 'It would be difficult for the Church to dispel the impression that it has begun to remarry all comers' (pp.82–4).

But there is a more profound reason for not holding services of blessing where there has been a divorce. What the couple have done (in getting married) denies the lifelong nature of their previous marriage. The Bishop of Chelmsford, writing in his diocesan magazine in September 1978, wrote: 'This [a service of blessing in church, but no remarriage] is logically and theologically absurd. But it is an absurdity that arises out of compassion and many find comfort in it as they start a new venture in marriage.' Of course he is right. The comfort stems from the fact that the Church (at least partly) *accepts* their marriage, which is what they want. But true compassion cannot be based on a 'theological absurdity', on a denial – in fact a direct contradiction – of Christ's teaching. Christian compassion is all about 'speaking the truth in love' (Eph. 4:15) and is not about pretending that Christ did not mean what he said, because we do not want to upset anybody.

But are those who deny a service of blessing also caught up in an inconsistency? Can it be right later on to pray for the healing of a second marriage that has run into difficulties or for the continued growth of a happy remarriage? We saw in chapter 10 that the new couple have entered into a marriage covenant. They should not have done so, but they have; and that covenant is now binding on them. They cannot repudiate it at will; they should not repudiate it, even if they subsequently realise it was a mistake (cf Eccles. 5:4–7). Therefore it is entirely right that Christians should pray for a second marriage that has run into difficulties to be sustained. But it cannot be right at the very beginning of the marriage for the Church to give its seal of approval (which is how it is inevitably seen) by offering a service of blessing. This must be withheld.

And a further way in which the Church bears witness to the lifelong nature of marriage is by disciplining its members who by their deliberate actions deny this vital Christian truth. Where a church member separates from, or divorces, his partner for no reason that the New Testament sanctions, or where a church member has gone ahead with a remarriage despite having Christ's teaching explained to him, there thoughtful disciplinary action, designed to lead the church member(s) to repentance, must be taken (see chapter 10). This gives a tremendously important message to both the church and the world: Christians take Christ's teaching on the indissolubility of marriage with the utmost seriousness, including his condemnation of divorce (except for adultery) and of remarriage. For a church to do nothing and carry on as if nothing had happened gives a totally different message. As one example: a churchgoing couple were friends with another couple where the husband went to church and the wife did not. The wife of the first couple left her husband and lived with – soon married – the husband of the second couple. No disciplinary action was taken by the church and within months the new couple had become leaders of the choir. What message does this give church and world about how seriously we take Christ's teaching on marriage: that God joins a couple together, that God makes them one flesh for life?

Every church bears witness to a view of the nature of marriage by its wedding policy and by its discipline (or lack of it). Our calling is to bear witness to the lifelong nature of marriage, as taught by Christ.

## 4. To the wrong of remarriage

It would be very pleasant if our message could be entirely positive: marriage is lifelong. But as the last section has clearly shown, if our message is to be consistent, it has to be negative as well. If marriage really is lifelong, then remarriage is not appropriate – or, more exactly, it is wrong – in the lifetime of a partner.

Whenever the New Testament speaks about remarriage, it does so, without exception, negatively. Undeniably Christ taught that remarriage is wrong under most circumstances. It is the argument of this book that he taught that remarriage was wrong under all circumstances during the lifetime of a partner. Therefore it is quite impossible for any church to announce as its policy: 'We remarry divorcees.' The basic stance must be 'We are not able to marry divorcees.'

This must be the case even where the view is taken (in our view, mistakenly) that Christ does allow remarriage after divorce-for-adultery. The Church of England Report *Marriage and the Church's Task* recognises this clearly. It does (though not unanimously) advocate remarriage in certain limited circumstances, but states: 'It must be clear that the occasions when remarriage in church occur are exceptional and determined by a consistent policy', and the first of its proposed Draft Regulations is: 'It is not normally the practice of the Church of England to solemnise the marriage of anyone who has been divorced and has a former partner still living' (pp.85, 163). Obviously those convinced that Christ forbade remarriage after divorce under all circumstances would have to make even this statement stronger still: It is never our practice to marry anyone whose original partner is still alive.

But what of those denominations where remarriage is allowed under certain circumstances and where a higher authority – often, a bishop – has to give permission in each case? What if the bishop, by virtue of belonging to the denomination, feels unable to refuse permission in all cases? He must be extremely careful as he decides whether to withhold, and especially whether to give, permission.

*Marriage and the Church's Task*, in its Draft Regulations, states that 'special permission [for remarriage] . . . may [only] be given when the incumbent can give *adequate assurances* to the bishop that', among other things, 'the divorced person shows evidence of insight into the causes of the breakdown of the previous marriage, acknowledges with penitence whatever responsibility may have been his for that breakdown, seeks the forgiveness of God and is forgiving himself, and intends to make new vows in confidence in God's promises of renewal' (p.163. My emphasis). Indeed, such written assurance is not deemed enough. 'The bishop shall . . . see the couple', or, if he delegates his responsibility to a panel of advisers, 'it would be usual for at least one of the advisers to meet the couple wishing to marry' (pp.164, 162).

One US Episcopal Diocese has similarly exacting 'Standards of Marriage Preparation for Divorced Persons'. 'Couples are to meet a minimum of five times . . . for premarital counseling . . . in addition to the meeting to discuss a wedding date and wedding plans.' Nine marriage-related topics are specifically required to be covered in these sessions. A full questionnaire is provided, asking searching questions about the original marriage and divorce, relations with the original partner and family, and the Christian faith of both prospective partners; this is to be both filled out and discussed in the preparation sessions. A great deal of space is left for the answers to these questions. The bishop then has to receive this questionnaire at least forty days before the proposed wedding, together with details from the incumbent of when the five counselling sessions took place and what topics were discussed and the reasons for the incumbent's believing that 'this marriage is soundly intended'. If the marriage is permitted and the wedding takes place, then 'the bishop must receive a report on the marriage during the second year of the marriage'.

Once one has allowed that remarriages may under certain circumstances be permitted (which we maintain that Christ's teaching does *not* allow), all this sounds admirably thorough. The sad fact is that in most cases the practice gets nowhere close to the theory. In the case of the American Diocese mentioned above, the bishop showed me a recent application which he particularly commended for its thoroughness, to show how well his system was working. It was quite clear that he had not looked carefully at the application at all. The incumbent had reported to him that the couple 'have worked very hard on dealing with Steve's previous marriage and divorce'; yet in his written answer to the question 'What circumstances led to the dissolution of the former marriage?' the prospective husband had shown very little awareness of any faults he may have contributed. He merely said that he was 'too immature' at the time of his first marriage, and in speaking of specific faults only mentioned those of his wife, none of his own. In answering the question: 'What continuing care and ongoing support have you been maintaining for your former spouse?', for which the questionnaire set aside a whole page to give the answer, the man simply wrote 'None' – with no further explanation.

The papers showed that discussions with the church about re-marriage had already begun by 20 March, the date on which the canonically required Declaration of Intent, in which the couple 'solemnly declare that we hold marriage to be a lifelong union', was signed by the couple. Yet the papers also made clear that the divorce did not come through until the same month, so that the couple were engaged only days after (perhaps even before?) Steve was legally divorced, and the church accepted this situation. *Marriage and the Church's Task*, by contrast, has a Draft Regulation: 'No application shall normally be considered within a year of the decree absolute being pronounced' (p.163).

Moreover, the application by the incumbent was sent on 10 September and initialled by the diocesan staff member granting permission on 19 September. Since the wedding was planned for 5 October, this made it extraordinarily difficult for the bishop to refuse permission, as obviously by then all the wedding preparations would be largely in place.

And this was an example that the bishop himself put forward as showing how well the system worked. This has happened all over the United States. It is exactly what *Marriage and the Church's Task* fears might happen in England. It states: 'No one has come forward in [giving] evidence to argue in favour of this [remarriage of *all* divorcees]' but warns: 'Whichever approach [of enquiry into the circumstances, past and present, of the proposed couple] were adopted, there would be a built-in tendency to avoid hard cases and relax standards, leading in the end to indiscriminate remarriage' (pp. 84, 95).

The Church of England is currently in a muddle over its position on the practice and theology of remarriage. At present, a degree of anarchy reigns in which, in many dioceses, each incumbent 'does what is right in his own eyes' (cf Judg. 21:25) without any guidance or restraint from higher authority. Sooner or later decisions are going to have to be taken and incorporated into canon law. It is my hope that the present official practice of the Church of England will be maintained and the teaching of Christ that marriage is dissoluble only by death will be affirmed. But if (in my view, mistakenly) some limited exceptions are made, it must be clear – in the Church's practice as well as in theory – that the Church's basic stance is that remarriage is wrong; that it is, in Christ's own assessment, adultery.

Once any exceptions are made, it is the practice which is so exceptionally difficult. Where the Church refuses all remarriages or services of blessing, the policy is clear and understandable, even when it is not agreed with. But once an enquiry has to be made into the circumstances of the original marriage and divorce, once a judgment has to be made on whether the divorcee has genuinely repented of his part in the marital breakdown, then it will be impossible to avoid a much greater sense of injustice and a sense, wherever permission is refused, that this is a negative verdict specifically on them, the new couple. This will lead to a much greater 'alienation from the Church' than the current refusal to all. The only alternative is 'in practice to grant every request' which is what no one in theory wants and what in practice happens where divorce discipline is relaxed (*Marriage and the Church's Task* pp.59f).

The Roman Catholic route round these difficulties has been greatly to extend the concept of nullity. In 1983 the Catholic Church issued a new Code of Laws, and Canon 1101.2 states: 'If either or both of the parties by a positive act of the will exclude marriage itself or any essential element of marriage, such party contracts invalidly.' Church courts, asked for a decision about whether an original marriage was in fact null, decide whether each partner has 'adequately considered and evaluated . . . marriage . . . with this particular person' and has freely chosen marriage and is capable of fulfilling this undertaking. With such wide criteria, it is perhaps not surprising that in the USA almost all marriages brought before the Catholic judicial authorities are annulled (Flood pp. 85, 83, 90f). The official Roman Catholic statistics for 1990 in Britain (excluding Northern Ireland) are: Sentences in favour of Nullity: 1,116; Sentences contrary to Nullity: 157 (678 cases were withdrawn).

These last figures alone should cast considerable doubt on the wisdom and justice of the Catholic canons. They can be stretched to include almost any case. Indeed, the very drafters of the 1983 Code stated: 'These essential elements [of marriage, which both parties must accept for a marriage to be valid and without which a marriage can be declared null] are yet to be decided by Church teaching and the reflections of Church judges' (Flood p.85).

Almost every other denomination has found the Catholic approach a most unsatisfactory solution. The Church of England Report *The Church and the Law of Nullity* stated: 'We are opposed to any extension [of nullity] which could leave the validity of a marriage dependent upon the private stipulations and mental reservations of the parties' (p.64); these are far too subjective and difficult to prove. 'It would appear that [if nullity were extended] people could never in this life be absolutely certain whether they were married or not. Uncertainty, also, whether their marriage was in law void, or merely voidable, would leave the legitimate status of their children seriously in question' (*Marriage, Divorce and the Church* p.64). Catholic judicial rulings about nullity rely heavily on the concept of psychological immaturity at the time of the original marriage; yet not only is there no agreement on what constitutes psychological maturity but also 'in a fundamental sense all of us are engaged in a process of growing towards maturity throughout our lives and are necessarily immature at the outset of a relationship which makes such a significant contribution to that growth' (*Marriage and the Church's Task* pp.8of). Since it is quite frequent within Catholic judgments for one or both parties to be declared to be, or to have been, *incapable* of a true marriage, one wonders how often, if ever, such a person is refused a second marriage because his incapacity will clearly lead to another invalid ceremony?

If then we reject this unjustifiable extension of nullity, what is the alternative? In practice, many Protestant pastors remarry all comers, yet do so with a bad conscience. They know that whenever Jesus speaks of remarriage, he condemns it; they are therefore uneasy as they find themselves conducting more and more remarriages but they find it hard to know what they should do.

Unpopular as it may be with some, we must take our stand and bear witness to the wrong of remarriage. Pastors being interviewed for positions will need to make clear that this will be their policy and explain why. Pastors who at present are in churches which have allowed remarriage should, we suggest, set up a review group from the appropriate body (elders or Church Council) to review the present policy in the light of Christ's teaching and bring forward proposals for change.

## 5.   *To the difficulty and joy of happy marriages*

It is vital that all Christians, and Christian leaders in particular, are realistic about the difficulties that every married couple face. It is still all too common for wedding sermons to give the impression that, with a minimum of effort, unremitting happiness awaits the new couple, for talks on marriage at Christian youth groups to dwell only on the positive aspects of the experience, for church leaders to give the impression that their marriage is, and has been, completely troublefree.

Far removed from this is the realism of the Bible which speaks openly of sexual temptation, mutual irritation, jealousy, vindictiveness and self-absorption within marriage and gives many examples, particularly in the Old Testament, of marriages that run into difficulties (as just some examples: Adam, Abraham, Isaac, Jacob, Samson, David, Solomon and Hosea). Happily, this realism is increasingly being reflected in sermons and Christian talks which are prepared to speak about sexual and marital difficulties, and in which clergy and other Christian speakers are increasingly willing to be open about the struggles that they have been, or are, going through. This is only unhealthy if the content focuses wholly on the problems and offers no suggestions as to God's way through, or if it draws attention too much to the speaker and away from God, or if it seriously undermines confidence in the speaker's leadership (as opposed to just showing, helpfully, that he too has feet of clay).

But in most circumstances, and for almost all people, such candour is healthy. For the young it means that as they approach marriage they do not see it through rose-tinted spectacles. Many of the difficulties of marriage have to do with the discrepancy between expectations and reality. Far too often the problems that Christian marriages go through can be (at least partly) laid at the door of Christian parents and youth leaders who presented an idealistic picture of marriage with no acknowledgment of the very real difficulties that will be encountered. For my own part, I well remember hearing in a youth group talk a couple saying that sex had actually proved much less important within their continuing marriage than they had thought it would be in anticipation. This had a very definite impact on me and has certainly helped me come to terms with sexual disappointments within myself and my own marriage.

Honesty about marital difficulties can also be very helpful for unmarried adults. Many struggle to feel contented in their singleness and part of the reason for this is that they have a quite unrealistic idea of what marriage is like. They know the disadvantages, as they experience them, of being single. They not only need help to see the very real advantages of singleness which the Bible puts forward, but also to appreciate the difficulties and problems of marriage. These are so often never mentioned. When only the happiness of marriage is discussed, it is not surprising if the unmarried hanker after marriage and feel cheated.

But also the married are greatly helped when there is realism, in sermons and talks, about the difficulties of married life. Few will want to unburden themselves to a pastor who seems perfect and whose marriage is entirely problem-free. But once difficulties are acknowledged, in the Bible's picture of marriage and in personal experience, the response is likely to be: 'He understands! I can go to him for help.'

Yet this is of course only one side of married life. Marriage is a mixture of difficulties and joys, in which the joy is meant to – and often does – predominate. It is Proverbs, and the Wisdom Literature in general, which is so realistic about both aspects of marital experience and they speak openly and directly about the joys of a good marriage: the committed companionship, the sexual pleasure, the contented family life and the financial security (see chapter 4). The Wisdom Literature is perhaps the most neglected area of the Bible in Christian preaching.

And here too teaching needs to go hand in hand with example. Perhaps the best testimony to the joy and fulfilment of married life is a good Christian marriage. It is especially important that a Christian leader's family life should be strong and healthy, as the Pastoral Epistles recognise (1 Tim. 3:1–5; Titus 1:5f). It has been my experience that where a pastor's marriage has been rocky, this has become widely known in the church (even though he may have sought to conceal it) and has had a destabilising effect on the church as a whole. Where, by contrast, the pastor's marriage is strong, this has provided the same kind of security to the church as it undoubtedly has for the pastor's own children.

This is not of course to argue for living a lie, in which the pastor pretends that all is well within his marriage when it is not. Rather, it is to advocate a pastor's working to keep his marriage healthy and develop his relationship with his wife and family and to see this as a very important prerequisite for his ministry. This of course means investing 'quality time' and effort in his marriage. A friend of mine, senior pastor of a large church, says: 'In order to be the best possible husband to my wife, I must spend time alone with God each day. In order to be the best possible father to my children, I must spend time with my wife alone each day. In order to be the best possible pastor to the church, I must spend time with my children each day.' And he practises what he advocates: he jealously guards time for meditation and prayer, and time for the family, every day and will not normally let the telephone or even friends (as I know to my cost) break into that time.

# Conclusions

This book has sought to wrestle with the issues of divorce and remarriage, both in biblical teaching (particularly the teaching of Christ himself) and in pastoral experience and practice. The order of the book has of course been deliberate: to tackle the biblical material first. The temptation for all pastors is to react in precisely the reverse order: to start with human desires and aspirations, especially when we understand them well and feel them very acutely, and to mould our theology to fit these desires. It is a temptation which I as a pastor have fallen into many times.

Yet it is a temptation. And it is precisely because these desires, particularly as expressed in the late twentieth century, often conflict with the teaching of the New Testament that our churches find themselves in such confusion today. We must again reverse the order. We must first work through to conclusions about Christ's teaching. This is the essential starting point. We cannot simply shrug our shoulders and say: 'It is so difficult to decide what he is saying', because our pastoral practice will in fact be based on a set of theological assumptions whether we recognise this or not. But having come to a conclusion (which is always open to revision if we are proved wrong), then we must work out its implications for our teaching, our caring, our ministry of reconciliation, our ministry of bearing witness to Christ's truth.

One of Proverbs' pithy sayings sums up God's call to us: 'Many a man claims to have unfailing love, but a faithful man who can find?' (20:6).

This is intended by Proverbs not principally to point out the rarity of faithfulness, but to challenge its readers to be faithful. It is a double challenge to us. In the first place it is a challenge to Christians in our relations with each other and specifically (in the context of this book) with our marriage partners. We may frequently say 'I love you', but our determination must be to remain faithful in practice: even in the rocky times, even if our partner were to desert us or commit adultery against us.

And in the second place, this is a challenge to remain faithful to God. Again, we frequently tell him that we are devoted to him; in contemporary Christian songs we often sing directly: 'I love you'. But our determination must be to remain faithful in practice: to commend Christ's teaching on the lifelong nature of marriage, permanent even after divorce, to explain that teaching and uphold it, and to work so that it may again be accepted within the Church and within the world.

# Acknowledgments

Material reprinted from *Divorce – the Pain and Healing* by Judith Mattison, copyright © 1985 Augsburg Publishing House, is used by permission of Augsburg Fortress.

Material quoted from *Four Major Plays* by H. Ibsen (translated by J. McFarlane), 1981, is reproduced by permission of Oxford University Press.

Material quoted from *Road to Divorce* by L. Stone, 1990, is reproduced by permission of Oxford University Press.

# Abbreviations

| | |
|---|---|
| *1 Apol.* | *First Apology* (Justin Martyr) |
| *Ant.* | *Jewish Antiquities* (Josephus) |
| *b. Git* | Babylonian Talmud, tractate *Gittin* |
| *Ketub.* | *Ketuboth* |
| *Yeb.* | *Yebamoth* |
| BHS | *Biblica Hebraic Stuttgartensia* |
| CD | Cairo Genizak Document of the Damascus Covenanters (the Zadokite Documents) |
| *Comm. in. Matt.* | *Commentaries in Matthaeum* |
| *De Spec. Leg.* | *De Specialibus Legibus* (Philo) |
| ET | English Translation |
| *Gen. Rab.* | *Genesis Rabbah* |
| GNB | Good News Bible |
| *Leg. pro. Chr.* | *Legatio pro Christianis* (Athenagoras) |
| LXX | Septuagint |
| *m. Arak.* | Mishnah, tractate *Arakhin* |
| *Git.* | *Gittin* |
| *Ketub.* | *Ketuboth* |
| NEB | New English Bible |
| NIV | New International Version |
| NRSV | New Revised Standard Version |
| *Or.* | *Orationes* |
| RSV | Revised Standard Version |
| *Strom.* | *Stromata* (Clement of Alexandria) |
| *War* | *The Jewish War* (Josephus) |

# Bibliography

This bibliography is confined almost exclusively to works cited in the text. This fact is especially noticeable in the Commentary section which makes no attempt to be exhaustive and where important commentaries, not cited in the text, are not normally listed.

In the text, commentaries are normally cited by author only and can be assumed to be *ad loc.* except where indicated. Other Works are normally cited by author and page number only; where two 'other works' by the same author occur, a shortened form of the title is also given.

## A. Commentaries

### 1. Genesis

BRUEGGEMANN, W. *Genesis.* Interpretation Commentary. Atlanta: John Knox, 1982.

CALVIN, J. *Genesis.* ET. Grand Rapids: Eerdmans, 1948.

CASSUTO, U. *A Commentary on the Book of Genesis. Part I: 1:1–6:8.* ET. Jerusalem: Magnes, 1961.

DELITZSCH, F. *A New Commentary on Genesis.* ET. Edinburgh: T. and T. Clark, 1899.

*Genesis Rabbah: The Judaic Commentary to the Book of Genesis, volume 1: 1:1–8:14.* ET. Atlanta: Scholars, 1985.

KIDNER, D. *Genesis – An Introduction and Commentary.* Tyndale Commentary. London: Tyndale, 1967.

RAD, G. von *Genesis*. Old Testament Library. ET. London: SCM, 1972².
VAWTER, B. *On Genesis: A New Reading*. London: Chapman, 1977.
WENHAM, G. J. *Genesis 1–15*. Word Biblical Commentary. Waco, TX: Word, 1987.
WESTERMANN, C. *Genesis 1–11 – A Commentary*. Biblischer Kommentar. ET. London: SPCK, 1984.

## 2. Deuteronomy

CRAIGIE, P. C. *The Book of Deuteronomy*. New International Commentary. London: Hodder and Stoughton, 1976.
DRIVER, S. R. *A Critical and Exegetical Commentary on Deuteronomy*. International Critical Commentary. Edinburgh: T. and T. Clark, 1895.
RAD, G. von *Deuteronomy – A Commentary*. Old Testament Library. London: SCM, 1966.
WRIGHT, G. E. *The Book of Deuteronomy*. The Interpreter's Bible. Nashville: Abingdon-Cokesbury, 1953.

## 3. Proverbs

KIDNER, D. *Proverbs*. Tyndale Commentary. London: Tyndale, 1964.
McKANE, W. *Proverbs*. Old Testament Library. London: SCM, 1970.

## 4. Isaiah

LEUPOLD, H, C. *Exposition of Isaiah*. Grand Rapids: Baker Book House, 1968.
NORTH, C. R. *The Second Isaiah*. Oxford: OUP, 1964.
WESTERMANN, C. *Isaiah 40–66 – A Commentary*. Old Testament Library. ET. London: SCM, 1969.

## 5. Jeremiah

CARROLL, R. P. *Jeremiah*. Old Testament Library. London: SCM, 1986.
ELLIOTT BINNS, L. *The Book of the Prophet Jeremiah*. Westminster Commentaries. London: Methuen, 1919.
HOLLADAY, W. L. *Jeremiah. Volume I: 1–25*. Hermeneia. Philadelphia: Fortress, 1986.
McKANE, W. *A Critical and Exegetical Commentary on Jeremiah. Volume I: 1–25*. Edinburgh: T. and T. Clark, 1986.
THOMPSON, J.A. *The Book of Jeremiah*. New International Commentary. Grand Rapids: Eerdmans, 1980.

## 6. Ezekiel

EICHRODT, W. *Ezekiel*. Old Testament Library. ET. London: SCM, 1970.
SKINNER, J. *The Book of Ezekiel*. London: Hodder and Stoughton, 1895.

## 7. Hosea

ANDERSEN, F. I. and FREEDMAN, D. N. *Hosea*. Anchor Bible. Garden City, NY: Doubleday, 1980.
KIDNER, D. *The Message of Hosea*. The Bible Speaks Today. Leicester: IVP, 1981.
WOLFF, H. W. *Hosea*. Hermeneia. ET. Philadelphia: Fortress, 1974.

## 8. Malachi

BALDWIN, J.G. *Haggai, Zechariah, Malachi*. Tyndale Commentary. London: Tyndale, 1972.
CHARY, T. *Aggée, Zacharie. Malachie*. Sources Bibliques. Paris: Gabalda, 1969.
PEROWNE, T. T. *Haggai. Zechariah and Malachi*. The Cambridge Bible for Schools and Colleges. Cambridge: CUP, 1901–2.
SMITH, R.L. *Micah-Malachi*. Word Biblical Commentary. Waco, TX: Word, 1984.

VERHOEF, P. A. *The Books of Haggai and Malachi*. New International Commentary. Grand Rapids: Eerdmans, 1987.

## 9. Matthew (including the Sermon on the Mount)

AQUINAS, T. *Catena Aurea – Commentary on the Four Gospels collected out of the works of the Fathers, Volume I Part II*. ET. Oxford: Parker, 1841.

BEARE, F. W. *The Gospel according to Matthew*. Oxford: Blackwell, 1981.

BONNARD, P. *L'Évangile selon S. Matthieu*. Commentaire du NT. Neuchâtel: Delachaux et Niestlé, 1963.

CALVIN, J. *Commentary on a Harmony of the Evangelists Matthew, Mark and Luke*. 3 volumes. ET. Edinburgh: Calvin Translation Society, 1845.

CARSON, D. *Matthew*. Expositor's Bible volume 8. Grand Rapids: Zondervan, 1984.

DAVIES, W. D. *The Setting of the Sermon on the Mount*. Cambridge: CUP, 1964.

DAVIES, W. D. and ALLISON, D. C. *The Gospel according to St Matthew. volume I: 1–7*. International Critical Commentary. Edinburgh: T. and T. Clark, 1988.

FILSON, F. V. *A Commentary on the Gospel according to St Matthew*. Black's Commentaries. London: A. and C. Black, 1972.

GUELICH, R. A. *The Sermon on the Mount – a Foundation for Understanding*. Waco, TX: Word, 1982.

GUNDRY, R. H. *Matthew – A Commentary on his Literary and Theological Art*. Grand Rapids: Eerdmans, 1982.

HILL, D. *The Gospel of Matthew*. New Century Bible. London: Oliphants, 1972.

LAGRANGE, M-J. *Évangile selon S. Matthieu*. Études Bibliques. Paris: Gabalda, 1923.

LENSKI, R. C. H. *Interpretation of St Matthew's Gospel*. Columbus, Ohio: Lutheran Book Concern, 1932.

LLOYD-JONES, D. M. *Studies in the Sermon on the Mount*. 2 volumes. London: IVP, 1959 and 1960.

McNEILE, A. H. *The Gospel according to St Matthew*. London: Macmillan, 1915.

PLUMMER, A. *An Exegetical Commentary on the Gospel*

*according to St Matthew.* London: James Clarke, c. 1910².

SCHWEIZER, E. *The Good News according to Matthew.* ET. London: SPCK, 1976.

STOTT, J. R. W. *Christian Counter-culture – The Message of the Sermon on the Mount.* The Bible Speaks Today. Leicester: IVP, 1978.

## 10. Mark

CRANFIELD, C. E. B. *The Gospel according to St Mark.* The Cambridge Greek Text Commentary. Cambridge: CUP, 1977.

LANE, W. L. *The Gospel of Mark.* New London Commentary. London: Marshal, Morgan and Scott, 1974.

SCHWEIZER, E. *The Good News according to Mark.* ET. London: SPCK, 1971 .

SWETE, H. B. *The Gospel according to St Mark.* London: Macmillan, 1902².

## 11. Luke

ELLIS, E. E. *The Gospel of Luke.* New Century Bible. London: Nelson, 1966.

FITZMYER, J. A. *The Gospel according to Luke.* 2 volumes. Anchor Bible. Garden City, NY: Doubleday, 1985.

MARSHALL, I. H. *The Gospel of Luke.* New International Greek Testament Commentary. Exeter: Paternoster, 1978.

PLUMMER, A. *The Gospel according to St Luke.* International Critical Commentary. Edinburgh: T. and T. Clark, 1901⁴.

## 12. Romans

BARRETT, C. K. *The Epistle to the Romans.* Black's Commentaries. London: A. and C. Black, 1962.

CRANFIELD, C. E. B. *A Critical and Exegetical Commentary on the Epistle to the Romans.* 2 volumes. International Critical Commentary. Edinburgh: T. and T. Clark, 1975 and 1979.

DUNN, J. D. G. *Romans.* Word Biblical Commentary. Dallas: Word, 1988.

## 13. 1 Corinthians

BARRETT, C. K. *The First Epistle to the Corinthians.* Black's Commentaries. London: A. and C. Black, 1971[2].
BENGEL, J. A. *Gnomon of the New Testament.* ET. Edinburgh: T & T Clark, 1863.
BRUCE, F. F. *1 and 2 Corinthians.* New Century Bible. London: Oliphants, 1971.
CALVIN, J. *Commentary on the Epistles of Paul the Apostle to the Corinthians.* 2 volumes. ET. Edinburgh: Calvin Translation Society, 1848.
CALVIN, J. *The First Epistle of Paul the Apostle to the Corinthians.* ET. Edinburgh: Oliver and Boyd, 1960.
CONZELMANN, H. *1 Corinthians.* Hermeneia. ET. Philadelphia: Fortress, 1975.
FEE, G. D. *The First Epistle to the Corinthians.* New International Commentary. Grand Rapids: Eerdmans, 1987.
GODET, F. *Commentary on St Paul's First Epistle to the Corinthians.* 2 volumes. ET. Edinburgh: T. and T. Clark, n.d.
PRIOR, D. *The Message of 1 Corinthians.* The Bible Speaks Today. Leicester: IVP, 1985.
ROBERTSON, A. and PLUMMER, A. *A Critical and Exegetical Commentary on the 1st Epistle of St Paul to the Corinthians.* ICC. Edinburgh: T & T Clark, 1911[2].

## 14. Ephesians

BARTH, M. *Ephesians.* 2 volumes. Anchor Bible. Garden City, NY: Doubleday, 1974.
BRUCE, F. F. *The Epistles to the Colossians, to Philemon and to the Ephesians.* New International Commentary. Grand Rapids: Eerdmans, 1984.
DALE, R. W. *The Epistle to the Ephesians.* London: Hodder and Stoughton, 1901.
MASSON, C. *L'Épître de St Paul aux Éphésiens.* Commentaire du NT. Neuchâtel: Delachaux et Niestlé, 1953.
MITTON, C. L. *Ephesians.* New Century Bible. London: Oliphants, 1976.
STOTT, J. R. W. *God's New Society.* The Bible Speaks Today. Leicester: IVP, 1979.

## 15. Pastoral Epistles

BARRETT, C. K. *The Pastoral Epistles.* The New Clarendon Bible. Oxford: OUP, 1963.

DIBELIUS, M. and CONZELMANN, H. *The Pastoral Epistles.* Hermeneia. ET. Philadelphia: Fortress, 1972.

ELLICOTT, C. J. *The Pastoral Epistles of St Paul.* London: Longmans, 1883[5].

HANSON, A. T. *The Pastoral Epistles.* New Century Bible. Grand Rapids: Eerdmans, 1982.

KELLY, J. N. D. *A Commentary on the Pastoral Epistles.* Black's Commentaries. London: A. and C. Black, 1963.

PLUMMER, A. *The Pastoral Epistles.* The Expositor's Bible. London: Hodder and Stoughton, 1888.

SPICQ, C. *Les Épîtres Pastorales.* Études Bibliques. Paris: Gabalda, 1947.

## B. Other Works

ABULAFIA, J. *Men and Divorce.* London: Fontana, 1990.

ALBEE, E. *Who's Afraid of Virginia Woolf?* Harmondsworth: Penguin, 1965.

ARNDT and GINGRICH (cited as): BAUER, E., ARNDT, W. F., GINGRICH, F. W. and DANKER, F. *Greek-English Lexicon of the New Testament.* Chicago: University of Chicago, 1979[2],

ATKINSON, D. *To Have and to Hold – The Marriage Covenant and the Discipline of Divorce.* London: Collins, 1979.

BAUGHEN, M. *et al. The Church.* Basingstoke: Marshall Pickering, 1987.

BELLAH, R. N. *et al. Habits of the Heart.* New York: Harper and Row, 1985.

BHS: ELLIGER, K. and RUDOLPH, W. (eds.) *Biblia Hebraica Stuttgartensia.* Stuttgart: Deutsche Bibelgesellschaft, 1976–7.

*The Book of Common Prayer according to the use of the Episcopal Church.* The Church Hymnal Corporation, 1977.

BROMILEY, G. W. *God and Marriage.* Edinburgh: T. and T. Clark, 1981.

BROWN, C. (ed.) *The New International Dictionary of New*

*Testament Theology.* 3 volumes. Exeter: Paternoster, 1975, 1976 and 1978.

BROWN, F., DRIVER, S.R. and BRIGGS, C. A. *A Hebrew and English Lexicon of the Old Testament.* Oxford: OUP, 1906.

BROWN, P. *The Body and Society – Men, Women and Sexual Renunciation in Early Christianity.* London: Faber and Faber, 1989.

BURGOYNE, J., ORMROD, R. and RICHARDS, M. *Divorce Matters.* Harmondsworth: Penguin, 1987.

*The Canons of the Church of England.* London: Church House Publishing, 1986[4].

CHAPMAN, G. *Hope for the Separated.* Chicago: Moody, 1982.

CHAPMAN, G. *Now That You Are Single Again.* San Bernadino, CA: Here's Life, 1985.

CHURCH OF ENGLAND REPORT *The Church and the Law of Nullity.* London: SPCK, 1955.

CLIFFORD, P. *Divorced Christians and the Love of God.* London: Triangle, 1987.

CLULOW, C. and MATTINSON, J. *Marriage Inside Out.* Harmondsworth: Penguin, 1989.

COLLINGWOOD, J. 'Divorce and Remarriage' in *Anvil* 3:1 (1986) pp.66–75.

*Constitution and Canons for the Government of the Protestant Episcopal Church in the USA.* No publisher, 1985.

CRISPIN, K. *Divorce – The Forgivable Sin?* London: Hodder and Stoughton, 1989.

CROUZEL, H. *L'église primitive face au divorce du premier au cinquième siècle.* Paris: Beauchesne, 1971.

DANBY, H. (ed. and transl.) The Mishnah ET. Oxford: OUP, 1933.

DODD, C.H. *According to the Scriptures.* London: Nisbet, 1952.

DOMINIAN, J. *Marital Breakdown.* Harmondsworth: Penguin, 1968.

DULLEY, F. *How Christian is Divorce and Remarriage?* Bramcote, Notts: Grove, 1974.

DUPONT, J. *Mariage et Divorce dans l'Évangile.* Bruges: Desclée de Brouwer, 1959.

EPSTEIN, M. *Marriage Laws in the Bible and the Talmud.* Cambridge, MA: Harvard University, 1942.

*Eurostat: Demographic Statistics 1990.* Brussels: Statistical Office of the European Communities, 1990.

EVENING, M. *Who Walk Alone – A Consideration of the Single Life.* London: Hodder and Stoughton, 1974.

FETTERMAN, J. J. *et al. Pastoral Response to the AIDS Crisis.* Pittsburgh: Calvary Episcopal Church, n.d.

FLOOD, E. *The Divorced Catholic.* Glasgow: Collins, 1987.

FREEMAN, D. R. *Couples in Conflict.* Milton Keynes: Open University, 1990.

*Fresh Start.* Wayne, PA: Fresh Start Seminars, c.1983.

GREEN, W. *The Christian and Divorce.* London: Mowbray, 1981.

HAVARD, A. and M. *Death and Rebirth of a Marriage.* Wheaton: Tyndale House, 1969.

HENSLEY, J. C. *Coping with Being Single Again.* Nashville: Broadman, 1978.

HETH, W. A. and WENHAM, G. J. *Jesus and Divorce.* Nashville: Nelson, 1985.

HOSIER, H. K. *To Love Again: Remarriage for the Christian.* Nashville: Abingdon, 1985.

HUGENBERGER, G. P. *Marriage as Covenant: A Study of Biblical Law and Ethics governing Marriage, developed from the Perspective of Malachi.* Unpublished Ph.D. thesis, The College of St Paul and St Mary, Cheltenham, 1991.

HUGGETT, J. *Marriage on the Mend.* Eastbourne: Kingsway, 1987.

HURDING, R. F. *Restoring the Image.* Exeter: Paternoster, 1980.

HURLEY, J. B. *Man and Woman in Biblical Perspective.* Leicester: IVP, 1981.

IBSEN, H. *Four Major Plays.* ET. Oxford: OUP, 1987.

ISAKSSON, A. *Marriage and Ministry in the New Temple,* Lund: Gleerup, 1965.

JEREMIAS, J. *Jerusalem in the Time of Jesus.* ET. London: SCM, 1969.

JOSEPHUS, F. *The Works of Flavius Josephus.* ET. Edinburgh: Nimmo, 1867.

KASPER, W. *Theology of Christian Marriage.* ET. London: Burns and Oates, 1980.

KASTER, J. 'Education, Old Testament' in BUTTRICK, G. A. (ed.) *The Interpreter's Dictionary of the Bible*. Volume II. Nashville: Abingdon, 1962.

KIERNAN, K. and WICKS, M. *Family Change and Future Policy*. London: Family Policy Studies Centre, 1990.

KIRK, K. E. *Marriage and Divorce*. London: Hodder and Stoughton, 1948.

KISEMBO, B. MAGESA, L. and SHORTER, A. *African Christian Marriage*. London: Geoffrey Chapman, 1977.

LANEY, J. C. *The Divorce Myth*. Minneapolis: Bethany, 1981.

LEHMANN, M. R. *Genesis 2:24 as the Basis for Divorce in Halakah and the New Testament* in *ZAW (Zeitschrift für die alttestamentliche Wissenschaft)* 31 (1960) pp.263–7.

LEWIS, C. S. *Mere Christianity*. London: Collins, 1952.

LIDDELL and SCOTT (cited as): LIDDELL, H. G., SCOTT, R. and JONES, H. S. *A Greek-English Lexicon*. Oxford: OUP, 1940.

LUCK, W. F. *Divorce and Remarriage – Recovering the Biblical View*. San Francisco: Harper and Row, 1987.

*Marriage and the Church's Task – The Report of the General Synod Marriage Commission*. London: CIO, 1978.

*Marriage and Divorce – A Report of the Study Panel of the Free Church of Scotland*. Edinburgh: The Free Church of Scotland, 1988.

*Marriage and Divorce Statistics 1837–1983*. London: HMSO, 1990.

*Marriage and Divorce Statistics 1989*. London: HMSO, 1991.

*Marriage, Divorce and the Church – The Report of the Commission on the Christian Doctrine of Marriage*. London: SPCK, 1971.

MATTISON, J. *Divorce – The Pain and the Healing*. Minneapolis: Augsburg, 1985.

MAYLE, P. *Where did I come from?* Secaucus, NJ: Lyle Stuart, 1973.

McCASLAND, S. V. 'Education, New Testament' in BUTTRICK G. A. (ed.) *The Interpreter's Dictionary of the Bible*, Volume II. Nashville: Abingdon, 1962.

MURRAY, J. *Divorce*. Phillipsburg, NJ: Presbyterian and Reformed Publishing, 1961[2].

NESTLE, E., ALAND, K. *et al. Novum Testamentum Graece*. Stuttgart: Deutsche Bibelstiftung, 1979–81[26].

NIDNTT: see BROWN, C.

O'DONOVAN, O. M. T. *Marriage and the Family* in KAYE, B. (ed.) *Obeying Christ in a Changing World. Volume III: The Changing World.* Glasgow: Collins, 1977.

O'DONOVAN, O. M. T. *Marriage and Permanence.* Bramcote, Notts: Grove, 1978.

OPPENHEIMER, H. 'Is the Marriage Bond an Indissoluble Vinculum'? in *Theology* 78 (1975), pp.236–44.

THE ORDER OF CHRISTIAN UNITY (A Committee of). *Reconciliation and Conciliation in the Context of Divorce.* London: Order of Christian Unity, c.1985[2].

PARKES, C. M. *Bereavement.* Harmondsworth: Penguin, 1986.

PARKINSON, L. *Marriage Breakdown and Conciliation.* London: Board for Social Responsibility Newsletter No. 111, 1982.

PHYPERS, D. *Christian Marriage in Crisis.* Bromley, Kent: MARC Europe, 1985.

POWERS, B. W. *Marriage and Divorce – The New Testament Teaching.* Concord, NSW: Family Life Movement of Australia, 1987.

RAHLFS, A. *Septuaginta.* 2 volumes. Stuttgart: Deutsche Bibelgesellschaft, 1935.

RICHARDSON, C. C. (ed.) *Early Christian Fathers.* ET. London: SCM, 1953.

RICHMOND, G. *The Divorce Decision.* Waco, TX: Word, 1988.

RUBINSTEIN, H. (ed.) *The Oxford Book of Marriage.* Oxford: OUP, 1990.

SCHILLEBEECKX, E. *Marriage: Human Reality and Saving Mystery.* ET. London: Sheed and Ward, 1965.

SCOTT, M. *Divorced but not Defeated.* Paignton, Devon: Torbay Publishing, 1984.

*Second Wind.* Wayne, PA: Fresh Start Seminars, 1988.

*Services of Prayer and Dedication after Civil Marriage.* London: Church House Publishing, 1985.

*Statistical Abstract of the United States 1990.* Washington DC: Bureau of the Census, US Department of Commerce, 1990.

STONE, L. *Road to Divorce: England 1530–1987.* Oxford: OUP, 1990.

STOTT, J. R. W. *Basic Christianity.* London: IVP, 1971[2].

STOTT, J. R. W. *Issues Facing Christians Today.* Basingstoke, Hants.: Marshall, Morgan and Scott, 1984.

TAYLOR, A. J. P. *English History 1914–1945.* Oxford: OUP, 1965.

THIELICKE, H. *The Ethics of Sex.* ET. London: James Clarke, 1964.

THRALL, M. E. *Greek Particles in the New Testament.* Grand Rapids, 1962.

THURIAN, M. *Marriage and Celibacy.* London: SCM.

TOYNBEE, P. 'Children Who Never Forgive' in the *Observer Review,* 3 September 1989, pp.33f.

TOYNBEE, P. 'The Worm Turned Syndrome' in the *Observer,* 10 September 1989.

VERMES, G. *The Dead Sea Scrolls in English.* ET. Sheffield: JSOT, 1987 .

WALLERSTEIN, J. S. and BLAKESLEE, S. *Second Chances.* Ealing, London: Corgi, 1990.

WALLERSTEIN, J. S. and KELLY, J. B. *Surviving the Breakup: How Children and Parents Cope with Divorce.* New York: Basic Books, 1980.

WENHAM, D. *The Jesus Tradition Outside the Gospels.* Gospel Perspectives volume V. Sheffield: JSOT, 1985.

WENHAM, G. J. *The Book of Leviticus.* NICOT, London, Hodder & Stoughton, 1979.

WENHAM, G. J. 'Gospel Definitions of Adultery and Women's Rights' in *The Expository Times* 95 (1984), pp.330–2.

WENHAM, G. J. 'Matthew and Divorce: An Old Crux Revisited' in *Journal for the Study of the New Testament* 22 (1984), pp.95–107.

WILSON, R. F. 'Don't pay the price of counterfeit forgiveness' in *Moody Magazine,* October 1985.

WINNETT, A. R. *The Church and Divorce.* London: Mowbrays, 1968.

YATES, J. W. *For the Life of the Family.* Wilton, CT: Morehouse-Barlow, 1986.

# Index of Biblical References

References in bold indicate pages where there is a major discussion of the designated biblical text.

# Index of Authors

# Index of Ancient Literature

# Index of Subjects